To ~~Mike Suttard~~ Clifford Germen
with warm regards &
many thanks for Your
contribution at Beals

THE CODER SPECIAL
ARCHIVE

The untold story of Naval national servicemen learning
and using Russian during the Cold War

BY

TONY CASH & MIKE GERRARD

Great pleasure to meet you.

Very best wishes,

Mike Gerrard

First published in Great Britain by Hodgson Press 2012

Hodgson Press
4 River Court
Portsmouth Road
Surbiton
Surrey
KT6 4EY
United Kingdom
enquiries@hodgsonpress.co.uk
www.hodgsonpress.co.uk

A CIP catalogue record for this book is available from the British Library.

ISBN: 978-1-906164-25-6

Printed in Great Britain by Lightning Source Ltd.

Cover design by Sofia Stevi.

THE CODER SPECIAL ARCHIVE

ARCHIVE

**The untold story of Naval national servicemen learning
and using Russian during the Cold War**

BY

TONY CASH & MIKE GERRARD

Hodgson Press

NOTE FOR READERS UNACQUAINTED
WITH THE RUSSIAN ALPHABET

The graphic conceit RN И Я on the front and back of our book displays the usual abbreviation for the Royal Navy followed by a mirror image. The two reversed letters happen to be the Russian words 'and' and 'I'. Taken together, the four symbols can be understood to mean - 'the Royal Navy and Me' - one of the essential themes of this publication.

Contents

Illustrations

FOREWORD

I am happy to write a foreword to THE CODER SPECIAL ARCHIVE while at the same time feeling that my own experience learning Russian was not typical, nor was I ever a coder. Many of the contributors to this book had more interesting and varied experiences than I had; the Russian I learned never put to practical use; I did not go abroad; I did not monitor Soviet air waves, so that learning Russian was, certainly to begin with, just school carried on by other means.

School was Leeds Modern School, a grammar school in Leeds where I was in the sixth form with Tony Cash. I was very young for my age, and at 17 it was a toss-up which would come first puberty or the call-up. At 18 I had never been in a pub or had a cigarette or a girl friend. Compared with most of the men quoted in this book I was an innocent.

I knew though about the Russian course and, dreading national service as I did, that it was a possible lifeline. I opted for the Navy, a choice of service dictated in part by aesthetic considerations – I thought a coder's uniform looked more becoming. At the same time at 17 I saw the three services, Navy, Air Force and Army as approximating to, corresponding with the class system – Navy as upper class, Air Force as middle – the Army as working. So putting down for the Navy I knew I was being over-aspirational, and it was no surprise at all when I ended up in the Army where I belonged.

Some of my classmates did manage to get into the Navy, though: one of my closest friends John Totterdill becoming a midshipman and having, it seemed to me, an ideal life swanning round the Mediterranean as office- boy cum valet to Admiral Sir Philip Vian. John Scaife and Tony Cash both became coders so I knew it could be done. But not by me, and when my papers came and I found I hadn't got into the Navy I also found it was far from certain I was going to be able to do Russian. Certainly nobody seemed to have heard of the course at Pontefract Barracks where I did my basic training with the York and Lancaster Regiment. But though not by nature tenacious I persisted so that when at the end of six weeks most of my platoon were drafted into the Duke of Wellington's Regiment for eventual transfer to Korea I kicked my heels at Pontefract with another would-be Russian course candidate, Thomas Pearce, both of us eventually ending up at Coulsdon where we embarked on our study of the Russian language.

In memoirs that I've read by others on the course much has been made of how hard one had to work. While this was hardly true of the later stages it was certainly the case during those first six weeks at Coulsdon. This was when one was learning the alphabet and the basic grammar and coming to terms with the daily word lists that one had to master and on which one was tested at the end of each week.

The pressure, though, was to some extent self-imposed. We knew that the course at Coulsdon would end in an examination, with the top 25% going on to Cambridge. The prospect of Cambridge would have been incentive enough but what made it seem almost beyond imagining was that did we get into the top 25%, at Cambridge we would no longer have to wear uniform, do drill or bull our kit – all the irksome and sometimes humiliating burdens that had been visited upon us would fall away. No more guard duty or the threat of jankers or being put on a charge. One would be a person again not a soldier. No wonder we worked.

I am told that I am by nature competitive but I have never since been in a situation where one had to compete so directly with one's fellows and so relentlessly that it coloured sociability and almost ruled out friendship. This was certainly true of the first pre-university period of the course and continued for some time afterwards though less unremittingly – or maybe one just got used to it. Hanging over us was always the threat of being RTU'd – returned to one's unit, in my case Pontefract. I can't recall this ever happening to anybody, however poorly they did in the weekly tests, but it was perhaps because existence was to some extent precarious that I remember it as in many ways the most idyllic period of my life, and much more so than university proper which came a year or two later.

We were housed to begin with at Cecil Lodge in Newmarket from which we were bussed in every morning to the course HQ in Salisbury Villas on Station Road in Cambridge. At the end of the first term the lucky ones were allocated to a house in Newnham

Terrace in the centre of Cambridge (and subsequently part of New Hall). The rest of us were relegated to Foxton Hall, a square lavatory-bricked villa just outside Cambridge on the main line to King's Cross. Gone now, it was where I had my first gin and tonic and my first cigarette and used to stand on the lawn at dusk listening to the bats.

Finally we were all reunited at Douglas House on Trumpington Road, both Foxton and Douglas House having an after-life as convalescent homes before being demolished. If I dwell on these houses it's because they rather than Salisbury Villas are what remain in the memory, so much so that walking up the road to the station a few weeks ago I couldn't even pick out which villa it was where we'd studied half a century ago.

After Cambridge it was back to uniform and six months at Bodmin, living in the Spider, a conglomeration of Nissen huts heated only by coke stoves. Morning parades were a shambles with pyjamas sometimes worn under uniforms the weather was so bitter and classrooms so cold. Again it's the extra-curricular activities I remember most vividly – the poker fever that gripped the camp for a few months then ceased as abruptly as it had started; swimming at a surely insanitary water-hole on the moors followed by stupendous farmhouse teas at Mrs Penhaligon's. Cornwall then was criss-crossed by railways so there were trips to Fowey and Lostwithiel with week-ends spent at St Columb Minor and Polzeath, surfing yet to be discovered.

Bodmin was also a reunion with the Navy students who to me remained as enviable and out of reach as they'd been when I first tried to join their number at the start of national service. Huddled on the parade ground in army fatigues one saw these lofty and elegant creatures – Mark Frankland, Jeremy Wolfenden, Robin Hope – sauntering to their places, their social and academic skills making me feel still the uncouth squaddy I'd been in basic training.

It was around this time we all sat the Civil Service exam in Russian, a hurdle I failed ignominiously. This was a surprise as I'd earlier got a distinction in the A level exam but then the Army hadn't bothered to explain that doing well in the Civil Service exam would mean a pay increase, so there was no incentive. The hectic competition of the first months of the course was long forgotten.

At some point, too, we went off to take the WOSB, the board that would decide whether having been officer cadets for the last year we really were proper officer material. To my surprise (and already being something of an actor) I passed this first hurdle, the second being two weeks at Mons, the officer training unit at Aldershot. This proved more of a trial and I was failed. It dismayed me then and shames me now how much I wanted to pass. It was the first failure I'd ever had, but it was salutary. I had begun my national service as a committed Christian, a Conservative and, I'm sure a prig. Now, priggishness apart, I was none of these things quite, and though I didn't know it at the time it had cured me for life of any desire to join. It's this rather than the Russian word for 'rolling barrage', say, that sixty years later remains with me.

© Alan Bennett 25 June 2012

1.   Hamish Baillie at Cuxhaven 1955. Courtesy R Pearce.

INTRODUCTION

This 1955 photograph shows Hamish Baillie at a Royal Naval base in the north of West Germany, engaged in what was then a highly secret operation - logging and recording a message from the USSR Admiralty in Leningrad, making its daily broadcast to the Soviet fleet, using the call sign KROKODIL (Crocodile).

Hamish was one of around 4,000-5,000 national service conscripts who, at the government's instigation, were taught Russian in Joint Services Schools for Linguists (JSSLs) so that they could intercept Soviet military radio traffic. The purpose of these covert listening activities was to keep track of the disposition of the USSR armed forces, enabling the West to be forewarned of any threatening movements or manoeuvres on the borders between our then two worlds.

The first JSSLs were established in October 1951, at the height of a Cold War which had turned torrid. That year Western allied troops on the Korean peninsula were pitted in bloody battle against Chinese and North Korean forces, widely believed to be Stalin's proxies. In Britain, as in most other western democracies, the fear of Soviet-led communist aggression was extensive, pervading most of the political spectrum from right to left: there was not, nor likely to be, significant political opposition in this country to the creation of a large cohort of Russian linguists to counter that perceived threat. Nevertheless, the discussions led by the Joint Intelligence Committee of the Chiefs of Staff about establishing the Russian courses were ascribed 'Top Secret' status.

For the next nine years, until 1960, the JSSLs trained national service interpreters and translators from the Navy, Army, and Air Force, providing the young conscripts with a solid grounding in Russian grammar, vocabulary and conversational usage. *Kursanty*, as course students were known, were introduced to Russian literature, song and Soviet films, as well as being crammed with the technical military terminology particular to their Service. All those classified as translators (some four-fifths of the total) also received instruction in radio technology. In consequence, coders, privates and aircraftmen spent at least half their compulsory 24-month national service employed in much the same labour, often in each others' company. But there was no especially dedicated Army or RAF branch for soldiers and airmen who opted or were selected for the Russian course. (It was, though, normal practice for Army personnel, on successful <u>completion</u> of their training, to transfer to the Intelligence Corps, whatever their original corps or regiment might have been.) The Admiralty adopted a distinct policy of its own, originating a new division to accommodate its linguists, albeit with a name similar to an existing one.

Before 1951 there were coders (educational) in the Navy; their principal work was to teach sailors to read and write, rather as sergeants in the Army Education Corps instructed soldiers whose schooling had been inadequate. As the name suggests, coders were also trained in cryptography, the art of rendering clear text into ciphers or codes. In 1951 the first coders (special) materialised – the word 'special' specifically denoting 'trained in the Russian language for signals intelligence (sigint) work'.

For several reasons our service lives, before and after language training, differed markedly from those of our Army and Air Force colleagues. Much smaller than the other two, the 'senior service' has always been exclusive, deeply conscious of tradition and whole-heartedly committed to inculcating in its crews the skills required to maintain the fighting efficiency of warships at sea. Only a handful of national servicemen were taken into the Navy, usually those with strong naval connections and a consequent predisposition to accept, possibly even revere, seafaring customs and ritual. The overwhelming majority of coders (S) were different, neither knowledgeable about, nor automatically inclined to be respectful of the Navy, into which they would never have been enrolled had not the Service a need for their linguistic talent. Whereas the Army and Air Force were accustomed to dealing with many thousands of conscripts, most of whom might reasonably be assumed to be unwilling, the Navy found its few 'pressed' men something of an alien species: mutual incomprehension is a recurring theme in our narrative.

The thrust of the book is essentially chronological. It charts the setting-up of the JSSLs in the first instance, and the haphazard recruitment process that followed. The focus thereafter is on the typical coder's landmark experiences - the relatively benign (in comparison with Army and Air Force practice) basic training; learning Russian on Army and RAF camps; manning ships on anti-submarine and NATO exercises; recording Soviet military radio traffic in northern West Germany, for analysis at Government Communication Headquarters in the UK. In comparison, a fascinating account by two Soviet counterparts reveals how similar were their experiences to ours. Final chapters report how, over several decades, the civilian work of former coders illuminated, and sometimes even impinged on, the Cold War.

Much of our story derives from personal verbatim recollections volunteered by more than 70 contributing ex-coders (S), all now in their eighth or ninth decade. Yet this is not an oral history. The overwhelming majority of the direct quotations printed here came to us electronically. Dare we suggest that this is one of the first ever email histories?

It has been the authors' aim to keep the number of footnotes to a minimum, since our primary audience is expected to be the general reader. We are, however, mindful of future social, political and military historians, for whose benefit we have provided more, and more detailed, footnotes than non-specialist purchasers of the book might have anticipated. The notes provide references or guideposts which will lead scholars to a fuller appreciation and interpretation of the coder special experience within the general context of early post-World War II history. That context includes, for example, the decision-making process in government, the post-war shortage of labour, and the distinct problems facing the Admiralty, as well as the more immediate and obvious concerns for the security of the country in the early Cold War years.

Wherever square brackets [ ] are used in quoted text, the words inside are additions, comments or amendments made by the authors, Tony Cash and Mike Gerrard. Footnote citations of published material appearing in the reading list, with full bibliographical details, give only author and title.

xx

CHAPTER 1
DEVISING THE JSSLS

В ТЕМНОТЕ, ДА НЕ В ОБИДЕ
(Russian saying – 'In the dark, but not mad')

The plan to train Russian linguists for war

This book is the story of some 1,500 Naval national servicemen born roughly in the period 1929-39. All of us were schoolboys during the second world war, and, for several reasons, a fortunate generation – old enough to remember the conflict, young enough not to have been called up for it, lucky enough to benefit from the post-war boom and the expansion of tertiary education.

Those now aged 80 or so would have seen older siblings and friends in uniform, conjuring up in our childish imaginings action on the front line. But the wildest scenario would never have featured us in combat with Red Army men, so firm seemed the Anglo-Soviet coalition. Yet, even as the Allies battled together against Nazi Germany, the authorities in Britain were assessing what kind of threat the Soviets might pose when the war was over.

The Labour administration elected in 1945 did not always see eye to eye with the Chiefs of Staff, who, like war-time Prime Minister Winston Churchill, were more belligerent in their thinking about future relations with the USSR, some even convinced conflict was inevitable. The imposition of communist rule in parts of eastern Europe was characterised by Churchill as an 'Iron Curtain' coming down. His Fulton speech of March 1946 accurately anticipated, if it did not actually help foment, the Cold War. By 1948 British intelligence operations, having been run down three years earlier, were expanding once more, including several different types of covert action. Ahead of the more widely publicised American U-2 flights, the RAF was already over-flying the Soviet Union and its 'satellite' countries on aerial photographic missions. For fifteen months over 1948-49 the Soviets provoked a crisis by enforcing a land siege of West Berlin. They aimed to assimilate into what was becoming communist East Germany the three sectors of the old German capital occupied by the western Allies. It took many thousands of daily sorties by American and British planes loaded with food and fuel to relieve the blockade. Over the course of those same two years communists assumed control of both Czechoslovakia and Hungary. The exploding of the first Soviet atomic bomb in 1949 caught Western intelligence by surprise, and made Britain even more anxious to discover Soviet intentions. The Korean war erupted in June 1950, resulting in a rapid growth in the size of the Government Communications Headquarters. Based from 1951 in Cheltenham, GCHQ has for 60 years furnished signals intelligence (sigint) to ensure the nation's security. A further spur to this expansion was the difficulty of breaking Soviet encrypted messages, which made the low grade intelligence that coders collected more valuable than it might otherwise have been.[1]

In March 1946 and August 1947 the Joint Intelligence Committee (JIC) of the Chiefs of Staff issued reports examining Soviet strategic interests, intentions and capabilities. They stressed the need to have early warnings of any possible Soviet attack. An increased effort was put into intelligence work, now largely based on signals intercepts and electronic sources, as human intelligence was hard to come by.[2] The JIC would have been very conscious of the tremendous contribution made to victory in the recent war by GCHQ at Bletchley Park and its network of Y stations picking up German signals. Only a tiny number of Britons could speak Russian, so as early as 1944 Anthony Eden, then Foreign Secretary, had suggested that the Civil Service entrance examiners should add that language as an option. By the end of the year the School of Slavonic and East European Studies in London University was running six-month courses for small numbers of Army and RAF personnel, most of them non-officers. Cambridge University began Service courses in 1945, with 75 men of all ranks, Army and RAF. Again the Navy did not figure, although the Admiralty had run a course during the

---

1   Richard Aldrich, *The Hidden Hand, passim,* but especially pp 10, 66, 215, 217, 231, 394-96; also, his *GCHQ,* especially pp. 68, 100, 103, 107-08. Peter Hennessy, *The Secret State: Whitehall and the Cold War,* Allen Lane, The Penguin Press, 2002, ch 1. Geoffrey Elliott and Harold Shukman, *Secret Classrooms,* pp 25-29. Dennis R. Mills, 'Signals intelligence and the Coder Special Branch of the Royal Navy in the 1950s', pp 639-55, quoting from pp. 639-41.

2   Peter Hennessy, *The Secret State,* pp 1, 11, 13.

war, but few Naval officers had gained qualifications as interpreters in Russian.[3]

Whitehall debates, April 1949-March 1951

For the following analysis we have drawn on Admiralty documents which were once all classified but are now accessible to everyone in the National Archives.[4] The authors have also had the benefit of recollections from over 70 former Naval national servicemen who were trained as Russian interpreters and translators. What they recall indicates how official first intentions were not always realised.

As early as 1948 the JIC recommended to the Chiefs of Staff that they should set up a large Russian-language training school. Instead, in 1949 the RAF started courses at Kidbrooke, south-east London, with only 30-40 students a year, mostly RAF officers and men. The RAF may have led the way because one school of thought was then emphasising the possibility of a Soviet attack on Britain starting with air action, making the air element of sigint very important.[5]

We know[6] that the Kidbrooke course was organised along lines that established a pattern for the whole project to teach Russian

---

3   James Muckle, *The Russian Language in Britain*, pp 110-2, 119-20.

4   TNA/ADM 116/6331-34. These documents run to some 170 pages, mostly foolscap, closely typed; we gained access by the kindness of Richard Aldrich, who copied them on his digital camera.

5   Geoffrey Elliott and Harold Shukman, *Secret Classrooms*, pp 28-29, 38-39. RAF Kidbrooke was located in the area of Greenwich borough known as Kidbrooke. According to entries on the internet, it had served as a barrage balloon centre to help protect London from *Luftwaffe* raids in the recent war. Terry Hancock, aviation historian, confirms that the station never had an airfield.

6   Conversation, March 2012, with Tony McGrath, who joined RAF, 1947; became corporal, 1951; went to Kidbrooke, 1952. His was a 12-month intensive course, four and a half days a week, with a tutor-student ratio of 1:5; classes were divided into grammar and conversation, with native Russian speakers concentrating on the latter. Occasionally all 30 or so students received lectures in Russian on various topics. Though the JSSL's tutor-student ratio was significantly smaller, McGrath's description of the Kidbrooke curriculum is similar to the experience of the overwhelming majority of national service students of Russian, with one important exception: the 30 students comprised RAF regulars of all ranks from Flt Lt down to aircraftman, with a sprinkling of RN ratings and Army 'other

4

2. JSSL Bodmin, c 1953 Courtesy former Coder Bernard Smyth.

to national servicemen: it was the forerunner of the Joint Services Schools for Linguists. The first JSSL opened at Bodmin in October 1951, with university courses for interpreters in Cambridge and London at the same date. The authorities were working on a largely blank sheet, as up to this point inter-Service training had generally been limited in scope and duration. When there had been reasons for instructing Navy, Army and RAF personnel together, it was for 'technical' rather than the 'academic' subjects associated with secondary grammar schools and universities. A vigorous, and not entirely productive, debate about ways and means went on for two and a half years. How many Russian linguists would the Services need? How were they to be recruited? Where were they to be trained, and by whom? Were they to be officers or not? What was the ideal balance between military training and language instruction? Would civilians study alongside them for the civil departments of government?

All this discussion and the results had to be kept as secret as possible, since the Russians were known to be suspicious of the intentions of Westerners who learned their language.[7] Even the composition and size of the permanent staffs of the JSSLs were classified as SECRET, since from this information a potential enemy could estimate the size of each school. The fact that JSSL Coulsdon had a public right of way through it, giving a clear view of its 500 Russian linguists parading every morning at 8.00 am, makes the classification seem comical now.

In 1949 a civil servant in the Ministry of Education was put in charge of a committee to calculate how many Russian linguists (RLs) would be required, should hostilities break out. Thereafter, a plethora of committees, sub-committees and working parties were set up to address the issue. These were largely now reporting to both the Ministry of Defence (MoD) and the three independent ministries which in those days were responsible for the individual armed forces. Had the Ministry of Education maintained the lead position, we RLs might have enjoyed more academic, and less military, instruction. There might also have been far less stumbling around in the dark.

---

ranks' The officers were to be interpreters; the men to work as intercept operators.

7   James Muckle, *Russian Language*, pp 125-26.

The first concern of these committees was to determine the numbers of RLs to be trained. At one point they opted for 3,600, roughly a third to be interpreters and first-class translators, the remainder second-class translators. Later they upped the over-all figure to 4,100, but, by the time the scheme came to an end, we know that closer to 5,000 were selected and trained.

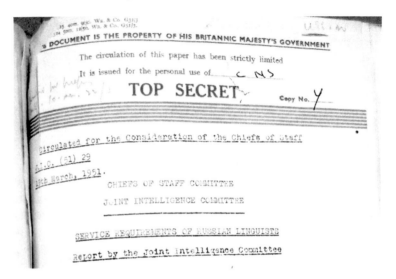

3.   JIC Paper, March 1951. Photograph taken by Professor Richard Aldrich at the National Archives in Kew, London.

An important JIC paper of March 1951 indicated that all three armed forces were able to list the exact additional numbers that would be needed, with their ranks and specific skills, should hostilities break out. In Table 1, perhaps the most interesting statistic is that almost all of the 438 translators projected for the Navy would have gone to sea, there, presumably, to search the air waves for plain language radio messages transmitted within the Soviet fleet, and between it and shore bases. The numbers quoted are not round estimates: the personnel department appears to have added up the additional individuals required, ship by ship, perhaps, to obtain figures that give a spurious sense of accuracy. They would have been mindful, no doubt, of men such as Alan Ross intercepting German radio messages during the late war. As a seaman, he had served on board a destroyer escorting convoys up the East Coast under attack from E-boats. He was able to brief his captain about German intentions, as enemy commands were communicated in plain language.[8]

At the outset of official discussions in 1949 national servicemen were being recruited for 18 months.[9] A year and a half did not allow enough time for a minimum of 'military' training, a long language programme, a continuation course to cover military Russian, and a follow-up period to practise the newly acquired skills. Consequently, the committees discussed at some length other means of procuring suitable recruits for RL training. The JIC paper of 19 March 1951 brought the debate to a head more than two years after planning had started. They proposed that for all three Services 2,688 RLs should be trained. Of these, fewer than half, only 1,216, were to be national servicemen. Making up the other 1,452 recruits were 741 women (probably all service women), 146 men above military age, 440 men of lower medical category and 125 foreigners. The Navy's requirement was for 833 RLs, of whom 477 would be national servicemen, and the remaining 356 made up of 258 women, 39 men above military age, 39 men of lower medical category (young men implied) and 20 foreigners (Table 1).

The proposed solutions to the shortfall in numbers of conscripted men bristled with difficulties. True, the country had received a great number of aliens from eastern Europe who had no cause to favour the Soviet Union, and many of them had a good knowledge of Russian, as did Ukrainians and Balts, who, as Soviet citizens, had been compelled to learn the language at school. After much debate, however, the JIC decided that this category would be useful only as potential censors in time of war, and should not be employed on any secret work. Though women were believed to be better at picking up languages than men, they posed quite different problems. (According to the written record, the committees did not contemplate co-education, which we would have found attractive!

---

8   Alan Ross, *Blindfold Games.*

9   After the 1939-45 war national service was continued on an *ad hoc* basis, until the National Service Act 1948 set a period of 12 months full-time military service for all young men, increased to 18 months before the Act even came into force on 1 January 1949. The Korean War occasioned an increase to two years full-time service, from September 1950. After full-time service, three and a half years had to be served on the reserve, with a liability to three stints of recall training/service of up to twenty days each.

Category	Interpreters	Translators	Total	Remarks
Fit men of military age	39	438	477	Of the 438 translators, 400 are for service at sea.
Women	63	195	258	
Men above military age	21	18	39	
Men of lower medical category	39		39	
Foreigners	10	10	20	
Totals	172	661	833	Of this total, 697 are for Signals Intelligence duties, 136 for Intelligence duties.

Table 1 Quotas of Russian Linguists proposed for the Admiralty by the JIC

Source: JIC (51) 29, 19 March 1951 in TNA/ADM 116/6332.

Notes: The authors have changed slightly the terms used to distinguish the classes of linguists. The interpreter column above includes 21 1st class translators (being men above military age) shown separately in the original; and the JIC's 2nd class translators have been labelled simply translators. This table and parallel tables for the other Services are the first mention of Signals Intelligence in the document collection; over 70% of the RLs were earmarked for such duties.

However, as Bill Hetherington has pointed out to us, at least one woman was eventually recruited, by the Women's Royal Air Force. She joined the 5th Intake at Coulsdon, being made a sergeant to keep her separate from the men students, except for actual JSSL classes.)

Within two days of the JIC meeting, Mr C G H Cardo, head of Commission and Warrant branch at the Admiralty (CW - responsible for recruiting officers), issued this forceful rejoinder:

> Women cannot be coerced; and even if inducement is offered to them to learn Russian, this must be followed by persuasion to keep their knowledge brushed up and further persuasion to be ready for duty when required – all this without any guarantee that they will in fact be available when required. Men over military age would, in general, find the study of Russian too hard. Men of lower medical categories might be exploited with the assistance of the Ministry of Labour [and National Service] … As regards foreigners, the JIC have themselves set the limitation. [Cardo's emphases][10]

From this point (21 March 1951) none of the 'other' categories was mentioned in the surviving documents, which refer only to national servicemen, apart from an occasional aside about regulars.

Cardo, however, was anxious to get on with the job, and proposed that the MoD should approach the Treasury and the Cabinet defence committee for funding to cover 1,216 national servicemen in the first instance, and to expand up to 2,600 as soon as 'supplementary arrangements can be made'. This was to be the programme up to 1954, which in due course was intended to go for another five years to 1959. On 24 April 1951 potential wastage was estimated as up to 37 per cent on interpreter, and 23 per cent on translator, courses - figures that turned out to be pessimistic for most intakes, judging by the recollections we have gathered. Yet, as the Navy was experiencing 25 per cent failure rates among regular recruits on technical courses, one can understand the pessimism associated with the very great leap in the dark that RL training entailed.[11]

---

10 Elliott and Shukman printed the JIC's list of reservations about aliens in *Secret Classrooms,* p 37.

11 The 25 per cent is quoted in *Naval Review,* 1949 (1), p 23. For the Coulsdon intake of August 1952 we have had a report of about 60 per cent fall-out of naval personnel from the translator course. This intake was made up of men who were recruited in the spring of 1952, a time of year

Whitehall exerts itself - summer and autumn 1951

With the Universities of London and Cambridge established as the first homes for training Russian language interpreters, it is not surprising that the mandarins should turn their attention to finding within the nearby Home Counties suitable military accommodation for the translator schools. Having both sorts of course in close proximity would be convenient and perhaps ensure high standards at the latter. Whitehall's alleged prejudice against the provinces may also have played a part in official thinking. Ironically, however, the choice for the first translator school fell on a partly disused Army camp on faraway Bodmin Moor, in Cornwall. Though, to be fair to the administrators, Coulsdon Common, a few miles south of Croydon, was picked for the second school, even if it only lasted about two years before everything was concentrated on Bodmin until the summer of 1956. Then the whole enterprise was transported by special train to Crail, in even further away Fife, Scotland, where it survived until the scheme came to an end in March 1960.

The first mention of Bodmin and Coulsdon came on 14 August 1951, in a War Office note saying the sites would be made available from 1 October 1951 and 1 February 1952, respectively (in those days it was the War Office that was responsible for the Army, as a single service). Thus it fell to the Army to provide lodging and canteens at the translator schools for all the students who were to attend – to their chagrin: the broad consensus is that Army living quarters and food were significantly below RN and RAF standards, and the Army officers small-minded and out of sympathy with the schools' *raison d'être*. Of course, we did not expect *cordon bleu* cookery and boarding-school-quality accommodation, but some commonsense understanding of why we were there would have been welcome.

On 25 August 1951 Mr Cardo sent a one-page memo to 28 (!) different recipients inside the Admiralty that the inter-Service scheme for the *university* JSSLs would be put into practice on 1

when few graduates and sixth-form school leavers were available; in later years the August intakes at JSSLs were much smaller than the November and February intakes. Drop-out from most of the translator courses was probably well under five per cent, but higher figures were experienced on a number of interpreter courses, which were much more demanding, even for good linguists, 30 per cent being quoted for those who went up to London in January 1953 (from the Coulsdon intake of October 1952).

October. The Admiralty was taking on the responsibility for JSSL London, the lightest of the three administrative burdens, and an officer-in-charge had already been appointed. In the event, London sometimes took on Army and RAF interpreter students, as well as Naval, because on several occasions the Navy failed to provide enough candidates to make it an economic proposition for the university. At Cambridge the RAF, the responsible Service, had to fall back on two airfields to provide domestic accommodation for their Army and RAF students, who were housed there for several months until Foxton Hall, located a few miles out of town, could be bought and converted.

Then on 24 September 1951, one week before three JSSLs opened, the Secretary to the Admiralty sent copies of a two-page SECRET letter (presumably by confidential couriers) to the three home fleet Commanders-in-Chief, the commodores of the Royal Naval Barracks in Chatham, Plymouth and Portsmouth, as well as to the Commanding Officer of Victoria Barracks, Portsmouth. The CinC Plymouth had complained of not knowing what was afoot at nearby Bodmin, which had been attached to his command. However, the CO of Victoria Barracks was the most important recipient in practical terms, since men called up as coders special had to spend about three weeks there, being kitted out and taught to march before going to JSSL Bodmin; therefore, they could have been expected almost any day. The Secretary explained that in these exceptional circumstances men commissioned as midshipmen would start their course at JSSL London on 1 October, without a period of pre-university training as ratings. He also referred, in paragraph 4, to 'special radio duties' - the first mention in our Admiralty document collection of the sigint intercept work for which coders would be trained after the nine-month language course. Coders would wear Class III uniform (jacket and tie), would form a sub-division of Communications within the Executive Branch, and would be borne on the books of HMS *Drake* (Plymouth), if at Bodmin, and HMS *Victory* (Portsmouth), if at Coulsdon.

The secret letter states:

> The first course for second class translators will start at Bodmin on 1 October. There will be no Coders (Sp) on this course. The second course at Bodmin will start on 1 November.

In the event, these two courses appear to have been combined. Patrick Miller, one of our contacts, and about 40 other coders were on the 1 November course. Alan Gosling and five other recruits seem to have been 'mislaid' later in November, spending six weeks at Victoria Barracks to form part of a national service guard of honour for a visit of the Second Sea Lord. They were sent to London as ratings on an interpreter course, but transferred to Coulsdon in February 1952, as part of the first intake there. Future courses were scheduled to start at Bodmin or Coulsdon on approximately 1 February, 1 August and 1 November each year, with 250 students on each course, of whom it was hoped normally about 90 would be coders (S). At London, courses were to start on 1 October, 1 January and 1 April each year, a maximum of 50 on each course, of whom normally 25 would be midshipmen. These dates were adhered to, give or take a few days, probably until the JSSLs closed, but the numbers recruited are another matter.

The penultimate paragraph of the letter contained an apology for shortness of notice – effectively only three days:

> The preparation of this scheme has been made in conditions of urgency and the extent to which Naval ratings will be trained at Bodmin and Coulsdon was not decided until 21st ... This letter has been graded SECRET because of the special duties referred to in paragraph 4.
>
> BY COMMAND OF THEIR LORDSHIPS – W A Medrow (*for* the Secretary)

Running the show - the documentary record after 1 October 1951

On 1 October 1951 the initial hesitations were behind them, decisive action had been hurriedly taken, and now the Progressing Committee for the Training of RLs (later, the Inter-Departmental RLs Committee) was administering three JSSLs and setting up the fourth. Judging by the surviving documents, they were largely left to get on with it on their own, although there had to be contact with the Treasury in order to get funds for the period 1954-59. Recruiting competent linguists is a problem frequently referred to in the documents, and in the first year or so there was much nervous counting up of how many each Service had 'scored', alongside expressed anxieties about appointing suitable instructors, principals and commandants at both Bodmin and Coulsdon.

Another issue regularly cropping up was how men should be selected for the more advanced, interpreter courses. The complication for the Navy was the double hurdle it had erected: its insistence on officer-like qualities as well as academic ability. This argument ran on into the final years of JSSLs.

There had never been such a huge demand for Russian teaching materials - a small point, but one that underlines the newness of everything. Books had to be acquired, some only available from the continent. A Working Party on Syllabuses and Standards, the so-called 'moderating committee', was instituted, and it was realised that an Applied Language Course needed to be set up to fit translators for their 'Special (radio intercept) Duties'. Provision for refresher training had to be made, too.

The appointment of principals highlights how much of a headache the launching of the JSSL scheme caused the responsible military hierarchs, especially the basic 'Service' schools at Bodmin, Coulsdon and Crail. (There was no need to appoint principals for JSSLs London and Cambridge, as university academics were available.) Ideally, the Committee were looking for men with knowledge of Russian and some relevant teaching ability, as well as management experience in education at a suitably high level. At first, civilians were preferred, as the camp commandants were to be Army officers and the schools were to be managed by the Army, the first two on War Office property.

However, the Ministry of Education, if not common sense, could easily have told the military authorities that finding civilians for temporary appointments, and with such little notice, put them on a hiding to nothing. Short-term civil service posts were paid less than the established ones, a tricky point that was to crop up in a dispute about instructors' salaries (see chapter 5). Had the Ministry of Education played a bigger role in the scheme, salary scales would more likely have been those for technical college staff, where the distinction between established and unestablished posts did not arise. Apart from a few men returning from overseas and seeking new posts in the UK, practically all the appropriately qualified people would have been in permanent employment, and morally, if not legally, bound to give notice if they moved on. The JIC were making preparations on the assumption of an early war, but the country was at peace. Civilians could not be forcibly conscripted; even secondments would have been difficult to arrange.

Unlike civilians, however, Service officers could be posted where and when required, although there might be difficulty in persuading their departments to release them. Thus, as an interim measure, two RAF officers with Kidbrooke experience were appointed to take charge at Bodmin, effectively as principal and deputy; they must have been paid their contemporary Service salaries. The problem of a principal for Coulsdon was still exercising the committee as late as 4 January 1952, when no appointment had been made, although the school was due to open in February, and instructors to report in ten days time. The solution must have been temporary, as in May 1952 Wing-Commander A R D MacDonell was sent to Coulsdon for nine months.[12]

The appointment of instructors seems to have caused the committee much less head scratching. At a ratio of one instructor to ten students, significant numbers would be needed, and there would be as many as 50-60 at a JSSL when the build-up was complete. Professor Liza Hill, as Director of the Cambridge course, was responsible for interviewing many applicants for instructor posts ahead of the appointment of principals. Taking part in the process as members of the 'moderating committee' were the Director of the London course, Dr George Bolsover of the School of Slavonic and East European Studies, University of London, and Naky Doniach of GCHQ, who was to become inspector of JSSLs.[13] It is curious that none of our ex-coder contacts has reported principals or the 'inspector' sitting in with instructors to assess standards of teaching, as would have been the Ministry of Education's approach. Instead, exclusive reliance appears to have been placed on examination results, with the exception of one official visit to Bodmin on 24-25 November 1952.

---

12 Donald MacDonell, *From Dogfight to Diplomacy*, especially chs. 35, 43, 44. MacDonell was a Russian speaker, trained at Cambridge and in Paris, September 1951-April 1952, ahead of his projected appointment as Air Attaché, Moscow, which followed in 1956-58. He described his time at Coulsdon as 'the nadir of his career', but succeeded in getting sacked some instructors who could be blamed for a high failure rate.

13 Geoffrey Elliott and Harold Shukman, *Secret Classrooms*, pp 33-34.

The visiting officers on that occasion were Group-Captain W T Matthews of the Air Ministry's Education Service, Lieutenant-Colonel H K Evans of the Army Education Department, Lieutenant-Commander A E H Sladen of the Department of Naval Intelligence (not an instructor-officer), and Dr Bolsover, all members of the 'moderating committee'. They toured the campus, then split up and 'visited various classes while instruction was in progress, and talked with cadets in and out of class'. Reference to 'cadets' suggests that they only sat in with the interpreters' continuation classes, which had 'started under adverse conditions six weeks ago'. Attention was paid to deficiencies in the accommodation, both domestic and instructional, but, judging from the recollections of later students, this did not produce improvement to a decent standard. However, the main worry was on the teaching side, where the lack of well-qualified staff was the problem, and an effort was made to suggest more effective means of recruitment. They hoped to get two or three first-class honours graduates in Russian and six or seven native-language teachers with a university education. There was also a need to appoint several more Service officers for the orientation exercises, one of whom should be a Naval officer – the Navy had none such in post at the time. (In everyday terms, 'orientation' was to prevent students learning the Russian for words the English meaning of which was not understood.) So, nothing much appears to have been done about on-site assessment of translator training. The visitors expressed satisfaction, falling in with Bodmin's suggestion that translators would be capable of taking A-level Russian.

Planning how to train translators for sigint work

Having launched the first language courses, the Inter-Departmental Committee on RLs soon had to consider what was to follow for the translators, who would have nine months or more still to serve. References to post-language training are scarce in the documents consulted. This may have been a simple security precaution, or because the nature of the work we would have to do during a war had not been thought out, or a combination of the two factors, or even, possibly, the result of document loss or destruction. Whatever the truth, there ought to have been, even quite early on, some serious discussion of our eventual function in any war with the Soviet Union. Yet in 1949 the Services had responded hesitantly to a query about the numbers of RLs required. The bulk of coders special would have gone to sea, there, one assumes, to listen mainly to plain language radio messages between the Soviet Admiralty and its ships, and between the ships themselves and airplanes operating alongside them. Being at sea, we would have relayed intercepted messages to our captains, just as Alan Ross had done in WWII on convoy protection duties, or, as one retired Naval officer in a private communication told us, had occurred during the Korean war, when Russian voices were heard coming from the latest MiG fighters (although the Soviets were not officially engaged in that conflict).

A document of March 1952 noted that an '<u>Applied</u> [our emphasis] Language Course' was required for Navy and RAF *kursanty,* to last four months, the first intake to be on 1 July 1952. This was being planned under the leadership of Wing-Commander Hudson, of the RAF's Signals Branch, yet another example of the Navy relying on the RAF to take the lead. About three-quarters of the time was to be spent on 'specialist language study' (implying lots of new vocabulary), and the course was to take place at a JSSL. The men involved were those who went to Bodmin in the autumn of 1951 and would have had about nine months there by July. In the event, the course was organised in a much more appropriate location – the secure environment of RAF Wythall, a few miles south of Birmingham, which had been a barrage balloon station during the war. Here radios, tape recorder-players and other necessary equipment, comparable with that found in civilian language laboratories, were set up where prying eyes could not get a view, nor ears eavesdrop. It was only on 9 December 1953, when Wythall had been operational for over a year, that it got a mention as the place to which the 'lower-grade linguists' of the RN and RAF would continue to go for applied language training in the second phase of the scheme during 1955-59.

Y is for eavesdropping

Then there was the question what to do with many of us during the roughly six month period after Wythall - a problem entirely unmentioned in the document collection. Perhaps this is to be expected, as the archive was essentially concerned with inter-Service collaboration, and our time at monitoring stations at Cuxhaven and Kiel in the north of West Germany would be spent independently of both the Army and the RAF. However, it was not independent of GCHQ, which solved the problem of what all three sets of *kursanty* on special duties could do in peace time, when no Soviet forces, or hardly any, could be monitored in action. The most important objective of the scheme was being achieved as soon as men emerged from the first Wythall course in the autumn of 1952: they constituted a reserve which could be called up if war broke out. For GCHQ it was a very welcome bonus that several hundred men could be on watch at a number of places functioning like their Y (or monitoring) stations in the German war. These had been mainly run by the Army and the RAF, but the Navy had a large Y station at Scarborough and others dotted around Britain.[14]

Though little is known about it, as early as 1950 the Navy also had a 'forward listening station' tracking Soviet military activity. It was on the North Sea coast of West Germany, at Bremerhaven, in all likelihood at the same location as the later US sigint operation. Also around this time, Lieutenant-Commander John Harvey-Jones, afterwards a highly successful industrialist and TV business trouble-shooter, was directing the 'British Baltic Fishery Protection Service', which carried out clandestine intelligence gathering, using converted E-boats. Already by 1949 the RAF was conducting serious signals intelligence work from a number of sites in northern West Germany, and probably had the most advanced listening programme of the three services.[15]

By the time coders trained in sigint operations were sent to work at the Naval bases in Cuxhaven and Kiel, it was GCHQ that suggested wavelengths and bands to monitor and search; and it was to GCHQ that our intercepts were sent by teleprinter and confidential courier via Bremerhaven.

Refresher training for coder reservists on annual recall was discussed on 9 December 1953, when it was planned to send us back to RAF Wythall. This never happened, and, instead, we found ourselves going back to Cuxhaven (later, Kiel) for two or three

---

14 F H Hinsley and Alan Stripp (eds), *Code Breakers: the inside story of Bletchley Park*, Oxford University Press, 1993, p vi. Also private information from John Wise derived from his researches on Navy Y stations for a book provisionally entitled *Someone is Listening – a Brief History of Radio and Electronic Warfare 1900–1990*, awaiting publication.

15 Dennis Mills, 'Signals intelligence and the Coder Special Branch of the Royal Navy in the 1950s', pp 648-49.

weeks of somewhat desultory work on low priority wave-lengths, but we enjoyed our 'old boys reunions', and that is how Tony Cash and Mike Gerrard happened to meet, although belonging to intakes a couple of years apart.

CHAPTER 2
RAW RECRUITS

СAЛAКA — HE PЫБA, CAЛAГA — HE MOPЯК
(Russian naval saying – 'A sprat's not a fish, a sprog's not a sailor')

Received wisdom had it that the Royal Navy admitted no national service recruits. In fact, over the whole fifteen-year period of peacetime conscription less than two per cent of all those enlisted were sailors, the other ninety-eight per cent joining the Army or RAF.

The outbreak of war in Korea led to compulsory service being extended in September 1950 from eighteen months to two years. The longer time span made it possible for conscripts to receive training comparable with that for regular naval ratings, who normally had to sign on for a minimum term of seven years. Members of the Royal Naval Volunteer Reserve (RNVR) were eligible to be drafted into the Navy, provided they had completed at least three weeks' training and could satisfy certain medical conditions. This was a continuation of wartime practice, often encapsulated in the assertion, 'messing about in boats will get you into the "wavy Navy"' (a reference to RNVR officers' 'wavy' stripes). Many RNVR men lived in or near port towns, where the depot ships were located, and often came from seafaring backgrounds. Membership of the Sea Cadet Corps, the naval section of a school Combined Cadet Force (CCF), or the Sea Scouts was also helpful in gaining entry to the Senior Service.

Getting into the Navy –
with a bit of help from the Russians

Between 1951 and 1960 a second channel into the Navy, for sufficiently qualified conscripts, was through volunteering for the Russian language course at one of the newly created Joint Services' Schools for Linguists. An Admiralty document of April 1951 reveals that the Ministry of Labour and National Service had agreed to earmark potential Russian linguists as and when they first registered.

Those selected would be graduates or holders of the Higher School Certificate (about to be replaced by GCE A-level), with a language bias. Also to be considered were men currently studying languages, but so far not qualified beyond School Certificate (soon to be O-level).[1]

The two-year period of national service gave the Navy scope for training coders special in some basic naval skills, followed by a JSSL course at translator level, a radio course, and subsequent practice as Russian language radio operators. Alternatively, students with high marks at the first Russian progress test were interviewed for commissions in Intelligence, those successful transferring to much longer courses as interpreters. The Admiralty was very concerned about the possibility of high wastage rates: these could lead to too many men having to be transferred to an alternative role, for which the training would not be finished in time to allow any productive work.[2] Yet, over the nine-year period we are considering, more than 1,500 Navy men successfully followed one or other of the interpreter/translator routes, a figure very similar to that achieved by the other two services, despite the Navy being the smallest of the three – the Army was more than twice the size of the Navy.[3]

Recruitment of coders special was simple in principle, but haphazard in practice, albeit possibly less so than parallel Army and RAF procedures, whereby men were selected for JSSLs only after basic training; the Navy identified suitable candidates first, before calling them up.[4] News about the scheme trickled round recruiting

---

1   TNA/ADM 116/6332, RL/P 51.7, Selection and Intake for Training of RLs, 24 April 1951.

2   One early estimate calculated a failure rate as high as 37 per cent among interpreters, and even 23 per cent on the translator courses (TNA/ADM 116/6332, 8 May 1951). In the event, the drop-out levels were very much lower, perhaps under 5 per cent on the translator courses.

3   The 1948 Cabinet papers include a forecast of the sizes of the three Services for 31 March 1949: RN, 145,000; Army, 345,000; RAF, 226,000 (TNA/CAB 129.24, p 3). Also in 1948, and on the assumption of an 18-month period of national service, the sizes on 1 January 1952 were expected to be: RN, 152,000; Army, 381,000; RAF, 176,000 (TNA/CAB 129.31, p 34).

4   The Army appears to have excluded from JSSLs men with promising military or technical skills; likewise the RAF, in relation to potential aircrew.

centres and among young civilian men at a slow, uneven pace - the grapevine as significant a conduit into the JSSLs as official publicity. Viewed in nearly 60-year hindsight, recruitment for the Russian course appears casual and amateurish, in comparison with today's sophisticated, heavily advertised, campaigns to entice volunteers into the military. Examples given below demonstrate the widely disparate recruitment experiences of some early coders special.

The call-up of 18-year-olds for national service was essentially an extension of the process adopted in World War Two. Men were defined by quarterly cohorts according to date of birth. On four designated Saturdays each year, those born in the relevant quarter were required to register at a local Employment Exchange. At the registration, a form was completed by a clerk asking for personal details, including education and prior work experience. For registrants still at school, such as the majority of likely coders, there was a right to have call-up deferred until completion of A-levels. In some cases university entrants had call-up deferred until graduation, but many universities held places back until national service had been completed. The last question on registration was about choice of service, branch or regiment, but came with a warning that there was no guarantee one's predilection would be favoured. This was the first stage of the process, the second being selection for a particular service, branch and unit. Selection was sometimes carried out at the same time and place as registration, but more frequently local or other circumstances meant returning on a later date to a different building, even in another town. A full medical examination was also compulsory.

Varying motivations for joining the Navy

Beyond the need to have linguistic qualifications, a number of common factors influenced the would-be coder's choice of service. These included a positive wish to get into the Navy (sometimes supported by the experience of older relatives); membership of Sea Scouts, naval Cadets, or the RNVR; and, in a few instances, a simple hankering for something 'different'. Also notable were a negative wish to avoid the Army and a desire to continue 'academic' study. Most coders were drafted after leaving sixth forms in which they had studied French and often one other language. They came from all parts of Britain, including far away Shetland and even

NATIONAL SERVICE ACTS, 1948

ENLISTMENT NOTICE

MINISTRY OF LABOUR AND NATIONAL SERVICE ~~Regional~~ OFFICE,

DOMINIONS HOUSE,

17 MAY 1952 (Date)

> MR. BRIAN T. JONES.
> 39 MORDEN RD
> NEWPORT
> MON.

Registration No. NLT. 23223 .

DEAR SIR,

In accordance with the National Service Acts, 1948, you are called up for service in the ROYAL NAVY/~~ROYAL MARINES~~ and are required to present yourself on MONDay 2 JUN 1952 (date), between 9 a.m. and 4 p.m. to :—

VICTORIA BARRACKS.
SOUTHSEA
HANTS

PORTSMOUTH & SOUTHSEA (nearest railway station).

* A Travelling Warrant for your journey is enclosed. Before starting your journey you must exchange the warrant for a ticket at the booking office named on the warrant. If possible, this should be done a day or two before you are due to travel. If your warrant is made out to travel from London you may obtain a railway ticket at, and travel from, the most convenient station to your address.

A Postal Order for 4s. representing an advance of service pay, is also enclosed.

Immediately on receipt of this notice, you should inform your employer of the date upon which you are required to report for service.

Yours faithfully,

YOU SHOULD READ CAREFULLY THE NOTES OVERLEAF

*Delete if not applicable.

for ~~Regional~~ Controller.

N.S.12 (12/48) M17496 10M 4/49 CN&Co 749 (5630)

[P.T.O.

4. Prior to joining the Navy all coders would have received similar notification to report to Victoria Barracks. Courtesy Brian Jones.

the autonomous Isle of Man. Dennis Mills's intake at Coulsdon contained one New Zealander and one Canadian, neither of whom was obliged to do UK national service at all.

There were particular problems for the Navy, starting with the fact that it had a quota of only about 2,500 national servicemen a year, extended by 400 to make it possible to recruit men as coders (special).[5] Many smaller towns had no Navy representative in the selection process, but RAF recruiting sergeants seem to have been quite well briefed, and would sometimes put potential Russian linguists on the right track. Some men were only provisionally selected as coders, being sent for interviews by formal boards or for tests organised by the Admiralty, generally at Victoria Barracks (colloquially, Vicky Barracks, often Vicky B) or Royal Naval Barracks (RNB), both at Portsmouth, where successful applicants were eventually to join the Navy. Yet the authors cannot now discern any particular reason why the majority of our 'sample' were selected on the spot at their local centre, whilst some had to go on long journeys (even from Scotland), which must have meant significant Admiralty expense.

One of the first coders to be enrolled was Patrick Miller, product of an independent school, St John's, Leatherhead, who required a few months' deferment to take an examination. He had expressed a preference for the RN, and was asked to complete and return a couple of forms to the Navy. He was able to declare having obtained A-levels in French and Greek:

> So it came as no surprise when I was required to submit myself to medical examination on 5 September 1951 on the first floor of the South Western Hotel in Southampton. This involved a brisk and efficient poke about one's person and in my memory is linked with an interview and an IQ test, although I imagine these must have been at another place and time. The IQ test, I remember, included prose to be précis-ed, numbers manipulated, and shapes to be reassembled; one involved the picture of a nail to be associated with the appropriate tool (a chisel, saw and hammer were options, I recall). It was necessary to suppress a perverse choice.

---

5 TNA/ADM 116/6332, Director of Naval Intelligence to Cardo, re Requirements of RLs, 31 March 1951.

In the summer of 1952 Tony Cash, in Leeds, found out about the Russian language course from a friend with long-established RN connections, so when he registered for national service he said he was prepared to join the Navy, if this guaranteed entry to the course. He had studied languages at school and intended to do so again at university. Subsequently he was called up to Vicky Barracks for three weeks' basic training, which became a regular routine for most of us.

Bill Musker, in the same intake as Tony, lived in Southampton, had been in the Sea Scouts, and was an assistant Sea Scoutmaster at the time of his call-up, with knowledge of German, French and Latin at various levels. His troop was in contact with an admiral, no less, who, hearing of Bill's qualifications and sea-faring fervour, organised proceedings so that Bill never had an interview, and went direct to Vicky Barracks, knowing that he was to be a coder special.

Geoff Robson's situation, if not unique, was also unusual, as he had completed an honours degree in Russian and German at Nottingham University in June 1952. The national service centre there knew about the demand for Russian linguists, and he was soon summoned for an interview at the Admiralty, and on Monday 11 August he reported to Vicky Barracks. However, unlike the coder special intake of that date, he was not supplied with uniform, but told on the Friday to report the next week to the London JSSL. There he joined the second intake to the interpreter course, which had already been studying Russian for six months.

The Nottingham centre seems to have been well clued-up, as Geoff Sharp was also recruited there, having been a graduate student in the university department of pharmacology. Hearing about the Russian course, he asked if he might be considered on the strength of his matriculation (O-level) French, and his wish was granted. Presumably the Nottingham centre offered him the Navy entry because the route to JSSL through the Army and RAF was unreliable.

Another group of coders entered the Navy in 1952, through the RNVR: John Carter, Adam Pyke, John Wade and Dennis Mills. John Wade says he cannot now recall how he came to be re-categorised from seaman to coder special, which may lead us to conclude that the process was straightforward. By contrast, Dennis Mills could almost claim to have 'got in twice', once through the RNVR and once through volunteering to go on the Russian course, as he has explained:

> I was told at the Lincoln selection centre that it was impossible to get into the Navy, even for RNVR ratings. This led to a fairly acrimonious argument, which stopped when the civilian interviewing officer went quiet and started scrimmaging through papers in the drawers of his desk. Eventually he found a leaflet to consult, then looked at my form and said, 'I see you did French and Latin in the sixth form – would you consider learning Russian?' That was all three years before: I had taken a degree in geography since then. My head span momentarily, before I heard myself saying, 'Yes'.

Adam Pyke's case was very different. The example of his father, a gunnery officer in the RNVR during the war, is what led him also to join. His eyesight was below the standard required for a seaman, and he was offered the choice of sick berth attendant (not for the squeamish, he thought) and electrician's mate, second class (EM2), so he 'chose the screwdriver rather than the bedpan'. On call-up for national service, he reported to HMS *Collingwood*, the shore base that trained electricians, and found wielding screwdrivers, soldering irons, and the like stretched his practical competence too far. As a national serviceman, he could not transfer to become a writer (clerk), but meantime his father had heard about the Russian language course. A request through his divisional officer for transfer was speeded on its way by virtue of Adam's year at Grenoble University, spent in 'digs' with a French family. So after ten weeks as an EM2, and without going to Vicky Barracks, Adam joined the coders special.

Most of the erstwhile RNVR ratings experienced another of the Navy's rites of passage. Reporting to Vicky Barracks with their 'square rig' uniforms (traditional sailor suits) they exchanged these for 'fore-and-aft rigs' (uniforms comprising shirts and ties and conventional jackets and trousers). Dennis Mills reported wearing square rig, and was obliged by the leading wren in 'slops' (the stores) to strip down to vest and pants, in full view, before she would issue his new uniform – we suspect she enjoyed her chances to play this trick on 'sprogs' (raw recruits). Fore-and-aft rig was worn by all ratings in so-called 'miscellaneous' categories, such as cooks, stewards and writers, until 1957, when the Navy decided to issue to new entrants in all branches the modernised square rig worn by junior rates in such traditional Naval roles as seaman, signaller and stoker (engine-room mechanic).

Lionel Franklyn had graduated at Leeds in English, and remembers that he was recruited at a Navy office in Coventry:

> At first I was told there were no places for national servicemen, but after I had taken an easy intelligence test ('Cor blimey, you've got them all right') I was offered an interview. 'Was I any good at <u>modern</u> languages?' was the main question. 'Well', I said, 'I have done a lot of Latin and also a bit of Anglo-Saxon.' She seemed happy with that, perhaps knowing that Russian is a language like Latin, with many case endings - but probably not.

John Cole was older than most of us, having graduated BA and MA in geography, the second degree resulting from study in Italy; his languages also included French and Spanish. At the Blackheath centre a panel of officers turned him down for a commission in the RAF, and he was passed on to a naval petty officer; at that point the route to Vicky Barracks was probably obvious.

Bob Bower, in King's Lynn, knew about the Russian course through his sixth form teacher, and perhaps was thus better informed than those who did national service after taking a degree, or after a period at work. However, Bob had to prompt the people at the Cambridge centre – Cambridge, of all places, where one of the JSSL interpreter courses was already running. Perhaps its existence really was kept secret!

As a sixth-former in Manchester, Graham Young had no knowledge of the Russian course, nor any inclination to join the Navy, at least until he discovered that his first choice of service, the RAF, was not to be. Graham, a keen fell-walker, had from 1950 spent many a Sunday hiking in the Peak District, which was, he says:

> ... half an hour's ride and a few shillings' fare from Manchester by train. When I went for my interview I told the flight-sergeant that I wanted to join the Mountain Rescue Service (MRS) - there was a troop near Buxton, and I thought I knew the area. Perhaps, for the flight-sergeant, I looked too bookish or unlikely

to stand up to the physical demands of MRS work, I don't know. I have an idea he said that the branch was open only to regulars, but he didn't invite me to sign on. So he did me a good turn in suggesting that I learn Russian, to do which I should have to join the RN.

Sam Hindley and Mick Taylor were in the same sixth form in Bolton when they jointly decided to try for the Navy. As they had studied modern languages for their A-levels, they felt more or less qualified for the Russian course, about which they had vague information. The Bolton centre sent them to Salford for interviews, in which they were both successful. Was it, perhaps, the same flight-sergeant who had interviewed Graham Young?

At school in Northampton Clifford German had identified 'something academic' as a priority for his national service: he feared lest his intellectual faculties atrophy during the two years he would have to spend before taking up the place he had won at Cambridge University. The Russian course, he realised, would be attainable, even guaranteed, if he opted for the Navy rather than the Army or RAF.

Having an admiral in the family, might help you into the Navy, even one whose career had been somewhat turbulent. Old Etonian Robin Hope could boast an uncle, Admiral John Godfrey, who had been Director of Naval Intelligence at the start of World War Two:

> ... but was sacked by Churchill when the German battleship *Scharnhorst* sailed undetected through the English Channel one night. He was exiled to India and given the lovely title FOCRIN, Flag Officer Commanding Royal Indian Navy. Unfortunately for Uncle John, the Indian sailors at the end of the war became impatient of the delays in their demobilisation, and mutinied. As a punishment, he was denied the knighthood to which his rank of vice-admiral normally entitled him on retirement. In a lot of old papers not long ago I came across a letter from Admiral Godfrey to a colleague in the Admiralty, saying that his nephew was a fine young man who came into the Navy with his blessing and should do well.

Still fumbling their way in - coders conscripted from 1953

Arnold Bell joined the Navy from work as a clerk in a Blackburn office, having taken French and Latin among his O-levels. He was

5. Members of the Combined Cadet Force parading at Robin Pearce's grammar school in Grimbsy, early 1950s. Courtesy R Pearce.

studying French and geography at A-level in evening school when he reported for selection and was confronted by an Army sergeant, who told him he would be joining the local regiment, based at a barracks in Preston, for initial training:

> Every young man in Blackburn then was enlisted in the East Lancs, that's where you went. All of my age had heard in the town's pubs lurid tales of what went on there, the harshness, bullying and whipping. So I told the sergeant that I wanted to join the Navy. 'You can't do that: the only way to get in the Navy is' - he went off to search for papers in his desk, ruffled around, and then came up with - 'to DO Russian'; not, 'LEARN Russian'. 'Put me down for that', I replied - anything rather than the East Lancs, or other infantry regiment, was my only concern.

Arnold was summoned to Portsmouth, with several more candidates, for tests and interviews conducted by senior officers, and by 10 August 1953 he was at Vicky Barracks as a coder special.

Robin Pearce also belonged to the minority recruited from civilian employment rather than the educational sector. He had been to school in Grimsby, where a talk about national service in the Navy so impressed him he joined the school CCF. Robin had taken three science subjects, enabling him to find work at the Atomic Energy Research Establishment at Harwell. He had been there about a year when he was called for selection assessment at the nearby Reading centre. The interviewing Army officer seemed to know very little about coders special, and perhaps thought he was looking for men with three School Certificate passes in language subjects. Robin could offer a pass in French and some lower level tuition in German and Latin; his English Language pass, however, seems to have tipped the balance in his favour.

Devotees of the Navy

No-one at Humphrey Mildred's school in Hastings had any inkling how a youngster might do his national service in the Navy, but that is what he very much wanted to do, having harboured such an ambition from boyhood in the war. He had been told about the Russian course by an older friend, and with French and Latin qualifications under his belt he went to the Brighton centre looking for an entry on this basis. There a friendly RN warrant officer, who knew about JSSLs, sent him for tests and interviews with officers at RN Barracks, Portsmouth, lengthy enough to require an overnight stay.

At school Nigel Hawkins joined the Sea Cadets and then the RNVR, because he had been told that this was the surest way of getting into the Navy. He was accepted for naval entry at the Bristol selection centre, but his eye test detected short-sightedness, so he was admitted to the supply and secretariat branch, still hoping he might make the Russian course. At a preliminary interview at Coulsdon it was decided that Nigel was, indeed, a suitable candidate for JSSL: he was re-categorised as coder special and sent to Vicky Barracks for basic training, after which he proceeded to JSSL Bodmin, Coulsdon by then having closed.

Like Humphrey Mildred and Nigel Hawkins, Gareth Mulloy had nursed since childhood an overriding ambition to serve in the RN. The son of a diplomat from the Irish Republic, he could have avoided the draft altogether, but at school in London he chose to join the naval section of the CCF, whose officer-in-charge was also his Greek teacher. It seems to have been this gentleman who in the summer of 1956 suggested to Gareth the Russian course:

> He was aware of my all-consuming interest in the Navy, and probably had a misplaced optimism about my linguistic talents following my distinction mark in O-level Ancient Greek; my A-level course was French, Latin and English. I had taken the entry exam for Dartmouth [RN officer training college], but had failed the mathematics paper, so that ambition was nipped early in the bud. Nevertheless, my interest in the Navy was obsessive.
>
> So, when I presented myself at the selection interview I said I wanted to learn Russian, and was asked if I had a preference of service; I answered that I wanted to learn Russian in the Royal Navy. The answer was curt. 'Was you in the RNVR or Sea Cadets?' 'No, but I was an Instructor Cadet in the Naval Section of my CCF.' 'Never heard of a Russian course, and the CCF don't count for nuffing. You've gotter choose either the Army or the RAF.' When I persisted, I was put into another, much smaller queue leading to a chief petty officer, who showed similar incredulity but agreed to pass my request up the line.

A month or so later I was summoned for an interview in RNB Chatham [an unusual venue, possibly a failure of memory here] where I was intrigued to find myself sitting opposite two Wren officers, whom I found attractive. I was 18 years old and very immature, but found the interview more agreeable and less forbidding than any I had expected. I undertook and passed various tests, among which was probably the test I have subsequently assumed to be of potential to learn a difficult foreign language. (I discovered this test, used by Foreign and Commonwealth Office recruiters, thirty years later, when I worked with the FCO in recruiting the last expatriates into the Hong Kong Administrative Service.)

Sailor by chance

Mike Shotton had studied A-level Latin, French and German at Stafford Grammar School, and had won a place at Oriel College, Oxford, to read modern languages after national service. He was, he says, required in 1954 to register at his local post office. He describes himself as 'totally unprepared' when the lady behind the counter filling in the form asked which service he was opting for:

> As far as I knew, based on the experience of school friends who had gone before me, the choice was limited to the Army or the RAF. So, being of a somewhat independent, not to say rebellious, nature, I instinctively replied, 'Navy, please'. Pretty rich, coming from someone with no naval connections and living about as far from the ocean as one can in the UK.

Eventually, Mike received a summons to a medical in Stoke on Trent, which followed the time-honoured custom:

> … of stripping off, being prodded, closing my eyes and balancing on one leg, and coughing while someone clutched a sensitive part of my anatomy.

He was then told to report to the desk of the service for which he had applied. He queried the whereabouts of the Navy desk, which was conspicuous by its absence:

> I got a funny look. Navy - they didn't get many of those. In fact, I was the only one that day. After some discussion, I was issued with a bus warrant, and told to find my way to a RN recruiting office on the other

> side of Stoke. Later, I found myself outside a window adorned with white ensigns and pictures of jolly tars, obviously having a wonderful time. I entered. Behind the counter stood a middle-aged chap in a Royal Marine sergeant's uniform. I felt very scruffy and small.

The sergeant explained to Mike how rare it was for national servicemen to be taken into the Navy, and that the only possible openings were as seaman or stoker, which he really did not recommend. His elaboration on the theme almost persuaded Mike that he might, indeed, be better off in the Army or RAF, as the sergeant was proposing. It was only when Mike had reached the door to leave that his interviewer told him to hang on. By now the Marine NCO had had a chance to look at Mike's papers. Realising that he was dealing with a grammar school boy, he asked whether he was any good at languages, and hearing the answer 'Yes', enquired whether he fancied doing another one:

> I sometimes wonder, if I had got to that door ten seconds earlier where would my life have gone? I rather doubt that the good sergeant would have chased me down the street.

Had Mike returned to the Army/RAF recruiting centre, as urged, he would probably never have ended up in 1969 marrying a Soviet wife.

Screening out undesirables

In our researches for this publication we have had access to a large number of government files. One was a SECRET Ministry of Defence document, dated 2 October 1951, containing the following statement referring to those who, whether Navy, Army or RAF, might be enrolled in the JSSLs:

> ... in all cases the potential linguists are first identified by the Ministry of Labour and National Service and all are security screened.[6]

During our service we heard vague rumours that some, maybe all, of us had been vetted to ensure our political reliability. We speculated and even joked that our more left-wing comrades might

6 *Ibid*/6333, Progressing Committee for the Training of Russian Linguists: progress report made at the start of the first training courses, 2 October 1951, p 2.

be 'commie' sympathisers whose best friends had been prevented from becoming coders because of the individuals they were associating with. It was certainly easy to understand that members of the (British) Communist Party might not make ideal coders, but checking out all aspirants would have been unbelievably expensive and fraught with practical difficulties. There is an intriguing passage in the biography of a former RAF *kursant*, Leslie Woodhead, in later life a distinguished TV programme-maker. He relates how a fellow JSSL linguist had told him:

> ... that when he'd been accepted for the Russian course, his neighbours had been quizzed about his background by strange men in macs.[7]

Professor Richard Aldrich, an expert on security matters, suspects that, given the hundreds of conscripts needing to be investigated, the normal practice would have been 'negative vetting':

> ... in other words, the names would have been run through the MI5 registry, looking for a trace in the archives; if no trace was found they were clean. The process of positive vetting - actually sending out people to do background checks - was just too time-consuming to do for everyone. GCHQ were often behind with their positive vetting.[8]

Between our first reporting to barracks and joining a JSSL, the authorities had a window of opportunity to weed out any coder considered, for whatever reason, unsuitable. This was the three weeks of basic training, during which we received our Navy number, paybook (serving also as official identity document, but without a photo), and uniform, as well as acquainting ourselves with essential Naval lore and learning to drill to an often bewildering array of parade ground commands. Some intakes were also given various aptitude tests, and the results might have influenced the decision whether a probationary coder would be rejected for the Russian course and transferred to another branch. Joe Daracott suffered this fate for reasons that were not made clear to him, as he told Tony Cash of the same 1952 intake. It is highly unlikely his exclusion was on political or security grounds: his later career in arts administration and the academic world included a distinguished 14-year stint as Keeper of Art at the Imperial War Museum.

---

7   Leslie Woodhead, *My Life as a Spy*, Macmillan, 2005, p 40.
8   Email, R J Aldrich to Tony Cash, 3 October 2011.

Basic training – the religious issue

One of the first questions put to newly arrived probationary coders was what religion we adhered to. Laidon Alexander laconically reports:

> When I said, 'agnostic', the PO raised an eyebrow, wrote down, 'C of E', said, 'Church of Egypt', explained, 'keep it simple'.

Patrick Miller similarly reports another doubter being told:

> 'You don't know? Put C of E, then, it's easier; you just get in, press the button, and up you go.'

Patrick later studied theology at Cambridge, taking holy orders at Oxford, and for more than half a century has been a pillar of the Church of England.

In all the accounts of national service that we have come across we have discovered no evidence of discrimination against non-conformists, Catholics, Jews or non-believers; we know of no recruit who was then a Buddhist and only one Muslim, a convert to that faith. Bill Hetherington recalls being issued with the *Naval Rating's Handbook* when he joined the Navy in October 1952. Published the previous year, this 'dos and don'ts of naval life' specifically states:

> You are not compelled to profess a religion; you can as an alternative declare your self an Agnostic or as having no religion.[9]

Tony Cash's agnostic response was accepted without demur, and if he sometimes wonders whether his avowed lack of religion affected his chances of being commissioned, it is only because of the experience of a university friend who went on to become a professor of psychology:

> Liam Hudson did his national service in the Royal Artillery. He'd won a scholarship to Oxford from Whitgift School, where he'd played rugby in the First XV. Outgoing and articulate, easily commanding respect, he was an obvious candidate for a commission. His senior officers spent ages, he told me, badgering him to change his entry as an atheist. To his, and, I suppose, to their credit, he resisted and was still commissioned.

---

9 *Naval Rating's Handbook*, Admiralty, 1951, p 62.

Basic training - first impressions

A few coders, Gerald Seaman among them, were invited to Portsmouth for an initial weekend's introduction, even before officially joining the Navy. His description of the Vicky Barracks he then saw will chime for all of us, whenever we first set foot inside:

> To this day I can still remember a long, high brick wall surmounted by barbed wire and with armed naval guards at the gates. The barracks square was filled with young naval ratings with rifles, marching round the perimeter, commands being hurled at them by fierce-looking petty officers, while periodically the air resounded with bugle calls and incomprehensible orders blasting over the tannoy system.

The petty officers and chief petty officers (POs and CPOs) are the RN equivalent of Army sergeants and sergeant majors, and they may have looked just as forbidding to us raw Naval recruits, but they were, for the most part, a very different kettle of fish. In the 1950s, Army non-commissioned officers (NCOs) from lance-corporal up, were notorious for giving new conscripts an extremely hard time, resorting fairly often to overt brutality in order, as they justified it, to instil from the outset discipline absolutely vital in combat. No such notoriety attached to Naval NCOs, whose attitude to us probationary coders was only slightly less benign than Robin Hope has claimed:

> In three weeks at Portsmouth we learnt some basic things about the Navy. First, the people actually in charge are petty officers and chief petty officers, a corps of middle-aged men, cynical about everything that comes down from above and motherly to the recruits.

Friendly contact between ranks may have resulted from living cheek-by-jowl on the 'lower deck', as naval ratings and NCOs have traditionally done while at sea. Sharing a common enemy on the 'upper deck' possibly cemented the relationship, too, as Robin hinted, when he told us:

> Naval officers, known on the lower deck simply as 'pigs', are an alien breed, with whom sailors have as little contact as possible. The camaraderie is understated but tolerant and almost always kindly.

It has to be admitted that Naval NCOs often sounded vicious. The late Jack Rosenthal, former coder and author of many TV dramas beloved equally by audiences and critics, has Petty Officer Swift,

6. Probationary coder specials at Victoria Barracks in October 1952. Fourth from right, back row is Mike Duffy. Far right, semi seated between front and back rows is Dennis Mills. Courtesy M Duffy.

in *Bye, Bye, Baby*, address his bunch of newly arrived probationary coders thus:

> You may think you're clever little bastards. With your Higher School Certificates and fancy degrees. In other ways you're chalk and Chinese wedding cake. Some of you were born with a set of silver golf clubs in your mouth, others with a hobnail boot up your arse. Here, you're all the same – coder specials. Which means you're not special at all. Which means you're not such clever little bastards either. Because coder specials are the lowest branch in the Navy – and therefore the lowest known form of human life.[10]

Any probationary coder from a genteel or sheltered background might well have agreed with PO Swift's low opinion of all Naval personnel, if he had shared Brian Jones's experience on his arrival at Vicky Barracks:

> We were sent to top up the numbers in partially-occupied barrack-rooms on our first night, and in my case the existing occupants of most of the bunk-beds were trainee cooks who already had a few weeks' experience of the Navy. Just back from leave, they spent most of the night in raucous exchanges relating the frequency, intensity and originality of their sexual exploits, much to the distress of my unaccustomed ears.

Kitting-out

Early coders were supplied with 'fore-and-aft rig' uniform and kit, intended to survive the whole 24-month period of service: an overcoat and/or a burberry (raincoat), two navy blue serge suits (if you wanted to wear gold badges it was necessary to buy a tailor-made doeskin suit), white shirts, black tie, socks and heavy boots and shoes, a peaked cap with two white covers for summer use, and a grommet of metal or bamboo to ensure the cap stayed evenly flat and neatly circular. We were also given a working uniform, so-called No. 8s, comprising navy blue cotton trousers and a much lighter blue, heavy-duty cotton shirt with buttoned pockets (much like the later denim imitations or jeans); many of us were still wearing the No. 8 shirt years after everything else had disintegrated.

---

10 Jack Rosenthal, *An Autobiography in Six Acts*, p 83. This speech is greatly reduced in the transmitted TV play.

38

To sew on badges and for any running repairs we were provided with a 'hussif' (housewife) containing thread, needles and buttons. Brushes and tins of polish gave us no excuse for failing to make our boots shine fit to reflect the face of the inspecting CPO. To carry this gear they provisioned each of us with a kitbag and a small purser's cardboard attaché case. A khaki sling bag with a gas mask inside was to be carried whenever we transferred from one establishment to another. Then there was the hammock: it came with mattress, sheet, pillow, personal blanket, and strict rules governing how they should be bundled together and lashed for inspection. Some of us struggled with our 'micks' - John Griffiths, for one:

> Having got into severe trouble for asking what was the point of having to 'tie up a bed' I hoped never to have to sleep in, I 'kept my head down' - another old nautical phrase, by the way.

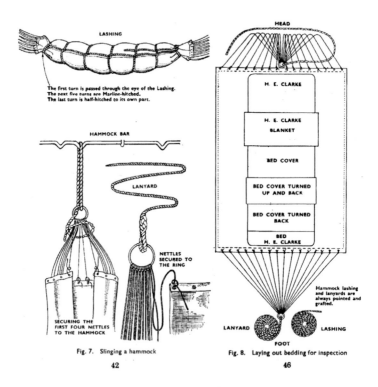

Fig. 7. Slinging a hammock
42

Fig. 8. Laying out bedding for inspection
46

7.   Hammock images from *The Rating's Handbook* p 42, Admiralty, 1951.

Tony Cash ran into difficulties, too, though he claims his hammock was shorter than the average, making it tricky to scrunch up all the bedding so that none peeped out of the ends when the whole was lashed together with the stipulated seven loops:

> I was quite pleased that I'd managed to get the hammock under control for the first inspection, though I noticed it looked a tad lumpy in comparison with other people's. The Chief on duty that morning was known as Obadiah – 'My name is Obadiah and I pull my little wire' was a phrase he obliged hapless victims to repeat loudly when he deemed them to have erred in some way. He was very tiny. He looked up at me and down to the offending article, then pressed his face close to mine and shouted, 'That's not a hammock; that's a fucking monkey's testicle filled with tin tacks'. I was laughing too much to feel humiliated, and relieved that I was not to be punished.

Learning the drill, and the ropes

Marching looks an easy enough skill, but in every batch of coders there appears always to have been one or more whose co-ordination of arms and legs was deficient. The intense effort to get it right would induce some wretch to lead with his left arm and left leg at the same time: the resulting shambles would render the drill instructor apoplectic, partly because it would be hard for him to detect who the culprit actually was. Understanding the mechanisms involved, we would occasionally use this ploy for our amusement, but only much later on: in basic training we would have been too frightened to swing the wrong arm deliberately.

Bill Hetherington has admitted that he was one of those coders whose square-bashing style wreaked confusion in any squad he happened to be marching with:

> One gunnery instructor was so concerned about me that he called me out and sent me for a special physical examination, as he thought I might have some hitherto undiagnosed physical defect. The medical officer was somewhat bemused, gave me a quick once-over, checked that I had no difficulty in normal walking and other movements and sent me back as fully fit. If there was any problem at all, I think it was due to the fact I have always been at the lower end of the height range,

and my short legs had difficulty in keeping pace with my longer-legged confrères. Clearly, I would never have made a guardsman, but I had no desire to be one. My legs have not prevented me walking ten or twenty miles at a stretch.

If pressed, most of us would probably admit that there were occasions when we positively enjoyed marching, as Brian Jones clearly did:

> There was much parade-ground drill to be rehearsed, but those in charge, chief gunnery instructors (GIs), were possessed of barks that were worse than their bites. There was a genuine concern to ensure we derived satisfaction as well as pride from our performance, and for the best division [squad] on Saturday morning Divisions - usually, it seemed, marching to *Sussex by the Sea*, rousingly played by the volunteer naval band - there was a prize of a large cake, quite a desirable reward in those days, and, as our GI said, 'something to write home to your parents about, so they know you are being well treated'.

Patrick Miller found drill easier than most, he says, because he had been in the CCF at school:

> But there were always those who looked like a sack of potatoes in uniform (**Dear mother, take me home ...**), failed to slope arms properly (**by yer left udder, you clown, not that udder, de udder udder ...**), or even dropped their rifle - a horrendous crime (**You are the only one of its kind outside captivity. At the sight of you, bulldogs shit and jump through hoops of fire ...**), or failed to co-ordinate arms and legs (**The Russians 'ad this trouble. Forget 'Left, Right'. They tied hay on one arm, straw on the other and shouted, 'Hay, Straw' ...**).

All ratings, including coders, were usually obliged to take a swimming test early in their Naval careers. Gareth Mulloy's experience must have been replicated by thousands of others:

> We went to Portsmouth [Vicky Barracks was in outlying Southsea] in a big blue charabanc, with *RN* emblazoned in white on each side, to have our swimming skills tested in a long pool. I had answered, 'Yes' to the question, 'Can you swim?' and claimed to be able to swim the required two lengths. To test this, I

was togged-out in a dry calico sailor's suit, and pushed
in at the deep end. At first the suit provided buoyancy,
and I exultantly struck out. The buoyancy soon gave
way to weight, as the suit absorbed water. Half way
through my second length I started to sink, and had to
be fished out with a boat hook, from the middle of the
pool, by the PTI [physical training instructor]. Despite
this humiliating failure, I was given a 'qualified
swimmer' mark. I should have admitted failure, as
this would have allowed me to make weekly visits
to Pompey for swimming lessons, which would have
been more useful than sweeping leaves or avoiding
sport.

Also on the sprogs' schedule were sessions explaining how to
deal with a conflagration and respond to a gas attack. These were
usually held at HMS *Phoenix*, the Royal Navy school of firefighting,
a shore establishment in Portsmouth. Gerald Seaman recalls being
treated to a vivid demonstration of what happens when water is
poured onto an oil fire by mistake:

A huge vat of diesel oil was ignited, water was
sprayed on to it, and eventually there was a gigantic
explosion, with flames shooting a hundred feet into
the air, as the water broke down into hydrogen and
oxygen under the heat. From a safe distance behind a
protective shield, a voice boomed over a loudspeaker,
'And that's what happens when some bloody fool
pours water on an oil fire without thinking!'

Gerald's next visit to *Phoenix* was for an official one-day course
in atomic, biological and chemical warfare, the last part of which
proved excruciating:

We were taken into a huge gas chamber with our gas
masks on. The chamber was then filled with tear gas
and we were told to take our gas masks *off*! Our eyes
streaming, the doors were opened, we were released
and obliged to run for half a mile to recuperate, to
liberate the gas from our lungs. The Navy certainly
believed in realism.

However hectic and time-consuming the training schedule was,
there were daytime moments for secluded contemplation, as Brian
Jones recalls in his summary of the 'Vicky B' ordeal:

Conditions had not been unduly Spartan, the food
had been acceptable in a period of general rationing,

and there was a quiet calm to be enjoyed away from the bustle of the parade-ground when ensconced in the 'heads' (lavatories), situated in the towers at the corners of the barrack blocks, and from which one could gaze out towards the distant Isle of Wight.

If at the end of three week's basic training our destined JSSL was not ready to accept a new intake, probationary coders would have to fill in time. Many would go on to HMS *Mercury*, a signals station and school near East Meon, Hampshire, for a course in cryptography, centred on the use of the *Typex* machine, a variant of the German *Enigma* device, which the boffins at Bletchley Park had learned to decode during World War II. An additional or alternative time filler was to go to sea for a short period – the subject of the next chapter.

Time-filling coders cause an elderly CPO to rejoice

While waiting for the Russian course to begin Mike Gerrard and three other coders from his intake were allocated to secret work which brought them tantalisingly close to ships without their actually going to sea. Based at the Signals School in Chatham, they were assigned to the updating of confidential books and *Queen's Regulations and Admiralty Instructions (QRAIs),* which had been gathering dust for years. In some instances World War II orders were still in place, and the coders had to update them by entering post-war amendments, including newer regulations and procedures. These had not yet been logged and entered, at least, not at Chatham, even though they were deemed necessary by virtue of British membership of NATO - by late 1954 the alliance had been operational for half a decade. Mike describes the work as mind-numbingly dull, but requiring close attention:

> It was imperative to read the older documents with care, to identify the changes needed, and to insert the new sections into the books in every case. The superseded sections had to be destroyed in accordance with the degree of security appropriate to each. Lack of attention to this task over the years had meant that in a number of instances existing orders had to be updated several times.

> One ageing and overworked CPO was in charge of confidential books, and the arrival of four bright and

completely green young ratings in his office was the best thing that had happened to him for years. The four coders had roughly twelve weeks to complete the task set for them, while for the Chief it amounted to three months' Rest and Recuperation.

Although their duties included a confidential books collection and delivery service for ships anchored in Chatham dockyard, these four coders had to serve eighteen months in the Navy before their first real shipboard experience.

44

CHAPTER 3

SPROGS AT SEA

ФЛОТ БЕЗ ХОРОШИХ МОРЯКОВ НЕ ФЛОТ, А СБРОД

(Russian naval saying – 'A fleet without good sailors is not a fleet, but a shambles')

Being mistaken for railway workers

At some stage in our Naval careers, either before or after months of language and radio courses, all coders were expected to put in 'sea-time', spending a few weeks, up to two months, aboard one of Her Majesty's vessels sailing from one of several bases around the United Kingdom. Carrying obligatory kitbags, hammocks and gasmasks, coders, in twos or threes, occasionally singletons, travelled to destinations as far apart as Plymouth, Devon; Londonderry, Northern Ireland; and Invergordon in the far north of Scotland. The sight of men in blue serge suits and peaked caps, lugging on one shoulder what looked to the uninitiated like postal bags and on the other shoulder large, rope-bound, sausage-shaped cloth packages, prompted civilian rail travellers, especially the elderly, to assume we were porters available for hire. Inevitably, there were arguments with genuine porters, who resented our commandeering their trolleys and consequent loss of tips. Such misunderstandings vanished when later intakes were kitted-out with bell-bottom trousers and traditional peak-less sailor caps in place of our 'fore-and-aft' gear.

The RNVR experience

Several coders were already supplied with the standard 'matelot' outfit, because they were in the RNVR (Royal Naval Volunteer Reserve), membership of which was one of the very few routes into the Navy for national servicemen. Such volunteers were expected to put in three weeks' sea time every year, though Dennis Mills did not get to do his first stint until shortly before being conscripted into the Navy proper. In summer 1952 he received orders to report to the aircraft-carrier HMS *Indefatigable,* docked in Portland, Dorset.

46

8. HMS *Indefatigable* berthed in Sydney, Australia *circa* 1946. Courtesy State Records, New South Wales.

Launched in 1942, the 26,000-ton vessel had served in the Far East in the war against Japan. Though it still bore its war scar - a large dent where a Japanese *kamikaze* (suicide pilot) had crashed his plane into the 'island' superstructure - seven years later the '*Indefat*' was much changed, as Dennis reports:

> The ship had no aircraft on board, having been converted to a training school for RNVR and RN ratings. Six hundred of us were housed in the upper hangar, extra ventilation being provided by keeping open the forward lift shaft, on which aircraft were normally transported up to the flight deck. We slung our hammocks in serried ranks both sides of a main gangway, from which we were screened by our lockers. Compared with what we had heard about Army square-bashing and the courses at the Naval Gunnery School, the regime was fairly benign, although we did have to rise at 5.45 am and the food was nothing to write home about. We RNVR ratings were given a sensible mix of instruction, on seamanship, elementary navigation, naval history and customs. We also did PT and gained practical experience of manning boats, as well as marching and drilling on the flight deck. We did our share of 'working part of ship', too - what the Army calls 'fatigues'. I remember scrubbing a strategic piece of deck, which every officer in the ship seemed to cross while I was trying to get on with my work; and chipping rust off an anti-aircraft gun turret, ready for someone to paint it.

Rites of passage – naval style

Rituals have always loomed large in the Navy, some more congenial to coders than others. Whatever their feelings about the service, most sailors will agree that it is always a highly emotional moment when a ship leaves or returns to port, and they are called upon to take up positions, standing at ease around the periphery of the open deck. Dennis recalls his first such experience:

> On the second Sunday we set sail overnight down the Channel to Devonport. The sea was dead calm, but we noticed a change in temperature, which made our single blankets (I still have mine) seem inadequate. Sailing into Plymouth Harbour and along the short passage up the Tamar to Devonport was

an unforgettable experience. We lined the deck in traditional fashion, and, as the ship twisted and turned in its gentle course, an ever-changing vista came into sight.

Brian Jones also served on the *Indefatigable*, only a few weeks later than Dennis. He says the ship:

... afforded great grey spaces and sponsons, seemingly undiscovered by those in authority, where coders could take refuge to smoke 'blue-liners' [duty-free cigarettes, a blue line along the side] and speculate upon their future training as Russian linguists: the lucky ones even had a much-prized *Penguin* paperback to read.

The wartime damage to the ship from the Japanese suicide attack was still very much in evidence:

The ship's company took great pride in pointing out the scars of battle, to which the coders seemed to be constantly applying coats of grey paint.

Brian recalls learning knots and bends, as well as practising as sea-boat's crew, but 'there was no sense of pressure', he says, as the ship crossed the North Sea on its way to visit Denmark. Like Dennis Mills and many other coders, Brian found that ceremonial occasions and pageantry could be as enjoyable as uplifting:

The flight deck was, of course, an ideal parade-ground, and by the time we were inspected by the Danish Royal Family we were fairly accomplished at cheering ship - lining the flight deck and, on the command, rotating one's white covered cap at arm's length in front of one to each of three cheers.

On going ashore at Arhus, we were generously hosted by the local citizens, but while Odense, because of its associations with Hans Christian Andersen, was much enjoyed, there was a certain frustration at only seeing Elsinore at a distance.

The location of Shakespeare's *Hamlet*, would be of great interest to any late teenager destined, like Brian, to study languages and literature at Oxford.

Relations between coders and regular ratings

In the eyes of volunteer sailors, national servicemen were an exotic breed, even more so if they happened to be highly educated products of grammar and public schools, as almost every coder actually was. But we were also self-evidently 'sprogs' - raw, green, untested. There was considerable scope for misunderstandings, if not hostility.

Gareth Mulloy, conscripted four years later than Brian Jones, has described his interest in the Navy as 'obsessive', for which he was known to his coder colleagues as extremely 'pusser' - in non-naval parlance, 'more papist than the Pope' - in his observance of rules and rituals. Gareth has made this observation:

> My short experience at sea opened my eyes to the rough conditions prevalent in mess decks. Without being unfriendly, our temporary shipmates kept their distance. Those were the days of a 15-year school leaving age, and I felt that my superior education and perhaps too overt and immature indications of a superior intellectual level put the regular matelots on their guard.

The following conversation perhaps illustrates my point. Coder Les Farthing was asked by a regular, 'Hey, Codes, what does *eureka* mean?' 'I have found it,' proudly proclaimed Les. Bitingly came back the retort, 'Well, fucking shit on it.'

Yet many of our coder contributors record a remarkable degree of tolerant amiability exhibited by men who, unlike us, had committed their working lives to the sea. Arriving at his designated ship, a coder, like any other naval rating, would be allocated a lower deck mess, his effective home for the duration of his 'sea time'. There, in extremely close proximity to a dozen or so other sailors, he would eat, spend his off-duty hours, and sleep. If he had not done so before, he would learn how to sling his hammock, a tough canvas piece easily capable of bearing the heaviest sailor's weight, along with personal blanket, sheets and pillow thoughtfully provided by the Admiralty. Robin Hope, old Etonian, nephew of an admiral and later to be commissioned as a midshipman, served as a rating on a frigate in December and January 1952-53. He described his first night on board:

> Our mates showed great kindness and patience in teaching us how to sling our hammocks from the stout hooks secured to the deckhead, and how to adjust the many cords so that we could, after clambering into the hammock from the tabletops, assume a sleeping

position. There is no tossing or turning in a sailor's hammock. You lie on your back, your bum the lowest point, and stay that way until some early hour, when the loudspeaker bursts into the Light Programme [forerunner of BBC Radio 2], and the sailors reach under their pillows for cigarettes and light the first of the day.

The more usual wake-up call broadcast over the tannoy was, 'Heave-ho! Heave-ho! Heave-ho! Lash up and stow!' possibly followed by 'Come on, my lubbers, chop-chop!' or 'Hands off cocks, hands on socks!' The first of these injunctions required the hammock, with bedding rolled lengthwise inside, to be lashed in seven equally spaced coils, then stashed away in lockers conveniently attached to the ship's steel side or the bulkhead (internal partition). In earlier times rolled-up hammocks were suspended over the rail as fenders, to protect the moored ship on impact with other vessels or quayside.

In June 1953 John Drummond and another coder, both, like Robin Hope, former public school boys, were sent to Chatham to join the cruiser HMS *Superb*. Well over six foot, imposing in manner and appearance, John spoke like a 1940s BBC announcer (he went on to have a distinguished career in that organisation as controller of *Radio 3* and director of the *Proms*). His entertaining, acerbic autobiographical memoir *Tainted by Experience* details his national service episode, including time aboard the flagship of the America and West Indies Squadron:

> I spent most of the time on deck getting in someone's way and resisting seasickness ... I enjoyed sleeping in a hammock, even if my feet hung out of the end, groaned with hunger at the poor and scanty food, and tried to keep my mouth shut. Here for the first time I was among real sailors - and very jolly, profane and good-humoured they were, too. But how they hated temporary national servicemen, especially with voices like ours! My fellow coder had a particularly grand and sardonic manner, which was not appreciated. I felt a kind of snobbery in reverse, but we were gradually accepted. The star turn was provided daily by a pair of East End twins, who used to stride about stark naked singing rude songs; they were abetted by a gloomy long-serviceman who had been under the command of the Duke of Edinburgh in Malta and told endless stories about his temper and his physical endowments

- stories that always ended, 'and you wonder why the Queen looks so miserable!'[1]

Tangling with an admiral

For Drummond the most memorable moment of his few weeks at sea came on 15 June 1953 when HMS *Superb*, alongside some 300 other vessels of the Royal, Commonwealth and foreign navies, gathered for inspection by HM Queen Elizabeth II at Spithead, in the Solent, off Portsmouth. The most spectacular of all naval pageants, the Spithead Review traditionally celebrates the coronation of a new monarch (Elizabeth had been crowned on 2 June, having acceded to the throne on the death of King George VI the previous year). As the Queen's vessel sailed through the lines, John was on deck with a telescope:

> At one moment a voice asked if I could make out the nationality of a ship some way away. 'How the hell do you expect ...', I started, and removing my eye from the lens saw beside me the largest amount of gold braid on a sleeve that I had ever encountered. I sprang to attention, scarlet in the face. Our admiral laughed. I wondered if he would have been quite so jolly had I had a different accent - the Navy was nothing, if not snobbish.[2]

Sailors' perks

Historically, life at sea had always been pretty tough - primitive living conditions, rudimentary cooking, and entertainment exclusively home-made, at least until the advent of radio. But duty-free tobacco and a regular free shot of alcohol, benefits of empire, afforded some consolation. Throughout the ten-year existence of coders (special) a rum ration, known as 'grog', was available to ratings from the age of twenty, the privilege not being abolished until 1970. The entitlement was a daily 'tot' (one-eighth of a pint) of the finest Caribbean rum, significantly more powerful than what was obtainable in civilian life, but diluted with a quarter pint of water. In the early 1950s, if you opted to register T (for Temperance) in the mess books - in distinction from those registered G (for Grog)

---

1   John Drummond, *Tainted by Experience: A Life in the Arts*, London, Faber and Faber, 2000, pp 55-56.

2   *Ibid*, p 56.

- your pay was increased by an extra threepence a day. Every dinner time, on shore establishments, a rating of the Regulating staff, superintended by the Master at Arms (equivalent to an Army sergeant major), dispensed grog at the entrance to the canteen in tumblers that had to be drained on the spot. At sea, 'muster for rum' (waggish alternative, 'cluster for bum') would be piped at noon, calling leading hands to collect the tipple for their messmates, who had leeway to drink it when they saw fit, though it would go off if kept for more than a day; indeed, part of the rationale for adding water was so that the tot could not be hoarded.[3] Robin Hope recalls taking his tot on a particularly rough day:

> The little ship rose and rose to the crest of a vast wave, hesitated (like Nijinsky at the summit of his high leaps), then plunged abruptly into a deep trough, hurling all our dinners into a corner of the mess deck. Before the midday dinner there was an important ceremony: the rum ration. We queued with our mugs, into which a petty officer carefully ladled the mixture of powerful Navy rum and water. Petty officers were allowed their own dilution of the same ration. Officers in the wardroom were, of course, chalking up their mess bills - two or three old pence for a shot of Pembroke gin, four pence for London or Plymouth gin. I think our rum ration must have been the equivalent to about a pub treble measure. Certainly you felt its effect.

Finding employment for greenhorns

Literally 'at sea', coders were often metaphorically so. Though more 'sea-worthy' than many of us, thanks to his RNVR experience and genuine and long-lasting interest in things naval, Dennis Mills recognises the problems our superiors had trying to give us a suitable maritime role. He did his second stint of sea time aboard HMS *Portchester Castle,* named after a third century Roman fortress near Portsmouth. He recalls it in some detail:

> The ship had been built as a corvette in 1943, but uprated to frigate when better armed. By 1952 it had

---

3   *Naval Rating's Handbook*, 1951, set out details for preparing and issuing grog, ending with: 'CAUTION ... if too much naval rum is drunk it is dangerous. Naval rum is only 4.5 under proof, whereas spirits sold on shore are 30 under proof; an overdose of Naval rum may therefore *kill* a man by suffocation.' pp 159-160.

a pair of 4-inch guns and squid guns for firing patterns of depth charges forward, as well as the usual facilities for firing them over the stern. In fact, it was one of the best known of its class, because it appeared as the second ship featured in the film *The Cruel Sea,* shooting for which had not long finished when I was drafted to her.

It was a struggle to find suitable work for Dennis:

It was immediately clear that the captain (a lieutenant-commander) and his officers were nonplussed as to how I should be kept occupied. With only eight weeks training, I could hardly be trusted to do anything 'naval', and there was no obvious senior rating to put in charge of me. What's more, I was a university graduate, and such a creature had never appeared before. In the event, I was allocated to the communications lieutenant, who found me various odd jobs. The ship's office happened to be next to the radio quarters, so he installed me there and sighed with relief when he discovered that I had taught myself to type with two fingers on the students' union typewriter. In effect, I became an acting writer (clerk), as the ship was too small to rate a permanent one. I found typing at sea even more difficult than on land, but luckily we had the most amazingly balmy weather for almost all but the last day or two of my two months in *Portchester Castle*. Each ship had a copy of *Queen's Regulations and Admiralty Instructions,* which had to be kept up to date by pasting in new items cut out from bulletins. Fortunately our copy was at least a year out of date, and this job was made to spread over several days. The high spots of my career as a writer were the fortnightly pay days, when the first lieutenant got me to set up the pay packets ahead of the payment muster, for which he allocated me exactly the correct amount of cash he had fetched from an office ashore.

Our daily duty involved a friendly submarine hiding itself in the exercise area in the Channel, whereupon we set out to hunt it with our *asdic* [named from Anti-Submarine Detective Investigation Committee], a transmitter-receiver which sent an underwater signal that bounced back from any object it hit. Contributing to these exercises was a very low-flying helicopter, also using underwater *asdic*, dangling below it. The name of the highly secret game was to see which method of hunting was the quickest. When the submarine had been found, a signal was sent to it by throwing a hand grenade into the sea a safe distance from ship and submarine. Then we could all go home for tea.

As I was an MX (miscellaneous) rating, I was a member of the MX mess, which comprised about a dozen men, one or two each of telegraphist, signalman, steward, cook, stores rating, electrician. The engine room ratings were right up forward in the fo'c'stle, ourselves and the seamen aft of them, to port and starboard. Broadside messing was in use, which meant that we prepared our own meals and took them to the galley for cooking. This duty was done in turn, by 'cooks of the mess', and one had to learn how to negotiate a companionway (steel ladder) with a tray of hot food when there was a bit more than a gentle swell running (the race off Portland Bill sets up a choppy sea on the quietest days). Having been brought up on country grub, I missed a decent breakfast, but otherwise the fare was not too bad. The leading hand of the mess was given a cash allowance on which to feed us, and the lads liked to save up for a big blow out now and then. I was a complete 'sprog', but they patiently put me right on how to 'go on'. A good sign straightaway was that they called me *Codes*, rather than using one of my own names, and they continued to treat me very well, accepting my different background and lack of interest in pub crawls. It probably helped that I did not speak with a standard English accent. They were all Devonport ratings, a system, like Army regiments, intended to give a sense of common identity. As well as men from the south-west of England, there was a sprinkling of Welsh and Scots and most notably Irish from the Republic. I was very surprised that, although not British subjects, the latter could and did serve in the Royal Navy as a matter of course. Lincoln, where I lived, was so far away from any other home town that I decided my allocation to Devonport had been a clerical error.

Ships colliding at sea

Apart from the obvious hazards that all sailors face in storm-tossed seas, coders doing their sea time were rarely in any kind of physical danger, though Arnold Bell was certainly in peril in a widely reported incident in 1953. He and two other coders were sent to Invergordon to join the light cruiser HMS *Swiftsure* prior to autumn exercises in the North Atlantic. Arnold takes up the story:

There were lots of vessels anchored, battleship *Vanguard* (a superb looking ship), carrier *Eagle,* couple of other cruisers, lots of destroyers, frigates, corvettes, minesweepers and submarines. The Home Fleet was some sight then, the Firth was full of vessels. The Navy had a fleet. The *Swiftsure* was 'chokka' [overcrowded], and there was no slinging space for a hammock in the communications mess deck for us three, so we had to sling our micks in the sick bay tiffy's [artificer, a trained mechanic, but here a sick bay attendant] space until room could be found for us in our mess, which happened in a couple of days. After a day or so all the fleet, except the *Swiftsure* and the submarines, left Invergordon. Over the tannoy the skipper announced to the crew that the aim of the exercise was to try to repeat the *Bismarck*'s venture in 1941 to get into the Atlantic via the Denmark Strait between Iceland and Greenland, and the rest of the fleet's job was to try to catch us. 'We'll be going as fast as possible, and, if it's a bit rough, it will help us, but hinder the *Eagle* and the other parts of the fleet. We've got the subs on our side to keep us informed where they are, and we'll batter through it - though it might get a bit 'towsy', the skipper finally said. And it was. Very rough, indeed, in a gale off north Iceland, and the whole ship was battened down, as it pitched, tossed and rolled 20 degrees, doing about 27 knots. I can't recall then ever seeing a level horizon. We had to progress along the ship in stages, for when it listed over, all the past days' meals - potatoes, carrots, peas and puddings - were swished in the sea water across every deck, so that you had to clamber on to a hammock bar to keep your feet dry, and just hang there till it went the other side. The coders' watch room was about two or three decks below sea level, down steep companionways way aft on the port side, just above the fast-turning shaft to the screw we could see through a hatch one deck below. 24-hour watch-keeping was necessary, so the three of us had to do our bit, too. The exercise extended for about three days before we were spotted by an aircraft the carrier *Eagle* had managed to get off, and we were caught by the faster destroyers.

Once that exercise was over, we were told the fleet would give the gunners some practice bombarding the ice sheets on the Greenland coast. The next night was to be on midnight manoeuvres, when all the fleet was to be blacked out, not a light showing anywhere. Bigger vessels in line astern, us leading the line, *Vanguard* behind us and *Eagle* and other cruisers in line. Destroyers and frigates provided a protective shield on either side. Message from the vice-admiral on *Vanguard* for all the shield vessels on port side to turn to port, all on starboard, to starboard. This sent in code. The skipper on a new destroyer, the *Diamond*, was a four-ringer [captain], who just beforehand had a desk job at the Admiralty. Somebody on that ship made a mistake - instead of going to starboard, it went to port and rammed us amidships, right into the sick bay on our starboard side, where we coders had been sleeping a few days before. In the bow of every vessel is the paint store, and as the *Diamond* went into us a fire immediately started in her fo'c'stle. The rammer went full astern, and pulled out from us after about two or three minutes, but the fire had taken hold on the *Swiftsure*, and then spread up almost to the bridge. The sole sick bay tiffy in his hammock there was badly burned. I was taking the first watch that night, and about 10.00 pm was called, 'You OK, Codes?' 'Yes', I replied. 'Well, get on deck as fast as you can, with as many clothes on as you can find'. As I did so, I noticed that the propeller screw was barely turning, so something was up. On deck the whole fleet was lit up like Blackpool illuminations, with every searchlight shining on us, the *Eagle* fleeing off as fast as she could, for fear we were about to explode and her aviation fuel go up, too. Lots of us on deck passing canvas buckets full of sea water along the line, to try to get the fire out. Only then did I notice that the davits that in Invergordon had held whalers [lifeboats] now were vacant - they had all been washed overboard from the battering seas we'd been through on the first part of the exercise, during the gales we'd had in the Denmark Strait.

9. HMS *Diamond* after ramming HMS *Swiftsure* in 1953.
Courtesy Colin Carter.

Both damaged vessels took refuge in a fiord on the
west side of Iceland, where the shipwrights got busy
repairing the hole on our side three or four decks
deep, that you could put a double-decker bus through.
Where the sleepers and timber bolted on our side came
from, I've no idea. The *Diamond* had no bow, just
crumpled battered steel. My mother in Blackburn saw
pictures of the *Swiftsure* in the newspapers, and was
greatly worried about my safety.

Meanwhile, the rest of the crew were put to work
clearing up the mess that resulted, and I can recall
vividly clearing the burnt-out chief and petty officers'
mess, where every steel locker had a big hole at the
back. CPOs and POs got neat bubbly[4] - a fearsome
tipple, whereas the lower deck got only two and one
-and they were in the habit of pouring a small amount

---

4 Arnold Bell refers to the CPO and PO spirit (rum) ration, which was
supplied neat. Junior ratings had what he calls 'two and one' - two
parts water, one part rum, the admixture becoming 'grog'. *Naval
Rating's Handbook*, 1951, pp 159-160.

each day into a bottle stored at the back of their lockers, in readiness for their next 'run ashore'. They'd all exploded in the fire. The *Swiftsure*, being a Chatham ship, limped back to the Medway at about two knots, taking days. The vessel was paid off and scrapped, but that's another story.

The following communication was said to have passed between rammed and rammer following the collision:

HMS *SWIFTSURE* : 'What are you going to do now?'

HMS *DIAMOND*: 'Buy a farm.'

CHAPTER 4
GRAPPLING WITH THE LANGUAGE

А ГДЕ ЩИ, ТУТ И НАС ИЩИ
(Russian saying – 'Where cabbage soup is, look for us there')

People who know Russian are frequently asked how difficult it is to learn; does the alphabet put you off before you even begin; are the words hard to pronounce; does it have any common roots with English; is the grammar complicated? Those were the typical questions posed by family members, friends and strangers when they heard we were enrolled in a Joint Services School for Linguists. Most of us had pretty good relevant qualifications, decent O- and A-levels in French, German, Latin and occasionally Greek. A handful even had language degrees. An intriguing exception, though, was Ian Wooldridge, later for many years the *Daily Mail's* leading sports correspondent: he had but two O-levels, neither in a modern language. Lack of proven skill did not prevent him from satisfactorily completing the course at Coulsdon and going on to monitor Soviet military radio traffic in West Germany, along with other coders.

We would like to explain to the uninitiated reader what it <u>felt</u> like grappling with Russian, to give him or her an inkling of the quirks and peculiarities of the language, and how it differs from English. What follows is a very brief, impressionistic, account, homing in on those features that impressed, surprised, delighted, or had us scratching our heads.

Russian letters and sounds

That the overwhelming majority of us achieved proficiency in Russian is testament to the teaching methods and materials used, as well as evidence that the language presents no insurmountable difficulty to the motivated student. Compared with managing short-hand for secretarial work, as many of our female relatives and friends did in the 1950s, mastering the Russian alphabet was a doddle, a few hours' study and practice. Of the 33 letters, largely derived from Greek, six are effectively the same as in English. Another six temptingly look the same, but are pronounced differently, e.g., 'C' always sounds as *s* in 'swim', likewise 'H' = *n,* and 'Y' = *oo.* The remaining 21 are novel, but make life easy by following consistently regular rules of pronunciation. By far the most outlandish letter of this group is 'Ж', usually represented in English as *zh* (the sound made by *s* in 'pleasure'). The letter resembles nothing so much as a beetle. It was helpful to recall that the Russian word for the creature actually is ЖУК, pronounced 'zhook'. (When the Beatles attracted the attention of Soviet youngsters in the mid-1960s, they were dubbed ЖУКИ-УДАРНИКИ, *zhooki-udarniki* – literally, 'beetle-drummers'.[1])

Though Russian words are on average markedly longer than their English counterparts, they are a lot easier for us to pronounce than French, only two sounds presenting any real difficulty. These are the letters Л and Ы. The first, sometimes called *dark L*, is not heard in the speech of any speaker of standard English, though the Scouse pronunciation of the initial letter of 'Liverpool' gets close. The Russian letter that looks like the number 61 (and was usually called that by JSSL students) is a version of our vowel *i*, not very different from the *i* in 'pit': the lips are relaxed, but the tongue is raised slightly more in the mouth than in English; small though the difference is, our teachers were quick to notice if we got it wrong.

Coders did not need to be versed in the history of the Indo-European language group to recognise that quite a few Russian words have roots in common with English – *mat'* for mother; *brat,* brother; *syestra,* sister; *dom,* house (cf 'domestic'). It was also comforting to discover how countless abstract nouns end in *-atsiya,* as ours end so often in '-ation' – the word for 'ventilation' (*ventilyatsiya*) is very similar to ours.

Those of us who knew Latin or German could readily appreciate that Russian grammar was uncannily similar: we saw that nouns and adjectives change endings depending on their role in a sentence – whether, for example, they are subjects, objects, possessives, or follow prepositions. It was particularly intriguing to discover deep, underlying patterns, like the tendency for words asking a question

---

1   It should be noted that here, as elsewhere in the book, we have transliterated Russian words in such a way as to facilitate pronunciation by the reader.

to begin with the sound *k* and the corresponding answering words to have an initial *t,* such as *kto?* (who?) and *tot* (that one); or *kogda* (when?) as opposed to *togda* (then). Couplets like *when/then*, *where/there* and *what/that* reveal that modern English preserves the system, if only in vestigial form.

We were all struck by an oddity of the Russian spelling system which seems to insist that the letter *h* beginning foreign names should be rendered by *g* - hence *Gamburg* for the north German city and *Gamlet* for the Danish prince. One instructor who pronounced a Black Country town as *Volvergampton* sparked amusement that still lingers.

We soon learned that native Russian speakers tend to have a fairly uniform accent. You can traverse seven time zones from Moscow as far as Vladivostok on the Pacific coast, and hear those names and most other words pronounced more or less identically. By contrast, in Britain, especially the north of England, pronunciation changes quite dramatically every twenty miles or so. Liverpudlians and Newcastle folk are not mutually very comprehensible when they speak broad Scouse and Geordie to each other. Even at the early stage in our study of Russian, however, we were made aware that Ukrainians and many others from southern regions tend to turn the letter *g* into a sound close to our *h* or Scottish *ch* as in 'loch'. Thus, former President Mikhail Gorbachev, born in the south-western city of Stavropol, may well have called the hero of Shakespeare's tragedy *Hamlet*, so often did he fall back on the speech habits of his youth. The joke was to ask a Russian southerner to say, 'the capital city of Holland is the Hague' - in standard form, *'glavny gorod Gollandii GaGa'* - and you would hear instead, *'hlavny horod Holandii Haha'*.

Troublesome aspects of Russian

Alan Smith, who learned his Russian at Crail in 1956, five years after the opening of the first JSSL, recalls a story going the rounds then, illustrating some of the stratagems we used to din Russian pronunciation into our heads:

> Several years previously a coder (maybe a legendary one) was asked to try to help during a formal ship's visit to Leningrad. He was called on to give the crew some simple words of Russian with which to charm the local population. *Spaseeba* (thanks) was simple for

the ratings to acquire, but *zdrazdvwityeh* (hello) was too much for the matelots, until some Liverpudlian wit suggested it would be easier to remember the question: 'Does your arse fit you?' - in Scouse, *Duzyerarsfeetyer?* – which, if repeated several times in sequence, sounds close to the Russian. Apparently, the crew loved this, and went around the city dispensing loud 'hellos' to everyone, and laughing with each greeting, because they felt they had been equipped with a marvellous insult, nonetheless pleasing the Russians, who must have thought that British sailors really were JOLLY jack tars, the happiest military in the world, provoking many handshakes and slaps on the back.

So, acquiring the language of Chekhov and Tolstoy was not all plain sailing. Most of us struggled to memorise the long lists of words we were constantly being given. John Drummond complained that for a period of his interpreter course he had to read ten pages a day of Dostoevsky's novel *Crime and Punishment*, and master every new item of vocabulary.[2] As we have seen, some Russian words have roots in common with our own and other European languages, but the overwhelming majority appear quite unrelated. Having to know which syllable to stress is a further impediment to speaking the language well. The emphasis in English words is not so audible, though we are able without difficulty to distinguish between *cOnvict* and *convIct*; *objEct* and *Object*; *recOrd* and *rEcord*: one pronunciation produces a verb, the other a noun. But how, for example, does the present Chelsea Football Club owner pronounce his surname? It is actually *AbramOvich,* not *AbrAmovich* – the former a family name, the latter a patronymic, meaning son of Abraham.

The trickiest poser to get our heads round was which form of a Russian verb to use. In nearly all cases the choice was between what are called the 'perfective' and 'imperfective' 'aspects', and, as the names suggest, there are marginally useful parallels with the 'perfect' and 'imperfect' in French. The present tense offers no problem – it has to be imperfective for a simple reason: if the action of the verb is happening now it cannot be viewed as completed. The complication arises when you are dealing with the past and future tenses. The distinction between the 'perfective' and 'imperfective' forms is tangible enough to the eye and ear – a change of vowel or

2   John Drummond, *Tainted by Experience*, p 58.

the addition of an extra syllable are the usual indicators. Without, however, going into superfluous detail, we can give a flavour of the distinction by reference to a near counterpart in English. There is a sense in which the verbs 'to kill', 'to persuade' (and, no doubt, others) are 'perfective'. If you say, 'Cain killed Abel', it necessarily implies that Cain completed the action, with the result that Abel died. If in this context you used the 'imperfective' of the Russian verb 'to kill', the meaning would be, 'Cain was trying to kill his brother', implying that he might not have succeeded. Fortunately, opting for the wrong aspect is not and was not a 'hanging offence', though choosing which to use could induce high anxiety.

All *kursanty* had a powerful incentive not to be kicked out of their JSSL. Failure in exams could result in a 'return to unit'. For a soldier this could be especially unfortunate, possibly entailing a posting to one or other of the several unpleasantnesses to which young male Britons were subjected (or subjected others to) in the 1950s - battling communist regular troops in Korea, red insurgents in the jungles of Malaya, Greek nationalists in Cyprus, Egyptian conscripts at Suez, anti-colonial Mau Mau adherents in Kenya. Because the Navy was only tangentially involved in these conflicts, the fate of a failed coder was not so awful to contemplate: being forced to tend the diesel engine of a warship as a stoker was the frequently cited threat. As it happens, neither Mike Gerrard nor Tony Cash knows any coder who actually flunked the exam, but in an earlier, the August 1952 Naval intake at Coulsdon, only 35 out of 100 passed their final course test. Recruitment and teaching methods had possibly not been refined as much as by a year later, and/or the exam standards might have been set too high.

Captivated by a foreign tongue

A factor in our success may well have been the very sounds of Russian itself: they are immensely attractive to the ear. It may ultimately be a metaphysical question whether one language can be inherently more beautiful than any other, but if asked to rate the appeal of Russian on a scale of one to ten, an overwhelming majority of us would have accorded it a significantly higher figure than other languages we knew or had heard spoken. There are objective reasons why this may be so.

Russian is full of palatalised sounds, which are made by pushing the body of the tongue close to the palate, as in the initial consonants of *dew, few, new, tutor*. 'Palatalisation', to give it its technical name, is very characteristic of Russian, and, arguably, one of the reasons why the spoken language can be so beguiling. The process is often referred to as 'softening', and, significantly, Russian has a *soft sign,* resembling a small letter *b* when printed; it produces a fleeting *y* sound as in *yellow*, and is sometimes represented in English by an apostrophe.

Consonants can be softened by palatalisation; so, too, can vowels. English has five basic vowels: *a, e, i, o and u.* Russian has these, and effectively five more, pronounced *ya, ye, yi* (or *yee*), *yo* and *yu.* Tens of thousands of Russian words end in sounds like *aya, ooyu, iye, yeye, oy, oye, oyu, yesh, yosh, ayem, ayetye, yat, ayut, yeyut.* The resulting richness is well illustrated by the first verse of a famous poem by Mikhail Lermontov (1814-1841), very familiar to former *kursanty*, *A Lone Sail Gleams White*:

> *Byilyeyet paroos adyinoky*
> *Ftoomanye morya galoobom.*
> *Shto ishchet on fstranye dalyoky?*
> *Shto kinool on fkrayoo radnom?*
> (A lone sail gleams white
> In pale blue sea mist.
> What does he seek so far abroad?
> What at home has he quit?)

Try speaking the four lines aloud, and, even if you understand not a single word and have no idea which syllables to stress, you should, we contend, experience something of the allure of spoken Russian.

A primer, a reader and classic fiction

Before we initiates were given access to the delights of Russian literature, we needed a grounding in the basics of the language, for which four books were provided - Anna H Semeonoff's *A New Russian Grammar* (her Anglicised surname usually referred to in the Russian feminine form, *Semeonova*); a short reader, *Ordinary People,* by Elizaveta Fen; and dictionaries from the Soviet state publishers covering translation each way.

From *Semeonova* we acquired our very first Russian saying, *shchi da kasha pishcha nasha*, 'cabbage soup and porridge (more specifically, buckwheat gruel) are our fare'. It was a useful phrase to learn because, properly pronounced, it allowed us to distinguish two tricky letters/sounds, Ш and Щ, normally represented as *sh* and *shch*. (You have to peer quite hard at the letters to see that the second has a small 'tail' at the bottom of the third stroke.) Having no real knowledge of the wretched lives of Russian peasants, most of us took the saying to be a complaint, rather than the brag it actually is. Those who made it to Russia after national service soon discovered that *shchi* is ubiquitous, tasty and nourishing, as well as the subject of many other ancient saws. From an early, brutally patriarchal, age, comes 'the more you beat your wife, the more delicious your cabbage soup'.

Whether by design or accident, the text of *Ordinary People* was relatively easy to learn by heart in chunks. One Polish teacher at JSSL Bodmin in the mid-1950s thought he would make it even easier for his class by having them sing a passage to the tune of *On Ilkla Moor Baht 'at*. You did not need to be a Yorkshire patriot to conclude that the county anthem boasts a lyric marginally more exciting than the story line of Elizaveta Fen's reader. Her fictional married couple, John and Mary, live in a new small house not far from London, both disgruntled: he, because his parents are not rich enough to have sent him to public school or university; she, because her husband comes home from work as a laboratory assistant too tired to listen properly to her account of conversations with the milkman.[3]

Fortunately for our embryonic interest in Russian culture, we eventually moved on to more substantial works of fiction, such as *The Overcoat*, by Nikolai Gogol (1809-1852). It is the tragicomic story of a lowly St Petersburg clerk who, robbed of his greatcoat and frustrated by bureaucracy, dies of 'flu, able to obtain revenge only as a *revenant*, or spirit. By the time we first met Gogol's Akaky Akakievich we probably had enough Russian to realise that the wretched hero-victim's name was derived from *kaka*, meaning faeces, as in some other Indo-European languages.

---

3 The story of Fen's own childhood in pre-revolution Russia and her family's escape to the west would have been both more interesting and more instructive.

> Taman is the most miserable dump of all Russian
> seaboard towns. I nearly perished of hunger there, and
> was almost drowned into the bargain.

These are the gripping first sentences of *Taman,* by Mikhail
Lermontov. The version some of us were given to read was in a
slim stand-alone volume, though it is in fact one of five linked short
stories in the poet's semi-autobiographical prose work *Hero of Our
Time.*[4] Pechorin, a young officer in the Tsarist army, is stationed
in the Crimea, where he gets embroiled with a mysterious group
of people – a small boy whose blindness may be more apparent
than real; a cantankerous old granny, perhaps feigning deafness; a
powerful oarsman successfully manoeuvring heavy loads through
choppy waters; and an enchanting young woman who speaks in
riddles, and embraces the hero passionately the better to remove his
pistol. He has fallen in with a bunch of smugglers.

Tony Cash and Mike Williams, though a year apart, both recall
reading at Coulsdon *Family Happiness,* by Leo Tolstoy (1828-
1910). Published in 1859 in a literary journal, the novella attracted
little attention at first, though one distinguished reviewer claimed
it was the best work Tolstoy had yet done. Rereading the story,
Tolstoy decided that the critics who had refrained from pronouncing
had better reason for their indifference than his admirer had for
praising it. He thereupon vowed to give up literature. Fortunately,
he eventually changed his mind otherwise the great novels *War and
Peace* and *Anna Karenina* would not today have pride of place on
the bookshelves of so many former coders. *Family Happiness,*
unusually for Tolstoy, is written in the first person, and even more
unusually, that person is a young woman, Anna. She loves the friend
of her late father, now her guardian. They marry; the relationship
cools; they quarrel. Tony Cash and Mike Williams were not alone
in finding it all rather tedious. The story's Russian title, *Semyeinoye
Schastye,* provoked some hilarity, and our colleagues decided a more
appropriate English title would be *Semi-Chastity,* or even *Seminary
Chastity.*

Far more engrossing for JSSL students lucky enough to be
offered it was the novella *Queen of Spades,* by Alexander Pushkin
(1799-1837). A young officer in the engineers is obsessed by the

---

4   Now out of copyright, a translation can be read at http://www.
    ibiblio.org/eldritch/myl/hero.htm.

idea that, if he can persuade an ageing countess to divulge her secret, he will have the key to winning at cards. His fixation has tragic consequences. The story furnished the plot and characters for Tchaikovsky's hugely successful opera, as well as for a 1949 British art film directed by Thorold Dickinson and hailed as a masterpiece by Martin Scorsese.

Another of Pushkin's works some of us studied was his historical novel *The Captain's Daughter,* set in the eighteenth century during the peasant uprising led by Emilian Pugachev. It, too, inspired an opera, written some ten years before the 1917 revolution by a lesser known Russian composer, César Cui (1835-1918). In 1999 Russian director Aleksandr Proshkin adapted the novel for the cinema with the film *Russky Bunt (Russian Revolt)*, a singularly appropriate title in view of Pushkin's oft cited entreaty 'Lord preserve us from the senseless, merciless Russian insurrection'.

That Pushkin was very special was made clear to us from the outset. In the pantheon of poets he might be compared with Shakespeare, but, arguably, even more influential for the development of Russian literature than the Bard had been for ours. Notoriously difficult to translate into impressive English verse, Pushkin's poems have resonated powerfully with Russian readers from their first appearance in the early decades of the nineteenth century to the present day. Professor Tony Briggs, himself a former RAF *kursant*, has drawn attention to an aspect of the poet's legacy which he calls:

> … a kind of unreligious spiritual fortification …
> He has accompanied Russian citizens into the darkest
> recesses of personal anguish, including persecution,
> the prison house and personal exile, and sustained
> their spirits against all the odds.[5]

Our JSSL teachers, many of them victims of communist brutality, would have said 'amen' to that. They were in no doubt about Pushkin's greatness. We students were able to obtain at least a glimpse from an intensely lyrical verse such as *Ya Vas Lyubil (I Once Loved You)*, which ends generously and surprisingly:

---

5   A D P Briggs, *Alexander Pushkin: A Critical Study,* London and Canberra, Croom Helm, 1983, p 17.

10. Painted portrait of Alexey Maresyev. Courtesy RIA Novosti.

I loved you wordlessly, hopelessly, tortured in turn
by timidity and jealousy. I loved you so sincerely, so
tenderly, as God grant you may be loved by another.

Soviet literature on war themes

The reading material on offer changed radically after the 9-11
months basic language course on Army-run camps at Coulsdon,
Bodmin and Crail. The Royal Air Force supervised the next stage
of our training, at establishments at Wythall, near Birmingham and,
for later intakes, Pucklechurch, Gloucestershire, and Tangmere,
West Sussex. Here, in preparation for eventual work in signals
intelligence, coders and our RAF equivalents undertook an intensive
course in radio technology and the Russian military terminology
associated with mid-twentieth century warfare and its attendant
paraphernalia. To familiarise us with the relevant vocabulary
we were given books such as *Boevye Budni (Days and Nights at
War)*, a Soviet pilot's account of his WWII exploits - not exactly
high literature, but significantly more engrossing than Elizaveta
Fen's soap opera about John and Mary. Luckier later intakes of
students had the pleasure of reading *Two Captains,* by Veniamin
Kaverin (1902-1989), about an Arctic explorer in the early years of
the twentieth century and his son, an air force pilot pitted against
the Nazis after the German invasion of the USSR in 1941. Written
in 1946, Kaverin's distinguished novel sold more than 100 million
copies in various languages and was successfully adapted for both
screen and TV.

Another Soviet classic novel of wartime derring-do is recalled
by RAF *kursant* Jack Doughty. *Story of a Real Man* (1947),[6] by
Boris Polevoy (1908-1981), is based on the essentially true account
of a Russian airman who suffered a similar fate to Douglas Bader's,
but worse, because both his legs were amputated above the knee.
The real-life Alexey Maresyev was a fighter pilot shot down by
the Germans in the region of Novgorod in March 1942. Despite
the injuries to his limbs, he managed to crash-land his damaged
plane behind enemy lines and crawl for eighteen days to Russian-
held territory. By then his legs were too devastated to save. In less
than sixteen months he was back in the air, wearing prosthetics and

---

6   The Russian text is available at http://lib.ru/PROZA/POLEWOJ/
    chelowek.txt.

70

70

11. Still from the Soviet film *Ballad Of A Soldier*. Courtesy RIA Novosti.

sufficiently in control to shoot down at least three German planes, giving him a tally of eleven by the war's end. He was awarded the highest Soviet military decoration, and his life was celebrated in one of the last operas Prokofiev ever wrote. Maresyev lived to be 85.

Russian language movies

To familiarise us with contemporary idiomatic Russian, as spoken in real situations, we were occasionally 'treated' to viewings of Soviet films, some more grim than entrancing, but nearly all a welcome change from grammar grind or conversation classes, and infinitely preferable to an afternoon spent on military exercises. Having studied languages in some depth before being conscripted, most of us had experience of foreign films, especially French ones. Russian movies, however, were effectively unknown. Tony Cash was probably alone of his intake to have seen *The Fall of Berlin*.[7] It was shown at a cinema in his home town, Leeds, shortly after its release in 1949. The accompanying publicity claimed that more than sixty cameramen had lost their lives shooting live action of the actual battle for the Nazi capital. To an impressionable teenager who had earlier followed radio news reports of the progress of the Red Army from Stalingrad to Berlin, the film's war scenes justified the hype, but the closing moments left him incredulous. Like a *deus ex machina*, Stalin descends from the skies to an airfield in Berlin, where thousands of troops and former concentration camp inmates flock round him, singing his praises in several languages. Some forty years later Tony Cash worked on a series of TV programmes about Stalin, from which he learned that the dictator was always extremely reluctant to fly and may have done so only once, when he went to Tehran in 1943 for a summit meeting with Churchill and Roosevelt.

Some coders studying during the last year of the national service Russian course had an opportunity to see one of the finest Soviet war films, *Ballad of a Soldier* (1959), in which a young infantryman, as a reward for an act of spontaneous bravery, is allowed leave to mend the roof of his mother's shanty. The film traces his difficult journey back home through war-torn towns and villages. Agitprop-free, Grigory Chukrai's elegy chronicles realistically the actions and

---

7   Many of the films and songs mentioned can be accessed in full or extract form on *YouTube*.

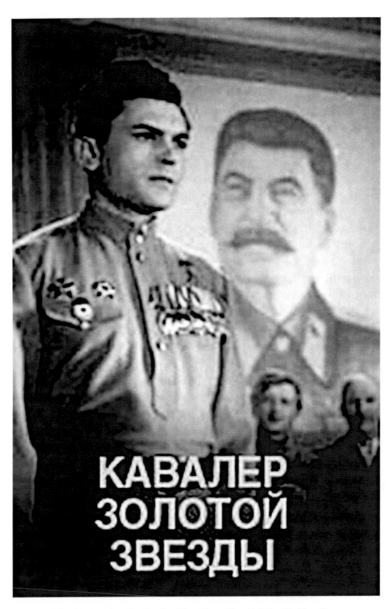

12. Poster for the Soviet film *Chevalier Of The Golden Star*.

attitudes of shirkers as well as the heroic. Midshipman Michael Waller, on RNVR recall, was one of those who saw it:

> I found it very moving - how can you accuse anything on that theme made at that time of being over-sentimental? I have to say that many of my fellow JSSLites were geared up to expect a dose of pure propaganda, and laughed their way through it.

A few films on offer did deserve derision. Former coder Mike Williams recalls one, though the title, perhaps understandably, now eludes him. He found memorably risible a scene:

> ... of young Ivan returning from the war to his *kolkhoz* [collective farm], to be greeted by someone he knew years before as a skinny kid, now transformed into the full bloom of awesomely insulated Russian womanhood (built like a T-62 tank). Complete with traditional headscarf and wellyboots, this elephantine damsel batted her eyelids at 'our Ivan' and took off, with a coy backward glance, into a conveniently close birch forest. She tripped over a well-placed log, as Ivan, pounding in pursuit, caught up with her and leaned purposefully over her. For what seemed an interminable pause he gazed intently into her eyes (while we hooted, yelled and urged him on to greater things), before he muttered those immortal words – 'Come with me, Natasha, and see our new State-produced tractor'.

Also, in what Mike Gerrard calls the '*kolkhoz* class of film', was *Kavalyer Zolotoi Zvyezdy* (*Chevalier of the Gold Star*) based on the 1948 Stalin-prize novel of that name by Semyon Babayevsky (1909-2000). Actor/Director Sergey Bondarchuk, whose epic version of *War and Peace* was later screened all over the world, plays the be-medalled hero of *Chevalier of the Gold Star* returning to his Cossack village at the end of World War II:

> ... an awful film, in which the All-Soviet Boy repeatedly outwits the brutal - and no doubt revisionist - section foreman, and by the end of the film collects the girl and the medal that gives the film its title.

More congenial to Mike Gerrard's taste was the 1953 film *Chuk and Gyek,* about two little boys whose mother takes them from their Moscow home to join father on a far-away geological expedition. The kids contrive to lose his telegram, unread by mum, with near

74

13. Image from the Soviet film Chuk and Gyek showing the boys with their mother. Courtesy RIA Novosti.

disastrous consequences for all involved. Lost in a forest, Chuk and Gyek face grave danger:

> This film is famous for the immortal line, '*Ukhodi, myedvyed. Ya nye boyus tebya*' ('Go away, bear. I'm not afraid of you'), when the little lads are confronted by a brown bear during their wanderings. After the showing, my mates at Bodmin nicknamed me *Myedvyed*, on account of my physical shape, and it became the standard greeting I received whenever I approached one of them.

Many years later I made use of that nickname in an (unpublished) short story, in which the first person hero served as trade attaché in the Moscow embassy during the 1960s, and was disgraced after seducing his glamorous KGB minder while on a trade visit to Prague. He's forced to resign from the British service and she, too, is dismissed from the KGB, and exiled to her home city of Leningrad. She disappears into obscurity there, having adopted the cover name *Medvedyev* (in memory of the affair), and in the fullness of time the highly gifted son she bears him becomes president of the Russian Federation when Putin runs out of time. The story was lost when the computer I had at the time blew up and everything on the hard disk was destroyed.

The bear as symbol of Russia is a notion that goes back at least four centuries – 'big, brutal and clumsy' the attributes alluded to by *Wikipedia*. Its cuddlier manifestation, the teddy bear, is as popular with Russian children as with our own, and is universally known over there as *Misha*, the diminutive of Mikhail (Michael). *Misha* was the mascot image for the 1980 Moscow Olympic Games.

A given of Soviet art was that it had to be positive and uplifting. With its happy ending, *Chuk and Gyek* is certainly that: think Disney, though, and you realise that the film need not be viewed as propaganda. Nor does propaganda necessarily preclude art, as at least one classic of Soviet cinema proves. Former coder John Griffiths, who later covered the 1959 Nixon-Khrushchev encounter in Moscow for the *Western Mail*, remembers viewing the classic silent film *Battleship Potemkin* (1925), directed by Sergey Eisenstein (1898-1948):

> Though my Russian was never up to interpreting the linguistic niceties, it appealed greatly to my radical tendencies, and on my subsequent travels through the

14. 1926 Poster for the Soviet film Battleship Potemkin.

Soviet Union as a journalist during the relative thaw of 1959 I found that, lost for conversation, asking my interlocutors whether they had seen it usually drew smiles and nods of approval. Whether they had actually done so, I often wondered.

There can be no doubt that viewing films improved, at least marginally, our language skills, though not necessarily in ways our teachers might have anticipated. A coder at Coulsdon in 1953, Graham Young, tells us:

The item which has remained most clearly in my memory is a parody of a Soviet film, a sods' opera, staged at a concert towards the end of the year. The actors spoke their lines in correct Russian. Every few minutes they froze, and two stagehands carried on an inept translation into English, written on a strip of paper, imitating the subtitling methods and quality of the Soviet originals. When the speech was long, the translation was short, and *vice versa*. 'Да' (*Yes*) was translated as, *On behalf of the Supreme Soviet etc. and the Autonomous Republic of the etc. I as the Chairman of the etc. agree.* The highlight came when one of the characters said in English, 'What's all this garbage?' The stagehands carried on, Что это значит? (*What does this mean?*).

Learning the songs of our Cold War foe

An intriguing irony of the JSSL story is that the British government got national servicemen to learn Russian to defend Britain from a country it considered a potential, if not actual, enemy; yet quite a few of us ended up Russophiles, in love with many aspects of Russian culture, not least its music. Tony Cash was unusual: he had a taste for it long before he joined the Navy, having fallen for the well-known Red Army anthem *Polyushko, Polye,* when he heard it on the radio at the age of seven, after the German invasion in June 1941, bringing the Soviet Union into World War II on the British side. The song, literally translated as *Little Field,* tells of Red Army heroes off to war, leaving their weeping girl friends behind. The words only became known to him at Coulsdon some twelve years later.

Most students were introduced to Russian songs very early in their training in JSSLs at Coulsdon, Bodmin and Crail. Anna Martin, *émigrée* daughter of Greek communists purged in Moscow in the

15. Cover of the Samovar song book. Courtesy T Cash.

1930s, possessed a singing voice as attractive as her features and personality. One of the youngest teachers at Coulsdon, Mrs Martin introduced her classes to the folk song *Chubchik* (*Lock of Hair*), in which a young woman laments the fate of the wind-blown, curly-haired fellow who languishes in Siberia, a land that holds no fear for her, since 'Siberia is also Russian soil'. A captivating rendition of the song inclined everyone who heard it to take a serious interest in this novel musical idiom.

Jozef Godlewski, a prominent teacher at Bodmin in 1955, is fondly remembered by Peter Hoare as a

> … great character who certainly sang with us in class. I remember that he would go off for a pee, saying, *Nu gospoda, sud'ba igraet chelovekom* ('Well, gentlemen, fate toys with man').

Godlewski was quoting from a very popular nineteenth century folk song he had taught Hoare and his classmates, about the conflagration that consumed Moscow after the French occupation in 1812. The all-devouring flames are observed by Napoleon Bonaparte himself. He is identified in the lyric, not by name but, ironically, as the 'great man in the grey frock coat, his arms crossed over his chest'. Having conquered all Europe, why, he asks, have I come to Russia? 'My troops will perish in the snow, their bones will rot, unburied, unmarked.' His final words are: 'Fate, ever fickle, toys with man, now raising him high, now casting him into the abyss without trace'.

We know that students at Crail held at least one concert of Russian songs in 1956. Cyclostyled song sheets circulated at Bodmin, as well as at Crail, but at Coulsdon in 1953, choir singing was a regular feature of service life. Informal classes were held in the NAAFI during service hours. In addition, there existed a formal choir membership of which was open to all students on the course, soldiers and airmen as well as coders. They simply had to pass an audition, though only a minority were minded to try. Testing would-be choristers was done by the choir-master, Mr H Niezbrzycki, who was also on the JSSL teaching staff. The front cover of the *Samovar* song book was designed by him. A talented all-round musician, Niezbrzycki sang the melodies and harmonies as required, accompanying himself on the guitar.

$\mathcal{S}$amovar $\mathcal{S}$ong $\mathcal{B}$ook

PREFACE

TO SECOND ENLARGED EDITION

The demand for our first edition has encouraged us to produce a second, with more Russian songs and twenty-nine Polish.

Presentation is in the main unaltered, but division into bars has not been continued.

We are most grateful to Mr A. Scobie for selecting and arranging all the additional Russian songs; to Mr H. A. Bazylko and to Mr Halski for selecting and arranging the Polish songs; and to Mr H. Niezbrzycki for designing the cover.

The Editorial Board has again been extended, but thanks to the unfailing help of Mr L. Ross, not impossibly so.

16. First page of the Samovar song book. Courtesy T Cash.

The song book is now something of a rarity. The second edition contains over 160 songs, a few in Polish and Ukrainian, the majority in Russian. Mingled together are ancient folk melodies, nineteenth century sentimental ballads, spirited Cossack airs with dramatically unexpected changes of tempo, Gipsy tunes, Soviet popular songs, and *chastushki*, a traditional satirical form, a cross between limerick and calypso, in four-line rhyming verses. *Samovar* is what jazz musicians call a 'fake book': it contains single-note melody lines with the underlying chords for accompaniment, indicated by letters of the alphabet.

Most of the songs had an immediate, exotic appeal to the young men learning to sing them, though the reader needs to be aware that any one *kursant*, even a member of the choir, would not necessarily have come across all the songs we are examining. In the early 1950s, post-adolescent Brits were familiar with a relatively narrow range of musical idioms – nursery rhymes, music hall ditties, popular songs of the 1940s dance halls, perhaps a handful of operatic arias - very few of which embodied the modal harmonies and abrupt changes between major and minor keys prominent in the Russian vocal repertoire. The latter was neither Cole Porter nor Puccini, and certainly not George Formby. The *Samovar* melodies were mostly fresh and original, perhaps only two or three commonly known. One such was *Ey, Ukhnyem* ('Yo, Heave Ho'), the *Song of the Volga Boatmen,* which had long ago firmly lodged in the national consciousness. As in the best of work songs, the very melodic line exemplifies the action of serfs hauling a barge with immense difficulty. We supposed that, being Russian, they habitually sang as they laboured, and what more natural than to hymn the sun, the 'curly' birch trees on the banks and the mighty 'mother-river' itself, especially when flowing free after the melting of winter ice.

Already known to some, from the repertoire of the bass singer Fyodor Shalyapin (1873-1938), was the melody of *Ochi Chornye*, a Gipsy-style lament, in which the singer bemoans how passion for his *Dark Eyes* has consumed him. The *Samovar* variant ends with lines strongly reminiscent of this verse from Robbie Burns's poem *Ae Fond Kiss*:

> Had we never lov'd sae kindly
> Had we never lov'd sae blindly
> Never met or never parted,

82

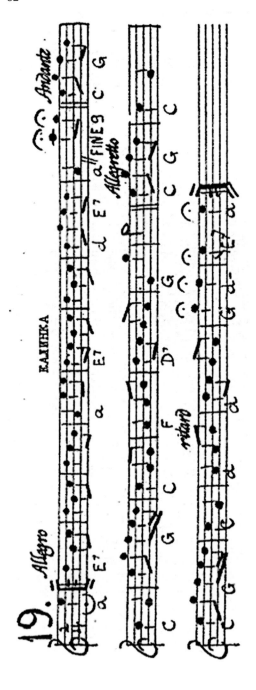

17. Music and chords For Kalinka as printed in the Samovar song book.

We had ne'er been broken-hearted.

Another Russian melody that may have rung bells with us because of a popular French version, was *Pomnyu, Pomnyu, Pomnyu Ya (I Remember, I Remember, I Remember)*. The vocal group les Compagnons de la Chanson had recorded *Le Galérien* in 1950, and it had been played occasionally on BBC radio request programmes such as Family Favourites and Housewives' Choice. In the first person, the lyric recalls a mother's warning not to mix with robbers or – 'My darling son, weighed down with chains, you'll be sent to do hard labour in Siberia'. The final, tragic verse has the narrator complaining bitterly that he neither stole nor robbed, but was nevertheless consigned to Siberia for loving freedom and the people too much.

Altogether jollier, though more enigmatic, was the traditional old folk song, *Kalinka* (meaning, possibly, *Snowberry, Juniper* or even *Guelder Rose* - no one seems sure). The singer asks to be laid to sleep under a pine tree. He commands it to make no noise above him. Finally, he calls on a beautiful girl to love him. Each verse is followed by a refrain that speeds up inexorably with every repeat. The *Kalinka* of the title, along with *Malinka* (raspberry) also featured in the song, may simply be affectionate diminutives for the girl herself.

The Coulsdon choristers were probably not aware that one of the most touching songs in the collection was a setting of a famous poem by Mikhail Lermontov, who has been dubbed Russia's second greatest poet, after Pushkin. *Spi Mladyenyets*, sometimes called *The Cradle Song of a Cossack Mother*, has the opening line 'Sleep, my handsome little fellow'. The scene is an outpost of the Russian empire in the Caucasus, where Christian troops sought to crush resistance from the mainly Muslim populations. The singer tells her baby boy that he, too, will grow up to be a warrior Cossack, and she will shed bitter tears as she watches him saddle up, rifle in hand, ready to join the battle; she will give him a holy icon to keep close, and will pray for him all day. One verse of the song has special resonance in the twenty-first century: it describes the 'evil Chechen crawling on to the bank of the river Terek, sharpening his dagger'. Over the decades, this has been one of the most popular of Russian lullabies.

Cossacks were traditionally Russia's imperial *gendarmes*, trained specifically to live and fight on the country's periphery, which for most of the nineteenth century was constantly expanding. They had not, however, always been willing servants of Tsarist autocracy. In the seventeenth century a Cossack revolutionary, Stepan Timofeevich Razin, wreaked mayhem up and down the Volga until his capture in 1671 by the Tsar's troops. Executed by being quartered alive in Moscow's Red Square, he was immortalised some two hundred years later in the song *Styenka Razin*, which recounts an extraordinary incident in his life - true or imaginary, we had no way of telling. As drunk as his Cossack oarsmen, Razin is seated at the prow of a long boat, embracing his newly-wed Persian princess. His underlings mutter mutinously that their leader has deserted them for a mere woman – 'One night with her, and he's turned into a woman himself'. Enraged at their taunts, he sings the refrain:

Volga, Volga, great Russian mother river,
Never have you seen a gift like this Don Cossack's.
To quell discord among us free men –
Here, receive this beautiful woman.

Whereupon, he hurls his unfortunate bride into the rushing tide.

One member of the Coulsdon choir who learned that song was an Army private and talented pianist, Tom O'Brien. He occasionally played jazz in the NAAFI with coders Tony Cash, on clarinet, and Malcolm Brown, on guitar. Twelve years later Tom turned the song to good account. Now using the surname Springfield (the celebrated singer, 'Dusty' Springfield, née O'Brien, was his sister), he took the old Russian melody, altered a couple of notes, added a new lyric (totally unrelated to anything in the original), and *The Carnival is Over* became a huge hit for the Australian group, The Seekers, holding the number one place in the charts for seventeen weeks in 1965. By then Tony Cash was broadcasting programmes of pop music to Soviet audiences for the BBC's Russian Service, and was able to introduce his listeners to the Anglicised version of their folk song. Fear of the Official Secrets Act made it impossible to explain to the audience the precise circumstances in which the song had come about.

If there was any one singer in the 1953 Coulsdon choir who stood out, it was the late Carwyn James. Native Welsh speaker, son of a miner, committed nationalist, Carwyn was blessed with a sweet, high tenor voice, which, coupled with his very slight build, made his hugely successful career in club and international rugby union difficult to envisage (until you saw him in action, that is). His *forte* was singing the lead on *Stanochek (The Spinning Loom)*,[8] an old folk-song melody with twentieth century words that tell of a young woman tending her machine, singing happily because she has fallen for an elegantly-dressed fellow factory hand, but ceasing to sing when, within a year, he ditches her for another. Never mind - very Soviet, this - she finds consolation toiling over her 'dear little friend, her irreplaceable loom'.

Had they been asked, a majority of Coulsdon choristers would have chosen *Tachanka* as the most stirring of songs learned in 1953. The name denotes a horse-drawn carriage bearing a machine gun and used on both sides during the Russian Civil War of 1918-1922. The *Samovar* version celebrates the *Rostovchanka*, from Rostov-on-Don, hurtling through the golden steppe land at the bidding of its young, tanned, dust-covered machine-gunner.

Of all the Russian songs taught to the choir, the closest to any popular western idiom of the period was *Syerdtse (Heart)*, from a 1930s Soviet film. An intimate tango ballad, it is more suited for solo than ensemble performance: 'So many attractive girls, so many endearing names, but only one troubles your heart, when you're in love ... Love comes upon you stealthily when least expected, and kindles in your body a tremulous fever.' Overblown perhaps, but an improvement on the banal lyric of another Soviet number of the period, *Vyesyoliye Ryebyata (Jolly Lads):* 'Song lightens the heart ... Hamlets, villages and cities love songs ... If you march through life with a song, you'll never fail', etc. Unsurprisingly, the melody was as mundane as the text.

Much more widely known to Soviet audiences was another song we learned, *Shiroka Strana Moya Rodnaya* (*My Native Land is a Broad One*), officially titled in Russian *Song of the Fatherland*. It was written for a 1936 film *The Circus*, and the opening phrase, performed on the vibraphone, was used for many decades by USSR

---

8 Carwyn can be seen singing this song on *YouTube* at http://www.youtube.com/watch?v=jEYsHm0KoMA.

All-State Radio as a signature tune. The melody is stirring enough, if a little tricky to sing because of an interval of a ninth that takes some negotiating. The singer proclaims he knows 'no other land where man breathes so freely', an assertion a Soviet citizen could confidently make, since he would have had no opportunity to visit any other land. Coder Mike Williams recalls a noisy rendering of the song at Coulsdon being suddenly interrupted by an elderly, somewhat aristocratic, Russian lady teacher, who complained bitterly to choirmaster Niezbrzycki that this sort of Soviet material was entirely unsuitable for his choir. He shrugged, smiled, and continued unabashed.

One of the songs in our repertoire remains extremely popular today with Russian audiences, but was perhaps even more so during World War II. Like the majority of *Samovar* numbers, *Katyusha* is a march, brisker than most, belying somewhat the lyrical text. The title is a diminutive of the Russian name Yekaterina, and may be translated as Kate, Katie or Cathy. She is described coming to the steep river bank when apple and pear are in blossom and the mist on the water has melted away. The subject of her song is the grey eagle of the steppes and the man she loves, whose letters she has kept. Defending the motherland on the far frontier, he is called upon to remember the simple, modest girl, while she should remain faithful to him. It is generally believed that the popularity of this song in Red Army ranks led to its name being appropriated for the fearsome rocket launchers which made such a contribution to the Soviet victory over Nazi Germany. In any event, we now know that a popular parody of the song's last verse was sung towards the end of that conflict to the effect, 'Let Fritz remember the Russian Katyusha, let her song rattle his soul and strengthen our resolve.'

Ex-coder choristers David Wills and Tony Cash both recall that the highlight of the 1953 Coulsdon choir's year was a concert we were invited to give in Cambridge at the student ADC (Amateur Dramatic Club) Theatre. Wills says:

> It was remarkable that we found the venue, as the Russian teacher in charge kept on stopping the coach to ask where Cambridge University was. [As a collegiate university, Cambridge has no single venue or campus.]

Neither remembers the evening's programme, though Tony has a recollection of playing *Syerdtse* on the clarinet, with Malcolm Brown on guitar, as a mainly instrumental number.

A measure of JSSL success

Hearing, speaking, reading, writing, singing (even dreaming) Russian under the tutelage of native speakers five hours a day for several months on end; having access to a variety of literature; stimulated, however bizarrely, hilariously or emotionally, by movies in the language, we unsurprisingly achieved considerable expertise - to the extent that quite a few coders volunteered to take the Cambridge A-level, thereby encountering an even wider range of fiction, poetry and drama, all to be digested in free time.

After demob, many of the national servicemen who trained as translators and interpreters opted to continue their study of the language and literature at university, so much so that by 1958 there were more students at Oxford taking Russian than those taking any other modern language except French. University departments of East European studies all over the UK received a tremendous boost from the influx of former JSSL scholars, providing a cohort of Russian-language secondary school teachers. In 1962 the then Conservative government set up the Annan Committee to investigate ways of increasing and improving the amount of Russian being taught in our schools; crash conversion courses were instigated for teachers of other modern languages.

If, at the time of writing, Russian studies are in serious decline, the principal reasons are the ending of the Cold War; the disintegration of the Soviet state after 1991; the rise in importance of Spanish and Chinese; and, ironically perhaps, the dominance of English in the European context, leading to a general decline in the study of modern languages in British educational institutions.

88

18. Jozef Godlewski, seated front row, with one of his classes at Bodmin. Courtesy RAF *kursant* John Mitchell, seated far left, second row from the bottom.

CHAPTER 5

THE TEACHING STAFF AT JSSL

ДРЕВО И УЧИТЕЛЬ ПОЗНАЮТСЯ ПО ПЛОДУ

(Russian saying - 'The tree and the teacher are known by their fruit')

From the moment the government conceived the scheme to have Russian taught to national servicemen it would have been aware that a pool of potentially suitable instructors was readily available. Hundreds of Russian speakers had been brought to our shores at the end of World War II, principally former citizens of the Soviet state or of East European countries which, post-1945, were firmly locked into the Communist orbit.

What the authorities planned

Government papers released to the general public since the mid-1990s reveal that in January 1951 a planning committee discussed, probably for the first time, the question of recruiting instructors. A staff-student ratio of 1:10 for training translators was proposed. They estimated a need for 120 instructors: 14 should be 'English' (though 'British' must be inferred), 67 to be native Russian speakers, and the remainder could be either:

> Fluency in the language is not enough; indeed we are advised that for certain types of linguistic teaching, such as grammar, an English teacher is definitely to be preferred to a foreigner who does not possess a wide command of English.

The value of having learned Russian as a foreign language in up-to-date institutions was noted. A supervisory committee was envisaged to monitor the work done at JSSLs,[1] though none of our 70-odd respondents remembers seeing anyone coming to their classroom who could conceivably have been an inspector.

In March 1952 the committee was still anxious to find the right balance between British teachers of Russian grammar, who were in

---

1   TNA/ADM 116/6332, RL P (51) 2, 17 January 1951, pp 5 and 8.

90

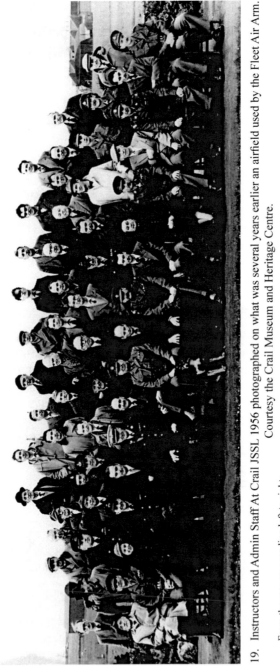

19. Instructors and Admin Staff At Crail JSSL 1956 photographed on what was several years earlier an airfield used by the Fleet Air Arm. Courtesy the Crail Museum and Heritage Centre.

From the rear row reading left to right:

REAR ROW   H A Bazylko, T L B Wade, H Sternbergs, J Klavins, H Rathfelders, J M D Steen, H A Malhomme, P Kazakowitz, S Nitich

THIRD ROW   Wolkowinski, J Krohin, W R Niezbrzycki, Pedersen, N D Bancroft, Campbell, G Mezulis, R C McDermott, N Kuznetsov, B Mandre-Methusalem, B K Jakutis, P Ancipovich, N Kravchenko, N Suslin,

SECOND ROW   Brewer, J Baykovski, Huracek, N Komarov, Kacznarczyk, V Volkonsky, F J de Ramer, J C Wilczynski, P H Meades, Ringer, A Scobie, L Ross, Sillitoe, Davies, F Rzeszowski,

FRONT ROW   C Bystram, Sanders, Koshevnikova, Grey, Brian Hawkins, Brig Griffiths, Lt Col Headmore, Lt Col Rose and Sally, N, Lunen, Maj Tod, J O Lewis, Mrs A M Nicholas-Eve, Collins, E Wassiljew, Mackie, G E L Bird, Small.

very short supply, and the far more numerous aliens from Eastern Europe. To attract well-qualified staff, it was proposed to urge the War Office to finance special extra responsibility allowances, perhaps by analogy with the Burnham scales applicable at that time to teachers in English schools.[2]

James Muckle, the leading authority on the teaching of Russian in Britain and a former RAF student of the JSSL, has unearthed a Crail staff list dated July 1956. Interestingly, the ratio of British to foreign personnel was almost exactly as envisaged by the authorities five years earlier. Nearly all the individuals named had previously taught coders, soldiers and airmen at Coulsdon in Surrey and/or Bodmin in Cornwall, both having been closed during the previous two years. Listed as 'civilian language instructors', 53 men and 4 women were cited, along with their ages, starting dates and whether their work was principally training interpreters or translators. Nearly half were said to be Russian, of whom 13 were specifically designated 'ex-Soviet' and one stateless. Eight were from the Baltic states of Estonia, Latvia and Lithuania and two from the Ukraine - all four countries then in Moscow's inflexible grip, just as they had been before the Bolshevik revolution. Eight were British, and there was a solitary Czech. The largest sub-group, after the Russians, were the Poles, who numbered 15. Not every teacher at the English JSSLs stayed in JSSL employment long enough to get to Crail in Scotland in 1956, which means that it is difficult to calculate how many instructors were employed altogether over the period 1951-60.

Relations between teachers and taught

During language training a coder would have direct dealings with only four or five tutors,[3] though he might glean information from mates about several more. Judging by the recollections we have gathered for this book, our teachers were generally well liked,

---

2 TNA/ADM 116/ 6334, TRL, 14 March 1952.

3 Each JSSL class had one teacher for grammar, and one for conversation and dictation practice, so individual coders were limited to two teachers, unless there were staff changes. Lectures, joint singing sessions and extra-curricular activities like the Russian choir and drama productions could give us access to a wider range of teachers. Further teachers would be encountered at Wythall or Pucklechurch.

despite not being professionally trained for, let alone dedicated to, such a vocation. That they found favour with us is not difficult to explain. Our fear of flunking the course and being relegated to mundane, possibly more dangerous, military duties was sufficient to instil constant respect. There were, too, conspiratorial pleasures to be had in membership of a small, select, privileged gang enlisted in an activity both exotic and exclusive. Much more than the British schoolmasters or university tutors under whom we had so recently studied, our new, mostly East European, teachers could relate personal stories that were by turns hilarious and hair-raising. Participants in revolutions, civil wars and two international conflicts; on occasion, victims of famine, imprisonment and torture; urbane, cosmopolitan and widely-travelled, they could hardly fail to impress young men whose furthest journey from home had, in many instances, been to report to naval barracks in Portsmouth. Though our memories of World War II persisted vividly, few of us had lost close relatives or experienced any significant deprivation. When our tutors regaled us with their life stories, we were an enthusiastic, albeit conscript, audience.

Teachers' hostility to communism

Former coder Gareth Mulloy went to Crail in November 1956. For small group conversation classes he was taught by Mr N Komarov. The 51-year old Russian, who may have originated from one of the Baltic states, is engraved in Mulloy's memory:

> The stories of the lives of these teachers under the Soviets were often horrendous. Komarov told us of being handcuffed with barbed wire. His description was so vivid that I still remember the Russian for it - *provolochnoye zagrazhdyeniye*. All were forced exiles from their native countries. Many had left families behind. None could ever contemplate returning whilst the Soviets remained in power. They had thrown their lot in with the West, and were considered as traitors by the Soviet Union. We were witnesses to the effects of the humiliating degrading system of government that communism brought to Russia and its satellite countries. The stoicism and courage of these people impressed us tremendously, as did their patience in teaching us.

Ian Phillips was at JSSL Crail at the same time as Gareth Mulloy, though in a different class. His abiding memory is of a diminutive Latvian called Sternbergs:

> He actually stood on a box in front of the class to gain enough height to stare down on his students. He claimed to be very lucky, because every other boy at his school joined the army and became officers. He was too short - so no officer. All the officers were shot by the Russians. 'Which,' he asked, 'is the biggest country in the world?' Answer – 'Latvia.' 'Why?' Broadly smiling Sternbergs: 'because all the land of Latvia is by the Baltic and most of the population is in Siberia'.

Peter Lord had come across Sternbergs in Bodmin in 1955:

> He was our grammar teacher. Middle-aged, short and plump, he was very serious and brooked no nonsense. He was rumoured to have been in the Gestapo. He was presumably a Latvian of German origin and amongst those who moved to Germany when the USSR and the Third Reich shared out northern Europe in their accord at the beginning of WWII. I don't see him strutting around in jackboots, but he would have been a valuable interpreter.

One former coder, Lawrie Douglas, believes he heard, perhaps from another teacher, that Sternbergs had translated for the Germans at the Treblinka extermination camp. We do not have independent evidence.

J Klavins, remembered by James Muckle as 'hard-working and efficient', was another Latvian teacher who very openly revealed the hatred he felt toward communists of all stripes, as the former midshipman Clifford German recalls:

> Mr Klavins was a ponderous and melancholy Balt with very anti-communist views. I can still remember the venom with which he denounced Patrice Lumbumba (so he pronounced the name), the head of the newly independent Democratic Republic of the Congo.[4]

---

4   Following the end of Belgian rule, Patrice Lumumba was in 1960 elected Prime Minister of the Democratic Republic of the Congo. A willing recipient of Soviet aid, he provoked western displeasure and was deposed and then murdered by Congolese opponents in 1961; CIA involvement has long been suspected. The Soviets created a new university in Moscow in

Just as virulently anti-communist was another of Clifford's instructors:

> Mr Melechowicz was a Pole with one eye, no forearms and one elbow, variously the result of a plane crash or an attempt to divert a grenade. He was a brave and courteous man, who could unerringly drink vodka from a small glass balanced on his wooden elbow, and another and another. I remember him coming into class one day [5 March 1953] saying. 'Stalin has died aged 72 years, 2 months, 4 days - 72 years, 2 months and 4 days too long.' The years months and days may be guesswork,[5] but there was no doubting the emotion.

Aged 46, Oleg Kravchenko was one of the younger teachers at Crail. He was in a very small minority on the staff to have fought against the Allies in World War II. Our RAF colleague James Muckle got to know him later, when he was looking for a native speaker to help his pupils studying Russian at Chichester High School in 1963:

> He was excellent. I came to know him quite well. Unfortunately, his wife died around 1962, leaving him with three young children under twelve. Certain things about Oleg may repel us today: he had fought in the Bulgarian army during the War. What!? Fought for Hitler? Yes – he was quite adamant. Hitler was the only person opposing Stalin, so Oleg fought for him. Now, I am no friend of Hitler, but at the same time, even during the Second World War there were many British people with grave misgivings about our alliance with Stalin. It is just another example of the way moral issues become a 'moral maze' and challenge our notions of justice and of right and wrong. A good thing we ourselves did not have to make some of these choices.

Yevgeniy Galko had also been sufficiently hostile to the communists to opt for the German side in the war.[6] He served in the

---

his name; it hosted students principally from the Third World. Clifford German was able to hear Klavins's tirade in 1960 through continued contact as a RNR officer, after the national service Russian programme had ended.

5   Stalin, born 18 December 1878, actually died aged 74 years, 2 months, 15 days; he created confusion after coming to power by insisting, despite official records, that he was born 21 December 1879, which would have made his age on death 73 years, 2 months, 12 days.

6   Prince Oleg Volkonsky, son of Prince Valentin Volkonsky (discussed later in the chapter), has posted recollections of his father teaching at JSSL Crail

Cossack Corps of the *Wehrmacht* General, Helmuth von Panwitz. Only by hiding in the mountains did he manage to avoid the tragic fate of the 17,000 fellow Cossacks who were forcibly repatriated to the Soviet Union: the British handed them over in the Austrian town of Lienz in spring 1945 – an episode for nearly twenty years effectively concealed from the general public. If Galko harboured any ill feelings towards the British for what he might justifiably have considered an act of treachery, he does not seem to have displayed them to his JSSL students.

Mike Williams was taught by Galko and found it an enjoyable experience:

> He was a great guy, with a powerful, booming voice that carried above any noise. His voice volume, so we were told by one of his colleagues, was developed by yelling orders across the thunder of Cossack horses' hooves in the charge. Having discovered my name was Mike, he nicknamed me *Mishen'ka* [diminutive of *Misha*, short form of *Mikhail*, Michael] – 'Ho, ho, Mishen'ka you are a teddy bear!' Apparently Russian kids call a teddy a *Mishen'ka*. If we had the dreadful watch [night guard duty] hours and I turned up looking like death, he would roar, 'Ah, Mishen'ka, it's the blinkin' girls, make you tired - you 'ave to give them up!' I used to think, 'I should be so bloody lucky, Sunshine', but never had the courage to say so. He set us an essay – *Lyubov' Matyeri* (*Mother Love*). Mine just clicked with him, apparently, and he took it to show several Russian ladies in his rather elevated social circle. He came back a couple of days later, saying – 'You make the ladies cry, Mishen'ka, they loved your essay. They say you must love your mother.'

The female teaching staff

For every ten men instructing on the Russian course there would be one woman. Tatiana Osipovna Gerasimova, Maurice Berrill's group teacher at Coulsdon in 1953, was one of those who did not make it to Crail, though she was eminently capable of motivating her students. In one of his letters home Maurice described what

on the Internet at http://www.volkonsky.com/Chapter05.html Galko was one of the elder Prince's closest friends there.

20. Mrs Levitskaya with class members and possibly an acting principal at Coulsdon 1952. Courtesy Bill Morgan, RAF *kursant.*

occurred when his intake completed the course and was leaving the JSSL:

> We gave a fountain pen and a cigarette case respectively to Miss Gerasimova (Group Teacher) and Mr Henry (Class Teacher). Miss Gerasimova (or Tatiana as we now call her) also had a surprise for us: a parcel of three books for each - one of poems, a novel, and a volume of pictures of Russian architecture - all of course, in Russian! She also handed out paper napkins and produced a great box of Russian pies - cabbage & meat & egg - though not pies as we know them, but rather like large doughnuts stuffed in the centre with the minced cabbage, etc. They were very tasty. Then again, today, she gave us all a little bag of sweets. She really is very kind and very comical and we shall miss her.

At Crail, Ian Phillips was taught by Helena Levitskaya, an altogether more ambiguous character than Miss Gerasimova:

> She had her own quarters at JSSL, and I think she had a pug dog. She certainly had her favourite *mal'chiki* (boys), mostly RAF *kursanty*. She would entertain them to tea and had, I think, her own *samovar*. Her *mal'chiki* apparently told her much about English traditions, habits and customs. They would paint touching watercolours to illustrate these and one, showing a typical fireplace and hearth, would be entitled, *One should not look at the mantelpiece when poking the fire*. She must have been seventy in those days.

She was actually stated to be 59 on the Crail staff list, the oldest of the four women instructors employed there. Robert Cox, one of the last students at Crail, had his own reasons for taking against her:

> Levitskaya was not a favourite of the RN contingent. We thought she was hopelessly reactionary. She thought some of us were atheist lefties, from discussion and the lecturettes; she wasn't wrong, either. We called her the 'black widow'.

John Curran, has fonder recollections of Helena - then, being an RAF linguist, he was one of her 'boys':

> She was so warm and friendly and showed great affection to us. She would often bring in cookies. I remember her as an old lady, but recently, when I

saw a picture of her with some students – on one of the websites – goodness me, she was quite young and attractive!

Another of Levitskaya's RAF *mal'chiki* was Jack Doughty, who emphasises a different aspect of her character:

> She was indeed an excellent teacher, the best one I ever had, but she had a fiery temper, which earned her the nickname of *vzryvchatoe sushchestvo* – 'explosive substance'.

Kosara Gavrilovic was a much younger instructor, and she certainly caused post-adolescent hearts to flutter. An alluring, divorced Serb, she was engaged to teach coders who had been commissioned as midshipmen at the JSSL attached to the School of Slavonic and East European Studies in London. Clifford German was (almost) smitten:

> Kosara Gavrilovic, a very sexy Serb, whose family owned a substantial business (possibly bakeries) in pre-WWII Belgrade. She was very definitely 'up for it', as I believe the expression goes, but was probably a tad too old at 30 for most of us. I think she suspected us of collective homosexuality, and was fond of saying, meaningfully, 'Serbia is a young and vigorous country; we have no homosexuals there!', while looking each of us directly in the eye.

More palpably beguiled was Mike Williams:

> Gavrilovic, of the divine body and gorgeous legs - who could ever forget her? Alas, she never taught me, but I kept hoping.

Kosara soon abandoned work for the military to become a university professor. Her extremely well-crafted English verse translations of Serb and Russian religious poems can be found today on the Internet. As recently as 2009 she was campaigning to support the Orthodox Church clinging on in Serb enclaves in newly independent Kosovo. Author of numerous pro-Serb articles, also available online, she can be heard and seen, fine features still very much in evidence, on YouTube, where she fulminates against the Kosovan authorities, the United Nations, the European Union and the present Serb government, all of them, in her view, conspiring to destroy an age-old Serb and Christian heritage.

The horny-handed son of toil, the aristocrat and class divisions

Not every JSSL teacher achieved an immediate rapport with their students, as John Griffiths (Coulsdon 1952-53) recalls:

> Mr Kotvitsky had been a Donbas miner and had led a strike against the harsh conditions under which he and his fellows had to work. He only just escaped being shot, by fleeing to the West. Not surprisingly, perhaps, after all he had undergone, he was devoid of any sense of humour whatsoever and so was mercilessly ribbed by the whole class. This he endured in patient bewilderment and incomprehension, but he forcefully demonstrated the man who would not be pushed around when one of the class put a wastepaper basket full of rubbish on top of the door, so that it fell on him when he entered. He said nothing, but striding to the front, turned and glared at us. After a few seconds fixing each of us with his stare as if to flush out the guilty party, he quietly told us, in his broken English, 'You have insulted me. All leave cancelled for a week.' We treated him with considerably greater respect thereafter.

At the opposite end of the social spectrum from Kotvitsky was Prince Valentin Mikhailovich Volkonsky,[7] who was born in 1898 and of an age, therefore, to serve in the Russian Navy during World War I, but hardly old enough to have been elevated to the rank of admiral, as one former coder imagines. Could Prince Volkonsky, said by David Talks to have 'chewed tobacco in class and spat into empty *Gold Block* tins on the desks', be the aristocrat recalled by John Drummond in his highly entertaining autobiographical memoir, *Tainted by Experience*:

> He looked like an eighteenth-century grandee ... with a hook nose, scraped-back hair and exquisite manners. A gold half-hunter watch and a gold-headed cane were all that remained of the Volkonsky inheritance. He had a most elegant St Petersburg accent, which I strove to imitate - not difficult, since I have never been

---

7   A detailed, Russian language, account of Prince Valentin Volkonsky's life can be read in the memoirs of his wife and son, posted on the Internet at http://www.volkonsky.com.

21. Prince Valentin Volkonsky (in civilian clothes) at Crail in 1957. Sitting front row far left is Commander Maitland-Makgill-Crichton. Courtesy Prince Oleg Volkonsky.

able to pronounce *r* as a rolling consonant but only as something much more French and throaty.[8]

Of course, being British, coders were pretty clued-up on class distinctions, especially those embodied in the grammar/public School divide. Discerning social distinctions in nationals of other countries was intriguing, instructive even. Like John Drummond, old Etonian Robin Hope was a midshipman studying in London. Ironies were not lost on Robin:

> The motley collection of refugee and other teachers did not all speak Russian as their first language. Teasing, we asked teacher A why he said the correct phrase was X, whilst teacher B said it was Y. I treasure A's reply, 'What do you expect from a Bulgarian peasant?'

---

8   John Drummond, *Tainted by Experience*, p 60.

In 1957 Peter Duskin, then a gunner in the Royal Artillery, was studying at JSSL Crail, where he kept a detailed diary. Some fifty years later he expanded it into a substantial memoir of his national service career, from which he has kindly given us permission to quote:

> Some of the older non-British instructors still carried about with them the atmosphere of Tsarist Russia; Mr Jakutis, for example, arriving to catch a train at Crail station, was heard informing the staff of his requirements for the journey: 'No smoking and no peasants!' He also recalled that, when he had been a high-ranking officer in the military in one of the Baltic successor states to the Tsar's empire between the two world wars, he had had the habit, when inspecting the men's food, of having the cooks flogged if his baton did not stand unsupported in the soup. I am not sure that I believed this, but it sounded quite impressive. Certainly it gave me an idea of what ought to have been done to the cooks at Crail for having the nerve to serve up the extraordinary gunge that we were expected to eat in their cookhouse.

What's in a name, or a swear-word?

Teachers' names were frequent subjects of speculation as well as deliberate distortion for comic effect. For reasons that are not entirely obvious, Mr A Danilochkin, an ex-Soviet citizen and one of the first to be appointed to work at a JSSL, was nicknamed *Sorok Odin* (Forty-one). Gareth Mulloy believes the name derived from the 63-year old Russian's devoting excessive amounts of time to ensure students pronounced that number correctly. Peter Crowther was at Crail the same time as Mulloy, and recalls that Danilochikin's wife was on the staff, too. No coder could forget:

> ... the motherly, middle-aged lady who called us 'impotent' (for impertinent) and regaled us with stories such as the tale of how, during the siege of Leningrad, she had snatched a Pekingese pet dog at a street corner, taken it home, and cooked it! Who, too, can forget 'Sorok Odin', the mad ex-Red Army major, who drove wildly around in his open sports car nick-named the *Neupravlyaemiy Snaryad* (Uncontrollable Projectile)?

To some classes Danilochkin was known as 'Danny'. James Muckle recalls an entirely believable story told by an RAF friend, who had the reputation of being a good driver and had agreed to give the old *émigré* driving lessons:

> Danny was the most harmless old fellow, but when he put his top coat and hat on - as he did even in summer - he looked really sinister. During the driving lesson he passed a young girl at the side of the road. He wound the window down. Staring at her over his spectacles and from underneath his floppy black hat, he said, scarcely invitingly in his thick Russian-English, 'You want the lift, yes?' 'No! No!' she shrieked, and fled in the opposite direction. Poor Danny. He meant it well, and she had no need to fear.

The prize for outlandish names surely went to the only Estonian on the books at Crail, Mr B Mandre-Methusalem. Peter Crowther found his teaching methods as intriguing as his monicker:

> The classroom was festooned with pictures cut from magazines and advertising brochures etc. The idea was that we should take a dozen or so of these pictures and make up a little story in Russian using the words that they represented. He must have been an ardent admirer of Gina Lollobrigida, because pictures of her featured prominently in his collection. A typical exercise would begin with something like, '**Gina Lollobrigida** carried the **kettle** to the **sink** and filled it with water in order to make a **cup** of **tea** in the **teapot**'. At some stage, however, Mandre's focus on teaching had transferred itself into an obsession with collecting new pictures to swell his collection, so that much of the time we spent cutting them out of magazines and brochures. Unbeknown to us, his passion for collecting had led him to apply to local firms for advertising brochures. I shall never forget the expression on his face one afternoon when there was a knock on the classroom door and a young soldier came in and said, 'Mr Methusaleh?' and, receiving a nod, said, 'There is a van outside with a man wanting to see you. He has brought the vacuum cleaner you ordered from Edinburgh'. Poor Mandre, his English can't have been all that good. He only wanted a brochure so that we could say *Gina Lollobrigida nosila pylesos* (Gina Lollobrigida was carrying a vacuum cleaner).

It would be of considerable interest to know what our language instructors thought of us. Mike Gerrard believes that Mr Stanislavski, his Russian numbers tutor at RAF Wythall, anticipated verbal abuse from students:

> To discourage us from cursing him, he told us in a bizarre mix of English and Russian '*Ya khorosho znayu* (I know a lot of) *Russk*i swearing, *Nemetski* (German) swearing, *Frantzuski* (French) *i* (and) *Angliiski* (English) swearing'.

Amongst ourselves swearing was commonplace, if not *de rigueur*, but we know of no incident where a teacher was the target. Understandably, though, they were not eager to hear swearing among their students, as Dennis Mills, courtesy the same Stanislavski, found - to his cost:

> I didn't very much like playing tombola (bingo) in Russian, although it was supposed to be a Friday afternoon treat for Mr Stanislavski's class at RAF Wythall. Sitting on the front row and seeing Stanislavski bringing into the room his box of tombola equipment, I said 'Oh, f*** me', thoughtlessly, and not sufficiently *sotto voce*. Stanislavski mounted the teacher's rostrum like a turkey cock and tore me off a terrific strip, then dished out the punishment. I was obliged to mount the rostrum and act as teller, but then the tables were turned as I went along at my own slow pace, instead of Stanislavski's gallop. And no, I didn't have to translate 'sixty-six, clickety-click' etc – just read out the numbers in Russian as they were drawn.

The age gap

The teachers were, of course, considerably older than us. Of the 52 whose ages were indicated on the Crail list of civilian instructors, only three were in their twenties; 13 in their sixties, and the average age was fifty. Knowing that life expectancy was significantly lower half a century ago adds poignancy to the remark with which Mr Dudariv opened each session:

> *Gospoda, vy budyetye DOLGO zhit', a ya skoro ... UMRU'* (Gentlemen, you will live a LONG time, and I will soon ... DIE).

Perhaps music was a consolation to him, for, as Michael Waller reports:

> He played the balalaika at professional level.

Polish teachers of Russian

If the uprooted *émigrés* who drilled us so effectively in the intricacies of Russian grammar and vocabulary were ever at loggerheads over ancient national animosities, we students were oblivious to it. In our late teens or early twenties, most of us would have known too little central and east European history to appreciate the potential for friction between individuals whose national armies had so recently rampaged over each other's territories inflicting unspeakable barbarities. We practically all knew, however, that Britain had declared war on Germany in 1939 because of the Nazi invasion of Poland. We were mindful, too, that thousands of Poles had come to Britain to form regiments and air force squadrons in aid of the Allies, and had made a significant contribution to victory in the Battle of Britain. That Soviet Russia had also invaded eastern Poland in 1939 was effectively universal knowledge. We might therefore have had reason to expect some antipathy on the part of our Polish teachers *vis-à-vis* their Russian counterparts.

One of Tony Cash's first teachers at Coulsdon in 1952 was Henryk A Malhomme, a Pole whose aristocratic forebears (full name - Malhomme de la Roche) had fled France following the 1789 revolution:

> Suave, dapper, dark hair oiled and neatly slicked back, he liked to wear his overcoat loosely draped over his shoulders, and was usually to be seen smoking from an elegant cigarette holder. He told me two things which I never forgot. 'A Pole,' he said, 'is someone who has been, is or will be in a Russian prison camp.' I took that to be an exaggeration. More tantalising was his assertion that 'whatever they tell you about Russia, you have to realise that it's true and untrue at the same time.' Perhaps Malhomme was guilty of national stereotyping; if so, he was in distinguished company: Winston Churchill described that country as 'a riddle wrapped in a mystery inside an enigma'.[9] In some twenty visits between 1959 and 2000 to Russian cities such as Moscow, Leningrad, Sochi, Naberezhnye Chelny, Magnitogorsk and Tambov, I can only say that it always seemed easy to discern a fascinating space between official and unofficial Russia, in which one might do many of the things claimed by some Western

---

9   BBC Radio broadcast, 1 October 1939.

commentators to be impossible – like playing jazz in the Communist days.

In preparation for writing this book we have researched at the library of the Polish Centre in Hammersmith, London, where records are kept relating to the lives of Polish exiles in the United Kingdom. We have seen obituaries published in various journals for nine of the JSSL teachers, including Malhomme. Surprisingly, perhaps, in only one obituary is there mention of the deceased having taught Russian to British servicemen. In some instances this omission may have arisen from fear of divulging what was thought to be an official secret. Yet one may speculate whether the Polish teachers and their relatives felt some remorse, shame even, for this period in their careers. If we accept at face value what is contained in these press cuttings, teaching may simply have been seen as a fall from grace. Malhomme, whose father had led a law practice in St Petersburg, was a graduate of that city's law school. When, following the 1917 revolution, Poland regained its independence from Russia, he joined the Polish diplomatic service and, according to a *Times* obituary,[10] went on to serve in France, Denmark and Yugoslavia, ending up in 1935 as First Secretary at the Polish embassy in Berlin. After the Nazi invasion of Poland four years later, he fought as a member of the Polish 1st Division in Lorraine, eventually joining Polish free forces in Britain. He was four times decorated for bravery and received the *Croix de Guerre*. For someone with such a distinguished career behind him, teaching must have seemed a come-down.

If our Polish teachers felt in any way aggrieved, they did not disclose it to their students. In dealings with us they were the embodiment of charm and intelligent sophistication. One, in particular, endeared himself enormously to John Griffiths, partly because he contrasted so sharply with ex-Donbas miner, Kotivitsky, described above:

> Count Mikhail Lubiensky was a Polish aristocrat who claimed to have led the last cavalry charge against the tanks of the Russian occupiers of his homeland. Most scoffed at his claim, but I believed it, for I felt him to be a man of integrity. Perhaps my good opinion may have been influenced by the fact that when he caught me scribbling away in English under my desk, when I should have been ingesting irregular verbs, he

---

10 *The Times*, 30 May 1977.

took the paper out of my hand, but said nothing. The next day he brought me in a book – *Trilby*, by George du Maurier, I think – returned my painful prose and declared, 'You will never be a great Russian scholar, Griffiths, but you may make a decent writer one day'. I like to think he would not have been too disappointed in his prophecy, as the fifteenth of my published books rolls off the press.

Both Malhomme and Lubiensky had an idiosyncratic way of pronouncing the Russian *dark L* sound, so that it resembled a W. Polish has a letter Ł, pronounced as a W. There were, however, suggestions that this pronunciation of the letter was not so much Polish but rather a characteristic of old, aristocratic St Petersburg speech. Some sixty years later the controversy remains to be resolved.

The Polish upper classes were very much in evidence at the JSSLs, and not all earned our respect and admiration as much as Malhomme and Lubiensky did. Graf (Count) Tyszkiewicz has been described to us by RAF Coulsdon *kursant* Tony Tindall as suave and condescending, endowed, to his disadvantage, with no understanding of British undergraduate humour:

A chain smoker who ostentatiously held his cigarettes the Russian way, between finger and thumb, Tyszkiewicz often came to class in a voluminous green cloak and wide brimmed hat. His considerable height and slow gait saved him from ridicule, but he was nevertheless extremely vain and often unwilling to admit he had forgotten the English for a particular Russian word or phrase. After a lengthy pause he would say, for example, 'Gentlemen, who knows the English for *podvodnaya lodka* (submarine)? 'Shitty underpants', someone would shout out helpfully from the back. 'Ah, yes, thank you', said Tish, 'I remember now.'

Of the fifteen Polish teachers on the 1956 Crail list, easily the most memorable was Jozef Godlewski, judging by the number of times his name has cropped up in email correspondence with our coder contributors. The flamboyant ex-colonel gave his students the impression that he had once, almost single-handedly, prevented the Russians capturing Warsaw. Godlewski was doubtless referring to a highly significant battle occurring at the height of the civil war

22. Jozef Godlewski. Courtesy former Coder Peter Hoare.

into which Russia was plunged shortly after the Bolshevik seizure of power in November 1917. The struggle between Reds and Whites, the latter supported by some fifteen anti-Bolshevik states, including Britain and the USA, played out over a vast land mass from Brest to Vladivostok and Murmansk to Odessa. It lasted more than three years. In April 1920 a Polish army invaded revolutionary Russia, reaching the gates of Kiev within a few weeks. A Bolshevik counter-offensive drove the Poles back to Warsaw, where Lenin and Trotsky fondly imagined the Polish proletariat would greet their besiegers as liberators. Predictably, Polish nationalism triumphed over whatever leftish leanings Warsaw workers might have entertained. The Poles, with Godlewski maybe in a prominent role, drove the Red Army back for hundreds of miles, resulting in the loss to the new Soviet state of large chunks of what are now Ukraine and Belarus, territory regained only when Stalin joined an unholy alliance with Hitler to invade Poland in 1939.

Peter Hoare was taught by Godlewski at Bodmin in 1955:

> A colourful character with a fund of stories about his past life, he told us that in the 1930s he had been professor of agriculture at a Polish university and had invented a new model of tractor; that the designs for this were stolen by Fergusons, and he never received any recompense for their successful marketing of the design. He was certainly strongly anti-Soviet, and told us about the Katyn Woods massacre long before it was accepted as a Soviet, not a Nazi, atrocity. On a more personal note I seem to remember bright red underpants (in which he was sometimes seen to sunbathe outside the officers' mess), and I think others have talked about his reminiscences of drinking champagne from ladies' slippers.

James Muckle also recalls Godlewski with affection:

> He was entrusted with the RAF men (including myself) who had passed the 'first major' exam, but had been rejected by the Air Ministry Selection Board as 'unsuitable for officer training'. Mr G. was a larger-than-life character; a good teacher, though he was far too keen to speak English in class rather than Russian. He would, in quiet moments, extract a little brush from his pocket to groom his moustache. He taught us Russian songs, but they were in corrupt versions – not that it mattered, as they were fun to sing.

From the Polish library in Hammersmith we have learned that Godlewski trained at an officers' school in St Petersburg, making his way to Warsaw after the 1917 revolution. In the short war against the new Soviet state he was captured by the Russians at Lvov but escaped. In 1937 he was elected as a senator in the Polish parliament. Two years later, when the Germans occupied Poland, he decided to continue the struggle in France, working in mine disposal; in 1940 he escaped to Britain, where he served with the Polish free forces as a communications officer.

Extraordinarily ingenious and enterprising, Godlewski left after his death in 1968 a very large cache of letters, documents and articles, among which is a design for THE FACILITY SET. Elegantly drawn on parchment paper approximately 30" x 20", it shows a toilet case with pockets and buckles to hold comb, nail file, razor blades, 'stypstic' (*sic* - his English was always idiosyncratic), needles, flints etc - 24 items in all, the highlight being a little drop-down compartment for soap. A smaller scale design offers five different kinds of SPORTS BUTTON, drawn in section, front and back. We found no evidence that these projects ever materialised.

The Godlewski archive reveals that over a period of some thirty years he positively bombarded the British and international press with articles, the principal, if not exclusive, purpose of which was to persuade the world that the Commies represented an appalling threat to our freedom and security and that the West was exceedingly pusillanimous in dealing with it. Prominent political figures like John Foster Dulles, US Secretary of State to President Eisenhower, and religious leaders were also targets of his campaign. In 1955 he wrote to Cardinal Griffin, Archbishop of Westminster, warning that we should not be seduced by Soviet blandishments. He refers to the:

> ... efforts the Soviets are making to win over the West by means of treacherous propaganda and diplomacy, and at the same time by making superficial concessions whilst continuing to retain the 'spoils of war' and following the utopian aims of Communism.

The Roman Catholic cleric's response was measured:

> Certainly at the moment we cannot close our eyes to the past in giving consideration to the new efforts being made by the Soviets.

In January 1950 Jozef wrote an article, 'Achilles Heel'. He saw the Soviets getting a foothold in Egypt, Suez and Syria, and warned the reader:

> The Great Powers through short sightedness and egoistic policies and owing to absolute incomprehension of the Russians have brought a catastrophic situation to the world. Russia, which was saved from Germany through the efforts, pains and blood of the West, today, only four years later, threatens not only European and Asiatic neighbours, but also her wartime allies and benefactors ... The character of the statesman and diplomat of the Western world is more than ever an Achilles heel of humanity.

We believe not many of Godlewski's JSSL students would have agreed then, even fewer today, that the West saved the Soviet Union from the Nazis. Yet, however exaggerated Godlewski's fears of Soviet Russian aggression may now seem, any Pole who had experienced what he had can be forgiven for being such a committed Cold War warrior. This is especially true when you can see from his archive how passionately he strove to make the world realise the truth of the Katyn massacre: he was writing about it as early as 1947. Unsurprisingly, he found himself a bed-fellow of some politically quite dodgy individuals, like D S Fraser Harris of the League of Empire Loyalists, with whom he corresponded. Harris was obviously enthusiastic for Godlewski's basic anti-Soviet line, but in a letter to Jozef dated 23 March 1958 he was at pains to point out:

> ... it is not only Moscow that is striving for World Government, but the international financiers (resident in New York). These all-powerful men financed the Bolshevik revolution in 1917.

According to Harris, they were still continuing to do so in 1958:

> Dollar imperialism and Russian imperialism are working hand-in-glove.

Jozef's response is not known, so we have no idea whether he shared Harris's views on the New York financiers, but we saw not a trace of anti-Semitism anywhere in the archive, though much of it is in Polish, so not accessible to us.

Godlewski was held in high esteem, not only by his students but by his superiors, too, judging from a testimonial held at the Hammersmith Polish Library. Written by Brigadier E K Page, Principal at JSSL Bodmin from September 1954, it states:

> He has worked hard and most willingly, and produced excellent results; he is popular with all, and for most of his stay in Bodmin he has been elected as the 'doyen' of the foreign staff.

All the evidence points to Godlewski being a born leader, and it was not surprising to learn he headed a four-year campaign for better pay and conditions for himself and his colleagues, first at Bodmin and continuing when the language school was moved to Crail. The dispute is mentioned in *Secret Classrooms*[11] with a reference to a 'former Senator of the Polish parliament', but at that point the book's authors were not sure of the outcome. The Godlewski archive contains a letter he received from Stanley Mayne, General Secretary of the Institute of Professional Civil Servants (IPCS), dated 21 November 1955:

---

11 Geoffrey Elliott & Harold Shukman, *Secret Classrooms*, p 102.

I hope that the result of your and our efforts at that
meeting will be to put right some, at least, of the wrongs
from which you and your colleagues are suffering.

Ironically, Mayne, if not actually a Communist Party member
was certainly a sympathiser or 'fellow traveller', to use the
expression current in the 1950s. An obituary in the *Morning Star*[12]
calls the former General Secretary of the IPCS a 'life-long supporter
of the *Daily Worker* and *Morning Star*' [successive names of the
same paper]. Whether Godlewski was aware of Mayne's political
affiliations is unknown. The fiercely anti-Red Pole was effectively
the IPCS shop steward embattled with the authorities on behalf
of himself and other disgruntled JSSL instructors. We suspect he
would have acted no differently whatever he might have learned
about Mayne. In any event, the dispute was resolved more or less
to the satisfaction of the complainants, judging by a letter from the
IPCS dated 8 September 1959:

The grant by the Admiralty of Scale 'A' posts seems
completely to clear the issue as far as we are concerned.

Further clarification comes a fortnight later, Godlewski and
colleagues are to be put in the:

General Section of the Admiralty Scientific and
Technical Staffs Branch. You are now a civil servant
employed by the Admiralty.

Henceforth, Godlewski and his instructor colleagues were
entitled to an annual salary of between £940 and £1135 for more than
40 hours of teaching per week. Tony Cash, a second class honours
graduate from Oxford University with a Diploma in Education,
began teaching at a grammar school in September 1958, and recalls
that the Burnham scale on which he was being paid was comparable,
but the hours of actual teaching could not have exceeded 30 a week.

Following national service, James Muckle, like Tony Cash, took
employment in a grammar school. He recalls the last time he saw
his old instructor Godlewski:

Some years after my time in JSSL I met him in the
street in Chichester: he had lost some of his sparkle,
and was keen to know what salary I received as a
young schoolmaster – was he looking for a way out?

---

12 *Morning Star*, 30 December 1988.

23. JSSL badge.

CHAPTER 6
THE LIFE AND TIMES OF JSSL STUDENTS

РАБОТАТЬ - ДЕНЬ КОРОТАТЬ; ОТДЫХАТЬ - НОЧЬ ИЗБЫВАТЬ
(Russian saying – 'Work shortens the day; play banishes the night')

The authors thought of calling this chapter ALL WORK AND NO PLAY MAKES JACK A DULL BOY, partly because 'Jack' has for centuries been synonymous with 'sailor'. Coders were, of course, sailors by definition since they had been conscripted into the Royal Navy, but we rarely referred to ourselves as such. To our way of thinking, 'Jack' was like 'mate', simply a term by which someone might address us when asking for directions or a light for a cigarette. A few weeks in naval barracks and at sea were too brief a time for us to feel truly sailors.

The next and longest phase of a coder's career had very little to do with the Navy, and not just because there is nothing essentially nautical about learning Russian. The service-run JSSLs where we studied the language were not directed by the Admiralty. Bodmin and Coulsdon belonged to the Army, as did Crail, though formerly a Fleet Air Arm base. All three had an Army officer in charge, with Navy, Air Force officers and NCOs in support. For nine or so months we were subject to Army routines and procedures, while still answerable to *The Articles of War*, as Part I of the Naval Discipline Act was fearsomely known. Although we lived in huts segregated as to service, we generally studied, ate, exercised and did weapon training alongside our soldier and airmen peers; however in later intakes, the three services paraded separately (but on the same ground) and had separate Russian classes.

Kursanty on parade

The late D M Thomas, poet and novelist, was one of the first Army men to study at Bodmin, arriving there in November 1951. In his introduction to *Secret Classrooms* he memorably described the widely disparate marching styles of the three services:[1]

> When we were summoned to 'Get on parade!' we soldiers advanced with exaggerated arm-swings and boot-thumps; the airmen moved with a nonchalant, easy superiority, as if they were Battle of Britain heroes; and the sailors ... the sailors trotted a few yards in a rollicking, self-parodying way.

It is no accident that the Army and Navy have opted for modes of drill that contrast so strikingly. In the Army, when turning in the standing position, or coming to a halt, great emphasis is placed on stamping the feet heavily and noisily. In the Navy, such a procedure could be disastrous given the historical need to avoid undue damage to old wooden decks.

John Roxburgh of the Royal Artillery, a Bodmin contemporary of Thomas's, witnessed a similar shambolic attempt to parade cohesively which, he says, resulted in square-bashing being abandoned to be replaced by regular route marches:

> This was much more acceptable to all concerned and we enjoyed tramping the lanes of Cornwall to the strains of 'Green Grow the Rushes-o' sung at the tops of our voices. An inspiring or terrifying sound, dependent on your point of view.

Bodmin town's amenities

For a coder, Bodmin army camp had two matchless advantages over the naval land- or sea-based establishments in which he had so far served: when he was off duty he did not have to wait for a liberty boat to escape, and, furthermore, he could exit unobserved through holes in the hedge. Unfortunately, there were few outside attractions luring him to do so. Sited on one of the bleakest, most desolate moors in Britain, the camp was nearly a mile from Bodmin itself. In the summer months the narrow High Street, a stretch of the A30 London to Lands End road, carried a non-stop line of cars travelling in each direction in the first post-war explosion of heavy holiday

---

1   Geoffrey Elliott and Harold Shukman, *Secret Classrooms* p 2.

traffic. With little over 6,000 inhabitants, the town had several pubs, including *The Hole in the Wall* in one of the back streets, where the speciality was a potent brew of real scrumpy served with floating lumps of apple. Two pints were said to be enough to render the drinker completely blotto. There was a cinema, a couple of churches, including St Petroc's (now a Grade I listed building), and St Laurence's Mental Hospital, which put on the occasional hop. Patrick Miller, one of the first ever coders, recalls:

> ... trying to dance with local girls in our heavy boots and being deserted in the middle of the floor.

When Mike Gerrard was at Bodmin four years later than Patrick, the admission cost was one shilling (5p), and non-alcoholic refreshments were available at a small extra charge. Generally, the shilling was all that national servicemen could afford, and aspiring Don Juans were forced to give up their hopes for want of the price of a fruit juice or a cup of tea. It was a long walk from the JSSL to the hospital, and an even longer one back again at the end of the evening, and in general, people stopped going to the dances after the first month or two.

None of our respondents recalls any significant success with the female population: perhaps unsophisticated country lasses of that period were intimidated by highly educated young men the like of which they had rarely before encountered; or, more likely, they had already given their hearts to the soldiers of the Duke of Cornwall's Light Infantry, whose barracks was next-door to the JSSL. After all, the regiment had been in the vicinity for well over fifty years. Whatever the truth, according to Chief Petty Officer Roach, who drilled coders at Bodmin, the targets of Patrick Miller's advances were no blushing maidens, as Mike Gerrard explained:

> CPO Roach took a group of us one afternoon to the old cemetery in the garden of *The Hole in the Wall* to see a gravestone commemorating Miss X (name unremembered) – 'Virgin, of this parish'. 'Boys', he told us beforehand, 'I'm taking you to meet the only virgin in Bodmin.'

Roach was the senior naval rating at Bodmin, a famous eccentric, capable of finding 'syphilis' (ie. dust) under the beds in the RN huts. When sent during the 1955 rail strike to keep the peace among travellers at Newquay station he told the disappointed commuters 'there's no trains today, so you can all f*** off!'

The Palace Cinema, a cheap, local 'fleapit' in comparison with the swish Odeon at St Austell some 12 miles away, was well patronised by JSSL *kursanty*. It had double seats for courting couples towards the back of the stalls. Movies shown there regularly provoked spontaneous commentary from the audience, as Mike Gerrard discovered:

> During a scene in *Moulin Rouge,* when Jose Ferrer (as the painter Toulouse-Lautrec) went through the process of sealing the door and window of his room, drawing the curtains and turning on the gas, a male voice was heard to say 'E's goin' to gas 'isself', as the penny dropped. Second features, especially of the cowboy or US country-fair genre, were certain to arouse deep reflection among the audience, with the prairie wisdom of the older cowhands drawing appreciative agreement from the locals.

Each programme at the Palace fell into two parts - the main film and second feature, itself sometimes quite a substantial work, even if in the 'B' category. In between, there was an interval, long enough for ice cream sales, adverts, and visiting the loos - all animated by music from *The Glenn Miller Story*, which was then very popular with the patrons. Although from time to time French or Italian films with sub-titles were shown, Russian cinema did not get a look in.

Bodmin enjoys greater status in Cornwall than Coulsdon in Surrey or Crail in Fife. In the mid-1950s it could boast a High Street of sixty or more shops, but very few of them of much relevance to *kursanty*. All the national servicemen on the camp were students attending classes on weekdays. At weekends they were either doing household chores or travelling on sporting activities. On Sundays, with very few exceptions, the shops were closed. The only 'free' time was Wednesday afternoon, but that was early-closing day. Boots was one of the few shops open when *kursanty* were free. Soap, toothpaste and other bathroom needs could be bought there as well as medicines and assorted toiletries. Coders, including Mike Gerrard, were familiar customers:

> On one occasion, as I came into the shop, I found Mr Galko, one of our Russian small-group tutors, engaged in a desperate attempt to make himself understood to the counter assistant, and getting nowhere. Sensing an impasse, I asked the shop assistant what the gentleman was trying to buy. 'He keeps asking me for Royal

Skin soap, and I keep explaining to him that we don't stock it', was her reply. 'Give him Imperial Leather, I said confidently, delighting the tutor and putting a big smile of relief on the face of the girl. How useful it can be to know a little Russian ...

The two St Petroc's

Bodmin was enlivened by the presence of St Petroc's Club, located on the road leading from the town centre to the JSSL, near one of the two railway stations. Mentioned in *Secret Classrooms*[2] as 'a very nice gay club', it was indeed a pleasant place to have a quiet drink, and visiting *kursanty* were not put under any kind of pressure. Given service pay levels, it was not to be visited very frequently, but a student could have a gin or whisky, and make it last a long time by judicious additions of water or tonic after each sip. Coders leaving Bodmin for Wythall in November 1955 were able to enjoy a celebratory evening at St Petroc's shortly before their departure without any embarrassment. About this time, the club sign was stolen as a memento by a group of coders, and transported away roped up in a hammock. By chance, it has recently been restored to the Bodmin Museum, where it now resides as a memory of the *loucher* side of life in Bodmin at the time of the JSSL.

Bodmin's Anglican parish church also bears the name of St Petroc. As described in *Secret Classrooms*,[3] it was the location for performances of religious music by students from the Russian course, some of whom clubbed together to donate a rather beautiful icon as a farewell gift. Sadly, within a few weeks of being installed in the church it was stolen and never recovered. Only a very wan, out-of-focus photograph survives. However, the visual information in it was sufficient to allow Peter Collingridge, an expert on icons who has worked for many years for the auctioneers Christie's, to tell us the following:

> The icon is of course Russian, circa 1900, and shows Christ Pantocrator (the All-powerful), realistically painted with His right hand raised in blessing, His left holding the open Gospels, in a chased and engraved silver *oklad* (cover) with applied pierced halo. It is typical of late 19th and early 20th-century icons of

2   *Ibid* p 89.

3   *Ibid* p 91.

Christ, the painting might have been in oil, rather than tempera on prepared panel, and it might have only been painted to show the face and hands, the background being left blank (a naughty painter's scam at the time). Whoever stole it thought the silver was probably worth more than it was. What a pity.

Ironically, St Petroc himself suffered theft. He was a 6th century monk who had lived as a hermit on Bodmin moor. In 1177 his relics were stolen from Bodmin and taken to Brittany, but restored through the intervention of Henry II.

Home-made diversions

The seriously religious received a warm welcome when they went to worship locally in Bodmin, but varied entertainment was in short supply, and cultural activities hard to come by - which may explain why *kursanty* and instructors felt impelled to shift for themselves. Readers interested in knowing more about the remarkable drama productions staged at the camp are recommended to read *Secret Classrooms*[4] which pays fitting and amusing homage to the theatrical talents of two of the teachers, Dimitri Makaroff and Vadim Koshevnikoff in the years 1953-5. Their Russian-language version of Shakespeare's *Twelfth Night* was extraordinary in combining modern-dress, the music of Richard Strauss, and dance by famous turn-of-the-century Russian choreographers best known for works such as *Swan Lake* and *Firebird*. The least startling element of the staging was the use of an all-male cast of *kursanty*. Robin Hope played Olivia, the beautiful, wealthy noble woman plagued by the priggish, social climber Malvolio. It was, Robin says:

> ... my first drag act since the Dragon School, and my last.

Over a hundred years and more, the Dragon School in Oxford has been famous for successfully preparing pupils to enter our leading public schools. Now totally co-educational, it had only a handful of girls when Robin studied there in the 1940s, hence his initial 'drag act' experience.

Although the authors have no social survey statistics about the prior schooling of JSSL students, it has always appeared that public school-boys were significantly more numerous in the ranks

---

4   *Ibid* pp 91-5.

of coders than among our Army and RAF equivalents. Anecdotal evidence certainly suggests this to be true, which might explain why coders generally seemed to have more money to throw around than other *kursanty*. Two RAF students at Bodmin have referred to coders buying an old hearse for £100 to transport them to London for weekend jaunts and to local beauty spots inland and on the coast. No coder has so far come forward to substantiate the story, but it has the ring of truth.

Tales from the Bodmin *Samovar*

In chapter 4 we discussed the *Samovar* song-book in use at Coulsdon in 1952 and 1953. Bodmin also had its *Samovar* but in this instance it was a cyclostyled periodical, a cross between a school magazine and a house journal, featuring articles, reviews and poems in English and Russian, written for the most part by students themselves. For a time in 1954 it was edited by the now celebrated dramatist Michael Frayn, then an Intelligence Corps interpreter in his final months of national service. Very few editions still exist outside specialist libraries, and we are very grateful to Mike Duffy, a former coder promoted to midshipman interpreter, who has very kindly let us have his only remaining copy, issue No. 8 for June of that year. The journal was edited by someone who used only initials (as did all the other authors). M J F happen to be the initials of Michael Frayn, so it is reasonable to assume he was the editor. One of the articles he commissioned that month tells the fascinating story of the sinking of the Russian warship, the *Varyag* during the Russo-Japanese War, which began in 1904.

The article is written in Russian and attributed to someone with the initials M A O - almost certainly an instructor, a Russian called Mr M A Oljhovikov, about whom we know very little for sure, except that he must have been in his early 50s and later taught at Crail. *Secret Classrooms*[5] mentions that he was one of several staff members who gave the students a hand with the publication. The book also cites a rumour that he was the son of a Ukrainian hetman (warlord). Oljhovikov's article states that to commemorate the 50th anniversary of the outbreak of the Russo-Japanese conflict it was hoped future editions of the magazine would devote space to the subject. One of the very first encounters of the war took place in that

---

5   *Ibid* p 110.

24. The *Varyag* and *Koreets* limping back to port after a severe pummelling from Japanese ships. Courtesy RIA Novosti.

stretch of the Pacific Ocean between China and Korea, known as the Yellow Sea. The *Varyag*, a cruiser of 6500 tonnes, accompanied by a much smaller gunboat, the *Koreyets*, was confronted by a bigger, and very heavily armed Japanese cruiser, the *Asama* (9700 tonnes) supported by a flotilla of six other cruisers and eight torpedo boats. Despite the odds, the Russians refused to surrender. In a battle that lasted around 45 minutes, their two vessels were subjected to relentless shelling. Having lost a third of the crew and almost all its artillery, the *Varyag* had no option but to limp back with its companion into Chemulpo harbour in Inchon Bay not far from Seoul. The survivors were offloaded onto neutral ships, the *Koreyets* blown up and the *Varyag* scuttled so that they should not fall into enemy hands.

Oljhovikov concludes by noting that within weeks of the disaster the newspaper *Rus* published a poem celebrating the Russian sailors' heroism. Appropriately, it was written by Yakov Repninskiy, the man said in the article to have founded the Boy Scout movement in Russia. In one of Repninskiy's 11 verses printed in *Samovar*, seagulls are called on to tell the whole world the latest news - that in the battle 'we did not yield to the enemy, but fell for the honour of Russia'. On the next page, a second poem called *Demise of the Varyag*, also given in Russian, ends with lines which might be roughly translated:

> No stone, no cross will ever say
> Where we our heads to rest did lay
> To glorify the Russian flag.
> Only waves till the end of day
> Will trumpet the heroic demise of the *Varyag*.

The author of this poem was 'unfortunately' not known to Oljhovikov. A quick trawl on the Internet has now established that it was the work of a poet called Evgyenia Studenskaya who died in 1906 and was quite renowned for her translations of foreign verse including one of Rudyard Kipling's barrack-room ballads. The two *Varyag* poems became well-known in Russia as the lyrics of songs which are still sung today, judging by the versions which are available on YouTube.

122

25. Carwyn James, seated left and Bill Musker, seated right at Coulsdon in 1953 along with members of their conversation class and unknown teacher. Courtesy Bill Musker.

Climatic trials and tribulations

One abiding, consistently reported memory of Bodmin is of the inadequacy of the heating arrangements to alleviate the severity of the winter cold. Coders tended to attribute this failing to Army incompetence and lack of concern for student morale. Scorching summers could be a trial too, as Mike Shotton discovered in 1955:

> One or two of our intake got thoroughly sunburnt by lying around in the sun - so much so that they were unable to attend classes for a few days. They were then threatened with being court-martialled for 'deliberately incapacitating themselves' or some such nonsense - rather like shooting yourself in the toe at the front. Fortunately, they got a reprieve.

The Coulsdon camp and the officers running it

Coulsdon JSSL had one huge advantage over Bodmin as a posting – its location on London's doorstep. A far richer variety of extra-curricular entertainments and activities was available to Tony Cash and his fellow coders than to Mike Gerrard and his. The biggest single group of naval respondents who have been sending us their email stories were Coulsdon trained; their recollections have also been more prolific. The Surrey school bulks larger in our narrative than the Cornwall school, even though the latter existed more than a year and a half longer.

Both schools were run by the Army, however, and similar complaints are voiced about the men who were given authority over us. Clifford German recalls an officer of the Royal Inniskilling Fusiliers:

> … whose party trick at Coulsdon was to hold a parade and keep the whole squad standing to attention to see how long they lasted before fainting. I managed about 75 minutes and was by no means the last to go down.

To be fair to the Army, we were not too impressed by the calibre of our own naval officers either. Lieutenant-Commander Inglis was in charge of coders at Coulsdon when Tony Cash's intake arrived in October 1952. He was said to have been relegated to what must have been a backwater in the eyes of any ambitious two-and-a-half ringer, for having run a ship under his command into a harbour wall. In 1953 he retired, but that was not the last we saw of him, as Bill Hetherington recalled:

> He returned a month or so later as a commercial rep for Gieves, naval outfitters – 'Can I measure you, sir, for a doeskin?'

His successor, Lieutenant-Commander Bourgat, was not felt to be much of an improvement. Bill again:

> He made a point of summoning a special parade of all coders soon after taking over as our Divisional Officer. He had heard that we were not showing the Navy in a good light. 'The trouble with you coders here is that you don't give a *raspberry* for the Navy' he said. 'You couldn't care *less*. I'll *make* you care less.' We collapsed into barely suppressed titters. End of pep talk.

When the Coulsdon operation was transferred to Bodmin in the summer of 1954, Bourgat decamped there too, so Mike Gerrard was also witness to his quaint invective:

> At pay parades, he regularly read to us the Article of War relating to Buggery with Man or Beast, dismissing us with the observation that we had much in common with 'detritus exuded from Chelsea at one in the morning'.

The Coulsdon camp was adjacent to the Caterham Guards' Depot. From there, occasional stories percolated through to us of conscripts committing suicide, prompted by cruel treatment during basic training. If a JSSL student fell ill he would have to go to the Guards Depot hospital, as Maurice Berrill did, when he succumbed to a particularly severe bout of 'flu in January 1953. He wrote about it later that month in a letter home which his father kept and which has been published in the journal of the Bourne Society.[6]

> The 'flu epidemic was quite serious with one death and over 200 in hospital. The 'flu then spread to our camp. I began to feel the first symptoms on Monday afternoon and so I reported 'Special Sick' straightaway. The M.O. put me on some rather pleasant medicine — all is now clear. PS: Guards' Depot doctors' names

---

6   Local History Records *The Journal of the Bourne Society* Vol 68 August 2011 p 9.

turn out to be Captain Blood and Lieutenant Butcher!
Positively Dickensian!

In a letter to Jack Doughty, a former RAF *kursant*, the selfsame Lt
Butcher said that if his memory served him, the dentist at Caterham
was called Captain Savage. He ended his message with the thought:

> I was always pretty certain in my own mind that our
> postings to Caterham were deliberately arranged as a
> sort of War Office joke and to strike terror into the
> hearts of the national servicemen!

The Army superior with whom we had most face-to-face dealings
was Regimental Sergeant-Major Ben Collis of the Lincolnshire
Regiment. We lined up before him every working day. Mike
Williams has specific reasons for calling him to mind:

> I came under his eagle eye during morning parade
> when he shrieked, 'Get that sailor off the front rank
> – he's syncopating the step'! Having been told,
> when on leave about a month earlier, by an adenoidal
> Birmingham ball-room dancing teacher (one
> 'Madame Powell', a squat and menacing woman, who
> wore off-putting spectacles like the bottoms of Milk
> of Magnesia bottles) – '*Ooh yo' 'aven't a nownce of
> rythum in yower body*', I was really quite flattered by
> dear Ben Collis's description.
>
> Small, compact and impeccably turned out, with
> perfectly creased trousers and gleaming boots, he
> implemented the iron law of oligarchy at Coulsdon.

When we left to go to RAF Wythall, we sang, on our last parade,
an impromptu 'For he's a jolly good fellow'. It was the only time I
saw a smile on his well lived-in face.

The legend was that RSM Collis's previous posting was as guard
for a petrol pump in Malaya – then rumour, it must be remembered,
is a weapon in the armoury of the otherwise defenceless subordinate.
Not that we were totally bereft of other retaliatory possibilities.
When fog was dense (in the winter of 1952-3 it was frequently so),
not all the 500-odd parading students could be clearly seen by the
RSM. Knowing this, we might sway gently with the intention, as
Bill Hetherington has reminded us of:

> ... inciting him to bark 'Stand still', and counting how many times he said it. I think 30 times in 28 minutes was the record.

In the summer of 1953, on the morning Bill's intake, the fourth, was due to leave Coulsdon, the departing coders contrived a farewell gesture to the RSM when he should arrive on the parade ground:

> He strutted out with his swagger stick only to find 'STAND STILL' painted immediately above his marker spot, tastefully adorned with a posy of bluebells, whilst we of the fourth peeped round the corner of the clothing store as we handed in our bedding, relishing our handiwork and knowing the RSM could do damn-all about it.

We have reason to believe photos were taken of flowers being taken away on the RSM's order. Whoever possesses them, the pictures would make a welcome addition to the larger coder archive which Dennis Mills is compiling.[7]

Combating the cold at Coulsdon

Unlike Bodmin and Crail, Coulsdon was not subject to protracted spells of extreme cold. Nevertheless temperatures could be nippy enough to make us regret the scant supply of heating materials we were allocated. Maurice Berrill told his family how he dealt with the problem[8]:

> 1st February 1953: Today being Sunday I got up late, i.e. at 8 a.m, had breakfast, then returned to bed for an hour with *The Observer*. I got up again and lit our stove, though our bunker was almost empty of coke for we haven't had an issue for more than a week. However, I grabbed another man and together we carried our dustbin of ashes and rubbish to a tip and emptied it. Thus we had an empty dustbin and, having found that the door of the Dental Centre boiler-house was providentially unlocked, we abstracted (polite word!) two bins of beautiful new coke and dragged them through the bushes back to our hut. A little initiative is all that's needed and I'm sure the Dental Centre, which is only used once a week, will not miss its fuel unduly. As I write, our stove glows dully red

---

7 See the Acknowledgement to Dennis Mills on pp. 405-6.

8 *The Journal of the Bourne Society ibid* p 9.

and we can go to sleep as warm as rabbits in their burrow. Further, we still have quite a lot of coke left to carry us over until Tuesday, when we should next have an 'official' issue.

The Coulsdon coders who left mid-course

Whatever gripes any of us had about the cold, the food or the discipline, we were very much aware that our military lot could have been immeasurably grimmer. If you had to do two years in the armed forces there were few more congenial ways of doing it than being a coder special. Yet one fourth intake coder was hell-bent on quitting the service. We have not been able to contact him so we will refer to him as Neil C. Tony Cash recalls his story (the outline of which was confirmed by Bill Musker):

> Neil got himself an appointment to see the Medical Officer at the Caterham Guards Depot and told him that he'd fallen in love with a soldier in the next-door hut. Getting wind of this consultation, Lt Cdr 'Bombhead' Inglis called Neil in to discover what the reason for his visit to the MO had been. Asked whether they couldn't discuss the matter 'man to man', Neil is alleged to have responded: 'That's just it, Sir, there's been too much of this man to man business.' It may well have been Neil himself who told the story. In any event, I have a very clear recollection of his dashing into the canteen where our Russian choir was rehearsing at full throttle, leaping onto the stage, flinging his arms around a friend and exclaiming – 'I'm free, I'm free'. They'd agreed to let him out of the Navy.

Coder TW was in the fourth intake too and has been similarly uncontactable. A good linguist (with a place waiting for him at Oxford after national service) he made quite an impression on his colleagues when he did a fair imitation of Johnnie Ray singing *Cry* and *I Believe for Every Drop of Rain that Falls*. Tony Cash knew him from his performing in the Russian choir:

> TW was a strange lad as well as a 'bit of a lad'. He was very left, and I seem to recall his father was a Communist, though if he'd actually been a member of the Party, I don't think TW would have been taken on as a coder. I have a very vivid memory of him on a bus trip back from Cambridge where the choir had been performing at the ADC Theatre. A fair amount

26. En route to the Derby, 6 June 1953. Left to right coders Michael Clay, Hugh Woodhouse, Tony Cash and Malcolm Brown with Hugh's father's car in which they made the journey from Coulsdon to Epsom. Courtesy T Cash.

of booze had been consumed, and the bus wasn't about to stop to ease anyone's bladder problems. TW found a bottle to piss in. He was immediately challenged to drink the whole bottle by Coder Hugh Woodhouse (ex-Bradfield College pupil and star of their triennial Greek play). For a bet of a fiver, Tony proceeded to do precisely that. He didn't take to discipline, and unlike most of us, hadn't learned dumb insolence. I remember all Coulsdon's coders being assembled to hear the inevitable punishment meted out, though his precise offence now evades me. He was escorted off the premises to spend time in Naval detention quarters, and we never saw him again.

Extra-curricular pursuits

Bill Musker and others so far unknown, managed to find a way of augmenting their pay working at local pubs and hotels:

The Selsdon Park Hotel was the favourite. I graced the Purley Railway Arms lounge bar, having to drop down behind the counter and crawl to the public bar when anyone in uniform came in.

More high-minded, a committed Christian, Maurice Berrill did not like to miss Sunday services, as may be gleaned from his letter home written 1 February 1953[9]:

After tea I went down into Purley for church - worth it - my goodness, for we had that very moving and beautiful hymn of Jean Ingelow's, *And didst Thou love that race that loved not Thee*. The 'flu has hit the congregation, though, for there were quite a few empty pews, whereas, normally, every seat has been occupied - a good and encouraging sight.

On 4 May 1953 Maurice reported a visit with a hut mate to nearby Croydon Aerodrome. The other coder already had a pilot's licence – an extremely rare achievement in those days for anyone in his late teens or early twenties not actually serving in the RAF or a commercial air line. He went up in a Tiger Moth, while Maurice was given a ride in a Percival Procktor with its owner:[10]

We had a delightful 40-minute flight over Surrey, and came down safely on the third run-in after two

---

9 *The Journal of the Bourne Society ibid* p 10.

10 *The Journal of the Bourne Society ibid* p 11.

27. Malcolm Brown learning jazz chords for the guitar with the help of clarinettist Tony Cash at Coulsdon 1953. Courtesy Tony Cash.

attempts had failed. If an aircraft bumps, even slightly, when touching down, it is absolutely necessary to open the throttle to the full and take off again, all in a matter of seconds, otherwise it will stall on the bump about 10-ft from the ground and just drop, with considerable damage to the undercarriage - and the occupants! Still, it's great fun, exciting and instructive too. We hope to go again, next time just the two of us in the Tiger Moth.

In that same letter, Maurice describes how he and four others travelled by car into London for a programme of Russian films organised by the British-Soviet Friendship Society, which, he says, somewhat delicately, is considered to be the 'centre of Communist feeling in London':

That, of course, we disregarded: while we were there we spoke Russian to each other, just to keep up the atmosphere which was certainly very un-English, with men in rags selling copies of *Pravda* and *Soviet Weekly* outside the cinema.

Jazz at Coulsdon 1952-3

In the early 1950s jazz was popular among an ever-increasing number of young Britons, despite (maybe partly because of) the disapproval of British establishment figures whose Soviet equivalents were believed to be even more hostile. Fortunately for would-be Louis Armstrongs and Sydney Bechets, no great skill was required to play the simplest forms of the music, and soon bands were proliferating throughout the land, especially in art schools and universities. By the mid-1950s, there were so many small jazz ensembles it was possible to organise inter-university jazz band competitions. Tony Cash had already been playing the clarinet for three years when he joined the Navy in September 1952:

I took my instrument to Coulsdon in the hope, if not expectation, that there must inevitably be at least a handful of potential band members in the hundreds of Army, RAF and Navy bods I would be studying with. One possible candidate turned out to be Malcolm Brown, who was allocated to the same hut as me. His 'potential' lay in the fact that he possessed, but didn't yet play a guitar. Together we worked out the shapes for the basic chords, and within a couple of weeks

28. Tug of war at Coulsdon during Coronation week 1953. Courtesy of
former Coder Laurie Fox, seen at the head of the rope.

we were away, able to play slowish blues and jazz standards that didn't require more than three or four harmonic changes. In November 1952, Malcolm and I heard that trumpeter Ken Colyer was about to launch a new band in London following his return from New Orleans, where the music we were committed to had originated. If anyone should know how to play Dixieland jazz, it must be Ken, we surmised. As we had leave that weekend we were able to attend the launch. Playing in the new band were Chris Barber on trombone, Monty Sunshine, clarinet, and Lonnie Donegan, guitar and banjo. The interweaving front-line instruments were supported by the sprightliest of rhythm sections which included string bass and drums. Along with the rest of the audience, we were entranced. Back at JSSL Coulsdon we soon found it possible, more or less, to replicate the Colyer line-up. Three soldiers joined us – Roy Smith on trombone, Brian Mulligan on trumpet and Tom O'Brien on piano for the occasional performance in the NAAFI. The five of us actually went up to London to make a record - for our own amazement, not for sale: Tom was really the only thoroughly proficient musician in the group. Inevitably the sounds we produced were pretty undistinguished. Ken Colyer's followers were often fanatical in believing that his brand of New Orleans jazz was the only legitimate one. It's not surprising that British 'Trad' (traditional jazz) bands soon began to resemble one another like an endless succession of monozygotic twins. By the end of the 1950s Rock 'n' Roll had largely replaced our music as the banner to rally disaffected youth.

A right royal occasion

By and large, coders were unlikely to feel alienated from mainstream society, and for one sufficient reason: a combination of education, family history and personal ambition had already propelled us far on the route to successful, fulfilling careers. However broad the spectrum of political opinion espoused by coders, very few displayed hippie or dropout tendencies. We were not adherents of any counter-culture: our drinking, skirt-chasing, sports-loving inclinations were not very different from our fathers' - we even dressed like them. Only our age and musical tastes differentiated us.

134

Attitudes to national symbols were put to the test when on 2 June 1953 Queen Elizabeth II's coronation took place. Tony Cash was at home on leave that day, and not having access to a TV but also wanting to escape the brouhaha, decided to sample rock climbing for the first time. He and a close friend hitch-hiked from Leeds to the beginners' rock, the 'Cow and Calf' at Ilkley:

> Un-roped, I managed the first 18 feet nimbly enough then got stuck. Petrified, I could see no way of progressing further, and, worse, the route back looked equally impossible. I assume shame has blurred the memory of how I extricated myself, or was rescued. Never again. I should have found someone with a TV.

Maurice Berrill opted to attend the royal proceedings as close to the action as could be managed. He found a position on the Thames Embankment to watch the hour-long fireworks display which finished at 11.30 p.m.:[11]

> Then I went to Westminster to see the Abbey and the beautiful temporary annexe and all the decorations, then by side streets to Buckingham Palace. I was just in time to see the Queen and the Duke of Edinburgh come out on to the balcony for the last time at midnight - very pretty - and we all shouted and sang. Then up The Mall, through Admiralty Arch to Trafalgar Square, with much singing and skylarking. Queued at 1 a.m. in Post Office in Charing Cross Road for special stamp - people buying £s and £s worth, whole sheets and sheets of all the various denominations. After that to Piccadilly Circus where I stayed until 2.30 a.m. It was glorious fun - singing & dancing and men (mostly sailors!) climbing lampposts and girls sitting on top of traffic lights, police trying to look serious, yet enjoying it just as much. After all that I walked back miles to St Pancras station, found an unoccupied bench there and tried to sleep but was cold, so waited until a policeman on duty had cleared the Waiting Room of vagrants, and then went in and lay down on a broad stone windowsill, using my scarf as a pillow. Slept from 4.00 till 5.45 a.m, then got up and caught the train back to camp. Had an hour in bed then on parade at 11.00. Everybody was going to sleep in lessons - very comical.

---

11 *The Journal of the Bourne Society ibid* p 12.

The Crail experience

In August 1954 Coulsdon JSSL closed and the whole Russian language enterprise was consolidated at Bodmin; there it remained for a further 18 months before transferring in March 1956 to the other end of the United Kingdom, to a site near the small fishing village of Crail on the north east coast of Scotland, in Fife, where sheep strayed regularly on to the camp, just as they had done at Bodmin. The creatures were not especially popular with the Crail *kursanty*, one of whom is reported to have called them 'shitty-arsed, infestation-ridden, disgustingly smelly creatures' - far removed from the notion of 'Wrens in duffle coats' of the old salt, bestiality joke.[12]

Alan Smith, who has spent a lifetime using foreign languages was always fascinated by the varieties of English he came across during national service - 'Jack talk' as much as regional dialect. Crail in November 1956 did not disappoint him:

> On arrival we were welcomed by Chief Petty Officer Robertson, who stood some five feet tall. In the main canteen he told us in his broad Scots accent to stand at ease and then fall out and, 'OK lads, Yee can relax now and hay yerselves a wet, a wad and a burrn' i.e. a drink of tea, a sandwich and a cigarette.

Gareth Mulloy, a close friend of Alan's, recalls most vividly the journey to Crail from Hampshire, partly because he was more encumbered than was usual for a coder travelling between postings:

> On the long train journey by steam locomotive to Edinburgh we experimented unsuccessfully with the netting luggage rack as a place to sleep. I had taken a tea chest converted into a crude double bass in the hope of taking part in a skiffle group. I stowed my kit bag into the upturned tea chest while the pole holding the string section protruded downwards through the luggage rack netting. Another steam-powered train journey (two plus hours) from Edinburgh Waverley Street to Crail, where we piled into the back of an Army truck to be taken to the JSSL about a mile from the station. No RN charabancs in Crail. It was an Army establishment with all its attendant discomfort, as we were soon to find out.

---

12 A seaman on a charge of shagging a sheep claims he was so drunk he mistook it for a 'Wren in a duffle coat'.

29. David Talks, third from left front row on the interpreters' course at Crail in 1957. Third from the left in the middle row stands Commander Maitland-Makgill-Crichton then in charge of the naval contingent. Standing on his left is Prince Valentin Volkonsky. Courtesy David Talks.

Formerly a Fleet Air Arm base, the station was divided in two
- the Lower Camp, basically the airfield area which contained the
teaching block, and the Upper Camp, which included all the living
accommodation, the administration and dining sectors, as well as
the parade ground, recreation facilities and NAAFI. The buildings
housing students were named after famous admirals of bygone days,
Anson, Benbow and Frobisher. Lodgings were generally inadequate
and in the winter they were very cold.

Food, too, was a constant cause of complaint. Alan Smith still
has gruesome memories of what the Army Catering Corps were
serving up:

> The cookhouse stoves were coal-fired and all food
> contained a fine coal dust condiment. 'Soup' was often
> coloured water. Hungry, vigorous young men felt
> driven to go to the cookhouse in the evening to make
> tomato ketchup sandwiches to satisfy their hunger.

RAF *kursant* Graham Boiling's account of life at Crail, *Secret
Students on Parade* (now, sadly, out of print and very difficult to
get hold of) is throughout scathing about the failure to provide
decent meals or even a healthy kitchen environment. A dysentery
epidemic led to the temporary closure of the dining facility and
the appointment of a new cook sergeant. This followed the Crail
'mutiny' in 1957, when the senior officers were greeted with catcalls
and shouted down when they tried to speak. Gareth Mulloy believes
that there had been a scam involving the sale on the black market
of a substantial part of the rations allocated to the camp (a similar
tale had circulated at Coulsdon). After leaving Crail, Alan Smith,
too, heard a rumour that some of the hierarchy had been discharged
dishonourably for misappropriating food funds.

In charge of coders was a Naval officer quite unlike the standard
issue. At least once, he actually invited some of the RN students to
Sunday afternoon tea to meet his aged mother. David Talks, who
trained as an interpreter, has kind(ish) words to say of this Divisional
Officer:

> I was very impressed by Commander Maitland-
> Makgill-Crichton DSO, DSC, who spoke twelve
> languages and who sentenced a small group of us for
> being late on parade to three days' potato peeling.

It is said that once when, as Officer of the Day, he was due to inspect the JSSL morning parade, he arrived in a chauffeur-driven car, wound down the window, looked at the awful weather, and told the Sergeant-Major to 'carry on'. He was widely regarded among *kursanty* as the least objectionable officer. Clifford German, another interpreter, has a slightly different take on the man, describing him as:

> ... an undeniably brave but lunatic officer and descendant of a venerable, distinguished old Scottish family with strong links to the Navy, who is supposed to have rammed his destroyer into something, hopefully German, during the war and been banned from going to sea again.

All the JSSLs seem to have attracted oddball regular officers and NCOs, or was it simply that the authorities felt they could best employ these individuals away from anything that smacked of preparations for serious military action?

The Army and RAF produced eccentrics of their own. Some even managed to acquire strange titles such as 'Corporal of Horse', who turned out to be a Korean War veteran called Charnley. Despite his stated rank, he was actually the equivalent of a sergeant. Inexplicably, he seems to have been connected to three regiments - the Honourable Artillery Company, the Life Guards and the Duke of Cornwall's Light Infantry. He served at Crail and previously at Bodmin, where Mike Gerrard came across him. He expected to be, and was, addressed as 'Horse'. The joke for the linguists was to ask 'When are we going to eat ... (pause) ... Horse?' He wore a distinctive helmet which was stolen from him at Crail (we would like to think by a coder).

Graham Boiling's book does not feature coders very prominently, concentrating, understandably as the editor was an RAF *kursant*, on incidents affecting personnel of his own service. Nevertheless, there are references to coders on parade. A particular problem for them was the prevailing blustery wind howling in from the sea, which made it extremely difficult to keep their (seaman-style) caps in place. These regularly took on a life of their, own rolling at high speed around the parade ground.

When Tony Cash and Mike Gerrard undertook to write this book Tony was unaware that coders of later intakes had been dressed differently from us. Gareth Mulloy has given us a detailed description of how his lot appeared when on parade:

> We always wore No. 3 rig, bellbottom trousers which followed the style of the 18th century with flaps in the place of the modern fly front, tight jumper, big blue collar, an itchy sea jersey and a round white cap whose tally was HMS *Cochrane*, our depot 'ship' for pay and admin. based in Rosyth. Against the cold winds from the North Sea we were issued with a Burberry raincoat with a thin serge lining. We envied the Army their greatcoats. The Navy did not give us greatcoats. We concluded that this was because we were to serve for only two years and therefore did not justify the expense of warm clothing. If we were to spend much time at sea, foul weather clothing would have been available.

Larking on parade

Opportunities to take the mickey out of those in charge sometimes occurred when classes were formally marched from the morning parade to their lessons. Alan Smith remembers such an occasion when the whole intake put their caps on back to front, with the ship's name behind:

> … which was only noticed by a passing NCO on a bicycle who suddenly braked and leapt off shouting at the lead coder ' … 'Ere, wait a minute, yer've got yer 'at on back to front', and then in amazement, 'Hey, yer've all got yer 'ats on back to front!'

> On another occasion we invented an odd way of marching with two normally timed steps followed by one step in slow time whilst raising the knee to waist level and then back to the two steps in normal time. This amused us enormously and of course it was duly spotted by a Petty Officer who curtly ordered us to 'Stop yer bloody nonsense'.

> One of my taller oppos, Mildmay, and I would exchange our gabardine raincoats for parade. Hence, the PO passing down the ranks would say to me, 'Smith, who, in 'ell, issued you with that coat? It's draggin' on the floor.' As he passed down the ranks he would come to Mildmay, in my raincoat, and say, 'Mildmay, that bloody coat's up to yer waist. Where

30. The Crail JSSL rugby team circa 1957. Seated with the ball is Robert Cox. Second from the right in the back row is Peter Hill. On Peter's left is Army *kursant* Geoffrey Robinson, later a Labour MP and for a time Postmaster General Courtesy Robert Cox.

did yer get that?' Then inevitably, ' ... 'Ere, wait a
minute, 'ave you two clowns put on the wrong coat?'
Many apologies followed and, 'Oh yes, you must be
right PO. We hadn't noticed.' And the PO saying,
'Bloody 'ell. Can learn Russian in a couple o' months
and can't recognise their own raincoat.'

Alan feels that we should record retrospective gratitude to CPO
Robertson and PO Mangan at Crail whose rule over coders was:

... generous, considerate, humorous and avuncular;
a great contrast to the bawling NCOs of most military
films.

Very few of us would deny that the naval NCOs we came across
during our two years had anything other than what Alan calls a
'really positive effect' on our lives.

A soldier reflects

If the Army way of doing things often irked coders, soldier
kursanty like Peter Duskin tended to count their blessings at Crail.
In his memoir of his service career Peter tells of the way he and
similarly schooled colleagues had to keep a careful watch on
what they said and did, in case they justified the commonly heard
accusation that they were 'educated fuckers'. Peter explains why, at
Crail, he felt released from that restraint:

We were all more or less equal academically, apart
from a few really exceptional linguists and a few
(very few) who were simply not up to mastering
Russian and had to be sent away. In consequence
there was much more wit and life at Crail than in any
of the other postings we had been in, which is why
I suggested that JSSL was a little like a university.
The difference could be felt nearly everywhere in
the camp, but one place where it was marked was,
curiously, the NAAFI. The Crail NAAFI was unique:
there was no screaming and shouting, no juke-box
surrounded by jiving MT drivers, none of the things
that had sometimes made the NAAFI in other camps
seem like a bad pub. Conversation was usually a quiet
buzz, there were always lots of people playing chess
or bridge and, if anyone was playing the piano, he was
probably playing Brahms or Chopin: it was all highly

civilised. The Navy were always particularly 'couth', as I recall, and certainly they thought so, judging from comments they made in the JSSL magazine, *Samovar*. This atmosphere was completely intolerable to the 'Permanent Staff', i.e. the MT drivers, Regimental Police, store-men, and PT instructors (one of the smallest of whom once memorably claimed that they 'had to change the women under' him), and they mostly retired to the Corporals' Club next door. This arrangement pleased us and, we supposed, them; but later we discovered that most of them thought we were terrible snobs and that some of them hated us. It says a lot for our naivety that we found this surprising.

The writer Alan Bennett was another Army *kursant* who found his naval colleagues more couth than the average JSSL student. He has described in the foreword to this publication how he came across them at both Coulsdon and Bodmin, in 1952 and 1954. In a letter to Tony Cash he referred to:

> ... those god like midshipmen – Robin Hope, Jeremy Wolfenden[13] – who seemed to have life worked out – their uniforms <u>fitted</u>, Robin H's I'm sure tailored – and well beyond our sphere.

---

13 See chapter 13.

CHAPTER 7
A SECRET WORLD

ОДИН - ТАЙНА, ДВА - ПОЛТАЙНЫ, ТРИ – НЕТ ТАЙНЫ
(Russian saying – 'With one person – you have a secret, with two – half a secret, with three – no secret')

By 1963, when the last national service man was demobbed, well over two million had passed through the ranks. At least 99 per cent of them had been <u>exclusively</u> committed to <u>one</u> of the three armed forces. A conscript squaddie saw nothing of the Navy or RAF. Sailors and airmen were similarly ignorant of the other services. Only coders, some 1,500 in all, had the privilege (if that is the right word) of spending lengthy periods on establishments of all three services. We found it intriguing to compare and contrast the different forms of discipline, quality of meals, customs, traditions, inter-rank relationships, as we were shunted back and forth between Navy, Army and Air Force bases.

Indoctrination

Having completed the translators' course of up to 11 months in Army camps at Bodmin, Coulsdon or Crail, coders in most intakes were sent to the Applied Languages School (ALS), run by the RAF. In 1952 the ALS was based at RAF Wythall, immediately south of Birmingham. Alongside RAF colleagues, (no soldiers were present) we here underwent intensive instruction in Russian military terminology, as well as learning about the radio and recording equipment we would go on to use when assigned to listening stations monitoring Red Army, Navy and Air Force voice communications. Before entering the course we had to sign a formal statement that we were aware our work was covered by the Official Secrets Acts,[1] and that we had been warned of the penalties for improper disclosure. The process of giving the warning and signing the statement was

---

1   Official Secrets Act 1911, as amended by the Official Secrets Act 1920.

termed 'indoctrination'. For nearly four decades thereafter we were deterred from breathing a word about our sigint training or labours.

There could not have been many other sailors stationed so far from the sea as we were on the outskirts of Birmingham, but the rationale was sensible enough. The RAF's 591 Signals Unit (SU) had been formed at Wythall on 1 Jun 1952. Its essential purpose was to protect air force communications from malfunction and hostile interception – its appropriate motto - *Vigilanter*, 'Watchfully'. More importantly, in the early 1950s the received wisdom was that the main Soviet threat was from air-launched weapons, so monitoring Russian planes was the first priority for signals intelligence. Hence the availability at Wythall of reams of tape-recordings of their pilots, whose plain language communications with ground controls, enlivened by occasional singing and swearing, had been intercepted in West Germany. This radio traffic, muddied by dense static and interference, was what we practised unravelling and transcribing; comparable Soviet naval interceptions were much harder to come by. True, the Royal Navy's prime concern was the danger from submarines rather than planes, but, whatever their nationality, submerged mariners are by the nature of their trade not much given to transmitting idle or any other chatter; a sub's ability to vacate a geographical location, if identified, is much more constrained than a fighter's or bomber's. In any event, neither Mike Gerrard nor Tony Cash ever heard a coder at Wythall complain that he was not hearing enough naval stuff. Naturally, being conscripts, some of our number had other beefs, to be examined later in this chapter.

By the time coders started the second phase of language training we appreciated at least one aspect of our lives that had measurably improved. Success in the first phase led to promotion to the rating leading coder (special), equivalent to an Army two-stripe corporal, with a consequent significant hike in pay. The fear of possible demotion was now a further spur to our meticulously respecting the vow of secrecy we had undertaken, though John Griffiths's story suggests that someone, by no means necessarily a coder, had let the cat out of the bag:

> This training was all very hush-hush, and no-one was supposed to know what went on at Wythall. Just before we were despatched to the real thing in the north of West Germany I was taught that there is no

such thing as a secret. Sitting next to an old lady on the bus going into the city one evening, resplendent in my leading coder's uniform, I was taken aback when she turned to me and said matter-of-factly in her best Brummie, 'You're one of them spy fellas from up the camp, then'.

Elements of technical training

An interesting feature of the Wythall course, especially for coders, who almost universally would have had no previous opportunity to visit a working aerodrome, was the trip laid on for one of the intakes to RAF Wellesbourne Mountford, just over three miles east of Stratford-on-Avon. There we were invited to watch and overhear the control tower procedures and communications for planes taking off and landing. Understanding these, it was felt, would help us more easily envisage what our target Soviet aircraft were up to.

Some students received training in direction-finding (D/F), a vital component of the work we would go on to do at listening stations in West Germany, Cyprus and Turkey. Coder-translators at Wythall were gearing up to monitor, transcribe and record USSR military radio traffic, for onward posting to GCHQ in Cheltenham. But our tapes and hand-written notes could only ever be part of the overall picture our superiors were trying to establish about Soviet intentions. It was important to locate as precisely as possible the whereabouts of their ships, planes and land-based units at the moment their radio signals were being intercepted: D/F was the key, and the success of the operation depended on linking one or more radio receivers to a special antenna array, such as the Adcock. The system essentially had a minimum of four, equally spaced, upright elements aligned in pairs along north-south, east-west axes. From the strengths of the signals received it was possible, using basic trigonometry, to deduce the probable location of their source. In other words, the transmitter's position could be 'triangulated': if, for any triangle, the size of two angles and the length of one side are known, the remaining angle and sides can be measured.

Only a minority of us actually trained in direction finding, but we were all introduced to the inner workings of the superheterodyne radio receiver, and eventually tested on our ability to put down on paper a diagram of its wiring system. In 1952 and for some years thereafter the choice of receiver was one or other model of the Navy's standard issue, the Murphy B 40. This was the device many of us went on to use in Cuxhaven or Kiel. It had five wavebands, one above another. You could tune into them by carefully turning a large, fly-wheel driven, black knob: when selected, a waveband would light up. The semi-circular housing for this part of the contraption has been aptly described as:

> … looking vaguely like the glass-fronted stairwells popular in up-market 1930s mansions around the Welwyn area.[2]

Able to pick up signals between 600 Kiloherz and 30.2 Megaherz, the B 40 boasted an inbuilt speaker, but the operator would normally listen via headphones: having the speaker on was against watchroom rules lest the sound reach beyond the building audible to unauthorised individuals. Extension speakers and line outputs were available so that colleagues and superiors could listen in, too.

A coder's technical training at the Applied Languages School also involved handling the Ferrograph tape recorder, for its time a state-of-the-art machine, as reliable as long-lived.

Wrestling with the numbers

Nearly all coders had studied arts subjects in their school sixth forms; science and technology were largely alien domains. Yet most of us were intrigued by the new equipment we were going to deal with for the next few, final months of our national service. It had more appeal than the 'drill' in Russian numbers we were subjected to, an exercise as boring as taxing, yet pedagogically effective. We spent hours listening to, learning and writing down the many different forms any one numerical entity can assume in that language. This may sound odd, but think of *three* and its variants *third, threesome* and *trio*. Imagine adding an *s*, or 'apostrophe *s*', or an '*s* apostrophe' to any one of those and you will appreciate a change of meaning from singular to plural, or an indication of possession. In fact, any English number may have around twelve different written forms (though not all are distinguishable to the ear). By contrast, Russian can have as many as twenty-five distinct forms and sounds, usually reflected in the word endings. A speaker or writer of Russian always

---

2   http://www.portabletubes.co.uk/boats/murphy3.htm.

has to distinguish singular and plural; masculine, feminine and neuter; as well as the required case, which depends on function in the sentence or what preposition precedes the number. Fortunately, the endings were basically the same as those we had earlier learned for nouns and adjectives in our grammar classes at Bodmin, Coulsdon and Crail.

Geoff Forbes was a rare bird, indeed, when he joined the Navy in August 1952. A university graduate with a BA in Russian, he was commissioned as a midshipman, and sent straight to the JSSL at London University to train as an interpreter. Within a year or so he became one of very few national servicemen to teach his fellow conscripts:

> After a divisional officers' course in Portsmouth I was sent to RAF Wythall. I seem to remember spending my time dictating Russian number groups to the classes there, and acting as the station Fire Officer.

Mike Gerrard was at Wythall a couple of years later than Geoff Forbes, and still ponders the possible danger to our brains of all that number-crunching:

> There was an RAF instructor named Wynn, who didn't teach us, but who made headlines some years later by killing his girl friend, who had broken with him, and then himself. I often wondered whether it wasn't the constant repetition of number sequences that drove him mad.

Bill Musker was taught by Wynn and remembers him most clearly:

> The 'Homicidal' was a strangely intense senior technician [equivalent to sergeant] radio-instructor, who introduced himself in our first lesson by asking us to call out a long series of digits, which he wrote on the blackboard. Then he asked for another long string of numbers, which he wrote under the first one. Then he asked us to multiply the first string by the second string. Needless to say, the Arts and Linguists were pants at maths, and none of us volunteered an answer. So he proceeded to write out the answer from right to left, taking pairs of numbers and muttering fiercely to himself. He subsequently explained his uncanny *savant*-like ability as the result of reading Trachtenberg's treatise *Speed Mathematics*: the

Ukrainian Professor Jakow Trachtenberg had been incarcerated by the Nazis in solitary confinement and kept himself sane by working out a perception of how the science of numbers worked. From this he evolved methods of addition, subtraction, multiplication and division. Many years later I bought the book and, though much of it was esoteric, there were some practical techniques which I used during my working life.

The significance of the Russian numbers dinned into us was not, however, to make us better mathematicians. Armed forces around the world have long used groups of digits (usually a series of 'squares' each comprising five rows of five figures) to encrypt messages, and the Soviets were particularly good at it. What we were called on to do was write them down accurately and leave it to the cryptanalysts at Cheltenham to figure out possible meanings. We were never to know how successful our efforts had been: they failed to tell us. But you knew whether you had passed the technical course – or did you? RAF *kursant* James Muckle, historian of Russian language teaching in Britain, was at Wythall in the autumn of 1956. On the testing of our ability accurately to transcribe Russian radio communications and handle numerals adequately he says:

Standards of assessment in these more practical skills were perhaps not as stringent as they had been on the language course. One former trainee remembers a sergeant announcing: 'You lot are having an exam next week, and, by the way, you've all passed!'

A top-secret Chinese JSSL

Coders who trained at Wythall or Pucklechurch were not always aware that close by were small groups of RAF national service men studying other languages – Czech, Polish and German: the communist satellite countries had their own air squadrons which would need to be monitored while the Cold War continued.

Even less were we aware that somewhat larger numbers were learning Chinese, around 300 according to an article published on the Internet by *BBC News Magazine* in 2010.[3] From documents now available at the National Archives and from research reported

---

3 'Mandarin Blue: RAF Chinese Linguists', February 2010 http://news. bbc.co.uk/1/hi/magazine/8490680.stm.

in the article we now know that the RAF Chinese linguists (CLs) were destined for Hong Kong, in that period still a British colony. At Batty's Belvedere, one of the highest points on the island, the RAF had a listening station where Chinese military traffic could be recorded and Chinese flights in the vicinity of Hong Kong monitored. Training in number groups must have played a major role in the Wythall Chinese course too, since four digits were used to symbolise one Chinese character. The article tells the story from its beginnings in 1951, when the first course was set up at the School of Oriental and African Studies at London University, through 1955, when the project was taken over by the RAF and subsumed into the Joint Services School for Linguists, to its end in 1962, when the last conscripts were returning to 'Civvy Street'. Participants have stressed how they were shielded from many of the mindless chores and bureaucratic indignities to which we coders were from time to time subject. On the other hand, the difficulties of assimilating spoken Chinese left little room for acquiring any skill in writing, let alone opportunities to learn about Chinese history and culture. The CLs were not introduced to songs, films or books, as we had been in most of the long, first-phase courses at Bodmin, Coulsdon and Crail. Even at Wythall, as we noted in chapter 4, Soviet war-time stories were on the agenda, if only to reinforce our learning of military terminology.

Military duties at Wythall

If asked their impression of life on a RAF base, most coders would have rated it more favourably than the Army equivalent: less 'bull' and drill; immeasurably better food; more comradely relations between officers and men. For the latter we had an explanation: war-time pilots, navigators and gunners were too preoccupied with mastering their technical skills to worry about appropriate attire and hierarchical precedence. We had all heard or read stories of devil-may-care aviators scrambling into their 'kites', throwing on whatever came to hand – maybe a woman's stocking for a foulard – in readiness to confront German fighters and bombers. We thought it likely that such men, a few of whom were still around in the 1950s, had set the tone. How did the Royal Navy compare? Those coders who had opted to study Russian in order to join the Navy may well have put the Senior Service in pole position, but even they would

Class 9, Joint Services School of Applied Languages

RAF Wythall, October 1953

Back row : Halliwell, Tomlins, Smith, Watson, Hinksman, Wills, Peers, Butcher, Wood, Pilley, Bucknell
Front row : Berrill, McCormick, Saunders, Mr Katkov, Fl/Lt Nettleton, S/Tech Docherty, Cash, Salmond, Harris

31. Maurice Berrill's captioned photo reveals how evenly the student force at Wythall was divided between Naval and RAF personnel.

admit that the upper/lower deck divide was in those days tantamount to an Indian caste distinction. The same coders would rightly have pointed out, however, that food on RN shore establishments was comparable in quality to the RAF's. Many of them would also have lamented the air force's lack of age-old tradition and ritual, part and parcel of the seafarer's vocation.

Fortunately, perhaps, for the nation's defences in the 1950s, easy-going, somewhat bohemian air crew were not the people actually running the RAF. Even at Wythall, despite the strong emphasis on Russian military terminology and number-bashing, as well as on radio and recording technology, there were occasional military exercises in which coders had to take part. James Muckle recalls an unusual one that carried on over several Saturday mornings, and which he thoroughly enjoyed:

> The idea was that a nuclear bomb had fallen on somewhere like Coventry, and that we had to prepare for this eventuality. I was designated a 'saboteur' – it was my job to penetrate our signals training compound, and I did it! In civilian clothes, I climbed into the Commanding Officer's garden, spoke to his wife, who was hanging out the washing and was very surprised, but didn't call the RAF Police, and eventually conned myself past Corporal Murgatroyd, RAF but immensely thick, who was guarding the compound. Terrific fun, for which I was roundly praised by the officeroriat. One of the coders' jobs was to represent 'refugees', and to cause chaos around the place, particularly the guardroom. I remember a hilarious scene there, when a mob of coders, dressed up mainly as women, appeared and caused hysterical mayhem, to prove that the camp had no provision for dealing with this possible emergency. The star turn was one young man playing the part of a pregnant woman and giving birth to a pillow in sensational manner. On another occasion, the same coder dressed up in RAF uniform, insinuated himself into our RAF sanctum, and threw a thunderflash in among us. We were half terrified and half tickled pink. We knew him, and weren't taken in, but we didn't expect the explosion! Incidentally, about the thick corporal – I was talking to coders once and I referred to him. They said, 'What? Is Murgatroyd really his name? – We called him that for a joke!'

We have been told that the CO at Wythall during the make-believe defence operation described above was much exercised by a delicate problem. How, in rudimentary, ill-provisioned nuclear bunkers, were servicemen to relieve themselves? He or one of his subordinates devised a cunning plan: everyone should carry a cardboard box in case of emergency. Soon dismissed as impractical, an alternative solution was proposed: latrine buckets must be located in strategic places. The following conversation was overheard in the stores one Saturday, before that week's exercise got under way:

Civilian stores man: 'What are all these buckets for?'

Airman: 'To shit in'.

RAF corporal: 'Don't talk to me like that, my lad.'

Airman: 'It's gen, that. They're to shit in. If you get stuck in an air-raid shelter for hours you may need it.'

Corporal: 'I don't think much of that!'

Civilian stores man: 'I tell you this – I'm not having anyone shitting in here!'

On this occasion the civilian view prevailed, though buckets were placed strategically around the camp, never, as far as we can tell, to be used for their intended purpose. Nothing more was heard of the CO's obsession.

The RAF commitment to sport

There would certainly have been a consensus among coders that in at least one respect the RAF had an advantage over its service rivals – in the provision it made for extra-curricular activities. At Wythall we were positively required every Wednesday afternoon to participate in one sport or another, the RAF being prepared to subsidise some that might otherwise have been beyond our reach. Tony Cash took advantage of their generosity to ride horses for the first time in his life:

The Air Force actually stumped up as much as five shillings a head payment to the stables, which were only a short bus journey from the camp. My introduction was a tad disconcerting. As a couple of fellow coders and I got off the bus, we saw a small group of people standing over an RAF classmate prostrate on the ground in very obvious pain. We learned that his mount, no longer to be seen, had just thrown him, causing him to fall on to a hard kerb fracturing his thigh bone: they were waiting for an ambulance to take him to hospital.

Never having been close to a horse before - the occasional pony ride on the sands at Scarborough during the war didn't count - I was surprised to realise how tall was the animal that I was soon given to ride. I struggled into the saddle, embarrassed by my clumsiness in front of the young, though experienced, stable girls who were to accompany us on our initial outing. Mounted, I was even more surprised that I felt quite secure, and my apprehensions quickly vanished. It took a few goes to learn how to 'post', to move up and down in synchrony with the trotting horse, but it was a great sense of achievement when I got the hang of it. For the next twelve or so weeks at Wythall I went riding every Wednesday, occasionally forking out of my own pocket to ride at the weekend, too. Naturally, the girls were an attraction, especially when they put on drinks parties at the stables. A young albino lad who worked there part-time was learning to play jazz on the clarinet – an opportunity to perform duets, especially if there was a guitarist on hand.

In 1954 midshipman interpreter Brian Jones, a keen and talented rugby player, was posted to Wythall:

I was appointed as an instructor and divisional officer. I inherited a good rugby team, thanks to Carwyn James, who had just left, and I organised quite a good run-ashore for the coders to a brewery - Mitchell & Butlers, in Birmingham - from which all returned in high spirits. On a more cultural plane I and my fellow midshipman, Mark Nightingale, who had an Armstrong-Siddeley *Sapphire*, were able to make frequent visits to Stratford, where we saw lots of leading actors, including Richard Burton.

For Bill Hetherington, Wednesday pm offered a chance to visit his folk:

The sport I chose was cycling, which enabled me to travel to my home in Birmingham by bus the first afternoon, collect my bike, ride it back that evening, and thereafter ride home and back each Wednesday, a journey of perhaps an hour each way, doing my own thing in between.

154

32. The stage crew for Bill Slater's production of *St Joan* at RAF Wythall in 1953. Second from left in the front row is David Wills. Fourth from left in the front row is Bill Musker, and on his left, we believe, is Slater himself. Courtesy Bill Musker.

Some coders were keen on more conventional competitive sports. Geoff Sharp and Keith Watkinson, excellent long-distance runners, had both raced in the 1953 Royal Navy cross-country championship while they were at Coulsdon. Geoff describes the outcome:

> I remember that win as so easy that Keith and I coasted over the finish line holding hands to secure joint first. I guess sailors don't have much chance to train for cross-country!

It was natural that Geoff and Keith would be picked for the RAF Wythall cross- country team in 1954, and likely that they would enable the putative 'RAF' line-up to do well:

> RAF Wythall won that year's RAF cross country championship. However, three or four members of the six-man team were coders. So, at the late afternoon awards ceremony the wing-commander and other brass giving out the cup and individual awards were astonished when coders in naval uniform marched up first to receive it.

The RAF personnel delegated to sanction the sports we could opt for were sometimes very liberal in their interpretation of what might reasonably constitute a sporting activity. Bill Musker was particularly impressed by the liberality of one RAF physical training instructor:

> The Wythall PTI initially offered cricket in the summer, football in the winter, cross-country running. 'Is that all?' we asked. 'Oh!' he said, 'if it's raining, there's shinty in the gym'. On being challenged again, he said, 'What do you want to do?' And we gave him a long list of things - roller skating, sailing, ice skating, horse riding and many more. Finally, Pat Bucknell suggested 'country house visiting' was his thing, his mother being very well connected. Pat drove some of us around in his classic 1926 Austin 12 (6-seater with open top). This was a sport where No. 1 doeskin fore-and-aft uniform was obligatory. I spent many happy Wednesday afternoons with him, visiting magnificent black-and-white piles and being given teas by the housekeepers.

Mike Gerrard, on a later intake than Bill Musker, has a more jaundiced view of his days on the RAF base:

156

33. The cast of *St Joan* with Mary Webster fifth from left (as Joan) and Hugh Woodhouse, seated, seventh from left. Courtesy Bill Musker.

I detested Wythall. It was an extremely cold autumn/ winter, and for several weeks the kitchens and dining rooms were out of order, with the result that we had to get our food under canvas despite the cold conditions.

The discipline was different. RAF NCOs were full of themselves, and pernickety to a fault. They seemed to resent us, and to use their seniority to make life unpleasant. One RAF corporal alleged that a coder had said 'balls to the flag', and the latter replied in his defence that what he'd said was addressed to the NCO, not to the ensign. It went right to the CO for adjudication, and finished with the coder getting 10 days' No. 10 punishment - confinement to unit, plus extra duties in off hours.

The group I was in played bridge in the evenings and at weekends. I used to try to get away from Wythall, hitch-hiking to Oxford, London, Manchester and other places of potentially greater interest when I had no weekend duties. This precluded my engagement in weekend sporting activities.

Encouraging drama at Wythall

Given that our work at Wythall was shrouded in secrecy, it may seem surprising that we could be allowed, let alone encouraged, to put on plays to which civilians from far and near would be invited. Yet that is what happened in 1953 and 1954. On both occasions the motivating force was Leading Coder (Special) William Slater, who later became a TV director and producer and finally Head of Serials at the BBC. In the latter capacity he was responsible for procuring actor Tom Baker for the role of *Dr Who*. With enthusiastic support from officers on the base as well as coders and airmen, Bill chose to stage Bernard Shaw's *St Joan*, the Irish playwright's highly original and controversial take on the martyrdom of French patriot Joan of Arc. Remarkably, finance was available for Bill's production. During World War II around 1,000 airmen and 'WAAFs' (members of the Women's Auxiliary Air Force) had been constructing and repairing barrage balloons at Wythall. Every week the state paid on behalf of each individual sixpence into the so-called PSI (President of the Services Institute) fund, set up nationally to provide welfare and social activities on military establishments. This, we believe, was the source for sports subsidies, as well as the Wythall dramas.

158

Finding a suitable space for the show was no problem. Almost every military base is provided with a substantial NAAFI (Navy, Army and Air Force Institutes) building, essentially a canteen and recreational area for the non-commissioned, where a variety of goods and commodities are sold at reasonable prices. Bill Musker stage-managed the production of Shaw's masterpiece:

> The NAAFI had a stage with an amazing back-drop and scenery of a South Sea island. It must have been left from the very last post-war dance, when there were over 1,000 erks stationed there with their balloons. Billy Slater looked at the stage and salivated, because he was sweet on Mary Webster, who was at the time studying drama at the Birmingham Rep school. His Machiavellian plan was to direct a production of *St Joan*, in which she could play the eponymous heroine and thus fall into his clutch.

Mary proved to be a very willing target for Slater's stratagem, agreeing not only to play Joan but also eventually to become his wife, and in the 1970s to play a leading role in the popular BBC TV series *The Onedin Line,* directed by Bill.

The principal lady for *St Joan* in place, and most roles filled by JSSL students who had acted previously at their schools, it remained to sort out the scenery and props. It was explained to Bill Musker that since the end-of-the-war money had continued to be paid into the PSI fund on the basis of a full complement, so purchasing some basic theatre equipment such as lanterns, goboes and 'strange devices which simulated clouds' would not be a problem. The zeal and ingenuity of certain officers helped make good any shortfalls:

> I recall the airmen's divisional officer, Flight-Lieutenant Nettleton, responding to my wish for drapes by saying that the accommodation huts should really have new curtains, and that gold was a pretty colour. So, yards of material went into the camp tailor's workshop, and pairs of magnificent lined curtains came out. Similarly, Billy Slater wanted a curved cyclorama to do ambitious light projections instead of scenery. The Navy DO said that our radio sets needed covers, and, strangely, the amount of canvas required proved to be about the coverage of the cyclorama. We built the wooden 'cyc' - a little challenge in itself - tacked the canvas down, and sized it, and when we finished

that night it looked magnificent. Alas, when we came in next day each panel had sagged. PANIK!!!

Bill Musker's spelling is deliberate. The Russian word is 'panika', as all coders would recall from Elizaveta Fen's reader *Ordinary People*, in which John regularly upbraids his flustered wife Mary with the phrase, *Nye vpadai v paniku* – 'Don't panic'.

> Then the Army Liaison Officer decided that we needed training in constructing latrines, and that two widths of the hessian was just the depth of the cyc. This time the whole lot went on, was sized and ended up as tight as a drum.

> We took out the lights and tested them. Dawn broke, night fell, storm clouds rushed over the horizon, and then about 1.00 am someone started making shadow figures with their hands and fingers. In no time we were screaming with hysterical laughter, helped by copious draughts retained after NAAFI closing time. The RAF Regiment guard turned out convinced that the strain had turned our tiny brains, and then were treated to the shadow show and reduced to writhing helplessness.

Not long before the opening night, the man playing the Inquisitor was taken ill. Flight-Lieutenant Nettleton, who had undertaken a small role himself, suggested his brother could fill the gap, because 'he does some acting'. Bill Slater enquired what and where? Bill Musker recalls the officer's response and what followed:

> 'Oh, he is at Stratford with the National Theatre.' One phone call later not only was John Nettleton part of the cast, but he had invited us to send a three-tonner down to collect costumes from the wardrobe - *quantum sufficit*! [Latin, 'as much as is necessary'] I remember that Dunois' breastplate had last adorned the copious breast of Sir Donald Wolfit when he played Tamberlaine. Sufficient to say that, with Billy's fabulous direction and the beautiful girls from Birmingham Rep, we gave the most amazing performance to a NAAFI full of top military brass, locals and God knows who.

When Bill Slater's intake left RAF Wythall at the end of 1953, he, unexpectedly remained behind, and continued directing drama. We have not yet discovered how this was possible: both the Navy and the Air Force must have agreed the arrangement. Ex-Leading

160

34. The cast of Bill Slater's production of *The Devil's Disciple* performed at Wythall in March 1954. Extreme left in the back row is Graham Young. Flight Lieutenant John Nettleton, who played the lead, stands fifth from left in the middle row (between two ladies). Far right, arms akimbo, is Dennis Mills and immediately on his right is Frank Abel. Courtesy D Mills.

Coder Graham Young, whose contingent turned up there in January 1954, told us this:

> I have two different stories as to why he had not left with the 4th intake. The first was that he had been ill at the time; the other was that he had been in charge of the (tape?) library. It may have been a combination of these two reasons that enabled him to stay on to produce *The Devil's Disciple*.

Bernard Shaw's drama of the American Revolution was the first of two shows Bill Slater produced in 1954. The other could not have been more different, as its author and Wythall *kursant*, Leading Coder (Special) Gerald Seaman, explains:

> I was able to have staged an hour-long episode from a nautical opera I had written entitled *Mal de Mer* ('Sea Sickness'). The authorities were most helpful in assisting with costumes, scenery and paint, and the opera was a great success, being reviewed by the *Birmingham Post* and other papers. The producer was Bill Slater, the cast being made up of coders among whom were some very good voices.

The technical Russian course quits the Midlands

In July 1957 the second-phase training of Naval and RAF Russian linguists was transferred to RAF Pucklechurch, near Bristol (the students of Chinese following a few months later). This base, like Wythall, had served as a barrage balloon centre in WWII. Its new purpose was encapsulated in the unit badge approved by the Queen (as is her prerogative) in July 1958. Over the background open book, symbolising language training, was the motto, *Alert*. A hind's head in the foreground recalled the original deer park, where kings in medieval times had hunted.

As far as we can calculate, all coders whose first-phase training was at Coulsdon or Bodmin passed on to Wythall, as Tony Cash and Mike Gerrard did. Unsurprisingly, the overwhelming majority of respondents to our archive followed the same route, which explains why their stories predominate in this chapter. Most Crail *kursanty*, on the other hand, would have studied at Pucklechurch, as did Alan Smith. The proud possessor of what in those days was a form of transport prized by many a young man, he decided to drive all the way from Fife to Gloucestershire:

> I travelled from Crail to Pucklechurch on my
> Lambretta scooter, loaded at the back with my kitbag
> and all excess gear in a rucksack on my back. Stopping
> at Shap Fell pub in the Lake District for a sandwich
> and drink, my sailor hat, tied on top of my kitbag, was
> spotted by a charabanc of holidaying Northern town
> ladies, who left their coach and collectively serenaded
> me with *All the nice girls love a sailor* ... It was very
> cheering, if slightly embarrassing.

Stopping at his home in Cheshire on his journey south, Alan fell
seriously ill with peritonitis, and had to spend a week in hospital and
another week convalescing, so turned up at Pucklechurch well after
the new training regime had begun:

> I had great difficulty hearing the practice taped
> Russian transmissions, and felt left behind by my
> mates. The instructor bawled at me for a week
> because of my lack of skill and total failure to achieve
> any results. Later in the week he lost all patience,
> rushed to my side, snatched the headphones from
> me and listened to my workstation. With a great cry,
> he threw the headphones into a corner, saying, 'Yer
> bloody headset don't work'. Phew, I was off the hook.

On the food front, Alan, and presumably his Naval and RAF
colleagues, must have been well pleased ('chuffed' – the military
term – springs to mind) with the situation on their new base:

> This RAF camp was a major improvement on the
> spartan conditions of Crail. We had an award-winning
> chef, who produced hotel quality food, took enormous
> pride in his product and was about to retire. It was a
> privilege to eat in his canteen.

Alan has the impression that the Pucklechurch constabulary were
eager to protect the integrity of their nearby RAF base, whether or
not they knew its function:

> Jack Slater with a couple of other coders, dressed in
> civvies, was arrested by the local bobby for speaking
> in a suspicious language close to a secret military
> establishment.

Pucklechurch (or 'Chuckleperch' as one facetious *kursant*
rechristened it) may have been chosen to supersede Wythall, as the
centre for the training of future Navy and RAF siginters, because
since 1951 it had hosted a Ground Radio Servicing Squadron.

As its name suggests, that outfit was well qualified to maintain and repair navigation aids and radar installations, as well as the telecommunications equipment linguists were learning to use. Within two years, however, both the language course and the servicing squadron moved on, this time to West Sussex, to RAF Tangmere, former Fighter Command base of ace pilot and war hero Douglas Bader. Between July and October 1940 Hurricanes and Spitfires from Tangmere tore up the skies, doing battle with German fighters and bombers during the Battle of Britain. By the end of the 1950s, with national service coming to a close, the Tangmere Applied Language Course was now catering essentially for regulars. In 1961 Graham Young, by this time a civil servant in the Ministry of Defence, found himself teaching technical Russian at Tangmere. His JSSL past made him popular with his students:

> When I admitted that I had served as a coder from 1952 to 1954, they made me feel like a grandfather, buying me drinks on social evenings.

Visitors to the sites of RAF Wythall, Pucklechurch and Tangmere will today see blue plaques commemorating the presence there during the Cold War of Joint Services Schools for Linguists. RAFLING, the Air Force Linguists' Association mounted the campaign to have all such locations honoured in this way. The presence of coders is not mentioned in the inscriptions.

35. Leading Coder (Special) Dennis Mills togged out in his doeskin No. 1
uniform the better to display the golden badges on each arm.
Courtesy D Mills.

CHAPTER 8

CODERS (FULLY FLEDGED) AT SEA

НА КОРАБЛЕ, ГДЕ КАЖДЫЙ ЗНАЕТ СВОЕ ДЕЛО, МОЖНО ПЛАВАТЬ СМЕЛО
(Russian naval saying - 'When everyone aboard knows his stuff it's plain sailing')

As we have seen in earlier chapters, many coders (special) spent between 12 and 14 months of their two-year spell of national service miles away from the Navy, on Army and RAF establishments learning the essentials of Russian, mastering military vocabulary, and listening to recordings of Russian voice communications distorted by fierce radio static. By now they were promoted to leading hands (the equivalent of Army, two-stripe corporals), resulting in a considerable hike in pay, if not in status. Evidence of the new rank was the anchor (a 'killick', in Naval slang) we now had to wear on the left sleeve.

Joining a ship as a killick (the term extended to wearers of the badge), a leading coder (special), even one who had had little experience of the bona fide Navy, was a different proposition from sailing as a probationary greenhorn. The regulars may have found us just as outlandish, but all the months of Russian study and official secrecy added an aura of mystery which we were only occasionally able to use to our advantage.

Discovering the whereabouts of your ship

The Admiralty took great pains to ensure that every one of us spent a minimum few weeks at sea. At an appropriate point in our Naval careers we would be despatched to various ports around the periphery of the United Kingdom. However, communications not being as sophisticated or instant half a century ago as they are now, finding your ship could be quite a conundrum, as Tony Cash and his colleagues discovered:

36. Leading Coders Tony Cash, Malcolm Chaplin and Malcolm Brown
(reading left to right) on the frigate in which they served in early 1954
(the closest they ever got to a naval gun). Courtesy T Cash.

In the early spring of 1954, Malcolm Brown, Malcolm Chaplin and I were given travel warrants to take us by train from London to the Naval base at Rothesay, near Glasgow, to join the frigate HMS *Loch Ruthven*. The eight-hour journey proved vain: not only was our designated ship no longer there, nobody was sure where it had gone. Fortunately, accommodation for the night was offered aboard a cruiser at anchor in the bay, though one sailor tried to persuade us that, rather than anchored, it was actually stuck on a bed of 'tickler' tins - the half-pound cans of duty-free tobacco available once a month and jettisoned overboard when empty. According to our informant, the crew were mightily bored after months immobilised in the Firth of Clyde, but were about to perk up, having learned the ship would have to travel the next day to Portsmouth to deliver an officer for court-martial. Sadly, we never discovered what his offence might have been, or, indeed, whether we were the victims of a leg-pull. Our search for the frigate proved just as fruitless in Belfast, our next port of call. It had left several days earlier for Derry; there, a Naval bus hastened us from the railway station to the quayside, where, with mixed feelings we watched the *Ruthven* speeding away up Lough Foyle to the Irish Sea.

On exercise at sea

When coders were sent to do their sea time there was one job they could perform just as well as every other sailor, namely clean ship. But for many, untrained in any specifically nautical skill, it was not at all obvious what they might contribute to a ship's success in military exercises, the peace-time Navy's *raison d'être*. When Tony Cash and his two companions were able eventually to board the *Loch Ruthven*, after a week kicking their heels in Derry's naval barracks, their first duty was to report to the Captain:

> He, quite naturally wanted to know what exactly we were. The badge on a coder's right sleeve with its open book and lightning streak indicated a sailor who might be in the instructor branch, all reasonably clear to any Naval man, but what did the letter 'S' signify? 'It means we've learned Russian, Sir'. 'For what purpose?' 'I'm afraid we've signed the Official Secrets Act, and we're not free to tell you.' I knew we

were taking a bit of a liberty here, but to my amazement this answer seemed to satisfy him. He acknowledged that we must be pretty well educated and therefore might fruitfully be employed keeping logs of all that went on in the watch room while the ship was on anti-submarine exercises. And this is what we went on to do … at least, tried to do. When, one night, my turn came to log proceedings I found the Captain sitting forlornly before a radar screen complaining resignedly, 'I think I'll be sick; then I'll have a cup of tea; then I'll be sick; then I'll have a sandwich; then I'll be sick; then I'll watch this monitor; then I'll be sick again'. Sea sickness seemed to affect some half of the crew every time they first set sail. Oblivious, the First Lieutenant was poring over charts, giving me the impression he'd heard this routine from the Skipper many times before.

In the middle of the watch room was a hefty wooden stand with an impressive-looking log-book on it, open for me to record events. I was told to register any communications between ourselves and the aeroplanes and other ships together searching for the target submarine. Half-an-hour or so into the watch, a torrent of noise erupted from the speakers. Pencil poised, I strained to distinguish through the intense static any comprehensible words. When at last I was able to confirm they were English, I simply didn't understand them: they were technical naval terms which I'd never heard, spoken or read during the previous 15 months spent on Army and RAF establishments learning the Russian language and Russian military terminology. I confessed as much to the Captain, who accepted my failure with surprising equanimity and suggested I return to my mess.

Ignorance of ship's jargon could cause problems in harbour just as readily as at sea, as Tony Cash recalls:

Back in Derry, the *Ruthven* was due for a repaint. The Buffer (chief bosun's mate, responsible for the ship's upkeep) handed me a paint brush and tin of white paint, and told me to paint the 'stanchions on the for'ard gun deck'. I was in a quandary: the ship was stationary so I had no idea in which direction to move; the 'gun deck' I would probably recognise, but I had no earthly idea what a 'stanchion' was. All this I explained politely to the Buffer. A very tall man, and strong with it, he seized me by the scruff of the neck and seat of the pants and marched me at the double to the railings that were in dire need of a new coat of paint. Old salts must have found us national service coders a bit of a trial.

Locating 'enemy' subs

The anti-submarine exercises occupying the *Loch Ruthven* in the early weeks of 1954 were small beer, indeed, compared with *Exercise Strikeback*, which involved over 200 ships, 650 airplanes and 750,000 seamen from the major NATO countries. It took place around Iceland over a ten-day period in September 1957, and was the biggest since the end of World War II. Some 36 submarines assigned to the 'Orange' fleet, were tasked with 'sinking' as many of the 'Blue' fleet as possible. This was viewed as a major test of NATO's battle-readiness. Several of the 'Blue' destroyers were equipped with highly secret new equipment designed to facilitate detecting a submarine's presence from any radar signal it transmitted.

Volunteers to man the hush-hush apparatus were sought from among coders then training at RAF Pucklechurch for later radio intercept work. Along with some fifteen other coders, Gareth Mulloy, Alan Smith and Hugh St John Mildmay agreed to be the guinea pigs. All three reported to Plymouth to join the C Class destroyer HMS *Cavendish*. Gareth has described his first impressions:

> After rejecting the homosexual advances of the first petty officer I met after crossing the brow of my ship, I found a small space in which to sling my hammock and looked forward to an exciting new adventure as a real sailor. My enthusiasm was doused quickly by permanent sea sickness, interrupted only when we put in for repairs at Pembroke Dock. A short run ashore in Pembroke. It was Sunday in Wales. The only place we could find a drink was at a working men's club, where I recall with shame that I pinched a woman's bum, as an alternative to pouring pints of awful Welsh beer down my throat. I suppose I thought I was living up to the image expected of 'Jack' ashore. Back to the ship, and a stormy passage up the Irish Sea towards Iceland and the Arctic.

Those in peril on the sea

Alan Smith recalls that extremely rough seas were the 'backdrop' to their first week staggering northward in the Atlantic. Tragically, as Alan was later to learn, that same storm sank the *Pamir*, a four-masted, square-rigged, sailing ship, with the loss of 80 seamen, of whom 51 were merchant navy cadets. The atrocious conditions which had done for the German training ship persisted for hours on end, with consequences that are deeply etched in Alan's memory:

> The heart-jolting fear of that unknown sailor's embrace at 2.00 am has been and will continue with me all my life. I had been woken from my hammock to go on night watch on the bridge The night sky was pitch black with driving rain and spray. We were in a storm of severe hurricane strength. It was much more difficult to maintain any normal walking posture, gripping guide rails as tightly as one could and forcing the feet with determination, trying to bend the face away from flying water. I was just stepping onto the catwalk when that sailor lunged and grabbed me. Of course he tried to explain, but his words were lost in the howls of the gale. In snatches, his mouth to my ear, I managed to understand that he had been placed there as sentry and was roped on. The steel catwalk had been carried away by the tons of crashing waters. His job was to prevent any of the crew falling to the deck below with certain injury and most likely being washed overboard. At daybreak the order was given, 'No-one allowed on upper deck,' which was maintained for six days.

That this was an exceptionally ferocious gale was brought home to Alan when the regulars told him that never in fifteen years on board had they endured such a battering:

> The waves seemed to measure a mile from wave peak to wave peak, but I imagine they were at least a quarter mile across. This meant that the boat spent five minutes or so in the trough with towering walls of water around us, and then, say, three minutes riding at the top of a vertiginous wave, from which point one could see many boats of the fleet. I saw a very large old flat-top going under the waves and felt that must be a fairly rare sight. These were the old and longer aircraft carriers before the introduction of the shortened ramped decks with vertical take-

off planes. It was rumoured that the Americans lost six aircraft from their carriers and the British one or two. These enormous waves not only took away the catwalk between poop and bridge but also all our wooden lifeboats, including the very substantial captain's pinnace. Our hull side plates were split in one place below our mess-deck, and when the repair team went into the oil tank to inspect the damage, one could see the split in the plate widen and close with the movement of the waves, and a shaft of light entered that gloomy pit.

Testing hush-hush apparatus

Alan believes that he and his fellow coders were invited to volunteer for *Exercise Strikeback* because they had signed the Official Secrets Act and could therefore be trusted to handle the secret submarine-detecting system with discretion:

> The new electronic device was designed to capture the radar sweep of other ships and display them on a small circular cathode ray tube, three inches diameter. The operator's skill was to learn to recognise the 'normal' and fairly dense scatter of surface radar 'blips' on the tiny Screen, and thus be able quickly to spot the single 'abnormal' and distinct signature of the intruding submarine radar sweep and blip. Detection was to be communicated immediately over a reserved fleet radio network with the identifier call sign.

Submarines surface as little as possible, and normally allow themselves a single sweep of their radar system, before submerging again. If the location of an enemy sub could be pinpointed, it would be vulnerable to attack by depth charge or from the air. In these exercises it was normal practice at that time to use hand grenades, and if they exploded close to the target it might be counted a 'kill'. But could the novel detector actually identify its prey? Gareth Mulloy soon had the answer:

> During the week of the exercise, when we were working in simulated war conditions, I detected one signal on my tiny screen which I thought was that of a submarine's radar. 'Switch, Switch. Target at 185'. I managed to relay the code words down the voice pipe between bouts of nausea. Immediately I felt the good ship *Cavendish*, built in 1941, change course towards

the target. It turned out that the 'target' was a large American aircraft carrier. I was assured later that one of her radars did indeed emit a signal similar to the one we had been trained to look for. As we were in the middle of a large and varied fleet, the blips on my screen resembled the rain on a car windscreen in a typhoon, and the submarine signal that I was looking for was almost impossible to detect.

Unsurprisingly, atomic-powered submarine USS *Nautilus* chalked up 16 successful attacks against 'Blue' vessels, leading Vice-Admiral John Eccles to complain that NATO's search and destroy technology was inadequate.[1]

Life below decks

Gareth Mulloy's persistent sea sickness may have dampened his ardour for the sea-faring life, but it did not diminish his high regard for the Navy and the comrades with whom he served:

> At the end of a watch I had to take my bucket of vomit down the ladder from my crow's nest to the heads for emptying and flushing out. Then a climb back up the ladder to put it back for the use of my relief. Sometimes I had to re-use it after reaching the top, so had to repeat the whole procedure.
>
> For the last two days of our return journey I stopped being sick. For the earlier part I was continually sick, except when in my 'mick'. My shipmates were regular Naval ratings, who showed me rough and jocular kindness and sympathy in my plight.

In those days on smaller ships such as Gareth's each mess deck had a roster which determined which duty 'cook' would go to the galley at meal times to collect enough food for his mates. The cooking itself was done in the galley by trained cooks. As a consequence of the storm damage, access to the galley had to be via the engine room:

> The gruffly tolerant regular matelots on my mess deck had tacitly excused me this task because of my sickness. In any case, I could not eat. When feeling better, I took my turn, but had to negotiate the ladders into and out of the engine room. Climbing up steep steel ladders in a ship which was still rolling heavily,

1   *Wikipedia* at http://en.wikipedia.org/wiki/Operation_Strikeback.

when carrying a heavy tray of food, was difficult. When I successfully placed my valuable cargo of pudding on the mess table my satisfaction was quickly dissipated by the reaction of my fellow diners: 'Not fucking duff!' My short experience aboard taught me that a life at sea was not for me. There is nothing quite as debilitating and miserable as chronic sea sickness. It is fortunate both for me and the Navy that I failed that Dartmouth entry examination and passed instead the open competition to join the Civil Service as an executive officer.

At sea three years earlier than Gareth, Tony Cash also found congenial mess-mates sailing aboard the *Loch Ruthven*. He was also fortunate that Leading Coder Malcolm Brown was allocated to the same mess:

> Eleven of us, including Malcolm, shared eleven cubic feet of foetid air, so tightly packed together there was no room for me to sling a hammock. I had to kip on a bench fortunately padded sufficiently to make sleep possible. I soon learned that in really rough seas I had an advantage over my be-hammocked comrades – they had further to fall, as some of them did when the pitching and tossing became too violent.
>
> Built for 104 men, the *Loch Ruthven* now carried 114, and some complained of the overcrowding. We consoled ourselves that there were more of us to share duties. At sea for a week at a time, and no longer required to log exercises, I had, in fact few tasks to perform. In consequence, Malcolm and I played a good deal of cribbage. Our clarinet-guitar duets were appreciated, and we were delighted when we learned that a long-serving Irish sailor in our mess had a tea-chest bass and a penchant for skiffle, which in the early 1950s was beginning to make headway with youngsters, thanks to club performances and recordings by Lonnie Donegan, as well as the Ken Colyer and Chris Barber jazz bands.
>
> Another regular seaman had a radio aboard. One morning, Malcolm and I came below to discover our mess-mate alone, glued to his receiver, totally absorbed by J S Bach's beautiful religious cantata *Sheep May Safely Graze*. As the last strain died, he declared, in the ruggedest of northern accents: 'Fucking shit-hot, that bastard'. Northerners ourselves, and as enthusiastic

37. HMS *Loch Ruthven*. Courtesy Paul Snook.

about Bach as Louis Armstrong, we felt he'd hit on the *mots justes.*

'Vacation' in the Med

Like Tony Cash, Mike Gerrard had to serve some eighteen months before he got the opportunity to go to sea. Whereas most coders did their sea time in home waters, Mike was lucky enough to be sent with colleagues to the Mediterranean, and for a while his luck held. Flown to Malta, the group had a breather because the ships to which they had been allocated were still at sea, many hours' sailing from Valletta:

> For three or four days we were accommodated in HMS *Ricasoli,* a mediaeval fort on the wall of Grand Harbour, which was the first experience several of us had of sleeping under mosquito nets. We spent the days in desultory forenoon duties and getting our tot of grog, before going ashore to explore the area around the harbour. This brought us very quickly to the square which housed the bus station to anywhere in the island, the impressive war memorial and - equally amazing to our young, inexperienced eyes - the famous *Phoenicia Hotel.* John Allen, who had gone to spend his last six months' service in Turkey, had asked me to pay his respects to his father, who is commemorated on the war memorial, which I duly did before venturing into the lobby of the hotel. I remember thinking, 'I could never afford to stay in a hotel as grand as this', not imagining for a moment that in 1967 I should be taking my wife there for a long weekend to celebrate her thirtieth birthday.

Coders' most boring job

Mike's experiences at sea were considerably less enjoyable than his 'holiday' in Malta. Along with seven other leading coders he was allocated to the then new aircraft carrier HMS *Ark Royal*, eight more coders going to the cruiser HMS *Birmingham*. Both ships were participating, with American and Australian vessels, in *Exercise Cascade* in the western Mediterranean and Atlantic in March 1956. Fleet orders called for the strictest observance of 'radio silence' throughout the exercise: no ship was allowed to transmit any electronic signal, voice or Morse - otherwise

38. HMS *Ark Royal.*

an eavesdropping 'enemy' could gauge its exact location. The Admiralty could be forgiven for deeming coders, thanks to radio training received courtesy of the RAF, ideal candidates to monitor the fleet's communications channels. Leading coders worked in four watches of two, with instructions to inform an executive officer if on any occasion radio silence were broken. It was not. Mike Gerrard had endured the boring job of updating the confidential books at Chatham Barracks a year earlier; this was potentially worse, though it did allow him the opportunity to read *Crime and Punishment* from start to finish in one 24-hour period on duty:

> Nothing could be duller than the constant monitoring of compulsorily silent wavelengths. But there were some positive compensations: the coders were watch-keepers, and as such, accommodated in watch-keepers' messes. Given the nature of their duties, there could be no certainty that any particular rating would be in his mess at any specific time. While this did not absolve them from their duties as leading hands in their own mess, it enabled them to find quiet boltholes in different parts of the ships where they could relax when off duty. The *Ark Royal* pilots' restroom was the best place for a quick nap. It was furnished for the comfort of off-duty operational aircrew. Fortunately, they were not a fiercely possessive bunch, provided that there was enough room for everyone wanting to use it at any one time. It was a surprise to us that some of the pilots (who were all officers) were national servicemen. Through contact with the coder (educational) we had found that the Education Officer was not averse to an occasional rubber of bridge at quiet times, and the presence of a few off-duty coders made agreeable company when needed. The slops flat (area for collection and delivery of supplies, adjacent to the main stores) was ideal for late-night reading, as it had 24-hour lighting, but was little used outside regular working hours.

While Mike and his fellow coders were glued to their receivers listening out for infringements of the radio silence command during *Exercise Cascade,* they were unaware of a tragedy occurring in the skies above them. On 7 March 1956, as reported in the House of Commons next day, two planes from the *Ark Royal,* a Venom jet fighter and an anti-submarine Gannet, were lost with five fatalities.

We have been in touch with more than 70 former coders whose Naval careers span the years 1951-59. Only one, David Culver, has reported hearing of a fellow serviceman dying on or off duty. David was one of the coders with Mike Gerrard aboard the *Ark Royal* that fateful night, and his recollection is that the tragic news was not formally announced to the crew, but learned via the grapevine. Seeing planes catapulted from the ship in daytime was an unnerving experience, he said: unimaginable that such a procedure could be used at night. In the 1950s most of us in the armed forces knew that taking off and landing on a moving surface was dicing with death. A Fleet Air Arm pilot, regular or conscript, was someone to admire rather than envy.

Decoding at sea

Ray Worgan, a coder from 1952 to 1954, is one of a small minority given the opportunity to use their cryptographic skills aboard ship. His 'gang of four', including Norman Hetherington, Geoff Sharp and Adam Pyke, reported to RNB Chatham:

> After the ritual of spending a day joining the barracks by registering at seven different sections (mess, clothing stores, medical etc) and then spending the next day going through the posting routine by de-registering at the same seven sections, we were shipped by lorry, train, lorry, train and lorry to the naval base at Invergordon, north of Edinburgh. Thence by the mail launch to the cruiser HMS *Jamaica*, which had put in briefly during NATO exercises in the North Sea. We were put in the Signals mess of some thirty full time signallers and telegraphists, from 30-year olds who had served everywhere to 16-year olds who had just signed on for twelve years. Despite being leading rate, we were below the boy telegraphists in the mess-deck pecking order, as we knew absolutely nothing about the running of a warship on 24-hour watch and watch about. We were treated very politely as intelligent imbeciles.

> Our duties were to put into practice the Naval de-coding we had learned all that time ago at the Devonport signals school - one-time pads, double-encoding etc, being assigned in pairs on full-watch rota to the signals receiving room, deep in the bowels of the ship. We soon found our way there, but often got lost trying to get back to the mess.

In the signals room there was a row of four boy telegraphists in headphones, sitting at typewriters taking down the constant flow of messages from the Admiralty and all the other ships on the NATO exercise. I was paired with Geoff Sharp, and we soon remembered the patterns of decoding. One particularly rough night, when all the boys were vomiting into buckets at their feet, so that taking down messages would not be interrupted, an urgent message came through from the Dutch admiral who had newly taken over command of the exercise. This was top priority, and the signals lieutenant-commander sent word for very fast decoding. Geoff and I worked through the intricacies of doing the first change of lettering, only to find that when we did the second set, the result was gibberish. Mistake somewhere. Did it all again, very carefully. Again, gibberish. Leading hand of the watch getting very agitated. Then one of us had the thought: 'What if the Dutch admiral has forgotten that the codes changed two hours ago at midnight, and has used yesterday's code?' We tried the old code. The message came out. The leading hand triumphantly took the message to the lieutenant-commander, whose reply enabled the Brits to take a very superior position over the Dutch.

Word quickly got round the mess the following day, and from then on we were treated as imbeciles who actually had their uses.

Grog rituals

Ray Worgan has described the formalities associated with the consumption of grog aboard the cruiser *Jamaica*:

People were given their tots when they came off watch, or when there was a sociable moment before supper, and we were soon involved in the ritual of giving and being given a drink of some one else's tot as a thank you for some act of helpfulness during the day - swapping a watch or helping with a letter home. A small favour was rewarded with 'sippers'. A greater favour was rewarded with 'gulpers'. Invited to see off the rest of the tot, the lucky recipient would hear the phrase 'sandy bottoms' – a reference to the sediment left in the glass.[2]

2   Although sharing of grog in this way was widely practised, it was contrary to regulations. 'It must be strictly understood that the spirit

Coder record for sea time

Keith Watkinson's sea time was considerably longer than the norm: it lasted about five months, preventing him and about twenty other coders from going to any listening or Y station like the one at Cuxhaven. Instead of monitoring Soviet military radio traffic, the job they had been gearing up for in the previous 18 months, they went to the training squadron at Portland, an important naval base in Dorset until it was transferred to exclusively civilian use in 1995.[3] Keith was drafted after Easter 1954 to HMS *Portchester Castle*, a frigate, an uprated wartime corvette, which had been engaged in air-sea rescue operations in the South Atlantic during the last weeks of World War II. He served aboard until early demob in October allowed him to start university:

> I was allocated to the fo'c'sle mess, the biggest onboard and in consequence used as the cinema. There were two other killicks, both with one 'badge' [a chevron indicating four years' good service], who were the senior hands. As both lived ashore, when we were alongside, I was left in charge. The others were mostly boy seamen, many had enlisted from Dr Barnardo's. I have to admit that I did not encounter any animosity, although I was careful not to antagonise anyone unduly. My 'hook' [killick's badge] also let me escape being mess cook, a duty heavy with opprobrium. I was always addressed as 'Codes'. I found my time onboard a mixture of boredom and interest. My main tasks were to bring all the Admiralty charts up to date and some cryptography work. On my first visit to the chart office, I was amused to find a stack of comics in

ration is issued solely for consumption by the individual entitled to it, and it must not be given away, bartered, or otherwise disposed of. Quite apart from any infringement of the regulations, it is dangerous.' *Naval Rating's Handbook*, p 160. There was a recorded case of a popular young sailor receiving birthday 'gulpers' from all his mates, only to die before the day was out.

3   No official reason was given as to why, after such lengthy training, these coders were not required to put that training into practice. It seems likely however, that the Admiralty regarded the number of coders in post at Cuxhaven at that time was sufficient for the current purpose; that would not mean their training had been wasted, as the principal use of a large pool of trained coders was always for sigint in a potential future war.

the bottom chart drawer. I can only wonder how many other bored matelots had sat supposedly amending charts for such exotic places as the South Sea Islands and untouched since the war. Sometimes, in the evenings, I would go to the communications centre and tune into the *Goons* (a comedy show) on the standard issue B 40 radio. I seem to recall hearing the commentary on Roger Bannister's four-minute mile [6 May 1954] in those circumstances.

I was, however, fortunate enough, to be sent down in an S Class submarine to experience what it was like to be the hunted, rather than the hunter. It was wet and cold, and one could imagine how frightening it would be in conflict. When the sub settled on the sea bed to avoid detection, it was frightening to hear the depth charges going off over one's head.

The most exciting experience was a NATO exercise in the north Atlantic. There were mock battles, when the ship was closed down and blacked out. My station was in the communications centre to monitor the traffic to and from the Soviet 'trawlers' which shadowed us, with their large listening and transmitting antennae. I also received and sent coded messages within our fleet, using the *Typex* coding machine. We refuelled at sea, a dangerous exercise, as the supply vessel and the ship had to sail only some 35 yards apart, keeping accurate parallel courses. Members of crews were exchanged by bosun's chair. The swell and waves made all these manoeuvres difficult. The experience gave me a little insight into the life my father must have experienced when he served throughout the war on north Atlantic convoy escort duty in his anti-submarine ship. He was always very reluctant to talk about it, and I can only surmise he saw some dreadful sights.

When I was due to leave the ship, I was summoned to the Captain's cabin. He told me that I would soon be back in the RN to fight another war. Luckily, that was never to be the case.

My last days in the RN were in HMS *Drake*, in Devonport, where I went through demob routine. At the time the gun crews were training, and all those in barracks had to muster to support them. Some were a sorry sight, with broken limbs and other injuries.

Needless to say, and luckily for us perhaps, coders were, as far as we can ascertain, never allowed to handle ships' cannon, our experience of weaponry limited to a very brief training in the use of rifles, bren and sten guns during our time on the Russian course at Army-run JSSLs.

Utilising ships requisitioned from the former enemy

A handful of coders had opportunities to acquaint themselves with ships that had previously belonged to the Germany navy until they were commandeered by the Allies after the Nazi surrender in 1945. At Cuxhaven, where coders were sent to carry out the radio monitoring work for which they had trained, the Navy had possession of a motor torpedo vessel or E-boat ('enemy boat'), as they had been nicknamed during World War II. In the early summer of 1954 Tony Cash got to sail on it for a week, but not this time at the Admiralty's behest:

> The officer commanding our listening station wanted a holiday on Borkum, a German island in the North Sea close to the Dutch coast 120 odd miles west of Cuxhaven. Along with two other coders, I was dragooned (or should that be pressed?) into crewing for a young sub-lieutenant, who steered us safely enough there and back through some pretty heavy seas. It was the only occasion during my time in the Navy (or indeed since) when I really felt sea-sick, but it was the diesel oil fumes I inadvertently inhaled, rather than the ship's pitching that caused the trouble. I leaned over the stanchions expecting to vomit, but to my immense relief, all sensations of nausea were instantly dispelled when a high wave broke over the ship drenching me to the skin.

Former Leading Coder Bill Musker, eavesdropping in Cuxhaven in 1954, made something of a study of the ships annexed after the Nazi defeat, especially the E- boats:

> The German engineers referred to them as *diese verscheissende Schüttelschiffe* ('these shitty shaking ships') a soubriquet well merited and pondered by their crews struggling to contend with fierce tides, shallow waters with shifting sand-banks, and the vicious North Sea winter gales, as the engines predictably seized up, coughed and died. The engines had been supposedly

deliberately buggered and couldn't reach max revs. They also had a solid gearbox and were started by cartridges in the top of the cylinders. So, to go astern, the engine was stopped in 'ahead', gear put 'astern', then the engine restarted. Inexperienced cox'ns were hated by the hairy-arsed stokers, who had to keep whipping the cartridges out of, and new ones back into, red-hot cylinder-heads. On occasions we were allowed aboard to go mine-hunting in the Elbe, which was extraordinary: shooting with 303 rifles and Smith and Wesson's amazing duck gun, it was hoped to either explode or sink the mine.

A greater perceived danger than mines laid in World War II was Soviet naval power. Bill Musker served in the so-called Elbe Flotilla, which he claims was ordered to be on full battle alert and to patrol and blockade the North Sea lock gates of the Kiel Canal at Brunsbuttel am Elbe, though his description does not inspire confidence that the tiny flotilla would have been any deterrent to cruisers such as the *Sverdlov*, *Ordzhonikidze* and *Dzerzhinsky*, all completed in 1952:

The Elbe Flotilla was a small force, consisting of the flagship *Royal Albert*, motor torpedo boats (MTBs), a landing craft and several Carley floats. The *Royal Albert* was an interesting craft. Long and narrow-gutted as an ocean greyhound, she was a pre-World War 1 German ex-pleasure steam yacht. Her armament consisted of one 2" gun forwards and two Lewis guns aft. The 2" gun could only be fired broadside as the deck mountings were suspect, and it was considered to be strategically preferable that in the event that the recoil from a firing should prove too much for the ancient mounting bolts, it would peacefully catapult itself overboard, rather than demolishing the bridge and the wardroom beneath. The key fighting quality of the *Royal Albert* was her small fore- and even smaller after-profile, coupled with her ability to roll violently and to dig into the waves and imitate a submarine in any weather above force three on the Beaufort scale. This would render her virtually invisible to a pursuing enemy and gave rise to her somewhat unusual ship's motto – *In Flight We Trust*.

The landing craft was full of high explosive and otherwise unarmed. The Carley floats regularly got

39. The floating HMS *Royal Albert*, courtesy Maurice Berrill, who was told that this had been the private vessel of Grand Admiral Karl Dönitz, briefly German head of state after the death of Adolf Hitler in April 1945.

in the way of everything else in the base harbour, and it was vaguely hoped that they might be of similar inconvenience to any invaders.

In the event, in the knowledge of my presence – monitoring their every move - and the presence of the Elbe Flotilla and our devotion to duty (in spite of all that wind, wave, weather, and the Reeperbahn[4] could do) it was enough to prevent the Russian fleet from breaking out of the Baltic through the Kiel canal and placing Britain in a position from which she would have been forced to declare war.

Bill Musker's tongue-in-cheek account reflects the scepticism many coders felt about the might of the British Navy, especially if they had first-hand knowledge of our ships at sea.

---

4   Red light district of Hamburg. See also chapter 10.

CHAPTER 9
ON THE JOB – UNTOLD
WATCHROOM STORIES

ХОРОШО, ЧТО ЕСТЬ РАБОТА. А ТО НЕПОНЯТНО ОТ ЧЕГО МОЖНО БЫЛО БЫ САЧКОВАТЬ

(Russian saying – 'It's as well there's work, otherwise we'd have no reason to skive')

The coders' experience of national service was out-of-the-ordinary, for several reasons. We spent anything from seven to ten months learning a foreign language that few in Britain could speak; in contrast, the skills acquired by most national servicemen were pretty useless in civilian life. Going into the Navy was unusual, involving less than two per cent of the total number conscripted. Those who became coders had specifically opted for the Navy, whereas most men who went into the Army would have preferred something else, and even some destined for the RAF felt the same way. Because we learned Russian on an Army camp and did radio training with the RAF, we got around the armed forces: we were able to make comparisons denied to non-coders (see chapter 7).

More importantly, in common with our Army and RAF *kursanty* friends we actually DID something directly connected with the Cold War, rather than just training for a hot war. The overwhelming majority of other conscripts, (except the unlucky minority who went to Korea, Malaya or Suez - and some lost their lives), were far removed from the shadow boxing. Finally, our sense of comradeship was heightened by the fact that, apart from a time at sea, and unlike almost all other national servicemen, we stayed together in our intakes for most of the two-year period of service. Our specific and exceptional experiences were recognisably shared with many others, and have allowed bonds to be created even with those we did not meet whilst in the Navy, as our recent 'virtual reunions' by email demonstrate.

40. The direction finding (DF) hut at Cuxhaven in 1954.
Courtesy of Robin Pearce, standing at the entrance.

Eavesdropping on the Soviets in Cuxhaven

It is fairly certain that the Navy occupied the *Kriegsmarine* base at Cuxhaven on the south bank of the mouth of the river Elbe around May 1945, when the E-boats found there were commandeered. This was a useful location from which the Kiel Canal could be blocked, should the Soviet Union commence hostilities. It also provided one centre for intelligence gathering activities, the other being at Kiel.

In the early post-war period the Navy maintained a chain of fixed listening stations in the UK and a forward listening station at Kiel.[1] Other early intelligence activities were conducted in the Baltic by Lieutenant.-Commander John Harvey-Jones (later Chairman of Imperial Chemical Industries), who had passed a six months' course in Russian at Cambridge in 1945, followed by command of the British Baltic Fishery Protection Service, which conducted clandestine sigint gathering using converted German E-boats (as discussed in chapter 1). He was awarded the military MBE in 1952 for his contribution to Naval intelligence, which probably included intercept work.[2]

However, the training of Russian linguists by the Navy at that time was limited to a very few officers. Only when the first contingent of coders arrived at JSSL Bodmin in November 1951, a month after the school opened, could the Navy look forward to having sufficient numbers to man a monitoring post, and it would be more than a year before they were adequately prepared.

After JSSL, coders did the same radio training as their RAF counterparts. In general, the next stage in our service trajectory was either to be sent to the fleet to do sea time or to complete a cryptography course – in each case a matter of only a few weeks. Only the final lap of some four to six months saw us engaged in the task for which the coder special division had been set up in the first place. Almost all those we have contacted were posted to West Germany to do this job, even if they moved on from there. Early intakes went to *Royal Albert* until July 1955, when the whole operation was transferred further north east to HMS *Royal Charlotte,* on the shores of Kiel Bay. Two small groups went from Germany

---

1   R. J. Aldrich, *The Hidden Hand: passim*, but especially pp 244,253, 527. The adjective 'forward' means nearer the Soviet Union than the UK.

2   Several sources reached by *Googling* 'John Harvey-Jones'.

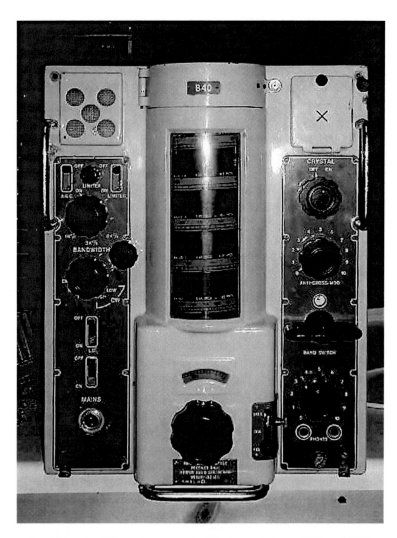

41. A Murphy B40 receiver as used at Cuxhaven between 1953 and 1954.
Note the large tuning knob at the bottom of the device: it worked on a
fly wheel allowing the operator to 'swing' between frequencies easily.
Courtesy of D Mills.

to Cyprus in 1956 and 1957. Another handful went to two GCHQ stations in northern Turkey in 1956.

HMS *Royal Albert*, the Naval shore base at Cuxhaven, contained a radio station established or enlarged, we believe, by the winter of 1952-53, when the first Bodmin intake would have been fully trained. On the site was a large wooden structure called *Ramsay Barracks*. It was barricaded from the living accommodation and admin offices by wire fencing. Entry was limited to personnel certified by a card to have been 'indoctrinated' under the Official Secrets Acts. The forest of tall aerials surrounding the building afforded hints of the work afoot. This was the watchroom where we were to do our eavesdropping.

Inside, there was a series of four or five long tables, divided into about three workstations, each equipped with a pair of radio sets, head phones and a Ferrograph tape recorder. Coders were split into watches of roughly fifteen men, individually allocated either a specific wave length to monitor continuously or a defined band within which to search or 'swing'. The task was to listen to and 'log' any spoken Soviet military radio traffic we found. The speech material had to be transcribed long-hand onto pads of forms on which were printed boxes for date, time, wavelength etc. The tape recorder was intended as a fail safe, when speech was too fast or too indistinct for effective simultaneous transcription. This could occur even when we wrote only 'speedword' abbreviations for frequently used phrases, such as, kms - *kak menya slyshetye?* (how do you read me?).

The Navy's Murphy B40 receivers were preferred to the RAF back-ups, partly because the former had a visual monitor that assisted tuning in to weak signals. Variable bandwidths allowed searches over a wide range. There was a facility to narrow the width to cut out interference if we found anything interesting. Also in use in the mid to later 1950s was the Hammerlund radio, which, as Bill Hetherington attests, possessed one advantage over its rivals:

> The top was hinged, allowing access to the interior where, on a night watch, one could place a pasty (curiously known as an 'Oggin, and previously bought at the NAAFI), to warm for assuaging boredom-induced hunger in the small hours.

42. Left to right – Malcolm Chaplin, Kevin Pilley, Maurice Berrill
and Midshipman Austin holding a tea fanny in front of the door to
Ramsay Barracks, entrance to which required the incomer to provide
proof of identity, Cuxhaven May 1954. Courtesy M Berrill.

Later intakes also had the use of Racal sets which were not popular with all operators, as Alan Smith recalls:

> At Kiel some of the few Racals bore the coder legend
> on the side, 'You'll get fuck-all on the Racal'.

Allocation of wavelengths was by the ex-coder midshipman in charge of the watch or one of the leading telegaphists assisting him, sitting at a raised desk giving a view of the whole operation. The four watches were divided in pairs, each pair sharing a 24-hour period, 8.00 am - 8.00 am, turn and turn about, with the next 24 hours off watch-keeping duty, though other work was required to be done until lunchtime. At weekends, one pair of watches shared the whole two days, while the other pair were 'off', absolved from morning duties.

If we were not aware at the time, we now know that we were on loan to GCHQ, and that the signals we monitored could have included those generated by the Soviet air force and army, their diplomatic service, and even the KGB (Committee for State Security) or its Stalin-era predecessor, the MGB (Ministry of State Security), in addition to those of the Soviet Navy.[3] Had war been declared, most of us would have joined the fleet, no doubt to carry out duties similar to the intercept operators in the German war – plain language work, interpreting signals of immediate interest to officers of the watch.

We got used to the call signs, such as that belonging at one time in 1954 to the Soviet admiralty: 'Я Крокодил!' (I'm Crocodile). Also very familiar was the counting of 1-10 or 1-5, forwards and backwards, for tuning purposes. There were 'oceans' of cipher groups which were simultaneously taxing and boring. Some non-tuning signals were sent in plain language, such as weather forecasts, or pilots reporting their movements on a bombing range. One contact who was at Kiel in the second half of the 1950s remembers a larger amount of plain language signals, which were more interesting than the 'grid', as we called the cipher groups.

The most promising of our data was sent by teleprinter to GCHQ in Cheltenham, message pads and tapes following by courier via the parallel US operation at Bremerhaven. Fred Wright, a midshipman of the watch in Cuxhaven in 1955 remembers that:

---

3   Information from Prof Richard Aldrich.

When we summoned GCHQ or Bremerhaven to prepare for our transmissions, we didn't use the phone, we used the typewriter, which was connected to the other two places via the *Enigma* machine and the teleprinter. We typed out something like 'Do you read me OM (old man)?' and they would reply 'Read you fives OM', meaning they were reading us O.K. I think this was to check we had set up the *Enigma* machine right. I don't remember ever finding I hadn't set it up right.

Bill Musker recalls that:

There were serious times in the watchroom when network frequencies and call signs changed unexpectedly and we prided ourselves in rapidly relocating our friends in крючник (*kryuchnik* - stevedore) and следопыт (*slyedopyt* - pathfinder) by their voices or traffic, quicker than our US partners in Bremerhaven. Caucasian or Georgian accents were prized for their uniqueness, though translating them was sometimes complex.

Recently, Dennis Mills and Clifford German, his watch officer, have pieced together what at the time seemed a most puzzling event that occurred in late September 1954. Clifford had been informed by our American colleagues in Bremerhaven that some Russian warships were sailing in our direction down the Norwegian coast, just outside national waters, and he was given the appropriate frequency to monitor closely with his watch. We also had radio direction-finding (D/F) equipment in a hut on wheels positioned on top of the nearby Elbe embankment to give it a good 'view'. Dennis reports that:

When the watches changed at 12 noon, I emerged from the watchroom to find a group of coders in earnest debate about the problems the D/F crew were having – the specified Russian signal was very loud – how far away were they? On the stroke of 12 o'clock, and about 100 yards away, a cement mixer stopped – being German, it would obviously stop precisely on time! This was followed by shouts of relief from the D/F hut. The cement mixer had been jamming all other signals. Although we did not realise it at the time, GCHQ were always anxious to ensure their collection stations were sited well away from passing motor traffic, knowing that it often created serious interference.

Eavesdropping on the Soviets in Kiel

At Cuxhaven it was normal practice for midshipmen who had trained as Russian interpreters to be placed in charge of watches to ensure coders were assiduously searching for, recording and logging Russian military traffic. Post-1955, when the listening station was transferred to Kiel, officer invigilators were no longer deemed necessary, judging from the accounts we have received from Alan Smith and Paddy Heazell. Alan told us:

> I don't remember us having any commissioned officer of the watch. I only remember this function fulfilled by a petty officer. He sat at a master console on a raised dais where he could observe any misbehaviour or sleeping coder. I have a feeling that at his console he could monitor what transmissions we were listening to at our individual stations. We had slight contact with our Captain and most contact with the hierarchy was via the 'Jimmy' [First Lieutenant, second in command].

Paddy Heazell, on an earlier intake than Alan, recalls an even less hierarchical watch-keeping set-up at Kiel:

> We did not have ex-coder midshipmen i/c our watches, but one of our own number. If a midshipman did turn up for any reason, I sense he got short shrift from us, because, smart they might be, but midshipmen, like the entire remainder of the Navy, could not do our job. I have to say that in no time we found our feet and felt pretty competent.

If supervision of monitoring work was more relaxed and haphazard at Kiel than at Cuxhaven, the resulting intercept material was processed more thoroughly before being passed on for analysis: recorded traffic was now transcribed by a coder allotted to this specific task, as Paddy explains:

> The idea was that operators would take down whatever they heard *verbatim* as it was received – with, of course, the recorder running. The Ferrographs were very good. Once the message was complete, the tape and the impression the operator had of the message was taken into a separate room, where the transcriber would beaver away trying to get a more accurate version. This, plus the original impression, was then dispatched to Cheltenham (we knew not how,

43. Maurice Berrill 'at my lonely post in the DF hut, to which I was regularly confined', Cuxhaven 1954. Courtesy M Berrill.

except that we had the impression that the very word *Cheltenham* was so secret we mustn't mention it).

Alan Smith recalls that transcription was sometimes a collaborative effort:

> The transcriber had time to listen to specific parts of the recording several times, rewinding the tape as much as needed and even asking other operators to listen in and give a second or third opinion on the recorded Russian. This could be very useful where the recording was poor quality, or where slang, colloquialisms, swearing or recondite technical terms were used. The operator would write out a much more complete, fair copy than the primary 'take'.

Whatever intercept messages we logged, there was only very rarely a feeling that the communication was of any particular consequence. Alan Smith, however, does recall an interesting exception:

> One significant message sequence continued for three days. It began with very low signal strength, and it took some effort to tune in for improved reception at an acceptable or usable level. We formed the opinion that it was a tank battle exercise, and much of it was transmitted in plain language with other parts in code. Later I received an informal congratulatory message from GCHQ that it had been a very useful intercept. I imagine it was forbidden for security reasons to pass a formal message back to the listening station. I have a memory that it had taken place beyond the Urals and that may be why the Russians had thought we would not overhear it, and hence had used plain language. I think it had been on shortwave and that we would not have received it without some deviation of the atmospheric conditions. Subsequent watches continued to monitor that frequency and we recorded the entire mock battle exercise.

Coders, whether at Cuxhaven or Kiel, were pretty well convinced that the Soviets were fully aware of our activities. Robin Pearce remembers seeing Soviet 'trawlers' with an armed sentry on duty in Cuxhaven harbour in 1955, no doubt monitoring us monitoring them. Paddy Heazell has a distinct memory of their proximity at Kiel:

There was always an element of 'playing games'. Soviet ships moored directly opposite the watchroom in Kiel Fiord, all visibly cluttered with monitoring aerials and intelligence-gathering paraphernalia. We knew they knew what we were doing: they could check on our aerials and observe our movements. Who was fooling whom? I recall no sense of serious apprehension about the Cold War. We were pretty close to the East German border, but we were amply inoculated with the optimism of youth. We were teenagers [or very recently so], and nothing would ever happen to us.

Most intakes did two to three weeks' reserve training at Cuxhaven or Kiel for three successive years after 'demob'. Lionel Franklyn was doing this at Kiel in 1956 when the Soviet leaders Bulganin and Khrushchev, *en route* for Britain, passed through the Kiel Canal in the cruiser *Ordzhonikidze,* with other naval vessels in attendance. All the coders on watch readied themselves to handle the Russian voice traffic they were expecting, but not a bleep was heard on the known Soviet frequencies – the conclusion must be that realising what we were up to, the *Ordzhonikidze* had established radio silence as it passed our station.

Monitoring on the Mediterranean and Black Seas

Peter Lord was one of a group of five coders who ended up in Cyprus, nominally HMS *Aphrodite,* at the 2nd Wireless Regiment at Four-Mile Point, Famagusta:

This was a fairly large Army camp with, I would guess, probably 30 to 40 listening stations, 10 to 20 of these manned by US Army personnel. The five of us ran an intercept desk. We had a watch-keeping system whereby two of us were on watch alternately, each doing 24 hours out of 48, and then had 48 hours off. We had a Ferrograph tape recorder and two receivers and the choice of four aerials. The odd man out collected the logs and tapes, then reviewed and edited them. He prepared call sign diagrams as an aid to analysing the traffic and finally prepared the intelligence for transmission to GCHQ by secure TELEX (teleprinter). We all took turns at this fifth man role. We had a typewriter with Cyrillic characters on normal mode, and English characters on the shift key.

This may have been to ensure standard transliteration for TELEX transmission.

There was a mix of traffic — cipher groups, reports from weather stations, weather forecasts and the like. However, I think we may have got more plain language than Cuxhaven, perhaps because we were just the one listening post and were able to range fairly freely across the wave bands. Our main objective was to pick up Soviet Navy traffic from the Black Sea. They had fairly regular low-key exercises, where it was basically plain language live interaction between ships. This was always interesting, and we learned some Russian swear words. The most dramatic incident was a near collision between (we reckoned) a destroyer and a submarine.

John Allen was in a party of four who went to northern Turkey to the Black Sea coast for the period April-September 1956, being split into two pairs, one to Sinope, the other to Asmara, quite close to the Soviet border. The main objective was to get data on Soviet rocket launches:

> Prior to going to Turkey, we were briefed at GCHQ, Cheltenham, and given our assignments and then sent to a centre to be kitted out with civvies, as we had been informed that we would travel as Foreign Office officials. Needless to say, the two-piece tweed suit, thick shirts and heavy brogues were not ideally suited to the Black Sea climate in summer. We flew out from Heathrow with BEA [British European Airways, nationalised airline] to Istanbul, where we stayed for a couple of days before travelling by ship to Sinope.
>
> The site was run by civil servants with RAF radar operators and us as radio operators. Our radio room was equipped with a VHF and an AM set. There were also two reel-to-reel tape recorders. A three-ton truck and Land Rover transported us to and from Sinope town, where we lived in a small scruffy hotel. Our operating hours were determined by GCHQ, I think. We had been allocated specific wave bands to monitor; one of us on VHF and the other on AM. As I recall, shifts were eight hours – usually through the day. We were situated right next to a US army base, complete with a mass of aerials, allegedly doing much the same as we were with our limited resources. We were supposed to share information, but I suspect it never happened. As we were 'civilians', our Navy pay was

44. Eavesdroppers at Cuxhaven taking a (probably unscheduled) break from
monitoring duties logging Russian military radio traffic.
Courtesy R Pearce.

paid into our UK bank account, and we drew expenses from the senior civil servant on site. There was no formal debriefing back in the UK.

Skiving, pranks, dissidence and silent strikes

The long hours of monitoring could be tedious and, as former midshipman Fred Wright has told us, it was not easy for anyone in charge constantly to check what coders were listening to, or, for that matter, recording. What he most vividly recalls of his stint in Cuxhaven is drinking hot chocolate in the night watch, not at all certain what his own actual duties were supposed to be. One coder friend later told him that listening to cricket scores was a common pastime.

A midshipman managing a watch, sometimes aided by a leading hand, had access to jack plug leads which could be connected to any coder's wireless, theoretically enabling him to check how diligently we were working, as Robin Pearce explains:

> Random checks would identify coders who were not searching or who were listening to commercial stations. I once listened to American Forces Network and heard, 'This is the 444 Transportation Corps. You call, we haul - that's all, you-all.'

John Griffiths was one of a group of half a dozen at Cuxhaven who did not always take their eavesdropping responsibilities very seriously:

> Our Russian supposedly fluent and our ears considered attuned to its varied accents, it was our role to monitor and write down every last trivial exchange of military conversation overheard. This was exceedingly boring ninety nine per cent of the time and we soon collectively devised ways round the boredom which would have had us court-martialled if they had ever come to light. We took it in turn one at a time to trawl all the frequencies that had been allotted to us, while the rest listened to more conventional radio stations broadcasting music, drama or whatever else we fancied. It was then that I developed my addiction to the Third Programme [forerunner of BBC Radio 3]. Whenever the 'trawlerman' heard traffic on any of our frequencies he would alert the appropriate colleague, who might or might not then deign to log it. I cannot

say that I ever came across any crucial military secrets, but I did learn that our supposed enemies were as human as we were. Part of our function was to try to identify the units involved by any characteristic idiosyncrasies or breaches of radio protocol. I became particularly attached to one Russian pilot who clearly shared my rebellious response to authority. If it were too foggy for easy observation, or he simply felt hungry, he would mutter the Russian equivalent of 'bugger this for a lark' and return to base.

Alan Smith recalls that coders given a waveband range rather than a fixed frequency to investigate were the lucky ones:

Many listened for a short time to American Forces Network, a source of good jazz programmes. Others listened to Radio Moscow and on one night watch I heard and recorded a retransmission of the bass Paul Robeson, singing one of the Russian anthems, *Shiroka Strana Moya Rodnaya* (My Native Land is a Broad One), which I taped, and it was quickly printed out in the transcription room. I still know the lyrics by heart and they give an excellent lesson in Russian grammar, declension case endings and short adjectival forms. There is now a fine hour long recording of Robeson's famous 1949 Moscow concert on YouTube, in which he addresses the audience in Russian.

Many coders had other priorities than spending time, especially the night hours, glued to their receivers, as Paddy Heazell reminded us:

We were instructed that reading matter was not permitted. Reading on watch was in breach of *Queen's Regulations and Admiralty Instructions*, and was a punishable offence. Nearly all of us had long reading lists to tackle in anticipation of forthcoming university degree courses. Salt was rubbed into the wound by the bland regulation that at 8.00 am we came off watch, had breakfast, then moved straight to 'clean ship' duties until 'dinner' (or lunch, as the more aggressively middle class - most of us - would prefer). We were not permitted to 'get our heads down' till about 12.30. We felt that we were being treated as if we were watch-keepers at sea. We weren't, and, moreover, the watches we were required to keep were untypical of Naval tradition. [There were three variations from standard Navy watch hours, including splitting the night into two watches of six hours, instead of three of four hours.]

Two other things grated. We felt that the equipment was grossly substandard and unreliable; and we also gained an impression that our labours were not really of the highest priority, as the Americans could cover all the frequencies we were allotted. I recall that probably in February or March 1956 our complaints over the feebleness of the B40 receivers led to a leading telegraphist coming into the watchroom with a large basket, which he proceeded to fill with useless valves – to the accompaniment of our cheers. The other source of mounting disaffection concerned the leadership we were given. I do not recall meeting or getting to know and be known by a single officer or senior rating. They seemed to us to be uninterested in what we were doing, and were evidently totally incompetent to do it themselves. I was forming a view that the RN was at a low ebb, with many regulars just waiting to leave the service, seemingly untuned to the possibility of a Cold War becoming Hot and certainly quite unable to relate with any sensitivity to the handling of national servicemen – particularly rather highly educated and potentially stroppy coders. I volunteered to visit the wardroom each week as the cinema projectionist. I recall no breaking of the ice barrier. We were different from your average matelot. On one occasion, we shared the 'liberty boat' minibus going into Kiel with the senior RN medic in the BAOR, a surgeon-commander. 'Going for a good run ashore, Jack?' was his greeting to a party of us. The response from a graduate of King's College, Cambridge, and former head boy at Charterhouse, voiced with that calm, understated self-assurance that betokened patient contempt, was that we were off to the Kiel Opera and, if time permitted, might visit a particularly impressive wine bar whose list we were working through.

Occasionally, activities in the watchroom might be more subversive, as Tony Cash recalls:

A fellow leading coder, still today anonymous, used a Ferrograph to make a looped tape bearing a simple, provocative message, delivered in a ludicrously exaggerated, plummy, public-school accent: THEY CALL THE NAVY THE ANDREW BECAUSE IT GIVES YOU THE SHITS. Neatly, even poetically, he had contrived to combine in one word references to both a notorious lieutenant press gang officer of the eighteenth century and the name of a mid-twentieth century, widely advertised, proprietary laxative liver salt. Over several days, whenever the midshipman in charge of the watch was absent, there was a strong chance the tape would be played. It invariably produced hysteria. When, in the summer of 1954, the first of our intake were due to return to England prior to demob, a phantom painter desecrated the watchroom building one dark night with huge letters on the exterior wall reading: THEY CALL THE NAVY THE ANDREW ... Someone somewhere has a photograph of the result.

Involved in the incident himself, Bill Hetherington, put to us the following question about the aftermath:

Do you also remember the petty officer in charge of the building, who, purple with rage in the morning, shouted, 'It's been done within the hour', as he touched it with his fingers, not realising that the wetness was the rain that had begun falling?

Robin Pearce, recalls an arguably more serious infringement of discipline in the watchroom in 1955:

An unfortunate man had repeatedly refused an order from a leading telegraphist to 'swing', that is, to search on a prescribed frequency range – probably in the small hours when there was little traffic. The telegraphist was doubtless acting on orders from further up the chain of command, making the offence a refusal to act on the order of a superior officer. This led to the coder concerned being reduced to able rate with a consequent proportionate loss of pay for the remaining weeks of his service. To underline the seriousness of the offence, 'lower deck' was cleared and all ratings mustered to witness the punishment being 'read out'. The coder's mates must have thought that he had been selected for punishment *pour encourager les autres*, as they had a 'whip round' to reinstate his lost earnings.

According to Graham Young, the leading telegraphist in question became the butt of another looped tape tune, sung to the tune of *Jealousy*:

> Davidowitz
>
> Gives me the screaming shits.

Mike Gerrard was much impressed by coders with more than average technological savvy, who recorded what sounded like gibberish until playing it backwards disclosed well-known rugby and other scurrilous ditties.

Not all coders wanted to use their tape machines creatively or even legitimately: Robin Pearce reports an incident open to several varying explanations:

> One day a member of our watch discovered that if you poked a pencil in one of the small sockets in the back of the Ferrograph, it would short. Half the sets in the watchroom were put out of action temporarily. That shows how stupid some of the coders could be.

Mischief, vandalism or sabotage – who knows?

Hitting back at Naval authority could take a more serious turn, as Tony Cash has explained:

> We had been told that we were doing an important job, effectively defending the realm from possible Commie invasion; we had the equivalent rank of corporal; we were in the last six months of our service, yet at Cuxhaven in my time (1954) we were often treated like raw recruits. Part of the problem was that we had to 'clean ship' first thing in the morning, regardless of the hours we had worked during the night watch. At the same time, we knew that our RAF compadres were positively obliged to rest after an eight-hour shift. At sea, of course, the rule is entirely comprehensible. An inevitable result at HMS *Royal Albert* was that the authorities had to find work for us, and all too frequently this resulted in us having to 'bull' the place or cut grass with nail scissors. Resentment was rife and led to a more or less unspoken decision to 'strike' - a refusal to hear or latch on to any Soviet military conversations long enough to record or log them. More than one 'striker' claimed that listening to the military traffic of a nation with whom we were not at war was contrary to the Geneva Conventions,

to which Britain was signatory. Whether this was actually true I have no idea,[4] but it was cited as a possible justification for this 'withdrawal of labour' in arguments with colleagues by nature more 'pusser'[5] than the dissidents. Of course, nothing was said to our superiors. Rumour had it that the commanding officer of the base was for a time worried that the Soviets must be planning some aggressive act, since they seemed to have initiated 'radio silence', generally understood to be a precursor to the launching of hostilities.

Alan Smith recounts a similar act of collective insubordination among coders:

We had a covert mutiny at Kiel once, which was expressed in the form of a well organised go-slow, and the amount of Russian traffic 'found' on the airwaves fell dramatically for one week. First the petty officers noticed the fall-off, and after some encouragement didn't work, the problem was passed upwards. This finally caused our Captain's fury and some form of punishment or threatened punishment.

A feeling of grievance was the principal cause of the 'industrial actions' at both Cuxhaven and Kiel, as Paddy Heazell makes clear:

Our sense of being undervalued and poorly handled, coupled with the fact that we were seemingly so much left to our own devices led inevitably to the quasi-mutiny of Easter 1956. It chiefly affected those long over-night watches, when we were happy to swing 'off net' and pick up no signals at all. By this stage I was in the happy position of being the transcriber. I was innocent of doing wrong because I was not required to tune in to anything, other than the tapes my colleagues delivered to me. I must have had half a dozen such night watches when I had nothing to do – for six long hours. But another astonishing thing about the situation was that we were so totally unsupervised

---

4   The Geneva Conventions, originating in 1864 and consolidated in 1949, concern treatment of victims of war - the injured, prisoners of war, civilian detainees and non-combatants generally. They therefore have no bearing on sigint and the work of coders, but it is not surprising that publicity about the 1949 consolidation may have been remembered by coders in the 1950s, without proper appreciation of the purport of the Conventions.

5   Naval slang for anyone overly conscientious in obeying orders or *Queen's Regulations*.

that we had the complete run of the station, including access to all the keys. I have to confess that more than once I availed myself of the comfortable sofa in the CO's office. Experience taught us that no one in authority would bother to check that all was going as it should. Was this dereliction of duty a crime against the state? I hardly think so. We were led to believe that the Americans were covering us with more expert equipment than ours.

Gareth Mulloy puts the blame for disaffection at the Kiel listening station at the door of the commanding officer, Lieutenant-Commander Cheetham and his first lieutenant, who both appear to have been die-hard traditionalists:

They found it difficult to deal with national servicemen, who were 'pressed' men, not volunteers, and whose level of education was significantly higher than that found generally in the lower deck at that time. This led to truculent petulant behaviour on our part.

Alan Smith, who served with Gareth, remaining a close friend to this day, believes that coders at Kiel might have been less insubordinate if they had known more about their commanding officer:

For me the biggest incentive to bad discipline and behaviour (taking for granted the bolshiness of a set of students forced into the military) was the total lack of empathy of our skipper, Lt-Commander Cheetham, who could easily have had us eating out of his hand, had he simply let us know his secret, that he had been shot down over the North Sea about 1941, and after some escape attempts had spent the rest of the war in Colditz [German castle used for officer prisoners of war].

Gareth Mulloy only learned in the late 1990s what Cheetham had been concealing from them:

We never realised the hardships endured by Cheetham during the war until long after leaving the Navy, when his obituary was published in the *Daily Telegraph*. He followed the old 'silent service' tight-lipped tradition and appeared to us immature schoolboys as a cold aloof figure. He did not communicate with us. He was ably supported in this role by his Jimmy (first lieutenant), a commissioned gunner whose dislike of us as a group was apparent from the day he first met us. In his eyes we were non-conformist. We questioned orders and expressed our disagreement when rules appeared unreasonable. We were not properly committed, as we were in for only a short term of service.

From conversations and email correspondence with coders of later intakes, we have concluded that acts of dissidence such as those described above were more the exception than the rule. Intercept work at Cuxhaven and Kiel was normally undertaken with a fair deal of enthusiasm, despite the 'beefs' and tedium. Ex Leading Coder Jack Rosenthal, wrote the 1992 Channel 4 TV drama, *Bye, Bye, Baby*. A meticulously accurate account of learning and using Russian in the Navy in the mid-1950s, it depicts fictional coders diligently scouring the radio airwaves in pursuit of their Soviet quarry, code-named *Albatross,* and rejoicing when they succeed.

Dicey intercept work at sea

Some men remember a very fast unmarked RN launch (probably a requisitioned German *schnell* boat), used for expeditions into the Baltic Sea. It was known regularly to carry a leading telegraphist who was a fluent Russian speaker, as well as the occasional coder. The nature of these missions was highly secret, prompting considerable speculation then and since. There were two possible, even likely, aims: close eavesdropping on communications between Soviet ships of the Baltic Fleet; and 'ferret' operations near or within Russian territorial waters. By the middle 1950s British and US planes had undertaken hundreds of patrolling missions along and across the borders of east European communist countries (some shot down for their pains). According to historian Richard Aldrich,[6] it was in the mid-1950s that Britain carried out some of its most intensive submarine surveillance operations into USSR territorial waters. Like the 'spy' planes, they were gathering 'elint' (electronic intelligence) such as the whereabouts of radar installations. Sometimes a speedy incursion was effected in order to cause panic in the local Soviet defence system thereby provoking unguarded voice communications for our Navy, Army and RAF monitors to intercept and record for eventual interpretation at GCHQ. It is not

---

6   Richard J Aldrich, *GCHQ*, pp 133-147.

fanciful to suggest, though we cannot be certain, that the *schnell* boats from Cuxhaven and Kiel were engaged in comparable actions.

In theory, however, national servicemen were not supposed to be employed on ferret operations. This may have been true in practice, too, but the Baltic trips undertaken by some of our colleagues raise doubts. In 1955 three coders volunteered to go on a Baltic mission. One of them, Arnold Bell, said he:

> … only did it for the extra money, to fund a holiday trip to Denmark. We had to parade buff naked, have all our clothing in the bag checked before getting dressed in normal working gear for coders, No. 8s. The listening post using VHF sets was below decks and when I asked the officer in charge where we were, or had been, was simply told it was none of my business, which was just to log any messages I picked up - all very secretive, on a 'need to know' basis. Briefed before setting off, we were told, if captured, to dump everything over the side - radios, recorders, tapes, code books etc - and just to give name, rank and number.

Gordon Clough, later to become a well known BBC Radio 4 producer, reporter and presenter, was stationed at Kiel in this period. His widow told Tony Cash that he had spoken to her of time spent 'bobbing up and down in a small boat in the Baltic'. The broadcaster Margaret Howard, who worked very closely for several years with Gordon on BBC Radio 4's *World this Weekend*, related his story that he had been involved in runs into Soviet territorial waters during his time in West Germany. He was not in uniform, she recalled him saying, but wore a Guernsey sweater. He told Margaret they were warned that if caught by the Soviets they would be disowned. Arnold Bell has no recollection of any similar warning.

Secrets and revelations – the *Isis* case

Prior to the transmission of Jack Rosenthal's TV play *Bye, Bye, Baby,* the public media carried almost no word of the radio intercept work of British forces in the period post World War II: the very existence of a network of military listening posts, working in collaboration with GCHQ, was itself a state secret. Yet, silence on the subject had been broken, some 34 years earlier, when in February 1958 two students at Oxford University, William Miller and Paul Thompson, both former coders, decided to go public with what they knew. They revealed hush-hush information in an article entitled 'Frontier Incidents – Exposure' in a special number of the undergraduate *Isis* magazine devoted to discussion of the Cold War and nuclear disarmament.[7] A key paragraph read:

> All along the frontier between east and west, from Iraq to the Baltic, perhaps farther, are monitoring stations, manned largely by national servicemen trained in Morse or Russian, avidly recording the least squeak from Russian transmitters – ships, tanks, aeroplanes, troops and control stations.

In passing, it should be pointed out that national servicemen in the Navy did not receive training in Morse. This was the province of telegraphists, who were all regular ratings. Provided the Morse signals being monitored were enciphered, i.e., only numbers were used, a telegraphist could record them accurately without a knowledge of Russian, as Morse codes for the numerals 0-9 are the same in any language.

William Miller was interviewed by the police some three weeks after *Isis* published the article. Committal proceedings began in May, by which time the national press had got in on the act. On 19 March, the one million-selling *News Chronicle* splashed the story on its front page with the banner headline 'SPY' PROBE AT OXFORD. It reprinted the offending paragraphs including the following:

> A plane 'loses' its way: while behind the frontier tape-recorders excitedly read the irritated exchanges of Russian pilots: and when the latter sometimes force the plane to land an international incident is created, and reported in the usual fashion.

In a moment of crisis irresponsibility of this kind could easily frighten the Russians into war.

We will never know whether the case would ever have come to court, had the story remained tucked away in *Isis*. However, the authorities probably made a tactical mistake. They allowed themselves to be provoked by what was a brief article, taking up only a half an A4 page, albeit including a striking photograph with the caption 'Mercedes-Benz Spy Boat'.[8] While the general public

---

7   'Frontier Incidents – Exposure', *Isis*, 26 February 1958, p 12 – the article was not signed.

8   Our thanks to Robin Pearce for drawing our attention to the court report

learned things they were not supposed to have heard about, the article certainly did not reveal anything new to the Soviets. Much later the *Guardian* referred to the government's prosecution of the case as taking 'a sledgehammer to crack a nut'.

William Miller, as sub-editor, and Paul Thompson, as author, were successfully charged under the Official Secrets Act of 'having in their possession secret official information to which they had access as persons who had been employed under Her Majesty [and of communicating] that information to ... a person other than one to whom they were authorised to communicate it'. The trial at the Old Bailey took place in July 1958. They were sentenced to three months in an open prison, of which they actually served one month.

If the authorities over-reacted, it is possible they were worried that more revelations of risky British incursions into Soviet waters and air-space would provide ammunition to the burgeoning Campaign for Nuclear Disarmament, launched only a few weeks earlier and attracting a great deal of attention by supporting the first protest march from Trafalgar Square to the Atomic Weapons Research Establishment at Aldermaston, near Reading.

In any event, the court case increased publicity for the article out of all proportion to its seriousness. The news had already spread in the USA to at least two minor provincial newspapers,[9] so perhaps the influence of the American government, or at least anxiety about American reactions to the security breach, could have entered into the equation. In this period the USA was taking a more aggressive stance than Britain towards the Soviet Union, and a firmer line on matters of domestic security. Miller and Thompson sincerely believed that the activities they revealed, especially those carried out near Soviet bloc frontiers, were dangerous enough to provoke the Soviets into military retaliation.

---

in the *Daily Telegraph*, 22 May 1958, in which a third undergraduate, Anthony Camacho, also an ex-coder special, is mentioned as the source of this photograph. It was taken from his college room by Miller, and he asked the latter not to publish it.

9   *Florence Times,* Florence, Alabama, 16 March 1958, and *Lewiston Evening Journal*, 18 March 1958.

FRONTIER INCIDENTS— EXPOSURE

THE doctrine of Western sincerity and the good fight against Russian wickedness is fostered in many little ways: and not the least of these is the misreporting of news. We wish to expose one variety of this. Frontier incidents are almost invariably reported as ferocious and unjust attacks by Russian fighters on innocent Western aircraft peacefully cruising well within their own frontiers. Sometimes it is conceded that the victim has lost its way. This is British understatement at its best. All along the frontier between east and west, from Iraq to the Baltic, perhaps farther, are monitoring stations, manned largely by National Servicemen trained in morse or Russian, avidly recording the least squeak from Russian transmitters— ships, tanks, aeroplanes, troops and control stations. It is believed, perhaps rightly, that this flagrant breach of the Geneva Convention can provide accurate estimates of the size and type of Russian armaments and troops, and the nature of their tactical methods.

In order to get this information the West has been willing to go to extraordinary lengths of deception. British Embassies usually contain monitoring spies. When the Fleet paid a 'goodwill' visit to Danzig in 1955 they were on board. And since the Russians do not always provide the required messages they are sometimes provoked.—A plane 'loses' its way; while behind the frontier tape recorders excitedly read the irritated exchanges of Russian pilots: and when the latter sometimes force the aeroplane to land an international incident is created, and reported in the usual fashion. The famous Lancaster bomber incident near Berlin was deliberately provoked in this way.

In a moment of crisis irresponsibility of this kind could well frighten the Russians into war. Certainly if Russian planes were to fly over American bases the American reply would be prompt. But there is no controlling the appetite of the statistical analysers at Cheltenham. Perhaps the best example of their activities is in the Baltic. After the war a

45. The 1958 *Isis* article which led to the imprisonment of former coders William Miller and Paul Thompson.

Mercedes-Benz Spy Boat

fleet of half-a-dozen exceedingly fast Mercedes-Benz tor-
pedo-type boats were built, and manned by sailors from
Hitler's navy, were sent out under English captains to
provoke and listen to the Russians. They would head
straight for the Russian Fleet at exercise and circle round
a battleship taking photographs. When they had succeeded in concentrating all the guns of the fleet and recorded enough messages they fled. When in Swedish
waters, contrary to all international conventions they flew
the Swedish flag. One British captain, who was suitably
equipped with a wooden leg which lent a certain glamour
to his Quixotic behaviour, so far exceeded the normal
practice, which was merely to enter Russian territorial
waters, as to go into Leningrad Harbour, and on another
occasion to land a small party in Russia. It is incredible
that this should have been allowed, but the irresponsibility bred and sheltered by the Official Secrets Act is
uncontrollable. In 1956 the new German Navy took over
the full control of these boats and are doubtless happily
continuing our own policy.

Aftermath of the *Isis* case

More than 70 former coders have contributed to this compilation of national service and Cold War reminiscences. Nearly all had to sign the Official Secrets Act (OSA) in connection with their Russian language activities. Not a single one has ever been informed that he was no longer bound by its terms. Five and more decades may have elapsed, but there appears to be no formal absolution from observing *omerta*.

As late as 1999-2000 John Drummond was sufficiently inhibited by the OSA to express the following thought when discussing in his autobiography the 1950s scheme to provide the armed forces with Russian linguists:

> In 1986 I took part in a radio documentary which was mysteriously withdrawn and never aired. The reason for all this seems to be a too literal interpretation of the Official Secrets Act ... So in what I write about the next two years of my life I will make no mention of the Navy.[10]

John was not alone in having this concern. Two of our ex-coder contributors invoked the Act as a reason for not divulging to us information at their disposal; a third worried that one of his emails might constitute a punishable breach. Perhaps all this anxiety sprang from recollections of the *Isis* trial of 1958.

Of a similar mind to the *Isis* dissidents was Bill Hetherington, who during national service, had come to the conclusion that our eavesdropping operations were immoral. On 10 May 1963 *Peace News* (circulation 12,000) carried an article entitled OFFICIAL SECRETS: MAN RENOUNCES UNDERTAKINGS. It recounted the story of former Leading Coder (Special) William Hetherington, now an activist in CND and 'leading member of the West Midlands Committee of 100', writing three days earlier to the Director of Naval Intelligence (DNI) renouncing undertakings under the Official Secrets Act he had made while on national service and reserve training between October 1952 and December 1957.

The article quotes Bill's admission that he signed relevant documents with misgivings:

> My doubts concerning the wisdom and morality of the undertaking I had made increased ... with my

10   John Drummond, *Tainted by Experience*, p 57.

abhorrence and disgust at the work in which I became involved.

A contemporary of William Miller and Paul Thompson at Oxford, Bill sympathised with their plight, and is quoted recalling what he terms the 'well-nigh totalitarian' verdict of Lord Chief Justice Goddard, the judge presiding over the case:

> 'It is not for young men employed in these matters to decide for themselves what is vital for the security of this country, and what secrets can be retained and what secrets are less valuable.' I felt, indeed, that there but for the grace of the devil, went I.

The *Peace News* article concludes with the final words from Bill's letter to the DNI:

> 'I hereby give you formal notice, Sir, that I ... reserve unto myself the right to publish whensoever, wheresoever, howsoever, and to whomsoever my conscience shall at any time dictate all or any part of any information or material that may have come or may in future come to me by virtue of the undertakings aforementioned.
>
> In taking this unilateral action I do not only wish to clear my own conscience, for that in itself might be construed as too selfish a motive, but to commend it as an appropriate course for all in like cases, including yourself.'[11]

A reply from the DNI was not forthcoming. Intriguingly, Bill comes from a family with strong Naval connections going, as he himself says:

> ... literally back to Nelson - my approximately four times great grandfather served as the admiral's bo'sun.

We do not imagine that Admiral Nelson would have approved the action of his bo'sun's distant descendant. Sadly, we have no idea what another admiral, the DNI -Vice-Admiral Sir Norman Egbert

---

11 *Peace News*, 10 May 1963, p 12. The period mentioned in the letter reflects the requirement for coders to renew OSA undertakings at the beginning of each stint of reserve service. Bill's last stint was in December 1957. In common with other coders he was subsequently informed of retention in the RNSR for a further ten years, and sent a travel warrant to be used for recall in the event of an emergency. Bill fulfilled the implied intention to reveal information about his work as a coder in a further article in *Peace News*, 'Open Secrets - confessions of a siginter', 25 August, 1978.

Denning, KBE, CB, made of Bill's *cri de coeur*, assuming it even crossed his desk. Sir Norman retired from the Navy in 1967, and was appointed Secretary of the Defence Press and Broadcasting Committee, known popularly as the D Notice Committee, (an essentially advisory body without punitive powers), which informs the media whether any proposed article or broadcast could endanger national security. Editors are entitled to ignore a D notice, but do so at their peril, since they may have to prove in court that publication or transmission did not wreak the feared damage. Sir Norman was in post for five years, during which time there appear to have been no media breaches of the OSA in relation to our sigint work. The *Isis* case ensured we kept our heads below the parapet. This remained the situation for a further 20 years.

TV playwright, Jack Rosenthal, might have made a very good stab at divining, if only in a fictional scene, the DNI's reaction to Bill Hetherington's cheeky letter abjuring the OSA. Jack's Channel 4 play *Bye, Bye, Baby*, a not entirely irreverent depiction of life in the Navy, derives a fair amount of its humour from the tensions between men on different rungs of the hierarchical ladder. The hero, Leo, is, like Jack, a Jewish northerner and university graduate with bolshie leanings. In her book on Jack's work for TV over a 36-year period, Professor Sue Vice refers to the dramatist's:

> … customary interest in power relations and authority in the workplace …[12]

Most of us who saw the play were impressed by how accurately Jack caught the nuances of class difference as much as those of rank. Some were quite startled by the vivid watchroom scenes disclosing to the world at large what had hitherto remained a state secret. One former coder actually wrote to Jack enquiring:

> Are you in fact still at liberty? I expect to hear news of your arrest at any moment, following this monumental breach of national security.

Sue Vice quotes this passage in her book on Jack's TV work and comments:

> This letter highlights the fact that *Bye, Bye, Baby*, a fictional film, strove for accuracy in terms of period and detail – the production company employed a naval consultant and another who had been through National

---

12   Sue Vice, *Jack Rosenthal*, p 68.

Service in the mid-1950s while Rosenthal himself drew upon, for instance, a *Dictionary of Dockyard Language*, a naval 'Drinks Guide to Kiel', and material on Russian phrases which he had kept since 1955. Yet, ironically, it was on the ground of its attention to period detail that the film was judged by lawyers to be a potential security risk which a production company's insurers might not want to take on.

Sue stated that in 1992 Jack was no longer bound by the OSA, which led Tony Cash to write to her expressing his admiration for the book but wanting to raise a tiny cavil about this assertion:

'Like all former coders special, I too signed the OSA, but have never been absolved from observing it. As an experienced TV Producer/Director myself, I can easily imagine the kind of conversation on this topic Jack may have had to assuage the apprehensions of wary lawyers. He could well have represented it to them that they had no reason to fear any repercussions in connection with a possible breach of the Act because it no longer applied to him (anything to get them off his back).'

Jack died in 2004. Fittingly, the Rosenthal archive went to the University of Sheffield where he had obtained his degree in English. The letter quoted above is held in the University Library Special Collections Department, along with draft versions of the screen-play for *Bye, Bye, Baby*, other correspondence and an audio tape of a small choir singing Russian folk-songs. It is evident from the documents held in Sheffield that lawyers concluded there was no need to seek clearance from the Ministry of Defence for the script to proceed into production. In the view of the MoD, coders special were said to be communication ratings, not members of the security and intelligence services, from whom a stricter form of *omerta* might apply. The OSA would only 'bite' (the term used by the lawyers) if the revelations were 'damaging'.[13]

---

13 The legal opinion requires some clarification: the OSAs do not make the distinction mentioned, or refer to national security. However, any OSA prosecution must be personally authorised by the Attorney General, who has discretion as to whether it is in the public interest, taking into account a range of factors.

By 1992, when *Bye, Bye, Baby* was transmitted, the Cold War was over, the USSR having disintegrated the previous year. It would have been exceptionally difficult to prove in court that Jack's play endangered national security with scenes such as that described in Jack's *An Autobiography in Six Acts* as an extract from the screen-play:[14]

INT WATCHROOM – HMS ROYAL ALBERT – CUXHAVEN - DAY - 1954

The walls are covered with maps of the Baltic and North Sea, charts of Soviet ships and submarines, and blackboards bearing Russian call signs.

Leading coder specials are seated three to a row at four benches of bays. Each of them is operating a B40 radio receiver and Ferrograph tape recorder. Before them are logging pads and pencils. They wear bulky headphones.

They've been on watch for almost four hours, swivelling their tuning dials through the manic wavebands, befuddled by listening to, recording and logging Russian naval messages, through a welter of Polish weather forecasts, atmospherics, interference and Eartha Kitt.

A midshipman is explaining watchroom procedure to Leo's group of new-boy coders.

MIDSHIPMAN

… one man per bay in four-hour watches, 24 hours a day, covering all Soviet radio transmissions from sea and air centred on the Baltic and North Sea.

(*beat*)

If you want a reason why, suffice it to say the Soviet Navy has 550 submarines and we have three. And we chaps, you and me, are the only ones stopping them marching down Oxford Street.

LEO

The submarines?

MIDSHIPMAN

Sorry?

---

14   Jack Rosenthal, *An Autobiography in Six Acts*, p 94.

Unfortunately, at the time of writing, there are no commercially available videos of *Bye, Bye, Baby*, though, given the general consensus about the high quality of Jack's TV dramas, we hope that sooner or later this lack may be remedied. In the meantime, readers and researchers wanting to see the play must contact the Sheffield University Library's Special Collections Department to negotiate a viewing.

220

CH 10
INNOCENTS ABROAD

В ЧУЖОЙ МОНАСТЫРЬ СО СВОИМ УСТАВОМ НЕ ХОДЯТ[1]
(Russian saying – 'When in Rome, do as the Romans do')

In comparison with students of the 1950s, today's eighteen to twenty-one-year olds are seasoned travellers. The 70-odd contributors to this publication are now in their eighth or ninth decade. A few may have visited France on school visits or exchanges, but most of what we knew about foreign countries was derived from newspapers, books and movies. In the early 1950s, television, by no means universal, was starting to give some of us an inkling what else was out there. For a national serviceman to be posted abroad was the nearest he got to having a gap year.

The Coder Special division was created expressly to monitor USSR military radio traffic, primarily in West Germany. For the overwhelming majority of coders this proved to be our eventual destination. Located on the North and Baltic Seas, Cuxhaven, and later Kiel, were the ports selected for us to eavesdrop on the Soviet fleet operating in those waters.

The journey out

There was no question of our being flown anywhere, and not just because flights were expensive: airlines in the 1950s were not geared to transport large numbers of people. Military ships and trains, both commanded by the Army, regularly conveyed men of all three armed forces, as required, to and from the British occupation zone, roughly the northern third of West Germany. The route to either of our listening posts was by ship from Harwich to the Hook of Holland, thence by train to Hamburg and onwards. The overnight sea voyage normally took no longer than seven or eight hours, though Tony Cash recalls a much more protracted crossing in

---

1   More literally, 'Follow the rules of the monastery you're in'.

46. View of Cuxhaven from Deichstrasse bridge. Courtesy D Mills.

the spring of 1954 with other coders, including his friend, guitarist Malcolm Brown:

> Just outside the Dutch port, the boat ran into nameless difficulties. A tannoy announcement told us we might have to wait a further three hours before pulling alongside. We were all quite hungry by now, and the thought of a wait that long before breakfast, scheduled ashore, was pretty discouraging. We could hear a great deal of threatful muttering from the sailors, soldiers and airmen overcrowding the passenger decks. Malcolm and I got our instruments out and began to play, about the same time that the Skipper decided to issue the ship's hard tack. To this day I still wonder which was the more effective in averting a mutiny - the tough, old biscuits or our crude, old Dixieland jazz.

Cuxhaven, on the mouth of the Elbe

Cuxhaven was fortunate in having largely escaped the attention of the Allied bombers which had all but obliterated nearby Hamburg, Lübeck and Kiel. The town could not have been considered a significant target, since its principal contribution to the German war effort was to host a mine-sweeping school. Crews and vessels of the local *Kriegsmarine* (literally, 'war navy'), as our German counterpart was called, continued mine-sweeping for some time after the cessation of hostilities, but under British supervision; by the time the first coders arrived in 1953 British involvement had ceased.

In the early 1950s the two Germanies (East and West) were still demilitarised in accordance with the agreement signed in 1945 by the four occupying powers, France, UK, USA and the USSR; the East Germans, though, had a large and very martial-looking police force. West Germany had been allowed to develop coast guard units and armed border police: Coders at Cuxhaven could see men from these outfits drilling beyond the perimeter of our base, and many of us suspected they were actually an embryonic military force. In May 1955, ten years after the war's end, West Germany was recognised as a sovereign state, and joined NATO (resident Allied troops, including coders, becoming guests rather than occupiers) The following November it established its own armed forces, collectively known as the *Bundeswehr*.

224

47. View of the fishing harbour at Cuxhaven in 1954. Courtesy D Mills.

48. Leading coder (specials) in No 8 working uniforms (with one exception)
outside the living accommodation of HMS *Royal Albert* in the winter of
1953-4. Courtesy R Pearce.

In the two to three years coders operated in Cuxhaven, the town had a population of around 40,000, many people dependent on the fishing industry for a living. The strongest enduring memory many of us have of Cuxhaven is the pungent, all-pervading, permanent reek of fish - not, of course, freshly caught, but being processed into glue, or fishmeal for animal feed. An auspicious wind may have helped Dennis Mills form a more favourable first impression:

> Cuxhaven was quite a nice drafting, the Hitler-period barracks more comfortable than anything most of us had so far experienced (Bodmin and Coulsdon were pretty dreadful), and the food livened up a lot when our numbers rose to a point enabling the Purser to dispense with BAOR[2] rations. The town had some pleasant coffee shops, a good American library, at least one small but good night club - where visiting musicians could sit in - an all-important camera shop, and a cinema.

How much we enjoyed being in Cuxhaven might depend on the season of year. John Griffiths would have preferred any other time to be there:

> Of my posting to Cuxhaven, only three things remain clear; the stink of fish, the beauty of local girl Antje von der Fecht, and that it was bloody cold. Not only could you walk across the frozen water of the harbour, but the temperature was so low that in the time it took to traverse the two hundred yards from canteen to barrack block the dregs in my enamel mug had already become an almost solid icy slush. I had hated the cold all my life since being made, as a small boy, to stand pointlessly about in it. Cuxhaven so confirmed my dislike that I vowed there and then never to travel in any but hot countries or, if in cold, such as Iceland and Russia, only at their warmest times of year. This is one of the relatively few vows I have managed to keep.

Following long-standing naval tradition, the Cuxhaven shore establishment (former *Kriegsmarine* barracks) in which we were billeted was named, ship-like, HMS *Royal Albert*. Just outside the main block stood a rather fine slightly larger-than-life statue of a capless German sailor about to cast a cable. Had it not been for his turned-up trouser bottoms, he might have been mistaken for a British

---

2   British Army of the Rhine

49. Memorial to a German sailor at HMS *Royal Albert* Cuxhaven.
Courtesy D Mills.

matelot - at least, in the eyes of coders who had only ever worn fore-and-aft uniform. Living quarters were modern and clean, with spacious rooms, marble floors and fine kitchens, but not obviously foreign. The loos, though, had an entirely novel feature: the pans were not the standard ovoid receptacles we were used to, but bowls with the back sloping down to form a shelf, which stretched half-way across. We wondered whether, on top of all the usual military tribulations, German sailors had been subjected to stool inspection.

Acquiring German

Meditating on the fate of the previous inhabitants of the site was not, it has to be said, our habit, though memories of the recent war were sufficiently acute to make us ever conscious we were part of an occupying force and might be resented by the townsfolk. Speaking German was the obvious way to establish good relations. Some coders, including Dennis Mills, took advantage of free German lessons given at the base by the principal of the town's commercial school:

> He invited us there to give conversation lessons to
> the students, and we were soon fraternising, myself

with Helga Wollenich. When I went back to do reserve training in 1955, Helga asked me to take her to see *The Cruel Sea*. I had already seen it twice and didn't relish sitting among several hundred Germans to watch it again. Fortunately, the blue passage in which matelots were fishing Germans out of the sea, and simultaneously giving vent to spleen, had been excised, and the evening passed off without incident.

Tony Cash took a few lessons in the language, but confesses to having mixed feelings about doing so:

> Unlike the sounds of Russian, which I always found very pleasurable to hear and speak, German seemed positively ugly, though not at all difficult to pronounce. I soon became aware that there were two versions of German spoken in Cuxhaven. This was borne in on me when one night I visited the local night club to play my clarinet with the dance band. When I got off the stand a fanciable girl beckoned and said, 'Come here', in an accent that sounded vaguely Yorkshire. When I replied in English, she didn't understand a word, and my German was insufficient to allow much progress in the relationship, though I managed to buy her a drink. Only later did I realise she was speaking *Plattdeutsch* or Low German, a form of the language then fairly common in the north, and nearer to English than *Hochdeutsch*, standard German.

Graham Young made greater progress learning German than Tony Cash, thanks partly to a working relationship with a former naval officer of the *Kriegsmarine*:

> I did the first hour of lessons, and the next day the Divisional Chief Petty Officer we had had foisted on us - Hinton, a torpedo-gunner - heard me using my halting German on the charlady for our floor. She was very thin, and moved so quickly she was known to us as 'The Galloping Hairpin'. I was trying to persuade her to iron some white shirts, when along came CPO Hinton and said, 'You don't need German lessons, but the PC3 needs a sweeper.' From then on I spent three mornings out of four washing the deck of the boat and generally cleaning her. I didn't lose on the deal in the end, because on one of these mornings there came along a member of the coastal protection police service. He claimed to be an ex two-and-a-

half [lieutenant-commander] and he'd come to run the engine and check the batteries. These done and my ostentatious deck-swabbing finished, we made ourselves coffee and chatted, half in English, half in German. And the PC3 was a good place to sleep, at the risk of being caught by Hinton, after a heavy night in the *Treffpunkt*.

50. The PC3 ship before renovation. Courtesy David Wills.

PC3 stood for Patrol Craft 3, which was moored in the harbour at the Cuxhaven base. It was rumoured she had been used during the war by the Grand Admiral (German equivalent of Admiral of the Fleet) in charge of the naval base at Kiel.

Literally, 'Meeting Place', the *Treffpunkt* was a night club with live music and dancing. A popular number there in those days was *Blueberry Hill* (made famous by Louis Armstrong). Dancers would foxtrot to it as readily as hop around to another hit of the day, a German polka, *Ach, Anneliese, ach, Anneliese, warum bist du böse auf mich?* ('Oh, Anneliese, oh, Anneliese, why are you angry with me? You're the only one I ever loved.'). Phrases from song lyrics, along with public announcements at rail stations, fleshed out the little stock of German expressions gleaned from war films we had seen as kids.

Finding the shortest way back to base after a boozy night out might be problematic, if you lacked the German to enquire the way. Fortunately, visibility was nearly always good, and bearings could be gauged from the *Wasserturm*, a landmark water tower, a splendid, late nineteenth century red brick structure dominating the town. Should you feel peckish *en route* there were always stalls selling *Bratwurst* and *Bockwurst*, variously spiced sausages, served in rolls with a sweetish dark mustard, if desired. We reckoned they predated American hot dogs by several centuries.

The food items that most enthused us were the locally produced *Kuchen* (tarts and gateaux) served in cafés in the late afternoon to accompany excellent *Kaffee*. A special favourite was *Ananastorte*, a pineapple sponge cake steeped in cream.

Coders and Cuxhaven citizenry

Our attitude towards the Germans was ambivalent. Those with whom we had dealings were friendly enough, but we had all lived through the Second World War and the appalling disclosures that followed it, including the liberation of the concentration camps and the later Nuremberg trials of Nazi war criminals. We had been brought up to regard Germans as 'The Enemy', and had lived through the Blitz, the V1 and V2 rockets, and the sinking of British ships by U-boats. We knew there was a substantial army of occupation in Germany, and we were regarded as part of it. Above all, we were uncertain how German people might take to us, but we were aware from history studies at school that a victorious army occupying any country is felt as a hateful burden by the occupied citizens; we had reason to expect the worst. Some of us had studied German at school or university, and were familiar with German philosophy, poetry and literature. The headmaster of Mike Gerrard's school in north London would not permit the teaching of German for several years after the war. As a result, although Mike studied languages, they were effectively confined to Latin and French, and it was only in his final year that a teacher was engaged for German studies, which had been confined to a limited scientific German course for students of physics and chemistry hoping to continue at university.

Our ambivalence to Germany and the Germans was nowhere expressed more starkly than by Jack Rosenthal in his TV play *Bye Bye, Baby*. A coder, Jewish like Jack, is off duty, travelling by train from Cuxhaven to Hamburg, and on the way is teased by some children. At one point he asks a young girl, 'What did your daddy do in the war?' to which she replies simply, '*Er starb*' ('He died'). Germans were Hitler's victims, too.

In Cuxhaven no one tried to discourage meetings with the local people, though we were warned often enough that we must not discuss with them, or even inadvertently let slip, the nature of our work. They were within easy reach and, by and large, willing to consort with us. Some inhabitants had jobs on base, but occasionally a specialist from the town might be required to deal with a problem. Lionel Franklyn recalls what happened when the teleprinter used in the watchroom to send data to GCHQ in Cheltenham broke down:

> The Navy could not help, nor could the American base. So we resorted to a German post office engineer. All pictures of Soviet warships were covered up, but he showed no curiosity, looking straight ahead between the lines of radio sets. But he did fix the teleprinter.

The Germans were surprisingly friendly and the local photo shop sold me an excellent Agfa Silette on credit. I paid it off quickly.

Bill Hetherington volunteered to help with groups of children at a youth centre, *Haus der Jugend*:

> This led to going camping in the Hunsrück with one group, and, unexpectedly, qualifying for a modest payment, as a helper, by the German government; and being invited by parents to meals etc. It became clear that some of the men were simply waiting for the day when we of the BAOR would march into the Soviet Zone (as it effectively still was in 1954) and 'recover' it. I responded non-committally, and changed the subject as soon as I could. Other home visits avoided any political slant, the parents clearly being keen to bring their children up to regard the British as friends.

Sporting activities

For a variety of obvious reasons the British armed forces have for generations attached great importance to sport. Talented footballers, rugby players and athletes have always been especially prized, and often excused onerous chores so that they can participate in significant competitions. A further stimulus to sport in West Germany was the opportunity it offered for cementing relations with host populations. Lawrie Douglas played for the *Royal Albert* Football XI:

> We were somewhat taken aback when we first met local teams. They wore hairnets or bands to keep their hair in place, and turned out in bright red or green shorts and lightweight cut-away boots. We wore long shorts, black or white, long socks and boots over the ankle - and no hairnets. Their appearance did not put us off because we lost only one game in the year I was there, 1955. The locals turned out in numbers, hoping to beat the English, and were very vocal in their support, making, we thought, a pretty hostile atmosphere. But after the games, they made sure we drained the glass boot of Märzen beer; at least they could laugh at us getting drunk. One of our coders, Colin Jones, was an outstanding player, a schoolboy international, I think, and he played for a local German league club. Most of our matches were against German teams, but we also took on visiting ships' teams from the Netherlands, Denmark and the RN.

Lawrie also played in a RN Northern Europe six-a-side football competition. His team, Coders B, with future TV dramatist Jack Rosenthal on board, won the tournament. Lawrie also played for a more select team, when the Elbe Squadron joined the Marines Rhine Squadron, HMS *Royal Prince*, Krefeld, to take part in an annual outing to show the flag in the Netherlands in honour of Queen Juliana's birthday. He travelled on a former pleasure steam yacht, also called *Royal Albert*:

> We sailed though the Frisian Islands, with fairy tale names Wangerooge, Spiekroog and Langeoog. I had read Erskine Childers's *The Riddle of the Sands,* which in 1903 described the islands as the base to launch an attack on our undefended east coast. I was given the opportunity to steer the ship for a while, under the supervision of AB Brown; he told me that his former ship, HMS *Birmingham,* had been used in filming *The Battle of the River Plate*, about the scuttling of the German pocket battleship *Admiral Graf Spee* in 1939. After exercises we docked in Den Helder, the main port of the Dutch Navy. The Rhine and Elbe Squadron teams played a match, and a joint team was selected to play against Dutch teams. The first was against the Dutch Navy side there. They won easily, and their

centre forward employed the tactic of standing on the goal line in front of our goalkeeper; this tactic was later used by Jack Charlton in his Leeds and England days.

Of all coders who could call themselves sportsmen, undoubtedly the greatest was Carwyn James. He was at Cuxhaven in 1954 at the same time as Ian Wooldridge, later to be hailed as one of the most revered of sports journalists. In the *Daily Mail* in 2001 Ian described occasions in his 'abysmal rugby career' when he had played with Carwyn against German-based Army and RAF XVs:

> Selection for the Navy team was almost inevitable if you were half fit and reasonably sober. We had only about 120 Navy men in Germany at the time, whereas the Army and RAF could choose from minimally 60,000 each. We were annihilated in both games, though I still have fond memories of the nurses in the RAF Hospital, Rostrup, where I finished up with a broken leg. So where was the magic in these grotesque encounters? Simply playing alongside Carwyn James, the greatest coach Wales has ever had and so intelligent and innovative that many rate him the best the world has ever seen.
>
> He played only twice for Wales, because the incomparable Cliff Morgan was resident fly half, but merely to be on the same pitch as Carwyn was to glimpse a game we didn't remotely understand.[3]

Cultural byways

One of the most remarkable manifestations of West Germany's post-war renaissance was the priority given to rebuilding shattered monuments, whether religious or secular, not only cathedrals and churches, but also playhouses and concert halls. By 1954 drama for a paying public was thriving in Cuxhaven, as Laidon Alexander discovered:

> I saw a performance of *Waiting for Godot* in German in a small theatre, two years, as it turned out, before it was performed at the *Players' Theatre* in London, and was thrilled. With hindsight, this, fewer than ten years since the end of the war, was impressive.

---

3   *Daily Mail* online, 17 March 2001.

Few coders could claim much knowledge of German theatre, and most were probably indifferent. But all of us would have known at least the names, if not many actual works, of the great composers of the German-speaking world. Goethe and Schiller may not have resonated; Mozart and Beethoven certainly did. One of our number could claim special expertise in this domain. On the train bringing him to Cuxhaven, Leading Coder Gerald Seaman had been delighted to read the sign *BUXTEHUDE* on one of the stations not far from his destination. Not many other members of his contingent would have realised that was the name of a very fine composer, highly respected in his lifetime by J S Bach. Then, Gerald was a music scholar with a place at Keble College, Oxford (Keble also took three other coders/interpreters in 1954); he eventually won a professorship, specialising in Russian instrumental and vocal works. The time he spent in Cuxhaven in 1954 was not lacking in musical events:

> The Naval barracks chapel had an excellent piano, and I spent many happy hours accompanying a fellow coder special, Mick Taylor, who sang *Lieder* in German with great sympathy and understanding. Although it was still only nine years after the war, the local Cuxhaven inhabitants were quite well disposed to the young *Matrosen*, and I was invited to join both the Male Voice Choir (*Männerchor*) and the Young People's Choir (*Knabenchor*). The Male Voice Choir had an elaborate initiation ceremony, complete with many songs of *Freundschaft* and *Brüderschaft* (friendship and brotherhood), all accompanied by generous drafts of lager. The attitude of the Young People's Choir towards Bach was particularly striking, with an element of deep devotion and reverence. My association with the choirs did much to improve my knowledge of German.

Fully six years before the Beatles famously began to learn their trade in Hamburg, that city was welcoming British jazz musicians. Tony Cash recalls a visit in the spring of 1954 to the *New Orleans Bierbar,* where the Ken Colyer jazz band had a residency:

> I was delighted to discover an old mate, Diz Disley, playing guitar with the band. He had been lodging at my home in Leeds while a student at the local College of Art, and I had learned a lot from him, most importantly, perhaps, that great jazz is not the exclusive preserve of major American cities. It was

234

A 108668

BRITISH FORCES MILITARY TRAIN DUTY TICKET
Britische Streitkräfte Militärzug-Dienstfahrkarte
Dienst Vervoer Bewijs voor Britse Militaire Trein

Valid for...officers/officer status

16 (Sechzen) ....OR/OR status for travel

From.....HAMBURG.................To.....HOOK of HOLLAND.

Via.....BLUE..........(train) ON.....21 AUG 57.....(date)

* Returning on..(date)

H.M.S. "ROYAL CHARLOTTE"
Authority for journey

Signature of issuing authority
(Name and rank in BLOCK capitals)

J. N. WILTSHIRE.
MIDSHIPMAN. RNVR.

SHIPS OFFICE
Unit Stamp
1 9 AUG 1957
Date of Issue
H.M.S. "ROYAL CHARLOTTE"

* To be deleted if not required

P. T. O.

51. Travel warrant in English, German and Dutch issued in Kiel.
Courtesy D Mills.

Diz who had introduced me to the music of Django Reinhardt, on whose playing he had modelled his own.

Jazz fans in West Germany in those days had an advantage over us, in that American artists were allowed to perform there; union restrictions prevented them from doing so in Britain. My first serious introduction to modern jazz was hearing the Woody Herman big band in Bremerhaven, just down the coast from Cuxhaven. I took a shine to the playing of baritone saxophonist Serge Chaloff. Had cancer not got him three years later, at the tender age of 33, he might have vied with Gerry Mulligan and Duke Ellington's sideman, Harry Carney, for the top spot on his instrument.

Travelling further afield

Assuming they had kept their noses clean, all national servicemen were entitled to a stipulated amount of leave every year. A leading coder stationed in West Germany would receive a free return rail warrant to a chosen destination in that country or up to fifty miles beyond the border, except to one of the communist 'satellites'. Tony Cash wanted to spend his summer leave in Paris, so took a train into Belgium, from where he hitchhiked, arriving in the French capital just as the news was breaking that Dien Bien Phu had fallen to Vietnamese communist insurgents, bringing to an end French colonial rule. Tony remembers the fierce political arguments that raged on the streets and in the media about who was to blame for the debacle:

> I spent a lot of my two weeks' leave frequenting the fairly international hippy-type community which congregated nightly under the Pont Neuf, the oldest bridge on the Seine. Naturally, they were pretty hostile to the whole idea of French domination of Indo-China, and not too bothered about the loss of French prestige, however much they may have regretted the tragic loss of life. But the French art students and drop-outs I talked to had a more pressing concern: to avoid the fate which had overtaken me - how could they get out of having to do military service? I was not much help to them.

Bill Hetherington and John Saunders used their travel warrants to take them to Bavaria and over the border into Austria, where

236

52. Heligoland, main island. Courtesy D Mills.

they, too, hitchhiked, to reach Vienna, their ultimate destination. In 1954 the city was, like Berlin, a small island in the middle of a Soviet occupation zone; the country was not reunited until July the following year, when four-power occupation ended with Austria agreeing not to join NATO, in return for seeing the back of Soviet troops. So, to complete their journey, Bill and John had to cross the Iron Curtain. That was daredevil enough, but by strolling into still Soviet-occupied East Vienna, they placed themselves in potentially great danger, only marginally less from our own Naval authorities than from would-be Soviet interrogators. We all knew that no serving coder was allowed to visit eastern Europe (leaving out of account occasions when an individual was possibly sent on a secret mission into Soviet territorial waters). By now we had enough German to realise such an action was *streng verboten* (strictly forbidden).

In many ways Naval authority was not always that strict – the master-at-arms in Cuxhaven was much less of a disciplinarian than his regimental sergeant-major equivalent at Coulsdon, as Bill Hetherington can attest:

> On a return journey from leave, a German railway official gave me wrong directions about changing trains. By the time I was back on the right route I realised I could not meet the midnight deadline for reaching *Royal Albert*. A railway police inspector said I could save time if I cadged a lift from a US military train which regularly passed through the Bremerhaven US enclave, but over which he had no control. I presented my plea to the US sergeant in charge of the train, who simply said, 'Sure', and I boarded to find myself the only passenger. I eventually arrived at *Albert* seven hours 'adrift', and explained all to the master-at-arms, who simply said, 'That's a likely story. On your way'.

Heligoland on false pretences

When Dennis Mills returned from leave one Sunday, apparently hours adrift, he did not get off as lightly as Bill Hetherington. He had decided to visit Heligoland, in the North Sea, just under 40 miles north-west of Cuxhaven. An ardent life-long geography student, Dennis knew the name from weather forecasts and from special maps issued during WWII, on which allied military breakthroughs could

238

S. 247a (Established June, 1933, Revised Aug., 1934) H.M.S. *ROYAL ALBERT*

SURNAME
MILLS

PART *COMMUNICATIONS*

CHRISTIAN NAME(S)
DENNIS
RICHARD

PART OF
SHIP *WATCH KEEPER*

MESS *C16*

RATING *L/CODER*

G. or T. *T G*

RELIGION *C of E*

(997) Wt. 31778/D8110 200M 10/44 S.E.R. Ltd. Gp **671**.

S.247a (Established June, 1933, Revised Aug., 1934) H.M.S. *R. ALBERT*

SURNAME
FRANKLYN

PART *Commy*

CHRISTIAN NAME(S)
LIONEL FRANCIS

PART OF
SHIP *WATCH - KEEPER*

MESS *C 16*

RATING *L/COR*

G. or T. *G*

RELIGION *R C.*

T91-9936 Wt. 1347 110,000 6/52 W.H.H.Ltd.

53. Station cards used by Dennis Mills and Lionel Franklyn while they were based in Cuxhaven. 'G. or T.' on the bottom line indicated whether the bearer had opted to take his daily tot of grog or was teetotal. Dennis appears to have changed his mind. Courtesy D Mills.

be charted. He had formed a habit of jumping on buses or trains in strange places, just for the pleasure of extending his geographical knowledge in a practical way. But Heligoland (British, 1807 to 1890, when it was ceded to Germany in exchange for Zanzibar) was out of bounds to all BAOR personnel, with good reason: it was too dangerous, having been very heavily bombed in 1944-45 on account of German submarine pens hidden in the cliffs, and the RAF had subsequently used the principal island as a practice bombing range. In 1947 a major operation destroyed 6,700 tonnes of explosives at one go – the biggest ever non-nuclear explosion. When Heligoland was returned to West German authority in 1952, there still remained unexploded bombs and shells to be dealt with.

Not only was Dennis not permitted to visit Heligoland, it was going to be difficult for him to get there on the chosen Sunday. The ferry left the quay at 10.00 am, but the only 'liberty boat' available to catch it was the 9.00 am bus, designated for sole use by Roman Catholic seamen going to mass. Dennis had agreed to make the trip with his friend Lionel Franklyn, who happened to be Catholic. Every seaman had a station card with an indication of his religion: Dennis's read 'C of E'. On exiting base to go 'ashore', it was mandatory to hand in your card, which you would be sure to pick up on return, otherwise you would be liable to be deemed 'absent without leave' (AWOL):

> So, in our civvies we presented ourselves at the regulating office at 8.55. The duty petty officer waved us through without looking properly at the cards or asking questions. We found the ferry, and learned that we could only go on Dunen, as the rocky island was still too dangerous for civilians to visit. The dunes ran parallel to the long sides of this sandy island, with tough grasses here and there, rising to a maximum of perhaps 15 feet above sea level. Lionel and I walked from the landing stage and the restaurant to the opposite end of the island, and most of the Germans got on with their sunbathing. Eventually we decided to wander back, take a few photos, have some afternoon tea in the restaurant, and drift towards the landing stage. The return journey was uneventful, and we got back to *Royal Albert* about 8.00-9.00 pm. Then

the fun started. When we went into the regulating office to retrieve our liberty cards I was dismayed to see on the chalk board 'Ldg Coder Mills - report to the Officer of the Day'. Lionel was given his card and tiptoed gingerly out of sight. I was told that I was so many hours AWOL, that my card was being kept in the office, and that I was already on the list for the morrow's 'Captain's Defaulters'.

Seeing Dennis's card lodged in the office that Sunday morning, the PO taking over from his predecessor had concluded that Leading Coder Mills had gone on leave the previous day, and must now be several hours adrift, since, as a Protestant, he could not have used the 'Catholic' 'liberty boat'. When Dennis was duly brought before the Captain, he paid a price for his deception, though he escaped the theoretical possibility of being sent to Navy detention quarters:

> The Captain consulted his notes, and asked the PO, 'How long absent?' The number of hours determined the length of No. 11 punishment, and it came out as four days' stoppage of leave and four days' loss of pay, at 17s 6d a day - a significant sum at that date. Marvellously, the Captain did not ask where I had been, probably assuming that I was late back from a Hamburg brothel, and maybe he was too much a gentleman to go into details. Or maybe he was just busy. For the record, my service documents show that my conduct on *Royal Albert* was exemplary.

Unsere warmen Brüder[4]

In all the submissions we have obtained from former coders, only one tells of bullying. 'Ragging', believed to be common enough in boarding schools of the period, is also singularly missing from our archive, though there were instances of 'apple-pie' beds being occasionally inflicted on someone who had irritated his mates - hardly worth recording for posterity. It was, therefore, all the more surprising to receive this Cuxhaven reminiscence from John Griffiths:

> Although I had only had a couple of beers, on returning with a group of messmates from an evening in town I was undoubtedly slightly drunk. One of our

---

4   Literally, 'our warm brothers', slang expression for 'gay' in West Germany in the 1950s.

number was a markedly effeminate homosexual in the days when tolerance for such differences was minimal. As we walked noisily and boisterously through the yard for marshalling the trucks that carried the Cuxhaven trawlers' catch to Hamburg, it was noticed that a couple were almost full of reeking fish guts. As one man, we seized our unfortunate comrade and tossed him over the side of the nearest one. Spluttering and choking, he just managed to haul himself up to its rim, and we relented and pulled him out. He stank for days, but only gradually did it dawn on us that he could have drowned. That realisation convinced me of the folly of drinking to the point where sense and compassion vanish in a blur of alcohol fumes, and I have never done so again.

Tony Cash was on very friendly terms with both John Griffiths and the victim of this story:

It's hard to imagine that in 2012 he would have any objection to his name being divulged, but I've been unable to trace him after all these years, so feel free only to reveal his first name, Barry. Unusually for our group, he was a graduate, having studied economics at Hull University. Charming, kindly and witty, he made no effort to conceal his sexual orientation, exploiting it rather, as a subject for self-deprecating jokes. But you didn't always know when he was being serious: was he, as he often claimed, as ardent a train-spotter in his twenties as he had been when a boy? It wasn't difficult to believe that he loved railway stations: he liked to amuse us by doing a pompous imitation of a German announcer proclaiming: *Achtung, bitte Bahnsteig vier, bei der Abfahrt des Zuges* ('Attention please, the train is about to depart from platform four'). However distressed he may have been by the ordeal John Griffiths has described, he was almost certainly much more worried by the outcome of a scandal in England which came to a head in March 1954. That was when Lord Montagu of Beaulieu was sentenced to twelve months imprisonment for homosexual activities with a couple of young airmen. Barry told anyone who would listen that he was burning his private letters and urging close friends to do likewise, because he feared the case was a prelude to a purge of gays in the armed forces.

In the 1950s 'gay' was not a synonym for homosexual. Three years elapsed between the Lord Montagu conviction and the publication of the *Wolfenden Report,* recommending decriminalisation of same-sex activities between consenting adults in private. A further ten years passed before the recommendations became law: Barry had good reason to 'keep his head down', or, as the Russian saying goes, stay 'quieter than water, lower than grass'.

The phantom Coder Ford

Depending on current manpower needs, it was common for leading coders to work in various offices around the base when they were not required for regular watches. We were, after all, eminently equipped to do most clerical jobs the Navy could throw at us. This fact, coupled with a strong sense of solidarity among a large group of men who had been together day and night for a year and half, made it possible for us to wind up our superiors in a way few other national servicemen could have dreamed of doing. Furthermore, it was possible to do so with little fear of repercussions. Tony Cash has described one jape that came off to the satisfaction of its perpetrators:

> A petty officer reprimanded my friend Malcolm Brown for some apparent infraction, and bellowed, 'I want to know your name'. The reply, 'What for?' was misheard as 'FORD', so Leading Coder Ford was born. It was relatively easy to give this figment a more or less convincing identity. His name appeared in the master-at-arms' office on a list of those entitled to have a pet on base; a telegram was received congratulating him on the birth of twins back home in England; he was even on the payroll. He had a bed and locker in 16 Mess in School Block. Finally, a station card in his name was created and left one Friday evening in the master-at-arms' office, as per *QRs*, just as one watch had weekend leave. On the Monday morning, when leave-takers returned and collected their cards, Ldg Cdr Ford's was conspicuous by its presence, an hour or so after he should have been back in base. Increasingly threatening tannoy calls for Ford to 'muster at the double' at the master-at-arms' office produced no result. I recall how the following day a PO came round our messes to inquire about the missing sailor. We told him that, to the best of our knowledge, Ford had taken

his bedding over to the watch room to kip there. I suspect the truth could not have been long in dawning: certainly, it would not have been hard to confirm that there was no Ldg Cdr Ford. The last most of us heard of the affair was that the lieutenant-commander in charge of pay at Cuxhaven had received a terrific bollocking from his seniors at Krefeld (RN HQ in West Germany) for trying illegitimately to augment the moneys paid to his outfit.

Kiel – recollections and highlights

In the summer of 1955 the Navy's eavesdropping operation was moved lock, stock and barrel, from Cuxhaven to Kiel, some 67 miles north east, as the crow flies. With a population more than five times that of Cuxhaven's, Kiel had played a cardinal role in Nazi Germany's war effort, thanks to its ample facilities for building, harbouring and supplying fighting vessels, notably 'U-boats' (submarines). In consequence, the city had been subjected to sustained campaigns of Allied bombing, wreaking as much destruction as that suffered by Coventry, with which in 1947 Kiel was twinned. During the ten years between war's end and the arrival of the first coders Kiel was largely rebuilt, in a manner befitting the capital of *Land* Schleswig-Holstein.

The only coders who had an opportunity to compare Cuxhaven and Kiel were those who worked in the former during full-time national service and then had a stint or two of a fortnight's reserve training at the latter, as Tony Cash and Dennis Mills did. They agree that seedy, downtown Cuxhaven was no match for Kiel's swish, newly-built centre. HMS *Royal Charlotte*, the Kiel shore establishment where the newly-arrived coders were to ply their trade, was in no measure inferior to *Royal Albert*: former German barrack-room accommodation was on a par, and the canteen served excellent meals. German sailors, at least in these two northern ports, had obviously lived in far greater comfort than we were accustomed to in Britain, whether housed by the Navy, the Army or the RAF.

Kiel's military significance was engraved on the skyline by three monumental structures, which gave Alan Smith one of his first and most abiding impressions of the listening station on the city outskirts when he came there in late 1957:

54. The huge crane on the Kiel Canal used during WWII to hoick sea planes out of the water. Courtesy Alan Smith.

55. Laboe memorial at Kiel erected in memory of German dead naval personnel in the 1914-18 War. Old postcard, courtesy Alan Smith.

Behind our watchroom were the great steel doors of the hangars for the huge, long-distance Dornier flying boats of WWII, which used to fly far out over the Atlantic to detect Allied convoys. In front of our watchroom and on the edge of the Kiel Canal was the immense crane (at least 120 feet in height), with its long gantry used to pick the Dorniers out of the water and place them on the runway to be trundled into their hangars. On the opposite bank of the Kieler Fjord was the Laboe memorial, commemorating German sailors killed in WWI, a concrete conning tower standing erect 100 feet into the air. A German friend of later years, who had been in the Hitler Youth, immediately gave me, when I told him of Laboe, his version of an old seafaring expression:

> *Wann habt man Laboe in Sicht,*
>
> *Dann kennt er sein Sacksgewicht.*

which seems to mean:

> 'When a man can see Laboe
>
> His balls' weight he doth know.'

It refers, in other words, to the lonely seafarers' eagerness to meet ladies of the town.

Embarking for Kiel two years earlier than Alan, Paddy Heazell's thoughts were focused on his travelling companions:

> My intake of, by now, trained coders special arrived just as a quite harsh winter set in. We came by rail via the Hook of Holland, and I recall our sense of superiority, as somewhat spurious sailors, at having to travel on board an Army-run troopship. We were duly proud of being the 'senior service'.

Paddy was impressed by the HMS *Royal Charlotte* complex of modern and well-appointed buildings, a mammoth contrast, he thought, to Victoria Barracks in Portsmouth:

> On the quay was a giant crane, which we felt at times would have made a far more effective aerial than the ones we had to use. There was an airstrip on high ground behind the barracks with a roadway climbing the long slope to it. Great for tobogganing. *En route* to the watchroom building, which was airy and again modern, we would see the huddled shapes of our patrolling guards, armed and sinister. They were refugees from the Iron Curtain countries, and our

56. Kiel harbour. Courtesy D Mills.

consolation was that if they had no brief for us, they had even less for the Russians. I doubt they spoke any English, and I recall no case of any fraternisation with them. I rather fancy we were instructed not to attempt it.

Alan Smith spent a winter in Kiel, and found it as frigid as any at JSSL Crail in northern Scotland:

One memory is our march to the watchroom on frosty nights. We had to pass the barracks of the much reduced German navy, which retained only a few small boats for coastal protection. We did enjoy the perverse singing of Russian marching songs as we crunched through the snow. We thought it a small joke to remind them of the collective Allied victory. If they did hear us, I would imagine that either it annoyed them, as intended, or made them laugh at our puerile provocation. We rarely met these sailors, but generally had quite good relations with them. Also, I remember that on winter nights coders stored their hats inside the radio sets, such that they were already warm for the walk back to barracks.[5]

The buildings comprising *Royal Charlotte* were well insulated against the bitterest cold spells, and we suspected that the previous inhabitants had also benefited from much warmer uniforms than those issued to us. That our clothing was inadequate for these northern climes was brought vividly home to Gareth Mulloy on his first encounter with American sailors and their opulent lifestyle. A group of coders were invited to see a film at the US Navy base in Lübeck, some fifty miles south-east of Kiel:

The invitation was most welcome. We set out one very cold and frosty day, dressed in our skimpy No. 1 suits and serge-lined Burberrys. We were accompanied by a bearded Royal Navy PO tightly enclosed in his fore-and-aft brass-buttoned suit. He was short, portly, but dignified; he had no topcoat, but was impressive in his PO's rig. We were met by his American opposite number, dressed like an extra for a film on the Scott expedition to the South Pole, in a fur-lined anorak with hood tightly tied at the neck and only a small portion of face showing. We entered the American answer

---

5   Presumably the radio sets were Hammerlunds, with a hinged top, as noted by Bill Hetherington in chapter 9, describing the keeping warm of pasties - different times, different priorities.

This card is to be handed to the attendant at the NAAFI Canteen servicing the Unit named below and entitles the holder to purchase 60 (Sixty) Cigarettes.

Space for Unit stamp.   Form W. E. 578C

H.M.S. "ROYAL ALBERT"

2 0 MAY 1954

BASE SUPPLY OFFICER

57. A voucher entitling the bearer to receive duty free cigarettes.
Courtesy D Mills.

to the NAAFI, where I was blasted for the first time in my life by American central heating. Our base in *Royal Charlotte* had all the comfort expected by, and provided for, its original *Wehrmacht* dwellers. The contrast to the comfort of the American facilities was striking. The cinema would not have looked out of place in the National Theatre on London's South Bank. For a few hours we experienced the luxurious lifestyle of the American serviceman. I remember with affection the stoicism of our grizzled PO, compared with the apparently hedonistic self-indulgence of his over-dressed American counterpart, when we went back into the reality of a Baltic winter. I cannot remember the film, but the hospitality was all-American and generous. I think we also had a dance arranged, where we were able to get fleetingly close to young German women. On the other hand, it was alcohol-free. Afterwards we had time for a glass of Löwenbrau beer and a visit to the beautiful medieval town of Lübeck, with its stolid twin towers marking the city gate.

Money-making opportunities

While abroad, we were entitled to buy our monthly ration of duty-free tobacco, just like any other sailor back home, but it was intended for our exclusively personal consumption. Severe sanctions could be imposed on anyone caught trading or facilitating the sale of what, for a small number of coders, became a form of currency. It was well known that there were people in Kiel willing to pay a premium in Deutschmarks (DM) for good quality British cigarettes, like Benson and Hedges. Alan Smith has told us in detail about his illegitimate earnings:

> Trading the contraband was very easy, since most of the service personnel on our station were German civilians willing to traffic the materials they obtained from us to their clients in the local populace. Rationing was formalised by issuing cards of A4 size and perforated into small squares, each line of squares representing a specified week's ration. We could spend them when we chose, but they expired after, I think, three months. A fellow coder and I valued the two-week visits of reservists, because they were allotted a full three-month card, with large crosses in indelible

pencil through the perforated squares before and after the period of their visit. They would, of course, spend the coupons to take home their supply of tobacco, but on departing for the UK they usually threw away the cancelled portions of their coupon sheet. My oppo and I made a point of immediately scouring the waste bins of the reservist mess rooms before any German cleaners appeared. We gathered the 'waste' coupons and clipped out any not touched by the indelible pencil, used them for buying duty-free cigarettes, and then sold them for Deutschmarks, thus making quite a substantial but illicit addition to our wages.

It is not the purpose of this book to bring elderly people to belated justice for misdemeanours of this kind, but equally it is safe to say that Naval regulations on smuggling appear to have been honoured more in the breach than the observance and, given the low pay for which people of high intelligence and ingenuity worked, this is scarcely surprising.[6]

Gareth Mulloy, to this day a close friend of Alan Smith, had a substantial reason for wanting extra money:

By 1957 West Germany had regained the reputation of the world's number one manufacturer of cameras. My photographic experience until then had been limited to my parents' Kodak Brownie and rare access to the school dark room. In Kiel I had set my sights on the acquisition of a Voigtländer Vito B camera. Even on a killick's pay this was beyond my means. Then I heard of the *Bludspendzentrale*. Here you could donate your blood, and get money and a glass of a particular *Verschnitt* (blend, but we called it 'fishnet') of brandy, and a piece of *Wurst mit Brötchen* [sausage and bread roll], if you feigned faintness. You were allowed

6 'Service tobacco may be taken up by officers and men on an individual monthly scale promulgated by *Admiralty Fleet Order*. It is issued, in the forms of pipe tobacco, in half-lb tins, or as made-up cigarettes, or as leaf tobacco, sold loose. Service tobacco is duty-free, as also are manufactured tobacco and cigarettes … and it must be understood that this is a very valuable concession which may be withdrawn if abused. The value of this concession has increased enormously of recent years and every single case of evasion of duty is another argument for its withdrawal. It cannot therefore be emphasised too strongly that *duty-free tobacco is for personal consumption of those to whom it is issued, and it is not allowed to be disposed of to any other person.*' *Naval Rating's Handbook*, 1951, pp 160-161 (emphasis in original).

to donate once every three months. That meant the chance of two visits, together worth 100 DM; I needed 150 DM for my camera. So I gave blood three times, lying about the intervals between donations. I also had to declare that I had abstained from alcohol for the preceding 24 hours. That was impossible, unless I were to give up my 'tot', so I lied again. Thus was I able to buy my first camera.[7]

Christmas shenanigans and clashes with authorities

Most men in the peacetime armed forces could normally expect to have leave at Christmas time. The watchrooms at listening stations such as Kiel, however, needed to be manned round the clock, regardless of season. Christmas 1958 was no exception. Having the festive lunch served to you by the officers was no compensation for missing out on your annual family gathering back home. Nor would it lighten your mood to be called upon to provide pre-Christmas entertainment for visiting NATO admirals when you had little dramatic skill or experience - the lot which befell Alan Smith and his colleagues that year:

> We were having great difficulty to imagine how to produce this major evening, but by great good fortune a group of Cambridge undergraduate reservists came during their Christmas vac. I have a vague memory that they were part of the Footlights group there. They quickly took charge of our pathetic efforts and dragooned us into performing the most ludicrously stupid small sketches (presumably an early example of the new UK satire and 'theatre of the absurd'). Eventually the great evening arrived with a glitter of much gold braid in the front row, and we performed our silly routines, which left the senior officers unsmiling and critical, but enthused the performers, all high on seasonal drinks.

Following the show, the cast and friends took themselves off to the local pub, which also served as a dance-hall. There they put on their 'preposterous theatre routines', which happened to involve cross-dressing. Gareth Mulloy was there, and takes up the story:

---

7   During their time at RAF Wythall some coders responded to an invitation to donate to the British blood transfusion service, a mobile facility visiting the camp for the purpose. In accordance with British practice, no payment was made other than tea or coffee and a biscuit.

Despite Berlin's reputation for this sort of behaviour in pre-Nazi times, it did not go down well with the local lads of the Prieser Strand. More oil was poured on troubled water when they accused us of killing their fathers. Some of us reciprocated with similar allegations. The result was a fight which was not very violent but unpleasant.

For Alan it was:

... the biggest brawl of my national service, and was only terminated by a major intervention of the Kiel police. I report with pride that the coders acquitted themselves quite well.

Alan Smith and Gareth Mulloy's long-lasting friendship may be just as much the consequence of their frequently getting into scrapes together as of shared interests. Gareth still distinctly remembers the pain of the loss of camaraderie with Alan and other coders when he returned to his Civil Service job in September 1958. One particular escapade on an outing from Kiel has remained lodged in his memory:

We were given a long weekend leave (Friday evening to Monday morning), which Alan and I decided to use for a trip to Copenhagen. This was aborted because I found myself 'in the rattle'[8] for nipping ashore in uniform to change a watch strap - a heinous offence. To avoid clashes with the local population, we always had to wear civilian clothes outside barracks. I was caught *in flagrante delicto* by our unloved First Lieutenant, who saw me from his car while driving home for lunch. The punishment was 24 hours stoppage of leave, which curtailed our Danish trip to a short stay in Sønderborg, just north of the German border. This time it was Alan's turn to get into trouble. With the benefit of hindsight, Alan and I agree that our worship at the shrine of Bacchus led to wasted opportunities for doing more worthwhile things; our visit to Sønderborg was no exception. We started our first evening in a new country at a dance. We had been told that because the occupation was still recent, Danish girls preferred British to Germans, and that their second language was invariably English. At the dance hall where we went to test these theories empirically we were disappointed

---

8   Naval slang meaning 'in serious trouble' (usually leading to confinement to barracks).

- the girls spoke Danish and German. Taking into account the amount of beer that we consumed, it was not surprising that we were not attractive to the local girls, despite our flaunted Britishness. Nevertheless, when I was starting to become friendly with a young Danish beauty, I noticed that Alan had disappeared. One of the girls said, '*Polizei*'. Misunderstanding? An accident? I had sufficient presence of mind to find my way to the local police station. Yes, there had been a minor confrontation. One effect of the recent occupation had been a transfusion of Nazi police methods to the Sønderbørg cops. Alan's indignant response to some uncouth behaviour of the police had provoked them into violence and arrest. By the time I arrived to rescue my chum he had been released with no charge and made his way back to the hotel. Our attempt at establishing an Anglo-Danish *entente cordiale* with the girls and constabulary of the town had failed dismally. A fairly typical matelot's run ashore.

Venues for dancing

In Britain in the early 1950s there were essentially two different kinds of public places where youngsters could dance – ballrooms and jazz clubs. For Tony Cash and most of his school and local friends, the former were primarily frequented with a view to picking up girls. To that end it seemed worthwhile learning the intricate steps of dances such as the quickstep, foxtrot, waltz, tango, rumba and samba, even, if pushed, old-time items like the valeta, the military two-step and reels. In jazz clubs, various forms of jive deriving from jitterbug were practised. Improvised and uninhibited, jive tended to appeal to any fan of the music. Spinning your partner round with either hand, in alternate directions, while swivelling your own body in sympathetic or contrary motion was the crux of the thing. By the second half of the 1950s jiving had become a wide-spread fashion all over Britain in clubs where traditional and modern jazz (and later rock 'n' roll) were played. The vogue for it spread abroad, as Alan Smith was delighted to discover:

> In all our northern trips, as in Kiel, a constant feature was the availability of good jazz clubs with a vibrant jive scene. These were often established in exciting venues like converted barges in port locations,

with decks cut through to make an intriguing club ambience, and with stunningly good-looking blonde ladies. I am not surprised that the Beatles first gained prominence in Hamburg. In fact, the sophistication of female and male fashion at that time (compared with the quaint, but brutish, UK teddy boy fashion scene) could convince me that the 'swinging sixties' started around the Baltic rather than in London.

What brought jive to a grinding halt was the advent of the 'twist', at the beginning of the new decade, by which time traditional jazz was beginning to decline in popularity. Surprisingly, in view of the fact that many of them were teenagers in the mid-1950s, none of our 70-odd contributors has described having had a passion for rock 'n' roll or any other form of pop music. Jazz and/or classical were the prevalent interests. For the fans of the latter, Kiel did not disappoint, as Paddy Heazell points out:

Little was more remarkable about post-war Germany than the restoration of its music and opera. Kiel was notable for its splendid provincial opera company and the public concerts held every week. In Hamburg we went to hear a number of operas, held in the half-destroyed opera house. One special weekend I attended two operas, a symphony concert (with the great pianist Claudio Arrau), a René Clair film and the international Picasso exhibition. Not bad in 36 hours.

An unpleasant incident

Coders at Kiel had fewer opportunities to consort with locals than their predecessors at Cuxhaven: HMS *Charlotte* was far from the town centre, whereas HMS *Albert* was in relatively easy walking distance of places where the public congregated. Alan Smith suspects that Kiel's proximity to the German Democratic Republic - as the Soviet Zone had been formally declared in 1949, although the USSR was still in effective control, with its thousands of troops - may also have made local Germans fearful of too close involvement with British resident forces; but parents almost certainly had many other reasons for not wanting their adolescent girls to strike up relationships with foreign sailors, however well-educated or talented. Alan felt that some of the merchant seamen of Kiel were inclined to be hostile, in contrast to the townspeople who worked on base. Every day, coders would come across the Germans who helped in the kitchen and served food; they were invariably friendly. Alan, however, recalls one episode that threatened a dangerous rift:

> One of the ugliest moments occurred in our canteen, when a particularly simple-minded civilian cook said of the cockroaches, 'We should gas them, like the Jews'. To make matters worse, he said it to our one Jewish coder - a very tough and burly rugby player - who reached across, seizing the cook by the neck of shirt and jacket, hoisted him above the steaming tureens and, nose to nose, hissed through gritted teeth, '*Ich bin Jude*' ('I am a Jew'). The rest of the kindly kitchen staff blanched with shock and fear.

Travel away from Kiel

Like their predecessors at Cuxhaven, most coders stationed in Kiel felt that Hamburg was too close and too significant a city not to be visited at least once. This, the largest of the North Sea ports, was thought to have been more hostile to Hitler than other German cities. In the 1934 plebiscite proposing full dictatorial powers for the Fuhrer some 20 per cent of Hamburg voters, more than twice the national average, expressed their opposition.[9] Needless to say, this was not the reason coders wanted to travel there. Gareth Mulloy's explanation is much nearer the mark:

> Its reputation for raunchiness compelled us to visit. First impression was of the huge areas of empty space caused by Allied bombing. Even as an immature 20-year-old, I felt moved when looking at the city where so many tens of thousands of people had died in the firestorms. Yet the *Wirtschaftswunder* [economic miracle] was in full swing, just over ten years after those horrific times. A visit to the Reeperbahn and then to Herbertstrasse, the brothel street closed to women and children, came high on our list of priorities. Attractive, scantily-clad women displayed in the windows of their little brothels were exciting for a bunch of sex-hungry, twenty-year-olds. Shortage of money, and probably moral probity mixed with fear of infection, deterred us from indulging. Similarly, an evening of carousing in the bars led to no more than the usual excessive consumption of beer. The invitation

---

9   Claim by Frederick T Birchall, journalist, *New York Times*, 19 August 1934, cited at http://www.spartacus.schoolnet.co.uk/GERhitler.htm.

by beautiful blonde girls to buy a bottle of bubbly, with the implication of more interesting sexual encounters to follow, was difficult to resist, but the bubbly would have cost a week's wages. Our puritanical (in my case, Catholic) education had inculcated inhibitions to such immorality. So we left reluctantly.

Alan Smith and Gareth Mulloy made a weekend visit to the old Hanseatic city of Lübeck, where they marvelled at the rapid reconstruction of the main square. They found two sides were totally rebuilt in a modern Baltic style splendidly complementing what had survived the Allied bombing. Alan says that, for a moment at least, he was stunned:

> I realised that objects of beauty of whatever period quickly establish a new harmony. This mood of artistic serenity was only broken when a seagull deposited its guano on Gareth's head, and he shouted to the sky, 'All these f***ing Germans and yer haff to choose a Paddy'.

As at Cuxhaven, Kiel coders were entitled to a scale of leave with rail warrants allowing them free travel as far as 50 miles over the West German border. Many used this travel concession to discover parts of Europe hitherto unknown to them. Alan Smith's pass took him first to Zurich for a family gathering. With a friend he then hitchhiked through Switzerland to Italy, familiar to him previously only from neo-realist films and reproductions of Renaissance painting:

> We were eager to discover the glories of Venice, old Bologna and the collections of the Uffizi in Florence. Impressionable youngsters, we were equally stunned by the beauty of the Italian ladies. As we sped past the rice paddies of the Po valley we thrilled at the sight of women in shorts, tee shirts and straw hats tending the rice plants in a real life re-enactment of Silvana Mangano in the film *Bitter Rice*. Other Italian movie clips seemed to play in front of our eyes on the beaches of Lake Garda and Viareggio and in the swimming pools of luxury hotels on the Tuscan hills. I was delighted to discover that my A-level Spanish easily converted into serviceable Italian.

Serious leisure-time activity at Kiel

At HMS *Royal Charlotte*, just as at *Royal Albert*, the coder's life was dominated by a 24-hours-a-day watch-keeping system that would now be described as at least anti-social and almost certainly an infringement of today's health and safety regulations. The watches, slightly adapted for coders, had not seriously changed since Nelson's time, breaking the day into odd periods and permitting only the occasional whole weekend leave. Organising regular social or cultural activities was tricky, whether they involved the theatre, concert hall or cinema. Snooker and billiards in the NAAFI were only marginal compensation. Nonetheless, whatever their interests, the priority pastime for most coders was consuming booze, looking for sex, listening and dancing to music. At Kiel, however, there was an activity which could compete with these intrinsically hormonal drives, and that was sailing. The city is famous for it. The boating contests for both the 1936 Berlin and the 1972 Munich Olympics were staged there. The annual summer regatta, known as the *Kieler Woche* (Kiel Week), is the largest such event in the world. As luck would have it, the BAOR Yacht Club was located only a hundred yards from the *Royal Charlotte* barracks. It was organised and staffed by the British Army. The Club's dinghies and 30-square metre yachts with six berths were freely available to coders, who were also allowed to work as crew in substantial Danish-built, wooden-walled yachts pinched by the Germans when they occupied Denmark in 1940, then requisitioned by the British in 1945. The Club instructors were national service soldiers, many of whom had lived in seaside towns working as fishermen: they knew the sea and were very good sailors. Before being permitted to use the smaller craft without supervision, coders had to complete a basic training course. Alan Smith was one who signed up, though with initial reservations about the men who were to teach him:

> We had the ignominy of the British Navy being trained as sailors by the British Army. They taught us yachting skills, and also to command the motorised cabin cruiser. The Club was well equipped with fifteen 30-square metre yachts, three of 50-square metres, and two 100-square metres. For the 1958 Kiel Week regatta, the Royal Artillery Yacht Club entered its two largest ocean-going vessels. These were very long boats and broad in the beam with an enormous main

258

58. Leading coders (special) in the NAAFI at Cuxhaven winter 1953, Alan Walker 3rd from left slightly behind 2nd from left. Courtesy A Walker.

59. Alan Smith (left) and Gareth Mulloy working in the BAOR Yacht Club in Kiel. Courtesy A Smith.

mast. Coders were invited to crew on one of them. It was really a joy to race through the water at full speed, close-hauled, under competent commanders and heeling at 45 degrees, with a rush of summer breeze tearing at your body and clothing.

Another advantage of the Club was the availability of duty-free spirits at ridiculously low prices. The only disadvantage was having to avoid the advances of the Club's skipper (a very strong advocate of physical fitness), who seemed to have an exaggerated liking for sailors.

A consular shindig

On the occasion of the Queen's birthday, HM Consul in Kiel decided to hold a Garden Party. *Royal Charlotte* was asked for volunteers to serve drinks to the officers, the local consular corps and city dignitaries. To lend a touch of colour to the proceedings, coders who put their names forward were told to dress in their No. 1 uniforms, gold badges prominent on each sleeve. Remuneration in kind - a meal and a beer - were sufficient to induce Gareth Mulloy and several oppos to wait on the distinguished guests, as Gareth recalls:

> The drinks tent was at the top of a knoll in the garden of the Residence, whilst guests were clustered around the base of the knoll. At the edge of the tent was a traditional German 'oompah' band. With the encouragement of the musicians, we would down a glass every time we loaded our drinks trays, and then gracefully glide down the path to the guests from the top of the knoll. The drink and the jovial reaction of the musicians had a very relaxing effect at the beginning. Inevitably, our behaviour and dress soon deteriorated, much to the amusement of the musicians and the concern of our Commanding Officer Cheetham and his First Lieutenant. Cap awry, speed of descent accelerated, and speech slurred, we were rapidly becoming a disgrace to our service. Our waiting was stopped, and we were sent back to barracks, where we spent the night in the cooler. Cheetham had concluded that we deserved a court-martial. Despite my earlier criticism of the First Lieutenant, we were saved from this by his intervention, when he learned of our remorse and the grim fate planned for us by Cheetham.

The next day we humbly sought the forgiveness of the Consul, which was graciously given.

Home for demob

Coders, whatever intake they were in, spent the last months of their national service abroad. To be demobbed they needed to return to England with all their kit, hammock, civilian clothes and the gas mask which had accompanied them on all their movements from one establishment to another. Carrying back home other items of any size was physically quite tricky, though temptations to smuggle were powerful: in the post-war period there were many restrictions on the exchange of currency and the import of luxury goods. Contraband fags and booze were sometimes hidden in a hammock in the belief that Customs officials would be deterred from too close an examination, because of all the lashing to be disentangled. Considering such faith in the hammock an excessively high risk, Gareth Mulloy came up with a scheme to create a false bottom in his kit bag. This involved folding a second, probably purloined kit bag to conceal the tobacco and other dutiable objects he was hoping to sneak into the UK. He confided his plan to a regular Army corporal who was a frequent passenger on the military ship from the Hook of Holland to Harwich:

> I suggested to him that HM Customs, many of whom were ex-RN, were likely to be lenient with returning servicemen, particularly those about to be demobbed. 'Not a bit of it, Jack. They'll take you to the cleaners if they find your baccy. You'll lose the goods, they'll fine you, and it'll go on your record. They know all the tricks – they'll find it.' I was about to re-enter the Civil Service I'd left two years previously. So a warning light came on in my head that if I were fined and suffered other retribution my renewed career with the Civil Service would not start well. I underwent an epiphany. I turned my back on the lifestyle of national service, which taught dodges for making life easier by breaking rules and (usually) getting away with it, and pointed myself to a new unblemished civilian life. I declared everything, then rejoiced inwardly when, despite a thorough search by the long-armed customs man, a few tins of Tickler escaped detection and I avoided payment of duty.

Ironically, Gareth ended his Civil Service career as Hong Kong's Commissioner for Narcotics.

Unlike Gareth, Alan Smith, his partner in so many authority-provoking capers, did risk a possible contretemps with HM Customs on his final lap to demob. He secreted on his person a small Russian FED camera, modelled on the much more famous German Leica. If he had realised the device owes its name to the initials of the first head of the Soviet fledgling state's secret police – Felix Edmundovich Dzerzhinsky - he might have thought twice about acquiring it. In any event, he and it crossed the frontier into Britain unscathed, as did another national service sailor whose inventive ploy to evade duty was observed by Alan:

> One quite distinguished pianist coder tied a large camera tightly into his groin at the junction of the legs. He walked, legs akimbo, past the Customs officials, simulating the roll of the seafaring matelot. His ruse tricked the officials, and I remember him, on the train to London, opening the flap of his bell-bottoms to retrieve the sharp-cornered box camera with a great sigh of relief - and tears in his eyes.

CHAPTER 11
THE INTERPRETERS

ПЕРЕВОДЧИКИ - ПОЧТОВЫЕ ЛОШАДИ ПРОСВЕЩЕНИЯ

('Interpreters are the post-horses of enlightenment' - Alexander Pushkin)

To become a Russian language interpreter in the Navy in the early 1950s you had to satisfy two conditions – achieve a sufficiently high mark in a JSSL first progress exam and pass an Admiralty interview for commission as a midshipman. Army and RAF personnel were spared the second ordeal at the preliminary stage: soldiers and airmen successful at the first exam were automatically promoted to officer cadets and only after a year or more of intensive training as interpreters was their suitability as 'officer material' finally assessed.[1]

Attaining the rank of midshipman

A midshipman is the lowest rank of naval officer, and his commission puts him in a different class from ratings and warrant officers. 'Class' is an appropriate word here, since historically midshipmen were frequently the sons of gentry. Most former coders would agree that it was unusual in our day to hear a Naval officer speak with a regional accent, the absence of which pretty reliably indicated a public school education. Alumni of private establishments may not have monopolised officer ranks, but they were very prominent. The experience of old Etonian Robin Hope at his AIB (Admiralty Interview Board) in 1952 is relevant:

> The interview went as follows: Visiting Officer - Name? Me - Hope. VO - Where were you at school? Me - Eton, sir. VO - Thank you. Next.

Though also privately educated, Patrick Miller was put to a sterner test at his AIB in Portsmouth, where he was confronted by:

---

1   The potential effects of this system are discussed by Alan Bennett in his foreword.

... a row of men in gold braid. It was disconcerting to see one of them constantly looking up and down at you as he scribbled (when I stood up I saw he had been merely drawing a cartoon). All I remember is being asked what kind of soil we had at home. I had learnt by then that an officer never says 'I don't know'. At most he might say, 'Come back later'. So I barked out, in total ignorance, 'Chalk, Sir', which seemed to work, as I was told later that I had been successful. Many years afterwards I was to see things from the other side of the clipboard, when, as a college principal, I was invited for about fifteen years to be the 'Headmaster' member of the AIB. By then it had become a much more professional and thorough testing over three days, to see if the candidates had 'officer-like qualities', or 'Oily Q's', as they were generally known.

One grammar school-educated coder with a distinct northern accent failed his AIB, though he is not convinced that pronunciation had anything to do with it. Tony Cash scored highly in the Russian exam, and was very keen indeed to study the language at greater depth than he would as a translator:

I recall being asked about my interests, and thought it more politic to talk about cricket than jazz. I told them I'd harboured an ambition to play for Yorkshire, and to that end used to go to practise in the nets at Headingley two or three times a week. They seemed very keen to know why I wanted to be a Naval officer, even repeating the question at the end of the interview. The honest truth was, and I was naively happy to declare it, that I'd joined the Navy because it guaranteed that I would get to study Russian – not what they were eager to hear. From my answers to other questions, it must have been fairly obvious that I knew little about, and wasn't too interested in, the Navy. It probably didn't help my case that on joining the force I'd written down that I was an agnostic - non-believers almost by definition subversive. Perhaps I should have admitted that I'd been brought up a Roman Catholic.

Clifford German, former head boy of Northampton Grammar School, had quite the opposite motivation to Tony Cash's:

I opted to study Russian only because I was medically grade three for national service, and the Russian course was the only way of aspiring to a commission, and joined the Navy because it offered the possibility of a commission, even if as a midshipman: the other services only held out hope of officer cadet status, and sent anyone who failed back to the ranks.

Clifford recalls that northern accents were not uncommon among his fellow midshipmen at the JSSL in London. If regular officers were prejudiced against national service midshipmen it would be for other reasons, he believes:

> I think the feelings of practical superiority and intellectual inferiority and resentment of the professionals towards the amateurs was fostered by the officer cadres, who also felt the linguists were better educated than themselves, just as there was a pecking order in the wardroom, with the executive officers [including communications, the interpreters' branch] at the top, the supply and secretariat (white sleeve rings between the gold) and specials (with curious turquoise rings) at the bottom.[2]

An evolving system

From Admiralty papers we have consulted, it is clear that the programme of Russian language training was under constant review, and by April 1954 the naval authorities were beginning to have second thoughts about the setup they had originally adopted. University teachers were reporting that some midshipmen were opting out of the intensive language course, tempted by 'more agreeable duties' in intelligence and cryptographic work. A decision was taken that henceforth commissions should only be granted to those who had successfully completed their interpreter studies. In the meantime they would be promoted to the rank of upper yardman, an approximate Naval equivalent of Army and Air Force officer cadets.[3]

---

2 The *Naval Ratings Handbook* placed ordnance officers, with dark blue rings, at the bottom; it listed no 'specials', but placed instructors, with light blue, immediately after supply and secretariat officers. *Naval Rating's Handbook*, p 14. Midshipmen wore no sleeve ring.

3 The new scheme was not exclusive to Russian linguists: 'Under the new officer structure, there will be three methods whereby ratings may obtain a commission. The first, the Upper Yardmen scheme, offers ratings with suitable qualifications the opportunity of obtaining a

Gareth Jones was subject to the new regime, but, like his predecessors, he had to undergo the AIB:

> The Board certainly probed naval interests. Luckily, I had two uncles who had served in the RN in the First and Second World Wars. One question I was asked was, 'What is the significance of this year (1955) for the Royal Navy?' I had not the faintest idea. Then from the corner of my eye I glimpsed Nelson on the top of his column in the adjoining square. I don't think I have ever thought as quickly. 'The 150th anniversary of the Battle of Trafalgar, Sir', I replied. I have often wondered since whether it was that response that secured my passage onto the London course. The commission was on condition that the interpreters' course in London was completed successfully. The immediate promotion was to 'upper yardman' - a designation even quainter than 'midshipman'.[4] We wore a petty officer's uniform with white lapel badges [a white patch with a buttonhole of white twist and a corresponding button, as worn by midshipmen].[5]

In 1957, when Peter Hill was interviewed for a commission, it was said the Admiralty were looking to select twelve officers, but in the event appointed twenty, mainly because of their impressive linguistic achievements. By this time the Board had widened to include someone from the teaching staff with appropriate language qualifications. If there had initially been discrimination against ex-grammar school boys, or lads with a Northern accent, it was all but eradicated not many years later. Whatever the criteria for appointing Navy officers in other categories, it was brains and application that won through in selection of Russian interpreters. The fact that the drop-out rate on the interpreters' course had continued as high as at the beginning may have led their lordships to rethink their selection procedure - by 1957, according to Peter, there were no drop-outs at all.

---

commission on the General List ...' *In Which We Serve*, Admiralty and Central Office of Information, October 1956, p 49.

4 *Midshipman* implies someone neither a rating nor a fully-fledged officer. A *yard* is a spar across a mast, to support a sail; how working on it became associated with aspiring officers is not known to the authors.

5 *Naval Rating's Handbook*, p 14.

60. JSSL Sussex Square, London 1953. Interpreter midshipmen with colleagues from other Services. Standing far right on the back row is Brian Jones. Seated far right on the second row from the front is Jeffrey Wickham. Courtesy B Jones.

Patrick Miller was among the first midshipmen to be admitted to the London JSSL. He did not complete the course, but not from any lack of ability. Originally, the fledgling officers lived in Sussex Square, Bayswater, very close to Hyde Park:

> The tale at the time was that the RN had bought up a former brothel, painted it all white inside and out, and stuck our group of midshipmen into it, assuming that former visitors would be deterred (incorrectly, as we soon found out when asked in the middle of the night if Big Bertha was in). We were put on the books of HMS *President*, were fitted out at Gieves for our officer's uniform and generally made to feel quite important. Our pay was at the rate of 7/6 a day, which at the time seemed like largesse, but later in HMS *Newcastle* I envied the longer service midshipmen who earned rather more.

Lectures and conversation classes were held at 47 Russell Square, Bloomsbury, an annex of London University's School for Slavonic Studies, six underground stations north-east of Sussex Square. For Patrick and his fellow midshipmen:

61. Midshipman Patrick Miller. Courtesy P Miller.

This meant commuting every day along the Central Line. Sometimes on our return in the evening, as a variation, we got out at Marble Arch and walked to Lancaster Gate through Hyde Park. The trick was to see how often we were accosted by the ladies of leisure who lurked by every tree, and to find out if it made any difference if one wore a hat (it did, the invitations increased by 50 per cent).

This indicates that *kursanty* midshipmen, in a civilian environment, wore plain clothes, in contrast to their coder counterparts on a military camp, who studied in uniform.

Falling by the wayside

The interpreter course was rigorously demanding. Not every commissioned midshipman matched up to expectations, as Nigel Hawkins recalls:

I had learnt Latin as a sort of minor subject, but found it very hard work in London, and was in constant fear of failing the fortnightly tests and being cashiered [dismissed]. Peter Mountfield unwisely got appendicitis, and when he left hospital after two weeks was immediately reduced to the ranks, and sent out to Singapore, though he was intelligent enough to go on to be a senior civil servant and might have caught up.

Nearly a third of Clifford German's intake came to grief:

The attrition rates on the interpreter courses were high - fail two consecutive fortnightly tests - pass mark, 60 - and you were busted. My course started with 60 middies and ended with 43. Those we kept in touch with ended variously as signals officers at Trincomalee and crewing the admiral's yacht in the Med.

One midshipman who for whatever reason failed to keep pace is known to have returned to JSSL Coulsdon as a coder, and completed the usual route to Cuxhaven.

Patrick Miller did not complete the course, but only because he was no longer motivated to do so:

Work was relentless, up to ten hours a day, homework with up to a hundred words a night, tests frequent and our places on the ladder made public. At first, I recall always being in the top half dozen,

270

62. The 4-inch guns of HMS *Newcastle* bombarding the Korean coast during the Korean war, early 1953. Courtesy P Miller.

but after six months some of us began to lose interest. We were immediately identified (*Don't you vant to learn Russian?*). Very soon an interview at Admiralty followed, and we were sent to HMS *Pembroke*, Royal Naval Barracks, Chatham, to learn ciphers and do the Pitman's typing course.

Patrick was one of no more than two or three former coders who went on to see military action, coming under fire from North Korean guns while serving as a cryptographic officer aboard HMS *Newcastle* for a 14-week period in 1953. On only one occasion during that time did he use his knowledge of Russian. This was in March 1953:

> ... when I heard two MIG pilots exchanging in plain language the news *Stalin umyer*, 'Stalin has died'. Passing this on caused a mild ripple of excitement on board; in fact you could say that I had my moment of fame, at least for a couple of hours, while we waited for the official signal from Admiralty.

Finding employment for trained interpreters

In 1956 Russian basic language and translators' courses for the non-commissioned were transferred from Bodmin to Crail - students, teachers, baggage, paraphernalia and all - though for a time interpreters continued to study in London. Robert Cox was stationed at Crail, and is one of a number of JSSL Naval officers to report to us that on completion of their interpreter training they found themselves at something of a loose end:

> I was possibly - even probably - in the last national service RN intake. By that time their lordships had no clue as to what to do with us so we stooged around doing odd jobs. I was told to read and appraise (not usually translate) snitched papers about Soviet navy technicalities, ranging from navigational gear to torpedoes. This was fairly daft, given my abysmal lack of anything approaching expertise in such arcane matters. But it was a pleasant six weeks in London at taxpayers' expense.

Two years earlier Nigel Hawkins had also felt underemployed as a fully qualified midshipman interpreter:

> We never did a useful job during NS. After finishing the last six-month course at Bodmin, I volunteered for

sea service, and this took me to minesweepers running in and out of Harwich harbour. There was still the odd mine which surfaced, and I am proud to think that we served in the RN when it was still probably the second largest navy in the world.

Unsurprisingly, quite a few interpreters eventually went on courses to learn interrogation techniques. Peter Hill, who had started his Russian studies at Crail in November 1956, was one, as were many of his colleagues, he says. In 1957 the Intelligence Corps's base at Maresfield boasted a newly-established 'Intelligence Research Unit' - perhaps the reason why the Admiralty chose this Army camp in East Sussex as a suitable place to instil into national service upper yardmen the skills necessary to prise information out of captives taken in war. Peter describes much of the course as 'practical':

> ... about keeping prisoners separate, keeping good records for comparison, deciding in advance what you needed to find out, and distinguishing between operational information and that for long-term analysis. Some of the permanent staff of the Intelligence Corps were Russian speakers, and dressed up in uniform when pretending to be prisoners. They also had Russian weapons, such as guns, in a field. I do not recall being instructed to use any form of violence on prisoners, although sleep deprivation, irregular meals, and use of light/dark were permissible. The main aim was working in a team and putting together the information gathered, like a jigsaw, to make a clear picture. One heard quite lurid stories about some of the permanent interrogators. Once, I recall, we were given a short talk by a visiting Russian general in full uniform before he returned to Moscow. Why he was there was not really explained. Many of us were taken in - I believe he was an instructor. They liked doing that sort of thing.

The call to interpret comes

Opportunities actually to practise newly acquired interrogation skills in real-life situations were not, of course, forthcoming – the Cold War never warmed up sufficiently. On the other hand, there were occasions when midshipmen's interpreting talents were on trial in friendly, peace-time, contexts. In 1955 Mike Duffy, then in the Royal Naval Special Reserve a year after completing full-time service, was in his second year at Oxford reading French and Russian. He was summoned by the Admiralty to interpret for Russian naval officers and men coming here on a goodwill visit, echoed on the other side of the East-West divide by a Royal Navy visit to Leningrad.[6] In October a squadron of two cruisers and four destroyers from the Baltic Fleet berthed in Portsmouth, bearing not far short of 3,000 men in need of entertainment. Mike recounts that he was joined by some forty other midshipmen interpreters. Before taking up their duties they were all briefed to keep their ears open for useful intelligence, and warned not to reveal anything of their own naval experiences, including how they knew the language of their guests. Invited to lunch on one of the Russian destroyers, Mike was struck by the Victorian style pervading the wardroom - fittings and fixtures, brilliant starched table-cloth, cutlery, crockery as well as crystal wine and vodka glasses, all too frequently replenished by stewards in white jackets. The ship's First Lieutenant was one of Mike's immediate dining companions; the other was the *Politruk*, Political Commissar responsible for ensuring loyalty and ideological purity in the whole crew. It was noticeable, Mike says, that the diners largely ignored the commissar, who drank so copiously he passed out and slid under the table before the three-hour meal had ended.

The interpreting stint lasted five days. Entertainment for one evening had Mike escorting a group of Soviet officers, now in mufti, to the wardroom at the gunnery school on nearby Whale Island, where a piper was laid on to provide music, so that they could learn Scottish reels and jigs. On another occasion he took a bus-load of Soviet ratings on a tour of Portsmouth and its environs. Undeviatingly smart in their best No. 1 uniforms, every sailor seemed to be kitted out with brand new shoes. A stop-off at a typical English tea-house caused Mike's charges some anguish. Traditional crustless cucumber sandwiches were the problem. Evidently, taught not to use his fingers for eating, one sailor was spotted trying to spear the delicate morsel with a fork.

For Mike the highlight of all this fraternising was the huge, impressive party which the Lord Mayor of Portsmouth hosted for

6   It is likely that the British to visit to Leningrad was the occasion of the *Duzyerarsfeetyer* story (see chapter 4).

63. Mike Gerrard, third from left in the back row, with some of the Soviet sailors for whom he interpreted at Portsmouth in 1955 and 1956.

the visiting Soviets in the Guildhall. He invited as many young women as possible from the surrounding area. To indicate his role as an interpreter, Mike had to wear a red rosette. He says it was all very hard work. He stepped out of the throng to take a breather, and shortly saw bearing down on him a beautiful, tiny, blonde dolly-bird in tight-fitting gear, holding the hand of a six-foot-six giant Russian matelot. She said to Mike:

> You're an interpreter, ain't you? What's the Russian for 'No'?

It was not only midshipmen who interpreted for the visiting Soviets. Mike Gerrard and a small group of other coders from Bodmin did so, two years running. With at least nine months study of Russian under their belts they were well qualified for the task. Their duties consisted chiefly of befriending the Russians, taking them on guided tours to naval establishments and places of interest, attending all the public occasions as interpreters and generally facilitating communication:

> This enabled us to see for ourselves the operations room at HMS *Dryad*, used during the Seconld World War for *Operation Overlord*, as the 1944 Normandy invasion was code-named.

Mike Gerrard also attended the same civic reception in Portsmouth Guildhall as Midshipman Mike Duffy, but not to use his Russian. Having a smattering of Spanish, Gerrard and another coder had been given the enviable task of interpreting for one of the Mayor's special guests, the Venezuelan Miss World 1955.

Mike Gerrard recalls that some of the selfsame sailors he met and shepherded around in October 1955 were back in Portsmouth in April the following year. Working unsupervised, Mike and his fellow coders took their responsibilities seriously:

> We regarded the question '*Ty - po·russki mozhesh?*' (Can you speak Russian?) as a call to duty, and protecting the ships' companies from the merchants of Portsmouth out to make a killing from the visiting sailors, as an imperative. '*To khvatit?*' (Is this enough?) almost invariably produced a positive answer from us, and a Russian went away with a bargain for his threepenny piece.

64. 1953 Spithead Review Souvenir Programme.

Commander Crabb incident

The flagship leading the 1955 flotilla to Britain was the 17,500 ton-cruiser *Sverdlov*, which had first approached British shores in June 1953. On that occasion its elegance, power and speed had impressed all those who watched it deploy two anchors - a tricky operation - as it took up its allotted place among the two hundred vessels participating in the Spithead Review for Queen Elizabeth II's coronation. The return visit to Portsmouth in October 1955 gave Naval Intelligence an opportunity to discover what was so special about the ship's hull or propeller system, allowing it to manoeuvre so deftly. We now know that frogman Commander Lionel 'Buster' Crabb undertook a mission with at least one other colleague to probe close-up the submerged working parts of the *Sverdlov*.

The Soviet squadron which arrived at Portsmouth in April 1956 comprised two destroyers and a very recent product of the Leningrad shipyards, the cruiser *Ordzhonikidze*, bringing the Soviet leaders Bulganin and Khrushchev on an official visit to Britain. Their schedule included extensive discussions with Prime Minister, Sir Anthony Eden and an outing to Oxford (where ex-coders studying at the University were among the onlookers). Named after a Georgian Bolshevik associate of Stalin, the warship had on its voyage passed our listening station in Kiel, while studiously observing radio silence.

For many readers the *Ordzhonikidze* will be more readily associated with Commander Crabb, the frogman who had dived under the *Sverdlov*. Two days after 'B and K' (as they were dubbed by the press) had left the country, the Admiralty announced his disappearance in Portsmouth harbour, and a fortnight later, after initially denying the matter had any connection with the Soviet ships, the government admitted that he had been doing 'underwater tests' on 'certain equipment': the presence of a sister ship of the same class as *Sverdlov* had been too good an opportunity for Naval Intelligence to miss. Crabb's headless, handless body washed up in June 1957. Mike Gerrard considers it:

> ... not beyond the bounds of possibility that some of the Russian sailors we met in 1955 might have been there to see off intruders.

Fishery protection

The Crabb incident apart, Anglo-Russian naval encounters in this period were largely amicable, even after the 1957 incidents when Soviet fishing vessels contrived to foul the nets trawled by drifters from Lowestoft and Aberdeen. To deal with the problem, the Admiralty despatched the minesweeper HMS *Bramble* from Chatham to the North Sea. Aboard was an official of the Ministry of Agriculture, Fisheries and Food (MAFF) aided by interpreter Midshipman Gareth Jones, now nearing the end of his national service:

> My first day at sea was spent translating an appeal explaining our concerns and asking the Russians to co-operate by keeping a fair distance from the British fishing boats. The plan was to invite the masters of the tanker and the factory ship to distribute cyclostyled copies of the appeal to the fleet of Soviet fishing boats they serviced during the months spent at sea. When the captain of HMS *Bramble*, the MAFF official and I boarded the tanker we were courteously greeted by the master, a native of Odessa, who regaled us with sweet Ukrainian wine and immediately offered to help by broadcasting the appeal to the fishing fleet. Our welcome aboard the factory ship, lying in the lee of Shetland, was equally warm, and we were treated to a full reception. A stern-faced political officer intervened to prompt the master to decline the proposed gift of the film *Doctor at Sea,* starring Brigitte Bardot, but a bottle of Scotch was gratefully accepted.

On returning to the Admiralty, Gareth discovered that the *Bramble's* intervention had been widely reported in the press, as well as being the subject of parliamentary questions. Christopher Soames, Financial Secretary to the Admiralty, told the House that the Soviets had been 'most friendly and co-operative'. When the Minister of Agriculture was questioned about the incidents he suggested diplomatic channels should be used to explore the possibility of compensation for the damaged nets. MP Marcus Lipton retorted:

> Would it not be better to authorise the captain and crew of the *Bramble* to handle the matter? They have dealt with it very satisfactorily up to now and seem to get on with the Russians better than the Foreign Office does.

Intelligence assignments

Fishery protection of the kind Gareth Jones was briefly engaged in did not come within the remit of the Official Secrets Act,[7] which all coders qualified for eavesdropping duties were obliged to sign as a matter of course. Midshipmen and upper yardmen would also have signed, if their post-training work involved access to classified papers and information about the Soviet Navy, or to intelligence material derived from signals interception. We are not aware of any midshipman called upon to deal with 'humint' (secret information derived from human sources), though such work would undoubtedly have also been subject to the Act. Midshipmen posted to non-sensitive jobs - mine-sweeping, for instance - may well have evaded the OSA's tentacles: Nigel Hawkins has no recollection of signing. A small number of trained interpreters went to the Admiralty to work in Naval Intelligence, certainly making them subject too. Fifty-five years later, Mike Shotton (JSSLs Bodmin and London, 1955-56) feels still bound by it, unable to divulge what he did. For ten years he was a lieutenant in the Royal Naval Reserve[8]:

> … during which time I did other things. However, I really don't think I am allowed to talk about them. So, not much help, I fear. Incidentally, I was obliged to resign my commission when I married a Soviet citizen (one of the 'potential enemy') in 1969. I remember clearly writing my formal letter of resignation to the Admiral Commanding Reserves – 'Sir, I have the honour', etc. etc. I no doubt jumped just before being pushed. Emma and I are still going strong after 41 years.

We know of no other former coder managing to acquire a Soviet wife – a notoriously formidable task; although the Soviets could not forbid a marriage, women who married foreigners were frequently refused an exit visa, so reluctant were the authorities ever to concede their citizens freedom of movement.

---

7   The authors are aware that more than one Official Secrets Act was involved. For convenience, we have followed a long-standing convention of usually referring to them in the singular.

8   In 1958 the RNVR was merged into the Royal Naval Reserve (previously comprising solely Merchant Navy members making themselves available for call-up by the RN in an emergency).

Nearly two years after Mike Shotton finished his clandestine term at the Admiralty, David Talks was posted there, and told us:

> My work (actually there wasn't much to do!) consisted of helping to plot movements of Soviet merchant and warships all over the world on a large wall map, thanks to reports received from GCHQ Cheltenham, and probably eavesdroppers in Cuxhaven. We operated in the bowels of the Admiralty. I walked to work in civvies from a Navy-rented flat in Chelsea, arriving at 10 am for coffee with some American liaison officers.
>
> On one occasion there was what was called a 'flap' concerning, I think, Yemen.[9] I was asked to spend a few nights in the 'Citadel' rabbit-warren. One night the phone went. Hesitatingly I answered. A voice from afar said, 'There is an unidentified submarine approaching the north-east coast. What should I do about it?' As a very green nineteen-year-old, I had no idea, so I replied, 'What would you do?' 'Send out a Shackleton, Sir,' was the response. 'Good idea,' I said, and that was the end of the phone call. To this day I have no idea what happened; my report the following day was met with apparent indifference.

Relations between midshipmen and coders

Midshipmen started their naval careers as coders, but once they had been commissioned to train as interpreters they were unlikely to have dealings with their former comrades, all destined to become translators-cum-eavesdroppers. In some years, however, at least eight to twelve midshipmen would be required to supervise coders logging and recording Soviet military voice communications in Cuxhaven. At any one time there needed to be four midshipmen available for the job, since radio monitoring was a 24-hour-every-day operation divided into watches. For many a coder, his initial spell monitoring the air waves for Russian sigint might well be the

---

9 It would have been the state of emergency declared in May 1958 by the Governor of Aden, then a British crown colony, which had been attacked by Yemeni tribesmen. Further attacks from 1963 led to British withdrawal in 1967 and incorporation into Southern Yemen, itself merged with North Yemen into the Republic of Yemen in 1990.

first occasion on which he would spend several hours at a stretch under the direct, in-your-face command of a naval officer.

In the 1950s most young men had heard horror stories of the 'best buddy' private soldier who, on receiving just one stripe of seniority, became an 'absolute bastard' to his former mates. It was even widely believed that the Army took a perverse pleasure in promoting innate bullies or saw the policy as a short cut to effective discipline. One of the Navy's attractions was that it had no such reputation. Indeed, former coders overwhelmingly agree that they were well treated by petty officers and chief petty officers responsible for their discipline and training. Significantly, countless amusing stories are told about POs and CPOs, but few concerning commissioned officers, apart from hearsay tales of ships being pranged through incompetence.

Relations between a coder on watch and the 'middie' in charge might reasonably be compared to those between a bright, if now and then recalcitrant, fifth-former and a highly intelligent, if not always conscientious, sixth-form prefect. Of course, there would usually be no age difference and occasionally, in the case of university graduates, the coder might be three years older than his supervisor. Several factors made for good relations: the common experience of learning a language and acquainting ourselves with its attendant culture; the shared grammar/public school educational background with the intellectual, artistic and musical interests it fostered; above all, the fact that we were all 'pressed' men – all conscripts, thereby a different breed from 95 per cent of the rest of the Navy. It would be difficult for a midshipman to be heavy-handed or high and mighty towards a coder with whom in a few weeks' time he would be sharing a college lecture or tutorial. Three days after leaving Cuxhaven on demob leave, ex-Leading Coder Dennis Mills returned to Nottingham University as a very junior member of staff. He remembers a chance meeting outside the senior common room with ex-Midshipman Vernon Atkins (one time cipher officer to Commander-in-Chief, Far East Station). After a matey chat, Dennis went into the staff room, but Vernon carried on to the students' refectory – tables had been turned, but neither of them looked at it that way.

Midshipman Fred Wright saw no hierarchical impropriety in travelling down the coast from Cuxhaven to Bremerhaven, to visit the American base with a coder friend he had first met in basic training, and with whom he is still on first name terms. A 1950s regular naval officer, as opposed to a national service one, would not have been best pleased, almost certainly would not have tolerated, being addressed by his Christian name, were the speaker a rating.

There was, however, one conscript midshipman in our midst who insisted on the prerogatives of rank: he chose to make himself quite unpleasant to his coder underlings. To spare his blushes we will refer to him by his first name only. Martin had been a colleague of Tony Cash's at Coulsdon:

> Of all the men from my intake, Martin seemed one of the least likely to be deemed 'officer material'. The coders who shared a hut with him thought enough of him to molly-coddle him, ensuring his boots were adequately bulled and his uniform sufficiently neat and tidy to pass inspection. He came across as very absent-minded, and was not at all well co-ordinated physically: his attempts to drill or march smartly were at best clumsy. Nevertheless, he was a good linguist, and had no trouble making the grade to qualify for the Admiralty interview. There was general disbelief when he passed it. Disbelief turned to dismay a year or so later, when he turned up in Cuxhaven in 1954, and began to treat his former colleagues as unfit to commune with. Unlike the other middies in charge of watches, his manner was peremptory and domineering: he gave the impression he positively enjoyed cracking the whip.

Clifford German was a midshipman who served with Martin and remembers him well:

> He had very belligerent right-wing views. I used to wind him up by telling him Martin was a Jewish name. 'No it's not', he shouted, 'What about Martin Bormann?' He became a school teacher in Bournemouth.

Clifford spent more than three months at the Cuxhaven listening station, HMS *Royal Albert*, overseeing monitoring operations, but not, he says, fraternising with coders during or outside working hours:

> … with all drinks at 4d a shot (gin at 3d) in the wardroom there was no real incentive to trudge into Cuxhaven for a drink, but I played a few games of cricket for the *Royal Albert* team in Hamburg, where

the batting order was strictly in rank order - the two lieutenant-commanders opened the batting, followed by two lieutenants and a sub-lieutenant, with me, as the only middie, at No. 6. But after the games the senior officers went back by car, and the coders and I were left to our own devices, and I am deeply sorry the photo I had of about six of us and a table containing probably sixty empty beer bottles was accidentally left in my rooms in Cambridge in 1957 - if anyone could trace a copy I would be for ever grateful.

The paths of midshipmen and coders also crossed at the Bodmin and Crail JSSLs - the former there to study specifically military Russian terminology - the latter undergoing the translators' course. Entirely segregated for their studies, they could find scope to associate in extra-curricular activities, whether sport, music or drama.

Midshipman Michael Waller made a contribution to the Russian version of *Hamlet* performed at Bodmin in 1954 (the exotic staging is amusingly described in *Secret Classrooms*:[10]

My own role was playing the violin in a mini-orchestra which accompanied the play within the play, which in turn was an opera composed by us.

Though the principal roles were taken by midshipmen, coders were also involved. Michael Waller gives Bodmin coders their due:

Having felt that we midshipmen were rather the tops, having been selected in the major progress test, we were mighty impressed on getting to Bodmin to find ourselves in the company of so many interesting coder people. Since we had been recruited, the overall ranks of JSSL men had swelled considerably, and it had become harder to top the interpreter hurdle.

Midshipman Brian Jones, who had played the first gravedigger in Makaroff's production of *Hamlet,* tried to organise some rugby at Bodmin:

… but local apathy and a vile winter - raiding the coal dump and burning classroom furniture were not unknown - prevented any sport, although we did go to see the All Blacks play Cornwall. I cannot honestly say I remember the coders at Bodmin, but I met up with them shortly afterwards at RAF Wythall, to which

10 Geoffrey Elliott and Harold Shukman, *Secret Classrooms,* p 92.

I was appointed as an instructor and divisional officer. I inherited a good rugby team, thanks to Carwyn James, who had just left, and I organised quite a good run-ashore for the coders to a brewery - Mitchell & Butlers, in Birmingham - from which all returned in high spirits.

The Russian teachers responsible for the Bodmin *Hamlet*, Dimitri Makaroff and Vladimir Koshevnikov, eventually transferred to Crail, and put on plays there, too. Again, coders and midshipmen collaborated, as they did in the very active Crail choir, organised by another teacher, the Latvian, Sternbergs.

Final qualifications

In the last six months or so of their service, midshipmen needed to be found employment – one of the reasons why they were induced to study for the Civil Service interpreters' exam, which came at the end of the course in Russian military terminology taken at Bodmin or Crail. Peter Hill says it was very demanding and:

> ... included 'orientation' i.e. knowledge of naval terminology - at least degree standard, if not higher. You could not be a reserve interpreter and go on the courses without getting above something like 60 per cent. A few, a very few, got 80 per cent or above, which meant you were a first class interpreter.

The overwhelming majority of midshipmen passed, several achieving firsts, including Jeffrey Wickham, who had played Hamlet in the celebrated Russian language version of the play and who later, as an established stage actor, became president of Equity, perhaps the only old Etonian ever to hold such a high union office.

Interpreting after demob

After full-time national service, coders were transferred to the Royal Naval Special Reserve (RNSR - Special, because it comprised only national servicemen) and had to do short periods of training in three consecutive years, usually involving two to three weeks' monitoring at Cuxhaven or Kiel. Interpreters were similarly transferred to the RNSR, and bound to report for annual training, but could change again to the RNVR (after 1958 the Royal Naval Reserve - RNR), continuing with it, in some instances, for as long as thirty years. Doing so gave them the opportunity of being promoted to lieutenant, lieutenant-commander if they persevered, or even, in Brian Jones's case, to the rank commander, RNR.

Clifford German was demobbed in the autumn of 1954 and eventually took up a career in journalism, remaining on the reserve until 1964:

> My then boss at *The Times* objected to my taking an 'extra' two weeks holiday and made it clear he would not be happy if I continued. So I 'retired' as a lieutenant RNR. The Navy also asked for volunteers in the Christmas holidays to act as interpreters on an official visit to Leningrad, and I know Peter Hill went, but my then supervisor at Cambridge, who had done his wartime service down the mines, talked me out of going.

Peter Hill is the archivist of the FRINTON Society (Former Russian Interpreters of the Navy), which was formed in 1985, when their RNR annual training scheme was brought to an end. It was felt to be a suitable reason for establishing a kind of old boys' club, through which members could keep in touch and organise regular dinners and get-togethers. To this day (2012) a newsletter, or 'signal', is regularly circulated to members.

In a 2007 number, Peter Hill recounted his trip to Leningrad. In 1966 he was called on by the Ministry of Defence to interpret on a goodwill mission to Russia's northern capital, by the cruiser HMS *Devonshire,* accompanied by HMS *Oleander,* an 'oiler' or refuelling ship, in which he was to travel. *En route* the cruiser collided with a stationary vessel:

> The bow of a moored tanker had torn away all the handrails on the port side of the upper deck, denting the Avgas tanks but without causing them to ignite or explode, and there was a fair amount of mangled metal. I believe there was an enquiry and court-martial some time later, but the immediate problem was to get it all covered up with tarpaulin before proceeding. The strategy apparently was that we should tell all Russian visitors to the ship that under the tarpaulins was secret equipment we were not allowed to show. With most Russians this was immediately accepted.
>
> The people of Leningrad were free to come aboard *Devonshire* and look round. The ship's ratings were

286

65. RNR Interpreters' refresher course at RAF Tangmere in 1963. Standing fifth from left is Gareth Jones. Seated far right is Mike Shotton with Mike Duffy on his right. Seated fourth from right is Brian Jones.
Courtesy B Jones.

smartly dressed and placed at key locations to help. However, it soon became clear that access to the ship was being controlled by a sort of guardhouse on the quay, and they only allowed those with tickets through to the boat ferrying visitors. Tickets had clearly been carefully distributed to party members, trade unionists, shop stewards, troublemakers, spies etc. I tried to get a couple of friendly youths who lacked tickets through the control in my company, but failed. Also admitted to the ship were nasty little groups of *Komsomoltsy* [Young Communists] wearing red armbands who went around the deck harassing the other Russians. I recall one old man coming up to me and saying, 'Do you have a doctor aboard? I'm a doctor and I would like to speak to him'. I went below to find the ship's doctor. When I returned the old fellow was being hustled towards the gangway by the teenage thought police, and that was that. I recall being extremely peeved.

One of Peter's duties was to take a selected number of ratings from the *Oleander* to the famous tourist attraction, Peter the Great's summer palace:

Two elderly ladies spouted facts like the fountains they were describing, and the torrent of statistics about hectares and cubic litres of water was too much for the somewhat subversive lads I was interpreting for. Discipline with them was a loose concept. Every time I turned round there seemed to be rather fewer than we set out with, until only a rather serious-minded chippie with good manners remained. I had earlier given the group a short lecture on behaviour when ashore: do not get drunk, do not get into fights, do not try to pick up women (there are no prostitutes in Leningrad, ha! ha!) and do not take British currency ashore and exchange it for roubles. When it came to departure time on the fifth day, there emerged onto the quay from the side streets all the lads in the *Oleander* crew, with their arms wrapped round the ladies of Leningrad. One later told me they had taken their money ashore, paid for women and parties, and spent most of the time drinking. Still, nobody, as far as I know, was arrested.

Aboard the *Devonshire* was Vice-Admiral Sir John Byng Frewen, KCB, Commander-in-Chief, Home Fleet. 'Black Jack', as he was known to his underlings, decided to invite a number of senior officers from the USSR Baltic Fleet to dine on the ship. Peter was there, too:

> The dinner for me was fairly tedious, as the English captain to my left, whom I was supposed to interpret for, insisted on practising his execrable Russian straight across me. But things warmed up towards the end, when Sir John, who had served in wartime escorts on convoys to Russia, as well as having commanded the aircraft carrier *Eagle*, made a speech reminding the Russians of the enormous amount of equipment and planes that had been brought round to Murmansk in the last war, at great cost. None of this appeared in the Russian press. He then sent out a steward, who brought in an engraving of his distant ancestor, Admiral John Byng, being shot on the quarterdeck of HMS *Monarch* in March 1757 for his failure to relieve Minorca. 'I always carry this at sea with me', he said with a wry smile, 'to remind me that admirals are not indispensable'. A bullet-headed colonel of the Leningrad garrison leaned forward and said to me in Russian, 'It is not unknown in our country'.

POST SCRIPT: The salvaging of the *Kursk*

How precarious the life of a sailor can be, whatever his rank or nationality, was vividly brought to the attention of the world when, on 12 August 2000, following an explosion caused by torpedo malfunction, the nuclear-powered Russian submarine, the *Kursk,* sank in the Barents Sea with the loss of all 118 officers and men. A year later, a Dutch salvage crew hired by the Russian authorities to raise the stricken vessel, was in need of a Russian speaker for a short spell. Former midshipman interpreter Anthony Hippisley, about to retire from his teaching post at the St Andrews University Russian Department, answered the call and flew to Kirkenes in the north of Norway where the name *Kursk* procured him a visa from the Russian consul in a matter of minutes. (It normally takes days.) He was then driven to Murmansk and helicoptered out to the diving support vessel, the *Mayo*. Anthony's main job, he says, was to attend morning meetings in the operations room where the salvage master went over the previous 24 hours' progress and detailed the day's plans:

> During the time I was on board the divers were cutting holes in the hull for the insertion of the grippers that were to raise the *Kursk*. All this discussion had to be translated for the Russian naval personnel present at the meetings, headed by their salvage chief whom I got to know quite well because we worked in the same office. When he came in each morning wearing his bright blue boiler suit (Russian No. 8s) I would greet him with the traditional 'Здравия желаю, товарищ адмирал' ('I wish you health, Comrade Admiral'). He would just smile and shake my hand. We were once looking down on the foredeck where some new rope was being stowed and he commented: 'Какие красивые концы!' ('what beautiful ropes', literally ends'). This remark took me back to Naval vocabulary classes in Crail, with Lt-Cdr Dick Howorth telling us that in the Soviet navy ropes are referred to as 'ends'.
>
> The MO on board the *Mayo* was a Russian naval officer, and since many of the health complaints were from British divers I would have to be on hand. The main problems were throat infections and skin rashes caused by long periods in saturation. Sometimes swabs were taken and flown to the lab in Murmansk, and I learned that a mould is called *gribok* 'little

mushroom'. We were once visited by another admiral, Admiral of the Fleet Vladimir Ivanovich Kuroedov who came to express his appreciation to all those involved. He went down to the saturation chambers and talked to the divers through the intercom. He presented them with jars of fresh loganberries, and they thanked him in voices made squeaky by the mixture they were breathing. Another Russian naval man I got to know slightly was the Northern Fleet's Chief of Staff who flew in from time to time to check on progress. We discussed the parallels between the present salvage operation and the Arctic convoys, and at our last meeting he gave me a book about the disastrous convoy PQ17. On the flyleaf he had written in Russian:

'To Anthony R Hippisley We have been brought to this place by the universal human duty to honour and remember the sailors who have perished.

These same values united our two peoples in the years of the Second World War.

May God help us!

Chief of Staff of the SF (Northern Fleet)

Hero of Russia

Vice Admiral M Motsak

September 2001

The Barents Sea

Site of the loss of the atomic-powered submarine *Kursk*.'

CHAPTER 12
SOVIET EAVESDROPPERS

КАЖДАЯ СКЛАДКА НА СОЛДАТСКОМ ОДЕЯЛЕ - ЛАЗЕЙКА ДЛЯ АГЕНТОВ МИРОВОГО ИМПЕРИАЛИЗМА

('Every fold in a soldier's blanket is a bolthole for agents of world imperialism' - Red Army aphorism)

From the moment the Coder Special Archive was conceived we wanted to glean whatever we could about our equivalents in the USSR. Even way back in the 1950s, while twiddling knobs in Cuxhaven, Kiel, Cyprus and Turkey, scouring the airwaves for Russian speech, we had mental images of young Soviet conscripts similarly engaged, but intercepting NATO military communications to forewarn their rulers of any aggressive moves from the West. Sadly, not one of our coder contributors to this publication, not even frequent visitors to the Soviet Union or its successor states, has ever come across a Soviet citizen to fit the bill. During the Cold War, the latter would understandably be reluctant to reveal themselves - the penalties for divulging state secrets so much harsher than in Britain.

Everything changed after the Soviet Union collapsed in 1991. Journalists, writers, political commentators, historians, even former military hierarchs now had an incentive to publish reminiscences and analyses of a great power rivalry which for forty years and more had threatened the annihilation of mankind. Public interest in the subject was considerable, witness the mammoth TV series, *The Cold War*, masterminded by Jeremy Isaacs and broadcast in 1998 by BBC2 in Britain and CNN in America. These 24 one-hour documentaries featured in-depth interviews with leading protagonists from both sides, such as Jimmy Carter, Fidel Castro, Lech Walesa and Mikhail Gorbachev. Since then, much has been printed in the West about Cold War topics, even those previously embargoed under the rubric of official secrets law. 'Sigint' operations, to which much of this book is devoted, were precisely such a sensitive area. We former coders regarded ourselves as able to talk and write about them in the second decade of the 21st century, but could our Soviet counterparts?

Appealing for witnesses

In September 2010 Tony Cash informed the BBC's Russian Service about the coder archive, and was invited to be interviewed in Russian to discuss the project. The programme's host was Seva Novgorodsev. Over several decades Seva has been enormously popular with Russian audiences, thanks principally to transmissions introducing his listeners to the best of otherwise inaccessible Western rock music. During the conversation, Tony had the opportunity to make an appeal along the following lines:

> We would very much like to contact former Soviet representatives of our profession, namely Russian military men who during the Cold War learned English to intercept military communications between our Western, especially British, planes, control towers; between tanks; between submarines and mother ships. Their recollections and photographs would be most welcome.

Reference was made in the interview to what was described as an interesting precedent for the proposed collaboration - the publication in 1997 and 2000 of English and Russian texts of *Battleground Berlin: CIA v KGB in the Cold War*. Written jointly by former high-ranking American and Soviet spooks the book recounts their rivalries and exploits in the divided German city.

The appeal fell on stony ground: no Russian listener contacted the BBC in response to Tony Cash's proposal. Speculation as to the reasons would be fruitless.

Evidence of Soviet eavesdropping

Yet we have very good reason for believing that thousands of Soviet conscripts manned listening posts to intercept Western military radio traffic. In May 1996 a branch of the US National Security Agency published a revised *Intelligence Threat Handbook*,[1] which claimed that the USSR had been maintaining 'one of the most sophisticated' sigint programmes in the world with 'collection sites'

---

1   See Section 3, entitled ADVERSARY FOREIGN INTELLIGENCE OPERATIONS, at http://www.fas.org/irp/nsa/ioss/threat96/part03.htm

in over sixty countries. The *Handbook* also refers to the Soviet practice of using disguised mobile collection platforms, such as 'tractor-trailers and other vehicles ... to gather intelligence in Western Europe'. It cites estimates made by Western intelligence officials that the Soviets 'conducted over 7,000 covert vehicular sigint operations in NATO countries annually' to obtain electronic order-of-battle data and to monitor NATO exercise communications.

There appears to be a general consensus that the USSR ran land-based sigint stations in the Warsaw Pact countries, in Afghanistan, Cuba and North Vietnam, but also in ostensibly non-aligned countries, such as Ethiopia, Syria and the Yemen, and possibly Iraq and Libya. Moreover, according to Norman Polmar,[2] of the United States Naval Institute, the Soviet Union had installed several hundred such listening posts 'along the land and sea borders' of its own territory. In the late 1940s, taking advantage of captured German technology, the Soviets had begun updating pre-World War II listening posts to create a large, elaborate network, incorporating high frequency direction finders (HF/DF), capable of pinpointing the location of any radio signal of interest, whether voice or Morse.

Responsibility for Soviet radio intercept operations directed at foreign military forces lay with the GRU, the Chief Intelligence Directorate of the General Staff, a branch of the armed forces comparable in power and authority to the KGB, the Committee for State Security. The GRU would have masterminded the acquisition of sigint material by Soviet military intelligence-gathering vessels (in US sailors' jargon, AGI's). It was widely believed that these ships hovered in the vicinity of Western ports and NATO naval exercises, posing as trawlers or tramp steamers. Polmar asserts that the Russians had in service more than 65 such 'intelligence-collectors'. but their ensign and radio antennae readily identified them as navy rather than civilian craft.

Siginter Mart's story

In our search for Soviet conscript eavesdroppers we have so far come across just two individuals who could be said to qualify. The first is an Estonian, Mart Aru. He was unearthed by a contributor to a draft history project created by former members of the 13th Signals

66. Mart Aru in Red Army uniform reading the official organ of the French
Communist Party. In the USSR the only western newspapers available
to ordinary Soviet readers were Party journals such as *L'Humanité*.
Courtesy M Aru.

Regiment who had served at an Army listening post in the tiny West German village of Langleben between 1951 and 1992. He wrote a memoir, *Mart's Life as a Spy*.[3]

Mart served in the Red Army between 1963 and 1966. In this period Estonia, like its Baltic neighbours Latvia and Lithuania, was one of the fifteen Soviet Socialist Republics of the USSR, and firmly controlled from Moscow. That he feels free now to write about his army experiences is probably due to Estonia being an independent state since 1991, following the break-up the Soviet Union: Mart is no longer constrained by official secrets legislation enacted by the former Communist regime.

Mart writes that he was conscripted into the 86th Independent (or 'Detached') Radio Technical Regiment OSNAZ – a frequently-used military acronym meaning 'for special purposes'. Such units were created specifically for radio intercept work, and Mart had excellent qualifications for the job. While still at school he had taught himself Spanish and German, and when called up was in his second year of English studies at university in Tartu, Estonia's second city. In exams required for university entrance he had scored five out of five in English, but only three in Russian, for reasons which he explains:

> Russian was not a popular subject in Estonian schools in those times ... so when preparing for entrance exams to the university I consulted my secondary school Russian teacher. However, the time was apparently too short, so my efforts in Russian were evaluated only with a 'satisfactory' mark ... I got a 'three', also, for my Estonian essay, in which I compared *The Ten Commandments* with *The Moral Code of the Builders of Communism*, finding that there was much in common between them. By the time of my conscription I had acquired a shallow background in quite a number of languages (I had even had a go at Kiswahili), and, filling in my conscription questionnaire, I naturally entered all the newly acquired linguistic skills in the respective box. I presume this rather impressive, although boastful, list may have decided my fate for the next three years. Nevertheless, I had no idea on 27 November what kind of service was in store for me, and visualised the horrors of three years in the infantry, a construction

3   Mart Aru's *Mart's Life as a Spy* can be read at http://www.langeleben.
co.uk/draftproject/draft_010.htm.

battalion, the strategic missile forces, or, worse still, the navy, where the term of service was four years.

Mart's call-up and basic training

With other young conscripts, Mart was escorted by rail from Tartu to Lepaja, a port on the Baltic Sea in Latvia, where his allocated regiment was based. He refers to stops at the Estonian and Latvian capitals of Tallin and Riga, forwarding stations, at which, presumably, some of his fellow-travellers would have gone their separate ways to other army destinations. Somewhere *en route*, all conscripts had their hair 'cropped', shaved entirely off, as has always been the Russian military custom:

> On arrival in Liepaja I was accommodated in barracks, perhaps 40 metres long by 30 wide, filled with double-deck bunks. Our uniforms were issued to us as soon as we arrived. We were taken to a sauna, left our own clothes there and emerged dressed in khaki.

Mart describes the everyday working uniform as including a trench coat, and adds in brackets the English transliteration of the

67. Mart Aru (extreme right) with fellow Red Army conscripts at a shooting range south of Liepaja in winter 1964 soon after they had taken their oath of allegiance. Courtesy M Aru.

Russian word *shinel'*.[4] This garment, he says, had to be carried over the shoulder rolled up when they were on guard duty or exercises, and was heavy enough to be a nuisance, though could be put to good use as a blanket.

The daily regime was evidently strict: within a minute of reveille sounding, they were expected to be in line, already garbed in trousers, boots and long-sleeved shirt. Failure to dress in time could be punished with extra duty assignments. Each day began with warm-up exercises and a run of over a mile, regardless of weather. Washing and shaving with cold water were followed by what in the British armed forces we have always called 'bull' – polishing boots and belt buckles. Much more taxing must have been the job of 'sewing a strip of white cotton cloth as a collar' to the army tunic. All our ex-coder contributors will recall that each sailor in the UK was provided with a sewing kit, known as a 'housewife', to be used during 'make and mend' sessions set aside for clothes repairs. Stitching, however, was never for us a daily necessity, as it was for Mart and his comrades:

> In the line-up for breakfast the sergeant carefully checked the results, and discovery of yesterday's collar or an insufficiently brilliant belt buckle inevitably brought punishment.

Though it was less than 40 yards to the canteen, the trainee soldiers were marched there in columns of three, and only on the appropriate order allowed to enter, in single file. Both sitting to and rising from the meal required specific commands. Provisions were strikingly more monotonous than those on offer on the navy, army and air force establishments where we coders served. For breakfast, Mart and his fellow recruits had:

> ... a few slices of black and white bread, potato mash or porridge washed down with tea. For lunch there was also soup and *kisel'* (a starchy sweet fruit drink) and sometimes, perhaps once a week, a minced-meat burger. We sat ten men to a table, and the meal was served by one of the chaps in the middle with a ladle

---

4 *Shinel'* would be familiar to coders as the title of Gogol's story of Akaky Akakievich (see chapter 4). Now normally rendered as 'great coat' or 'overcoat', 'trench coat' used to be the regular military term for that item of uniform. Coders wintering at Crail and Kiel would have appreciated Mart's coat.

from large metal pots and passed round. The cutlery
was limited to aluminium tablespoons.

Most of the men in Mart's squad were from the Baltic states.
Several were graduates. Others, like him, were part way through
their university courses. The majority had had no more than a
secondary education.

The basic training Mart describes will be very familiar to anyone
who has served in the forces, notably the army. It lasted some eight
weeks and comprised primarily square-bashing, physical training
and instruction in handling weapons. A Kalashnikov rifle (AK)
was issued to every soldier, but not in the first instance for personal
keeping. The AKs were locked away in special cupboards firmly
attached to the barrack walls. Soldiers had to learn how to assemble
and reassemble the weapon at speed, as well as clean it carefully
after use:

> Towards the end of the initial training period the
> young soldiers were taken to a firing range outside the
> city, where we were to demonstrate our marksmanship
> with our personal AKs. My performance was average,
> although I had done better shooting with an air rifle at
> secondary school military training classes.

The description Mart provides of the PT equipment available
will chime with British servicemen's recollections:

> There were parallel bars, a horizontal bar and
> vaulting horses in the barracks, and soldiers were
> encouraged to exercise on them in their free moments.

Less familiar to us is a subject Mart was taught called ZOMP,
a Soviet acronym from the initial letters for the words *Protection
against Weapons of Mass Destruction*. British naval personnel all
had some training in the use of gas masks, and, in the 1950s at least,
we had to carry them when we travelled on duty. But we received
no instruction how to counter the effects of biological devices or of
radiation from nuclear explosions.

Nor could it be said that we were politically indoctrinated in any
way. In the Red Army, though, so-called 'political education', was
always a vital component of the military curriculum. Mart and his
fellows had to attend special classes in the *Lenin Room:*

> It had a bust of Lenin, of course, and nearly all the
> walls of the room were covered with various political

posters,[5] notices with the soldiers' performance results and a panel of honour with the portraits of exemplary soldiers. There was also a billiard table, chess and draught tables as well as a TV set. Apart from political classes, it was the place where Komsomol [Young Communist] meetings took place and where the men spent most of their free time.

Mart makes the *Lenkomnata*, to give the room its Russian name, sound like a cross between a chapel, a traditional NAAFI and a lecture hall. It may well have been in the Lenin Room where the essentials of radio technology as well as the Morse code were instilled:

> During that stage I learned the American GI's phonetic alphabet, *Alpha*, *Bravo*, *Charlie*, *Delta*, etc., and will probably remember it to my dying day.

Basic training concluded with all recruits taking the Oath of Allegiance, a new version of which had been introduced in the USSR two years before Mart's call-up. Every individual member of the Soviet armed forces was obliged to swear that he would be 'an honest, brave, disciplined, vigilant warrior; strictly guard military and state secrets; unquestioningly fulfil all military commands'. He was called upon to dedicate his last breath to 'his people, his Soviet fatherland and Soviet government'. Should he break his solemn vow, then - 'may I suffer the severe retribution of Soviet law, universal hatred and the contempt of the working people'.[6]

Mart's sigint career

Mart was now ready to be assigned to what he calls a 'combat unit': we would term it 'active service'. In his case, it was to be on the outskirts of Liepaja:

> It was quite a large fenced territory consisting of the radio reception centre (PT),[7] garages for military

---

5   Mart would have been familiar from childhood with posters and slogans extolling the claimed achievements of Communism displayed across buildings in town centres, as was common in all the Soviet and 'satellite' states.

6   Whereas regulars enlisting in the UK armed forces have always been required to swear or affirm allegiance, this was not required of conscripts.

7   PT are the initials of the Russian *Priyomny Tsentr* - literally, 'Reception Centre', reception here referring to radio - in other words, 'watchroom'.

vehicles, the fuel depot, direction finders, the unit's pig farm, some potato plots and, last but not least, the guard room. I spent most of the rest of my service of two years and nine months either at the PTs or on guard duty. We normally worked six hours and then had 12, sometimes 18 or more, hours off before another six-hour shift at the PTs.

The PT was a single-storey building filled with radio receivers. There was a long corridor, the command room, a room for technicians and another one for radio monitors. There were four shifts in 24 hours, starting at 0900, 1500, 2100 and 0300 hours, each beginning with instruction by the duty officer for those on post for the next six hours, including D/F operators. The combat nature of the service was often underlined. The actual work consisted of monitoring certain frequencies and writing down all the communications we could hear.

Mart was expected to intercept not only voice but also teletypewriter (TTY) communications. This apparatus was not around when we coders were manning listening stations, only coming into existence in 1964. It allowed typed text to be conveyed by radio between operators using the same equipment. Mart admits that he did not find it easy at first to make out what was being spoken in English, because he had had little opportunity to hear native speakers, all his university teachers being non-English. With time, his ears attuned:

> For TTY there was a separate frequency and when we heard a station calling another and saying it had a TTY message, I was supposed to quickly tune one of the two receivers to the TTY frequency and switch on the TTY printer. All the communications were recorded in pencil on A4 sheets and handed over to the command room at the end of the shift. To help us out there was an army tape recorder, Zvuk-1, at the desk.

Mart describes listening to traffic passed on by international radio stations fixed on land in West Germany, Greenland, Iceland, Norway and the Faroe Isles. Many have now been superseded by satellites. By convention, such relay posts were identified by three-letter prefixes, OUN, for example, indicating the Faroe Isles:

> I only remember one incident during my whole service when there was open free voice communication between two stations of the OUN network. It happened

between DML in Sylt, [West] Germany, and VDB2 in Greenland. There was a new man at VDB2 and calling DML he enquired about life there and spoke about his own experiences, including meeting with bears in the neighbourhood. The conversation was interesting, but evidently of no value to the officers who were trying to crack the code the network was using in its TTY messages. We were supposed to keep only one of the two receivers on the OUN frequency, and were encouraged to search for stations of military relevance on the other one. Again, I remember only one occasion when I chanced upon open communication between units involved in war games in West Germany.

Mart tells us that on one of his receivers he used to listen to broadcasts in English by the BBC and Voice of America. Using the TTY system he could also pick up newspaper stories from agencies such as AFP (Agence France-Presse), Reuters, TASS (Telegraph Agency of the Soviet Union), UPI (United Press International) and others:

Teletype signals were easy to recognise and assess in terms of printing quality and so we were within easy reach of news no Soviet news channel would ever carry. I managed to smuggle out some of these news items and I still have them stacked away somewhere in my bookcase.

Mart describes in some detail the equipment he was working with such as the KROT (Russian for 'mole' - the animal) and R250M short-wave receivers, both capable of fine tuning and eminently fit for purpose. He calls the TTY printer noisy, despite its wooden casing:

… but when the signal was loud and clear it produced a faultless text, although only in lower case letters. The tape-recorder was also far better than similar civilian machines at the time.

By his own account, Mart was not especially diligent exploring the airwaves as instructed. Like British coders before him, he skived. Apart from listening to news, he would occasionally search for popular music, though doing so was strictly forbidden. His tastes ran to Italian ballads, British chart successes and what he calls 'German *Schlager* (jazz)' – if 'jazz', then presumably not the Eurovision Song Contest fare the word *Schlager* sometimes suggests. He implies that

68. Mart Aru with his girl friend and mother, summer 1965. Courtesy M Aru.

he and his colleagues made tape recordings of Western music and smuggled them out of the base:

> Yet another way of whiling away the long night hours was to take an English book on shift in the leg of my [shin-length] army boot. Often I managed to read it through in six hours. Night shifts were particularly suitable for this, as there was next to no fear of any officer suddenly turning up in the monitoring room. It was a good thing we were permitted to use dictionaries during the shift, as a detective story could easily be slid under the dictionary in case of trouble. Although no reading matter was allowed during the shift, some officers closed their eyes to such misconduct. Books could be borrowed from fellow-soldiers, all of whom had a small stock, but later we discovered a better source - an officer from our regiment who had served for a few years in Cuba, and had brought back several suitcases full of American paperbacks. Most were detective stories, but there were some Steinbecks among them.

Other soldiers in Mart's contingent were tasked with monitoring coded messages sent out by American B52 and B47 reconnaissance planes flying over international waters in the Baltic. It is now widely accepted that both British and US aircraft deliberately, if only occasionally, intruded into Soviet air space during the Cold War on spying missions, and some were shot down. By the middle 1960s, when Mart was serving at Liepaja, the Soviets must have been especially vigilant about Western overflights. Mart has described what would occur as soon as a signal from an American plane was detected:

> Orders were given to the D/F operators sitting at radar screens in their trucks in the Liepaja *pozitsiya* [post or position] as well as to posts in Kaliningrad, Ventspils, farther up the coast, and Kuressaare (then Kingissepa) in Estonia. If the tracks happened to come closer to shore than usual a *Vozdukh!* alarm was given. The idea was probably to raise the soldiers' vigilance, as no real attack could naturally be expected from a routine reconnaissance mission.

Vozdukh is the Russian for 'air' and in the context must be understood as a call for planes to take to the air. Mart clearly did not share his superiors' anxieties concerning foreign military encroachments, if he took it for granted they were only on 'routine reconnaissance missions'.

Eventually, Mart was given an intercept task that was not primarily military, though it had obvious military implications:

> Although I kept my OUN assignment all through my service, at certain times most regular duties were abandoned and all efforts switched to the US space programme. That was a time when the Soviets and Americans were neck and neck in the space race and the 86th Independent Radio Technical Regiment also apparently wanted to do its bit. We were sometimes given additional duties of monitoring US satellite tracking stations as far away as in Kano and Mauritius and the aerial system was even improved to intercept remote radio communications. On launch days, however, we were put on combat [action] duty to receive the press agencies and listen to the Voice of America. The UPI or AFP flash messages from the Cape Canaveral launch pad went immediately to the command room.

ПЛАНШЕТИСТ ПО ПЕЛЕНГАЦИИ
СЕРЖАНТ А.ОКУНЕВ.

69. Sergeant Alexander Okunev. The first line of the Russian caption
indicates that Okunev works as a direction finder. Courtesy A Okunev.

Siginter Okunev's story

We learned of Mart courtesy of former Army *kursanty* of the 13ᵗʰ Signals Regiment, who had manned a listening post in Langleben, West Germany. Aleksandr Okunev is known to us thanks to Jack Doughty, a former Air Force JSSL linguist. The two became acquainted via a Russian language forum hosted by a translators' website. Like Mart, Okunev is a citizen of a republic no longer part of the USSR – in his case, Belarus. It too gained effective independence in 1991, as did Estonia. Unlike its Baltic near neighbour, however, Belarus is the only European country ruled by an oppressive autocrat. Nevertheless, Okunev, like Mart, is shot of any obligations he undertook when pledging allegiance to the Soviet state and its laws: he can discuss his sigint activities with impunity. He gave an English language account of his military career to Jack, who arranged for it to be printed in *The Phoenix,*[8] a newsletter circulated among a group of former RAF *kursanty*. They adopted the name 'Old Eutonians', having served in the 1950s at a listening station in Uetersen, some 18 miles northwest of Hamburg. Like Mart before him, Okunev was conscripted after his first year at university, but in the 1980s rather than the 1960s:

> This was the time when the children of the war kids were getting called up, and there was a considerable lack of men everywhere … Out of about 50 students of the Department of Translation only two went to Air Defence Interception (your obedient servant and my buddy Yuri, we even made it into the same regiment) and another guy got into KGB reconnaissance … The rest of the boys were drivers, cooks, commandos, all sorts of stuff, a couple of guys even managed to get into the navy ... At the same time nearly all the men conscripted together with me were village boys with an embryonic knowledge of the 'German' which is taught in Belorussian villages and/or a vague knowledge of Russian. These were from the islands in the Baltic, kids of fishermen who honestly believed that Kazakhstan was a European country and a member of NATO.

Okunev's training course lasted six months, during which he had to learn 300 words of what he calls 'the Mumbo Jumbo language' – the lexicon of technical English military terms he might be expected

---

8   *The Phoenix*, March 2006.

to hear during his intercept duties. He also had practice listening to and transcribing recorded tapes. His other duties included:

> ... cleaning snow, tidying the barracks, 'mining' coal from a huge frozen heap of it for our boiler room, doing a lot of things and generally having a lot of fun, because it was only possible to survive and not to go nuts if you managed to preserve a bit of a sense of humour, and we were kidding and supporting each other.

Two of my friends are defending their Communist Motherland. That tool is called MASHKA, a piece of log with a handle, the bottom is lined with woollen cloth (remnants of someone's overcoat). The lino was thickly smeared with stinky wax and then the men on duty in the barrack polished the lino until it shone bright. What you see on the photo is probably anticipation of a visit by a stupid high-ranking officer, high-speed turbo polishing, I remember when the then Minister of Defence was due to come to Severodvinsk, our company Commander walked nervously up and down the strip of lino and the guys hurriedly polished the lino after him... ;)

70. Photo and text by Alexander Okunev. Courtesy A Okunev.

Training satisfactorily completed, Okunev spent the remainder of his compulsory service stint in the taiga, close to the northern city of Archangel, where, during the Civil War that followed the Revolution of 1917, British and American troops had fought the Bolsheviks. Some 65 years later, it was precisely British and American forces on whom Sergeant Aleksandr Okunev and his mates were directed to eavesdrop. A D(irection)/F(inding) Plotter, he was principally occupied in determining the precise direction of the incoming radio signals he wished to intercept. In this task he was skilled enough to have his photo posted on the Board of Honour.

He has explained the circumstances:

> I got it because I was a good guy and always knew where the B-52 or RC-135 was, even when our computer failed or there was full-blown aurora and nobody could hear anything. Do I impress you? Forget it, RAF and USAF do everything according to the schedule, and you can be 100% sure there was a P-3A in Eastern Mediterranean today, from 11 to 15 Zulu.

All three American planes referred to are employed for reconnaissance purposes. 'Zulu' is American military slang for 'Co-ordinated Universal Time', a standard in use world-wide and based on an atomic clock. Okunev is here making a big claim for his prowess in direction finding. There was, however, another explanation of why he was honoured:

> The real reason why I was a good soldier was that Captain N from the Technical Department at the HQ had told me that if we offered an improvement this would be a рационализаторское предложение (a sort of low-grade patent), and for that we were to be paid (!). Not too complex. E.g., you get tired of switching the intercom by hand, you make a foot switch, make a drawing, submit it to HQ and get 12 roubles (a sergeant's monthly salary) two weeks later! When we discovered this and got it rolling smoothly, we stopped going to the mess hall altogether, because we had all the money to buy milk and stuff at the officers' буфет (mini-bar). And I got to that Board as the best рационализатор (ideas man).

We former coders who had not always taken our allocated tasks seriously were gratified to discover that some of our Soviet opposite numbers were on occasions similarly inclined. Okunev describes a custom they called 'Lift-Off':

> It happened when an officer came in and said that today a couple of Buccaneers would be flying back from Canada, and anyone who missed it would get it in the neck. After several hours of intensive listening, when it was clear that the Buccaneers were either maintaining radio silence or had never taken off at

all, we would choose a frequency with 'ear-splitting' interference, and that would be the one for tracking the flight. The higher authorities took a dim view of this, but there were no unpleasant consequences, and eventually everyone became accustomed to the idea that if call-signs such as 'Boney-M' and 'Deep Purple' were 'intercepted' – we would call out 'We have lift-off!'

The Archangel climate is extreme – severely cold winters, with temperatures down to more than minus 40 degrees C, and very hot summers blighted by hordes of vicious mosquitoes:

> The place was really wild, although the city of Archangelsk [Russian name for Archangel] was quite close to the barracks, the 'pit' (our bunker) was far deeper in the taiga, and the NCO who used to check the antennas for the ultra long wave intercept (up to 18 km long, often torn by animals) told us stories about skeletons of American reconnaissance craft still rotting out there. Normally the pilot baled out and was rescued by a rescue team, and the Soviet military then stripped the electronics and engines from the aircraft, leaving the rest behind. Well, when I used to go to see my buddies at the direction finding (about a kilometre away from the pit, to reduce interference) and was walking along the wooden catwalk across the marsh, a lot of hares hiding under it used to dash off, scaring the hell out of me.

During his two-year spell snooping on NATO airmen close to the Arctic Circle, Okunev and his comrades speculated, just as we had done:

> … about what our colleagues on the other side of the Iron Curtain were up to. Around Christmas, when the threat of an attack by the dark forces of imperialism became simply unbearable, and we were working double shifts, there was nothing at all on the air apart from static, but the special interception gear periodically picked up from the teleprinters New Year greetings 'from the other side', written in awful Russian.

CHAPTER 13
ON THE MARGINS OF THE COLD WAR: THE KHRUSHCHEV ERA

ПОЛИТИКИ ВЕЗДЕ ОДИНАКОВЫ: ОНИ ОБЕЩАЮТ ПОСТРОИТЬ МОСТ ТАМ, ГДЕ И РЕКИ-ТО НЕТ

('Politicians are the same everywhere: they promise to build a bridge where there isn't even a river.' – Nikita Khrushchev[1])

By the time the first coder (special) had been restored to civvy street after his two-year national service stint, the parameters of the Cold War had changed: Stalin was dead, his passing marked in one Coulsdon JSSL class-room by *kursanty* standing to observe a minute's silence (more to irritate their Russian teacher than manifest sympathy for Uncle Joe, it must be said). The Soviet leaders who came to power in March 1953 may have shared some of the old tyrant's paranoia about the belligerent intentions of Western states, a mind-set also characteristic of both the Tsarist and the Putin regimes, but they were not imbued with Stalin's megalomaniac lust for personal power. In Nikita Sergeevich Khrushchev they also had a First Secretary of the Communist Party who genuinely believed in the inevitable world-wide triumph of socialism, and who was not averse to letting foreigners into the USSR to see progress being made to this end. Former coders keen to discover the reality of their putative enemies were now able to visit that country, though they were under an obligation to obtain prior clearance from the Admiralty. Permission came with strict admonishments to observe complete reticence at all times concerning any of our Service work.

John Bayliss tangles with Soviet security services
One of the first ex-coders to visit the Soviet Union after national service was the late John Bayliss, a keen jazz fan who dabbled on

---

1 Press conference, New York, October 1960.

310

МЫ ЗА ДРУЖБУ И МИР!

НАШ ГОРЯЧИЙ ПРИВЕТ ОБЛЕТАЕТ ВЕСЬ МИР!

МЫ ЗА ДРУЖБУ И МИР!

71. A poster for the International Youth Festival held in Moscow in the summer of 1957. The caption reads: WE'RE FOR PEACE AND FRIENDSHIP and OUR WARM GREETING FLIES ROUND THE WHOLE WORLD. Courtesy RIA Novosti.

the trumpet. In the summer following his graduation in French and Russian at Oxford University he tagged along with the Bruce Turner Jazz Band to act as their interpreter at the 1957 International Youth Festival in Moscow.

In the view of many commentators, the Festival was the first significant thaw in relations between the USSR and the West since the Cold War began. Khrushchev wanted the world to believe that the Soviet Union was a changed country since the demise of Stalin, whom he had so roundly condemned in his secret speech to the 20th Congress of the Soviet Communist Party in February 1956. Since most of the 30,000 or more young Festival guests from abroad were fairly carefully vetted before being allowed to travel to Moscow, it may be assumed that they were broadly sympathetic to the Soviet cause. Bruce Turner, a talented reed player who excelled when playing with the Humphrey Lyttelton Band, was himself, at least for a period, a member of the Communist Party of Great Britain. Rather than the West being persuaded that much had changed in the USSR, young Soviets, especially Muscovites, were seduced by their first encounter with live popular Western culture.

A warm reception for foreign visitors did not mean that they were free to exercise the freedoms and prerogatives they could take for granted in their home countries. Tony Cash, a fellow language undergraduate with Bayliss at St Edmund Hall, recalls John's account of his falling foul of Soviet officialdom:

> He had taken up with an attractive young Russian woman, but had to resort to clandestine meetings in the Moscow Underground, after the authorities conveyed their disapproval of the relationship. John let drop hints that his dealings with Soviet functionaries had developed beyond his being the passive butt of their displeasure. We only learned the fuller story, however, in 2011, a decade or so after his death. Penny Bayliss, John's widow, revealed that during the 1957 Festival he was caught selling a pair of jeans to a young Muscovite, in contravention of a Soviet law that specifically prohibited private individuals from trading. Hauled in to account for himself, John was told that if he went along with a certain proposal, all charges against him would be dropped. He therefore agreed to supply his interrogators with information from the UK. Returning home, he immediately divulged all to

the security services, and was effectively recruited by our spooks to feed stories to the Soviets, as well as make occasional visits to foreign countries to check on specified individuals. Penny recalls one such visit to Yugoslavia, possibly in 1968. She claims he was pretty well paid for his trouble.

We do not know which agency John was working for, whether MI5 or MI6; it might even have been Naval Intelligence, which had an autonomous existence until 1964. Yet he could not have been very active as an agent, since for most of his post-graduate life he was in full-time employment as a teacher in public schools, with a final, decades-long stint as head of modern languages at St Paul's School, London.

In 1964, however, John did have a break from teaching, when he travelled to the Soviet Union with author Douglas Botting (also a graduate of St Edmund Hall, though reading English and not a Russian speaker). They were there for more than four months, mostly in Siberia, eventually reaching Arctic territory unvisited by free Westerners since 1917. John acted as interpreter and assistant cameraman for the documentary film on Siberia that Douglas had been commissioned to shoot for the BBC. It was transmitted in 1965, the same year which saw the publication of Botting's *One Chilly Siberian Morning*, an intriguing, often hilarious account of their journey.

The travelogue reveals no action on the part of Bayliss, or indeed Botting, that could be interpreted as spying, though it is possible that John was keeping his eyes peeled to report back in London any signs of military installations. A postcard written jointly by the two men and the reply from London must seriously have perturbed Soviet securocrats, and caused their Russian minder-interpreter, Vadim, a good deal of heart-ache. On 4 June 1964 they heard a cuckoo in the region of the permafrost city Yakutsk, more than 3,000 miles east of Moscow. Believing this to be the first hearing of the bird that year at latitude 129'E., longitude 62'N, they thought the Editor of *The Times* should be informed - the newspaper's willingness to report these events being such a time-hallowed tradition. Several weeks later, back in Moscow, Vadim confronted them with a letter he said had come to his office for them, and which he had felt it necessary to open in case there was anything urgent in it. Reading it aloud, he enquired the significance of one passage. It was a slight variation of the standard reject letter from *The Times,* thanking them for the information, which was of:

> … great interest to us and though we will not make immediate use of it, we will keep it on our files for future reference. Please do not hesitate to send us any further information you may obtain.

They tried to explain the joke, but typically Soviet, literal-minded Vadim had great difficulty in understanding why obviously intelligent, highly educated Brits could be engaged in such a bizarre activity.[2]

Bayliss's and Botting's extended journey around the USSR would have been inconceivable in Stalin's time, as would the cultural exchanges which began to proliferate in the late 1950s between the Soviets and the West, and from which several ex-coders benefited. Nikita Sergeyevich Khrushchev is generally credited with having launched the policy eventually to be known in Russian as *mirnoye sosushchestvovanie* (peaceful coexistence) the notion that rival nuclear powers could tolerate each other's existence, if only for fear of mutual immolation. The doctrine was at loggerheads with the traditional Marxist-Leninist line that class struggle was inevitable and would necessarily lead to world-wide Communist supremacy (an issue which would soon cause friction between China and the USSR). Khrushchev may frequently have adopted a belligerent stance on the world stage, but many believe he was truly keen to improve the living standards of his people and to avoid war. He was particularly exasperated when the leaders of capitalist countries questioned his dedication to the cause of disarmament, though he should have realised that his brutal crushing of the 1956 Hungarian revolt would invalidate in most Western eyes his claim to be a peace-maker. Nevertheless, he did travel to the West, and was sufficiently impressed by what he saw to realise his country could benefit from greater trade, as well as from scientific and cultural contacts.

Teachers, including former *kursanty,* welcomed in USSR

One outcome of the Khrushchev 'thaw' was the teacher exchange scheme agreed between Britain and the USSR, and first implemented

---

2   Douglas Botting. *One Chilly Siberian Morning,* pp 120-121 and 177-178.

in 1958. Twenty or so British teachers of Russian, and a similar number of their Soviet equivalents, were given the opportunity to spend six weeks in the others' country, honing their conversational skills, lapping up the culture through visits to monuments, galleries, museums, theatres and concert halls. Tony Cash, then teaching at a grammar school in London, was fortunate enough to be selected for the second such exchange in 1959. He spent six weeks in Moscow and Leningrad. He has recounted an incident that seemed at the time to encapsulate how conflicted Soviet attitudes to Western popular music could be:

> Three Moscow University graduates, specialists in teaching Russian as a foreign language, were assigned to give us conversation classes every morning, and then later escort us sight-seeing and on cultural tours. The three young ladies were aware I played jazz semi-professionally and that I'd brought my clarinet with me. I knew that jazz in Russia was officially frowned upon, but thought that there might be a chance of contacting Soviet musicians. The day before the delegation's return flight to Britain, our hosts organised a party, and invited a dance-band contingent from a Red Army military orchestra to perform. I was told jazz numbers were in their repertoire and they'd be delighted if I were to sit in to blow with them. A brief interval for speech-making gave us the opportunity to work out a 12-bar blues arrangement, and before long we were into eight- and four-bar chase choruses in a succession of different keys. Toasts to Louis Armstrong, Duke Ellington and other jazz giants alternated with peace, friendship and international brotherhood. If our interpretation of the flashing lights was accurate, a good number of photographs were taken before the night ended.

> I kept in touch with some of my fellow delegates back in London, and learned that they'd received photo albums recording the highlights of our stay. I was told there were good shots of the farewell party and the band. I wrote to Moscow asking for an album but received no reply. In the end I borrowed one from a colleague. There was a picture of me playing, eyes clenched, cheeks and neck distended, oblivious to the outside world; underneath ran a caption in Russian: 'Mr Anthony Cash, a teacher from London, performs

a traditional Scottish folk tune on the clarinet'. Even in a semi-official document, not intended for general publication, they were chary of actually printing the word 'jazz'.

John Griffiths lands a scoop for his newspaper

One of Tony Cash's former Coulsdon colleagues, John Griffiths, was another beneficiary of Khrushchev's opening to the West. He has kindly allowed us to use extracts from his autobiography, *With Advantages*,[3] including one on his experiences in the Soviet Union in 1959 as a journalist on the staff of the *Western Mail*, the main newspaper of Wales. With two former fellow students of Peterhouse, Cambridge, along with a cousin and a colleague from the sister evening paper, he travelled through rural western Russia in a top-of-the range *Cresta*, which Vauxhall had specially modified so that it would run on the low-octane petrol available in the USSR. The vehicle created quite a stir in the villages through which it journeyed:

> If curiosity inevitably entailed fixed stares and the occasional tentative touch of a garment or a metal panel, we were always treated with the utmost courtesy, and our requests for food and fuel – particularly once I had expressed them in passable Russian – were always promptly and efficiently dealt with. Only when these practical obligations had been fulfilled, did the flow of questions follow. The orthodoxy or otherwise of those questions was conditioned by whether or not the village policeman, 'politico' or political fifth columnist happened to be listening. When uninhibited, the queries were penetrating, the comments frank and the eagerness to hear a view contrary to their own quite genuine. The scepticism of the villagers, particularly the women, was refreshing, and they obviously treated the propaganda outpourings of their own broadcasters and Voice of America with equal contempt. Gratifyingly, it was the BBC's World and European Services that they surreptitiously tuned into for a relatively balanced and objective account of what was going on in the world, from which their masters believed them precluded. I wonder if it was this response that encouraged me to apply a year or so later

---

3   John Griffiths, *With Advantages,* autobiography awaiting publication.

72. Photo of the Khrushchev/Nixon conversation in Moscow 1959 taken by John Griffiths while he was covering the American Vice-President's visit for the newspaper *The Western Mail.* Courtesy J Griffiths.

to join that very BBC service. It certainly convinced me once I was there of the value of the 'credibility items' we used to include in our programmes. These criticisms and arguments about the deficiencies and defects in our own society validated the positive claims we made for it and the observations we made about theirs.

John's mission to Moscow for the *Western Mail* was to cover the opening of the American Exhibition by US Vice-President Richard Nixon. The exhibits, ranging from the latest recreational devices to sophisticated industrial and agricultural implements, were designed seriously to impress Soviet visitors. Khrushchev's presence ensured security was tight at Sokolniki Park. John could have had a problem in being admitted:

My own habitually plain, some might even say slightly scruffy, attire secured me a journalistic coup of which I am still proud. The Russian security men took me for one of Nixon's bodyguards in very plain clothes and the American security men could not tell me apart from the drably dressed Russians keeping an eye out for Khrushchev. I was thus able to take photos and eavesdrop on the hostile exchanges over the bonnet of Chrysler's shiny pride and joy between the US and the Russian leaders. The gist of the exchange was an invitation by Nixon to look round at all the marvels consumer capitalism could bestow on its citizens. Khrushchev's not entirely convincing response was that Russians could have all these things, too, but without the debilitating capitalist ethos that went with them across the Atlantic. He had looked stony-faced as he walked round, but resumed his boisterous approach once the two entered into the exchange of toasts I reported in the *Western Mail* on 6 August 1959.

Nixon drank to 'the removal of military bases from foreign soil.' Khrushchev replied: 'If American deeds match American words, I will drink,' but made no move to raise his glass. Nixon tried to deflect attention in lighter vein: 'He doesn't like our drink'. Khrushchev, quick as a flash: 'I like your drinks and I like your people, but I do not like your policies'. Nixon then wished Khrushchev '100 years life', although he 'disagreed with his policies.' Khrushchev laughed; 'I willingly drink this toast, but when I reach 99 then we will discuss the matter further'. But this time Tricky Dicky got in the last word: 'You mean at 99 you will still be in power – no elections!'

British Council promotes cultural contacts between UK and USSR

The most prominent player in facilitating contacts with Russia has been the British Council. Founded in 1934, the organisation is registered as a charity, but receives substantial grants from the government. Its essential purpose is to promote abroad recognition of our civilisation and culture through visits and exchanges like the one that enabled Tony Cash to spend six weeks in the USSR in 1959. That same year, the Council also arranged an exchange of twenty research students in either direction. Former Leading Coder Gerald Seaman, then a research student at Oxford, took up post-graduate studies in the history of Russian music at the Leningrad Conservatory, where he had encounters with cellist Mstislav Rostropovich and composer Dmitri Shostakovich. His doctorate was incorporated into an account of the development of Russian music from early folk-song to the late 19th century, one of the first, substantial tomes on this period to be published in any language.[4] Shostakovich visited Britain to attend the 1962 Edinburgh Festival for the premiere performance in the West of his *Twelfth Symphony,* a commission from the Communist Party (that could hardly be refused) to celebrate the Bolshevik Revolution of 1917. The composer agreed to give Gerald Seaman an interview, which was published in the *Daily Telegraph*. In it he made clear that he was committed to the music-making principles of the classical era, and wanted no truck with modern music, whether electronic, serial or 12-tone, declaring that no outstanding work comparable to a Beethoven symphony had emerged from that source, or was ever likely to.[5]

In 1960 the British Council arranged with over sixty UK galleries and private owners to send 140 of their treasured paintings to Leningrad for display at the Hermitage Museum for four weeks in June and July. Presenting an overview of painting in Britain

---

4   Gerald R Seaman, *History of Russian Music*, Oxford, Basil Blackwell, 1967.

5   *Daily Telegraph,* 9 September 1962.

covering more than 250 years, with the emphasis strongly on the past, the show included canvases by our most talented and revered practitioners, such as Constable, Gainsborough, Hogarth, Reynolds and Turner; the post-World War II period was represented by Lucian Freud, Victor Pasmore, William Scott and Jack Smith. All in all, it was a serious effort to impress, and the accompanying catalogue was published only in Russian. This was the most significant exhibition of British art to travel abroad since the end of the 1939-45 conflict.

Whatever the means by which the art works reached Leningrad, they returned to Britain via a most unlikely form of transport: a fast minelayer, HMS *Apollo*, capable of 40 knots, and incidentally fitted out with sophisticated eavesdropping equipment, was assigned for the job. On board was an ex-coder, by then a Ministry of Defence civil servant in charge of radio monitoring. He believes it likely the ship was chosen because the Soviets were unwilling to pay the heavy insurance costs involved in other forms of conveyance. In any event, the *Apollo* was well suited to house this unusual cargo, thanks to the length and width of the tubes designed to propel mines into the release position.

While in port, the ship's company had a short run ashore, an organised visit to the Petrodvorets Palace, a half-hour drive from Leningrad, and by then largely restored to its former splendour, following its occupation and part destruction by German troops during the 900-day siege of the city over 1941-43. This trip apart, radio monitoring continued as usual, though pickings proved very thin. Our ex-coder recalls:

> I heard a young Russian voice start a call *raz, dva, tri* - the traditional 'one, two three ...' At this point an older voice cut in with a curt '*prekratitye razgovor!*' – 'Cut the chatter!' and nothing more was heard.

On returning to Portsmouth, the Captain gave an interview to the *Portsmouth News,* in which he praised his men for their good behaviour abroad, but what especially impressed him, he said, was the crane driver in Leningrad dockyard hoisting our precious, national treasures onto the *Apollo*:

> 'The crane driver was a woman, and she was extraordinarily efficient. Our boys really jumped to it.'[6]

---

6   *Portsmouth News,* 27 July 1960.

320

Patrick Procktor interprets for the British Council and American peace activists

Four years earlier than the Hermitage exhibition, the British Council had hired an interpreter who was himself to become a luminary of British painting – Patrick Procktor. In 1956, just out of the Navy, ex-Midshipman Procktor was invited by the Council's recently formed Soviet Relations Committee (SRC) to make a number of trips to the USSR. One trip, with a group of Lancashire textile workers, took him via Moscow to Tashkent, the capital of the then Soviet Socialist Republic of Uzbekistan, where, unsurprisingly, 'he had to look at a great deal of Russian cotton'. In compensation, the collective farm on the delegation's itinerary put on a magnificent spread, though Procktor rated the *shashlyk*, a regional kebab and the *kumys*, made from fermented mare's milk, as 'slightly problematical'.

On his return to London he received what he told the authors of *Secret Classrooms* was a 'weird little note', calling him to be interviewed at Queen Anne's Mansions, an outpost of the Admiralty. He had neglected to inform them of his intention to travel to the Soviet Union, let alone seek their permission, as required by his undertaking under the Official Secrets Acts. His interrogators asked him to explain the circumstances of his trip, reprimanded him, and told him that his application to join the RNVR would be rejected.

By his own admission gingerly sympathetic to the Communist cause,[7] Patrick Procktor may be thought to have made an odd decision in agreeing to work for the SRC: after all, the Committee could be considered a tool in the cultural struggle between East and West. In his autobiographical memoir, *Self Portrait*, he explains that the fees he earned interpreting in Britain as well as in the Soviet Union enabled him to live and paint for two months in St Ives, and to produce a portfolio of work that won him a place at the Slade School of Fine Art.

In *Self Portrait* Procktor describes a 650-mile journey he made on foot, from Brest-Litovsk, on the Polish/Soviet Union border, to Moscow. The year was 1961, and he was now a student at the Slade. He had responded to a request mediated through CND to march with, and be voluntary interpreter for, the last leg of the international

7   Patrick Procktor, *Self Portrait*, pp 22-3.

San Francisco-Moscow March, undertaken to promote the cause of world-wide nuclear disarmament. At this stage the footslogging peace lovers numbered 31, most of them religious Americans. As they processed through Byelorussian villages and towns where war-time devastation was still very much in evidence, they would often address large gatherings in theatres and halls. Procktor confesses that he sometimes found his colleagues 'naïve pacifists' and their leader capable of spouting 'ridiculous nonsense'. They met many Russians still sorely grieving for loved ones killed in the war and Nazi occupation:

> There would be big discussions of when it was ever right to start a war, which the Americans had trouble grasping, never having been occupied or threatened in that way.[8]

It was hoped that when the marchers reached Moscow they would be granted an audience with Khrushchev. The issue that most exercised them *en route* was what to say to the Soviet leader, a politician not at all inclined to agree with their policy that every nuclear power should unilaterally disarm. The meeting did not happen, but the group leader and nine women marchers, plus Procktor as interpreter, had tea in the Kremlin with a 'friendly but non-committal' Mrs Khrushchev. The march was allowed to hold the planned demonstration in Red Square, which gave Procktor an opportunity to visit the famous mausoleum containing the mummified bodies of Khrushchev's predecessors. There, the illustrious painter-to-be noted that 'Lenin was green, and Stalin crimson'.

Jeremy Wolfenden, former midshipman interpreter, of whom more later, reporting on the marchers for the *Daily Telegraph*, had a less sceptical take:

> The disarmament marchers may not have made much impact on the ordinary man in the street, if only because few of them speak Russian. But where they have met English-speaking people of their own age, they have clearly made a deep impression. Their discussion at the university yesterday was prolonged by nearly two hours beyond the time planned. Official representatives of the students made speeches condemning the policy of unilateral disarmament. But the marchers had several notes handed to them in

8   *Ibid*, p 43.

73. Tony Cash reporting in Scarborough on the 1965 Liberal Party
Conference for Soviet listeners of the BBC's Russian language
transmissions. Courtesy *The Scarborough Mercury*.

which the writers said, 'Don't take any notice of those official speeches. We do not all think like that'.[9]

Ex-coders broadcast to USSR for BBC Russian Section

By the middle of 1963 Soviet leaders seemed to appreciate that contact with the West did not necessarily lead to serious cultural contamination, let alone the collapse of the Communist project. They decided to stop jamming nearly all Western Russian-language programmes, including those emanating from the BBC's Bush House in London. For most of the next five years, Soviet listeners had relatively easy access over the air-waves to news, information, music and entertainment unmediated by Communist Party censors. Two former coders, the late Gordon Clough and Tony Cash, were by now employed in the BBC's Russian Section writing, producing and presenting talks and features for Soviet listeners about life, politics and culture in the UK. Tony Cash's first involvement with the Section had been when he was interviewed in connection with a recording he had made:

In 1961 the Dave Keir jazz band I played with recorded the song *Moscow Nights* for a cheap Woolworth label. A more polished version by the Kenny Ball band, with the title *Midnight in Moscow*, later went on to sell a million copies and reached No. 2 in US and UK charts. The Keir disc was distinguished from Ball's in having a vocal. This was sung in Russian by the pianist Mike Jefferson, who happened to be studying the language part-time for an extra A-level. At that time writing and presenting music programmes for the Russian Section was Vladimir Rodzianko. He was himself a composer and, incidentally, the great-grandson of Mikhail Rodzianko, President of the Russian Imperial Duma, swept away by the Bolshevik revolution. Rodzianko had heard our disc, and learned that the clarinet player was actually teaching Russian in London and so, at little expense, could be brought to the studio. I seem to recall it took more than a year before they paid me the twelve shillings and sixpence fee, in fact it was after I'd joined the Section myself. This was the only job

9   *Daily Telegraph*, 7 October 1961. Wolfenden's reports led to an editorial referring to an earlier one advising nuclear disarmers to 'go [to] the Kremlin', and went on, 'Honour clearly demands that they be promptly saluted, and here is a cordial and admiring salute'.

74. The actor Innokenty Smoktunovsky as Hamlet in the 'gravedigger scene'. A still from the black and white Soviet film of 1964. Courtesy RIA Novosti.

I'd ever applied for where being a jazz musician, albeit semi-professional, stood me in good stead. In those days a jazz player in Britain tended to be suspected of being a communist, an atheist, a sex-pervert and probably a drug addict. Fortunately for me, the BBC wanted someone who could not only speak Russian tolerably well but who was knowledgeable about popular music.

Within a month or two of starting at Bush House, I was hosting a regular late Friday night pop programme, featuring the latest releases by British artists such as the Beatles, Rolling Stones, The Who, Manfred Mann, The Searchers, Eric Burdon and the Animals, as well as leading American acts like The Supremes, Four Tops and Bob Dylan. For signature tune, I chose the opening bars of an instrumental number by James Brown and the Flames called *Mr Hip*, and persuaded my colleague Teddy Wigand, our best announcer and gifted sports commentator, to come up with a short verse that I could speak over the music. He devised a doggerel quatrain for the jingle that began: *U mikrofona Kash Antoniy, lyubitel' dzhazza i simfoniy*, and which might be translated roughly in its entirety as: 'At the mike here, Cash, Anthony – Fan of jazz and symphony – With all his might – Will bring you delight – Till the Moscow stroke of midnight'. Reversing the order of Christian and surname doesn't sound quite so barmy in Russian. It's difficult to judge whether the programme was widely listened to, but there was a statistic much bandied about in those days, that our Russian language broadcasts were generally being heard by as many as ten million people over the USSR as a whole. For much of the five-year period that I worked in the Section, four or five letters a week evaded the Soviet censor, and many of them referred to music programmes or contained specific musical requests. It was obvious that the Beatles, for example, were enormously popular. This was confirmed when one of Russia's greatest actors, Innokenty Smoktunovsky, who had played Hamlet in the much lauded film by Grigory Kozintsev, visited Bush House and in a *Desert Island Discs*-type programme for our Russian-speaking listeners chose a Beatles track, and spoke enthusiastically about their records.

326

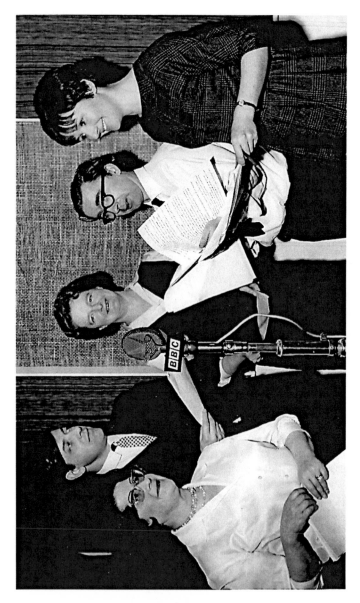

75. Gordon Cloough (2nd from right) recording with colleagues from the BBC Russian Section an episode from the radio serial soap The Lvov Family in the mid 1960s. Tony Cash is 2nd from left. Copyright the BBC.

Gordon Clough, who had learned his Russian in Bodmin, and done radio intercept work in Kiel, went up to Oxford a year later than Tony Cash to read French and Russian at Magdalen College. Graduating in 1958, he joined the BBC's Russian Section following a spell as a studio manager. He was already well established in the Section when Cash arrived. In April 1961, on the very morning that Yuriy Gagarin's momentous voyage into outer space in the *Vostok* spacecraft was announced, Clough wrote and presented for Soviet listeners a moving tribute to the astronaut's great achievement. A few weeks later he was allowed by the BBC to go to Moscow to interpret at the British Trade Fair, where the best of our industrial and consumer products were being displayed. A versatile writer, who could turn his hand to most subjects, Clough wrote and produced programmes on many topics – literature, theatre, sport, the visual arts, broadcasting and the media. He even penned one or two episodes of a *Mrs Dale*-type weekly soap opera in which he also acted: *The Lvov Family* series was reputed to have a fan club of older listeners in the Soviet Union, and letters of appreciation were not uncommon.

He was a speedy as well as exceptionally gifted translator. With help from Tony Cash and un-attributed editing by Alexander Lieven, head of the Section, Clough translated in a couple of weeks *Years of my Life* (*Voyny I Gody*), the memoirs of Alexander Gorbatov,[10] only the second officially sanctioned (as opposed to *samizdat*) account of imprisonment in the Gulag, Solzhenitsyn's *One Day in the Life of Ivan Denisovich* having preceded it two years earlier. A victim of the 1937 purge of officers that decimated the Red Army hierarchy, Gorbatov was released from imprisonment in Siberia after the Nazi invasion of the USSR in June 1941, and eventually rose to be Commandant of the Soviet Sector of Berlin.

Ex-coders as Moscow press correspondents

While Gordon Clough and Tony Cash were enlightening Russian audiences about life in Britain, Jeremy Wolfenden and Mark Frankland were reporting on Soviet affairs for British readers. Former midshipmen interpreters, they were employed in the early 1960s by *The Daily Telegraph* and *The Observer* respectively.

---

10 See Reading List.

76. Jane Bown's portrait of Mark Frankland in the *Observer* news room in 1985.
Copyright Guardian News & Media Ltd.

Wolfenden was widely considered one of the most gifted men of his generation. His tragic story is movingly told in Sebastian Faulks's *The Fatal Englishman*. An excessive liking for alcohol coupled with a tendency to flaunt his homosexuality made him an easy target for the rival intelligence agencies, which blackmailed him into supplying them both with information. He died in 1965, at the age of 31, having accomplished infinitely less than his hugely successful academic career had promised. His Eton school-mate and close friend, the journalist Neal Ascherson, pointed out that Wolfenden was reporting from Soviet Russia when the Berlin wall was erected, the Cuban missile crisis erupted, and Oleg Penkovsky was put on trial for spying for the British:

> ... yet I never read a really original or exciting article by Jeremy in all his three Moscow years. He produced competent, literate work: that was all. Deliberately, he was choosing not to achieve.[11]

Ascherson recalls that he and his friend had decided as schoolboys that it was some kind of laudably rebellious 'existential' act intentionally to fail when all around expect you to succeed magnificently. This explanation for Wolfenden's failure to write more enthralling material for the *Telegraph* is contested by both Mark Frankland and John Miller, a former Army *kursant* who spent most of his journalist career also working in Moscow. They offer a different explanation: Wolfenden was not called upon to analyse what he saw and heard, merely report on it; in-depth explanations of Soviet behaviour were the prerogative of the *Telegraph*'s senior Russian specialist in London, David Floyd. Frankland pointed out[12] that anyone who had been elected a Fellow of All Souls College, Oxford, could not conceivably have been contemplating a career of underachievement. No more than two Fellows are chosen in any one year, usually first class graduates, and they have to excel in one of the hardest exams in the world. According to Faulks,[13] Wolfenden strode out of a three-hour exam after only half an hour. The subject was 'Liberty, equality, democracy – three beautiful but incompatible ideals':

> Wolfenden did not write an essay, but merely jotted down a string of aphorisms. He won a prize fellowship.

11   *The Independent*, 5 May 1996.
12   Email, Mark Frankland to Tony Cash, 31 July 2010.
13   Sebastian Faulks, *The Fatal Englishman*, p 243.

The late Mark Frankland had been a contemporary of Wolfenden's at JSSL London. He had several publications to his credit, including very well received books on aspects of the Khrushchev and Gorbachev eras, as well as novels and a personal memoir, *Child of My Time* (subtitled *An Englishman's Journey in a Divided World*). Not long after graduating in history from Cambridge, Frankland was inveigled into joining MI6 (or SIS, the Security Intelligence Service, as it is more properly known). He believes he was approached because in the summer of 1955, three years earlier, he had helped smuggle a young Pole to the West out of Warsaw, while visiting the Communist World Youth Festival there. He was with a group of fellow Cambridge students who contrived to get the absconding dissident onto the train leaving for the West, and hiding him, when needs be, on the luggage rack. Feigning sickness, to conceal him, the only girl in their company lay on him, stripped to her briefs under a blanket. When the frontier guard entered the compartment to check its contents, he called on her to come down. Showing great presence of mind, Mark told the man in excellent Russian to:

... leave the girl alone: she's ill.

One can readily understand how, hearing a firm instruction in the language of his effective masters, a lowly-ranking Polish guard would jump to do as told.[14]

The ability to think so quickly, coupled with his language skills, would have made Mark a tempting target for our security services. He had not completed a year's training, however, when he decided that the spy's life was not for him. His principal reason was fear that he might be called on to effect policies with which he 'passionately disagreed'. Uppermost in his mind was the Suez venture of 1956, when the then Prime Minister, Anthony Eden, colluded secretly with the French and Israeli governments in an invasion of Egypt to regain control of the canal seized three months earlier by Colonel Nasser:

I was at Cambridge then, and with some friends published an anti-war pamphlet seditiously advising conscripts to ignore their call-up papers. I always knew that if there was another Suez I would walk out of Broadway Buildings right away.[15]

14 Story told by Neal Ascherson, in the presence of Tony Cash, at a commemorative lunch in Mark Frankland's honour hosted by Friends of the *Observer*, shortly after his death in May 2012.

15 Mark Frankland, *Child of My Time*, p 93.

MI6's loss was *The Observer*'s gain, though Frankland admits it took him some time to discover what he should ideally be writing about in Moscow. Inspiration came, he wrote in his memoir, from seeing youngsters congregating around the enormous statue of Pushkin in the square that bears the name of Russia's foremost poet. Frankland's initial thought was that this must be a 'spontaneous public meeting', an extremely rare Soviet phenomenon. Drawing nearer, he realised his mistake: the teenage boys and girls were taking it in turns to recite Pushkin's verse. It was the anniversary of the author's birth. Mark was obviously deeply moved. Such experiences could ignite the 'spark of sympathy' a reporter needs to go on discovering more and more about his subject, and develop:

> ... something of the lover's protectiveness, not towards regimes in power but the land and people that endured them.[16]

Frankland was at great pains to understand what motivated Soviet decision-makers and how their government functioned. In *Child of My Time* he describes making one extremely useful, if shady, contact capable of opening the necessary doors. The introduction was effected through a young man identified in the book simply as Vladimir, but now known to be Vladimir Pozner, who was later to appear quite frequently on US and British TV discussing President Gorbachev's reforms of the 1980s. Pozner had lived and studied in America, and when Mark met him in the early 1960s he was employed by the Soviet state news agency Novosti, allied to, if not actually controlled by, the KGB. An offer of lunch with Pozner's old history professor seemed too good an opportunity to turn down. The rendezvous was the Praga restaurant, at the time one of the most sumptuous in Moscow. Frankland was ushered to a private room, where he found Vladimir sitting with an older man at a large dining table laden with bottles of vodka and wine and platters of Russian hors d'oeuvres, *zakuski*, fit for a 'Kremlin banquet':

> Vladimir was taller by a head than his companion, but the smaller man was incontestably the more impressive figure. Strongly built, he had a short neck, heavy head and ruddy complexion. He seemed to me quite old, but I suspect he was only in his early fifties. Beady eyes, big teeth and a hooked nose completed the picture of a Russian Mr Punch who, given the chance,

---

16 *Ibid*, p 206.

would very much enjoy using his cudgel. This was
not my idea of how an eminent historian looked, and
I was not surprised that though we talked for almost
three hours the subject of history was not mentioned
once ... He asked me about myself and my views on
international affairs, and questioned me closely on
British politics ... he spoke only Russian and gave
no sign of understanding whenever Vladimir and I
exchanged a few words in English ... Before we broke
up he asked if there was anything he could do for me,
but did not seem put out when I shook my head. He
wrote a telephone number on a piece of paper and
gave it to me. Ring it, he said, if something (he did
not explain what that something might be) cropped up.
Just ask for Sergei Borisovich, he said, and bared his
long teeth in a smile.[17]

Frankland later took up the offer of help when *The Observer* asked
him to do a story in Siberia, which would have been impossible to
visit without official approval. Another meal at the Praga followed,
this time without Pozner. Before help could be agreed, Frankland
needed to answer a question:

Was I in any way 'culpable before Soviet power'?
That is the exact translation of his Russian words,
which I have never forgotten, not least because of
their archaic ring. He did not say guilty, but *culpable*,
sinful. And he did not say Soviet law or the Soviet
government, but power, *vlast*, a word that evoked the
might of the Russian state throughout the ages. Of
course I said 'no', but his little eyes were watching me
and his lips were parted as if in anticipation of some
rare delight.[18]

Frankland came to see Sergei Borisovich as a kind of KGB
godfather, who could smooth away irksome travel restrictions, but
whose subsequent attempts to entice the journalist into the Soviet
orbit were firmly, if gently, rebutted - as the memoir makes clear.

Frankland's first spell as Moscow correspondent for *The
Observer* provided him with ample material for his biography of
Khrushchev, first published in 1966, only two years after the Soviet
premier's removal from power. Since then, of course, a great deal
has been penned on the subject, and the retired former leader's own

17 *Ibid*, pp 69-70.
18 *Ibid*, p 70.

autobiographical writings were smuggled out of Russia in 1970. However, many of Frankland's judgements may still withstand scrutiny decades later, like his explanation why, in 1962, Khrushchev decided to put nuclear missiles on Cuba, only ninety miles from Florida. According to Frankland, one of the Soviet premier's overriding concerns was to shift the country's economy away, to some degree, from the interests of the military-industrial complex and more towards those of consumers. The arms race against a vastly wealthier and technologically superior USA was making this change difficult: the Americans were manufacturing more numerous and more sophisticated long-range rockets, intercontinental ballistic missiles, than the Soviets. Placing medium-range missiles in Cuba was a cheaper way of closing the missile gap.[19] When Khrushchev's colleagues in the Politburo conspired to oust him, they were able to point to his handling of the Cuban crisis as one of the factors why he should resign.

Frankland believed that Khrushchev was genuinely committed to the policies implied by the slogan 'peace abroad, prosperity at home', and that Khrushchev gave them priority over the global triumph of communism. As evidence to justify his belief, Frankland referred to the Soviet leader's willingness to quarrel with China on precisely this issue. Frankland considered it unfortunate that the West failed to recognise what motivated Khrushchev.

This relatively benevolent view of Khrushchev was not altogether shared by John Miller, the former Army *kursant*, who spent most of a 40-year career as a foreign correspondent in Moscow, reporting principally for the *Daily Telegraph*. His highly entertaining book *All them Cornfields and Ballet in the Evening* makes few if any concessions to the Soviet regime, whoever its leader happened to be. The title is a quotation from the self-serving, bolshie shop-steward, played by Peter Sellers in the Boulting Brothers' film *I'm Alright, Jack*, who believes the Soviet Union to be a worker's paradise. Miller does not go in for the kind of political analysis that characterises Frankland's work. The emphasis is much more on vivid personal anecdotes that are as amusing as illuminating. Miller had many opportunities to see Khrushchev, the 'journalist's dream', at close quarters. When Yuriy Gagarin returned from his epoch-making space flight, he was invited to the Kremlin to be honoured as

---

19　Mark Frankland, *Khrushchev*, pp 191-2.

77. Nikita Khrushchev and Mrs Khruschev receive Yuriy Gagarin and his wife in the Kremlin in April 1961. Courtesy RIA Novosti.

Hero of the Soviet Union. To the embarrassment of the assembled dignitaries, Khrushchev struggled to pin the gold medal award to the astronaut's chest:

> Finally the Soviet leader gave up, slapped the medal in the cosmonaut's hand and turning to the audience said with a grin: 'There you are, comrades, see how solid our Soviet cloth is. Even a pin cannot pierce it.' He knew as well as we all did, that the problem was not Soviet cloth. It was shoddy workmanship of the pin on the country's highest award for valour.[20]

If only because of the many hundreds of thousands of Gulag inmates released by him, Miller and Frankland agreed that Khrushchev left his country a better place than he found it – a claim that cannot be made for very many politicians.

20   John Miller, *All them Cornfields and Ballet in the Evening*, p 70.

78. Ian Wooldridge (far right) with unknowns, probably in Germany some time between 1952 and 1954. Courtesy Max Wooldridge.

CHAPTER 14

ON THE MARGINS OF THE COLD WAR: THE GERONTOCRAT ERA

СТУК В ДВЕРЬ. БРЕЖНЕВ ДОСТАЕТ ИЗ КАРМАНА ОЧКИ, БУМАЖКУ И ЧИТАЕТ: КТО ТАМ?

('There's a knock at the door. Brezhnev takes his glasses and a piece of paper out of his pocket and reads: "Who's there?"' – Russian joke)

The eighteen-year rule of Leonid Ilyich Brezhnev from 1964 to 1982 has often been branded as a period of economic stagnation and cultural repression at home, accompanied by a policy of stifling liberalising tendencies in the satellite communist regimes of Eastern Europe - Czechoslovakia being the crucial example. In 1966 Tony Cash at the BBC was producing for Soviet listeners a monthly magazine programme on cinema and the film industry. In one edition he interviewed Czech film-maker Milos Forman about his hugely successful films *Blonde in Love* and *Peter and Pavla*, sagas of adolescent disaffection and *angst*:

> I recall asking him how it was possible to make such apolitical films in a Communist country. Forman replied: 'Easy. There are so many of us and so few of them'.

The attempt to establish in Czechoslovakia 'socialism with a human face' led to the Russian invasion of August 1968. Thirty minutes before Red Army tanks crossed the border the Soviets began once again to jam BBC and other Russian language broadcasts.

Michael Connock compromised in Poland

It was always assumed during the Cold War that the security services of satellite countries such as East Germany, Hungary and Poland did not normally raise a finger against a Western visitor without at least consultation with the KGB in Moscow. In 1969 one former coder, Michael Connock, fell foul of the Polish authorities with disastrous consequences for his career in journalism. As a midshipman Connock was a contemporary of John Bayliss, Mark Frankland and Jeremy Wolfenden at the London JSSL. A brilliant linguist, he passed out top of his course, and went on to read modern languages at Worcester College, Oxford, where he had won an open scholarship. Between 1961 and 1969 he was the Soviet and East European correspondent of the *Financial Times*.

Connock described the calamity that befell him in an article in the Melbourne newspaper, *The Age*. His job at the FT took him to one or other East European country four or five times a year for periods of usually one to four weeks. The purpose of his last trip to Poland in February 1969 was to gather information for articles about politics, especially the so-called 'Jewish question', and economics. Intending to visit the shipyards on the Baltic coast, he was met at the seaside spa resort of Sopot by two men who drove him to a large building in a dark lane in the nearby port of Gdynia. He was taken up to a sizeable room with the Polish coat of arms – a white eagle on a red background – on one wall. Marek and Jozef, as they styled themselves, began to interrogate the journalist, one playing soft cop, the other, hard:

> 'Now, Panie Connock', said Jozef, addressing me in the vocative case which Polish, alone among the Slavonic languages, has kept, 'you are a journalist, and your profession is asking questions, but now we're going to ask you some questions …' I was still pretty frightened, but at the same time a certain excitement was taking hold of me. Here I was seeing at first hand the operations of the notorious UB, the Polish Secret Service.

While Marek plied their captive with sausages, tea and alcoholic drinks, Jozef wanted to know about Connock's Polish contacts:

> I told him the names of all I knew in Poland, because the UB was certain to know anyway, and to have omitted any name would only have put that person under suspicion … 'We don't want to put you in prison,' said Jozef, implying that they might have to. 'We want you to help us, then we'll help you.' By this time I was pretty sure that what it was all about was blackmail … (Jozef) asked in particular about a girl whom I shall call Anna Kowalska, whom I had

originally met in 1966. Then again, quite by chance, in Revolution Square in Moscow in 1967. In Moscow we had become very fond of each other.

Connock knew the lady was married, but he was under the impression that her husband was content to let her lead her own life. Before travelling to Poland in 1969, he had written to tell her he would shortly be back in that country:

> The day after my arrival, I had a telephone call from another woman saying that Anna had domestic trouble and could not ring herself, but would come to Warsaw. In the event, however, her husband came, and there was an unpleasant scene in which he demanded that I should make no further attempt to contact her. His worry was not concerned with marital jealousy, but with the trouble an association with a foreigner could bring.

To Connock's consternation, the interrogator, Jozef, produced incriminating documentary evidence – photographs of the journalist with Anna sightseeing in Moscow as well as a letter of complaint to the Polish Foreign Ministry. In it the husband begged officials to contact the British embassy to prevent Connock visiting Poland again. The price for not divulging this material to interested parties in Britain was Connock's signature on a document in which he would:

> ... 'voluntarily agree to co-operate with the Intelligence [*Service* omitted in the article but probably intended] of the Polish People's Republic in political, economic, intelligence and counter-intelligence matters'.[1]

A sentence was added to the declaration to cover expenses, and Connock was asked to sign. He was then given verbal instructions how to make contact with Marek and Jozef, now to be his handlers. An expression by them that they had read an article of his 'with interest' would signify that they were coming, 'whatever else they might go on to say'. He was to write down their phone number in some garbled form that only he would understand.

Throughout his ordeal, Connock was resolved to sign whatever was required, but immediately reveal all on his return to Britain. He realised that the compromising position he had put himself in would

---

1   All Connock article quotations: *The Age*, 17 March 1969, p 6.

mean he could no longer work in the USSR or Eastern Europe. Anticipating that he would be offered alternative employment by the *Financial Times* once the facts were known, he was gravely disappointed to be sacked, though given 16-months salary as per contract. His further career was principally teaching in higher education establishments.

Clifford German was for a couple of years a colleague of Michael Connock's on the *Financial Times*. He had also studied Russian as a midshipman at the London JSSL, going on to read Geography at Oxford, followed by teaching in American universities. He is co-author with Professor John Cole of *An Economic Geography of the USSR*, published in 1962, shortly after his change of career from academe to journalism. Connock's misfortune deterred Clifford from contemplating a correspondent's assignment in Eastern Europe:

> With hazards of that kind to confront, and with the stern warnings of DNI [Director of Naval Intelligence] to be wary of being compromised ringing in my ears, I turned down the opportunity to specialise in Russian affairs that the Cole & German book should have given me.

A career on the domestic front, working for *The Times* and *Daily Telegraph* proved a more attractive alternative. From 1987 to 1994 Clifford was the City Editor of *The Scotsman,* where his knowledge of Russian and of the Soviet economy stood him in good stead when it came to writing about the disintegration of the USSR in 1991.

Presenting a British jazz band in the USSR

Despite the worsening of relations between east and west in this period, cultural exchanges continued. In the summer of 1977 Tony Cash travelled with the National Youth Jazz Orchestra (NYJO) to Russia for a 16-day series of performances in Leningrad and Moscow. On his return to London he wrote an account of the tour for the BBC journal *The Listener*. The following draws on that article:

> When the orchestra's leader and director, Bill Ashton, first asked me if I'd like to interpret for and present his band on stage, I was delighted at the prospect of visiting Russia again, after an absence of 18 years, particularly since I might have an opportunity to meet

people who'd listened to my 1960s music programmes. At the same time, though, I was doubtful whether the Soviet authorities would allow me in as interpreter - not to speak of letting me loose on a Russian audience.

From the outset, it was clear that *Goskontsert*, the Soviet organisation sponsoring the tour, would provide their own interpreters. That they finally agreed to accept me in addition was probably due to the size of the party to be managed - 31 members - and its relative youth, the youngest musician being 15 and the oldest, 23. But the *Goskontsert* officials were not initially prepared to let me introduce the band to Soviet audiences; they preferred, they said, to rely, as they had in the past, on an actress qualified for the work. Anya, it transpired, actually possessed documentary evidence of her fitness to 'MC' concerts. She was not, however, qualified to improvise at the microphone and, 'if this was what was required, it should have been written into the contract'. Nor was she able, with decorum, either to pronounce or explain typical titles in the NYJO repertoire, like *Fuggles Fantastical Fugue*, or *Drink Tolley only with Meat Pies*. A satisfactory compromise was reached, whereby she and I would come on stage together at the beginning, middle and end of each concert, taking it in turns to present the numbers with introductory material prepared by myself. How this concession to Bill Ashton's wishes was granted, I do not know. Certainly, there were discussions at the highest levels in *Goskontsert*, maybe even the Ministry of Culture. A particular problem for them must have been what formula to use in announcing me on stage. I never concealed that I had once worked in the BBC's Russian Section (it would, in any event, have been difficult to do so, since many more people knew me than I could have imagined). They hit on a neat device. Anya eventually asked me if I would object to being introduced as a colleague from London radio and TV. I readily agreed. Our collaboration, thereafter, was most fruitful. Anya gave my Russian a more idiomatic turn of phrase; in return, I undertook to explain to our audiences the puns and references to mysterious English drinking habits contained in titles like *Home Brew*, *Black Velvet*, and *Samuel Smith and his Amazing Dancing Beer*.

If my presence caused any heartache, I was never made aware of it. NYJO's programme changed fairly radically with every concert, and introductions were always being written at the last minute. No one in authority ever asked what I was proposing to say. True, our audiences were regularly around the 2,000 mark. But the fact that Bill Ashton, Dave Gelly (a musician and critic accompanying us on the tour) and myself were interviewed, at length, for a Saturday lunchtime popular music radio show, with listeners numbering over 20 million, suggests at least a minor cultural thaw. The producer/presenter of the programme, Grigory Libergal, proved to be exceptionally well informed about the recent history of jazz and rock. He delighted me by quoting the four-line verse I used to open my late-night Friday pop-show beamed to Russia. Unlike me, he was also able to recall all the records I had played in my farewell programme in 1968, nine years earlier.

Later that summer Cash, by then a TV producer/director making films on music and the arts, was invited to Moscow with BBC recording engineers to help produce stereo versions of Bolshoi theatre productions of the opera *Boris Godunov* and the *Nutcracker* ballet – part of a major international co-production deal:

While I was in Moscow I had the opportunity to meet the USSR's greatest living composer, Aram Khachaturian. I wanted to propose filming a TV documentary portrait of him. Asked which of his contemporaries he especially admired, he surprised me greatly by replying Messiaen and Duke Ellington. Sadly, he took ill very shortly after that meeting, and died before the film biography could be made.

When Brezhnev assumed the Soviet leader's mantle after the deposition of Khrushchev, some Western commentators feared that the USSR would relapse into Stalinism. That did not happen. There was no plan to restore the mummified cadaver of the old tyrant to the Red Square mausoleum, where it had lain alongside Lenin's until its ignominious removal at Khrushchev's instigation in 1961. Dissident intellectuals, however, continued to be persecuted for merely expressing their ideas. Writers Andrei Sinyavsky and Yuly Daniel were incarcerated for several years in 'correctional' colonies far from Moscow, though still in European Russia.

Alexander Solzhenitsyn, author of *Gulag Archipelago*, the story of Soviet concentration camps, was sent into exile abroad. Nuclear physicist Andrei Sakharov, 'father' of the Soviet atomic bomb and campaigner for democratic rights, was banished from the capital to the city of Gorky. During Brezhnev's reign (as in Khrushchev's), dissent no longer called for a bullet in the back of the head, and most recalcitrants went through a legal process, albeit one which was rarely open to the public and press. But terror was no longer the State's first weapon of defence against its detractors: dissident historian Roy Medvedev could well claim that the Brezhnev era was 'the quietest in Soviet history'.[2]

Gordon Clough brings Soviet dissident to attention of English-speakers

In both the Khrushchev and Brezhnev periods, there was a jargon term, almost a catch-phrase, used by Communist Party propagandists to depict the glorious future beckoning a diligent, loyal Soviet citizenry. This was the cliché, *Gleaming Heights* -in Russian, *Siyayushchie Vysoty* – usually in the formula the 'gleaming heights of communism'.[3] The semi-religious nuance was altogether consistent with the Soviet Marxist lexicology in which Lenin could be said to be 'living yet'. The hallowed expression was intended to convey the notion of a kind of materialistic Nirvana to be realised in the not too distant future when, under a fully-realised communism, all earthly needs would be satisfied. By changing one letter – the initial *s* of *siyayushchie* to *z* – arch-dissident professor of logic, Alexander Zinoviev, invented *The Yawning Heights*. And that was his title for a vast, rambling, bawdy satire on the Soviet society of the middle 1970s. Its publication in the West in 1976 led to Zinoviev's losing his job in the philosophy faculty of Moscow University and expulsion from the Communist Party.

The story is set in a mythical country called *Ibansk* – Fucksville (from the Russian verb *yebat'*) – where the most common surname is *Ibanov* (combination of the ubiquitous Russian *Ivanov*, and the same verb). Prominent actual politicians, intellectuals and dissidents appear under thinly disguised monickers – 'Boss', for Stalin; 'Hog',

---

2   Quoted by Mark Frankland in *The Sixth Continent*, 1987, p 9.
3   British socialists have been known to use the less grandiose term 'sunny uplands'.

79. Ian Wooldridge dancing at a private party in Moscow in 1980 with
Olympic multi-gold medal winning gymnast, Olga Korbut.
Copyright the *Daily Mail*.

for Khrushchev; 'Truth-teller', for Solzhenitsyn; and 'Dauber', for the sculptor Ernst Neizviestny, who in 1962 had famously argued about modern art with Khrushchev at a public exhibition.

We owe the English translation of this 800-odd page epic to Gordon Clough, who says in the preface that it took him far longer than the six months Zinoviev spent on producing the original. It was not just the length which was daunting: the text is full of puns, and there are many pages of rhymed doggerel which Gordon has ingeniously rendered into comparable English verse. The quality of the translation may be judged from a sonnet, called by Zinoviev *The Legend*.[4] It is the heartfelt, dissident cry, echoing over the centuries, of every Russian patriot who finds himself in conflict with the regime, Tsarist or Communist.

> Why have you stayed, and not fled with the rest?
> I shrugged and shook my head, I felt depressed.
> I long have fought for this my motherland,
> For her I've lain and shivered in the frost,
> For her I've starved when no food came to hand,
> Here I grew up. I'm hers at any cost.
> I weep, but not a maudlin drunkard's tears;
> They're tender recollection I can't hide
> Of all the love I've given her down the years,
> My only love, my own grey land, my bride.
> Bereft of wife and babes one can survive;
> To leave one's land's a thought I can't endure.
> Better by far be buried here alive
> And feed her – be it only as manure.

Ian Wooldridge covers Moscow Olympics - upsets Soviet *apparatchiks*

Fortunately for mankind, the Cold War never actually became a 'hot' war, but there were during this period what came to be known as 'proxy' wars. These occurred when client states of the rival major powers clashed – the Arab-Israeli conflicts of 1956, 1967 and 1973 are obvious examples – or when one of the super powers took on a client state of the other – the deployment of American combat units

---

4   Alexander Zinoviev, *Yawning Heights*, trans. Gordon Clough, p 811.

346

Москва 1980

80. Poster for the Moscow 1980 Olympics featuring 'Misha' the Games'
mascot. Courtesy RIA Novosti.

in Vietnam in 1965 is the classic case. On Christmas Eve, 1979, the Soviets invaded Afghanistan to save a fellow Marxist-Leninist regime from being overthrown by the Mujahideen (much as the Americans had earlier tried to save non-Communist South Vietnam from being conquered by the Vietcong). The Afghan war was to last nine years with the West soon supplying the Mujahideen with cash and arms. But one of the first responses was a political gesture. In January 1980 US President Jimmy Carter announced a boycott of the forthcoming Moscow Olympics. British Prime Minister Margaret Thatcher eagerly agreed (although she had no authority over the British Olympic team, which ignored her), and some 60 nations eventually spurned what were to be the first ever Olympic Games staged in Eastern Europe.

President Carter's initiative was widely welcomed in America. The British were much more divided: some even of Margaret Thatcher's admirers were unwilling to agree with her on this issue. One such was ex-coder, Ian Wooldridge, doyen of sports commentators, who for decades wrote for the *Daily Mail* articles universally appreciated for their verve, originality and honesty. Wooldridge's views on the boycott were diametrically opposed to those of his newspaper which, nevertheless:

> ... still permitted me to write what I pleased, pointing out in a leader column that that was the difference between Britain and the Soviet Union. Mrs Thatcher didn't hold any grudges, either. One of Britain's rowing silver medallists at the Moscow Olympics was one Colin Moynihan. Later in the decade she was to appoint him her Minister of Sport.[5]

Wooldridge's essential point was that neither Thatcher nor Carter, nor their respective advisers, understood 'the quaint idealism' of the Olympics. In *Sport in the 80s*, a collection of the journalist's articles and columns from that decade, he tells the story of the 1936 Olympics, when Hitler wanted to decorate the Games with anti-Semitic messages. The then Olympic President, confronted the German chancellor, telling him that his signs violated Olympic principles. According to Wooldridge, Hitler pointed out that a guest does not tell a host how to run his house, to which the president retorted:

---

5   Ian Wooldridge, *Sport in the 80s A Personal View*, Centurion Books, 1989, p 9.

348

81. Soviet President Leonid Brezhnev waving to the crowds at the 1980 Moscow Olympic Games. Courtesy RIA Novosti.

'When the five-circled flag is raised over the stadium, it is no longer Germany. It is Olympia and we are the masters here.' The signs were removed.

The article concludes with an indirect reference to the invasion of Afghanistan:

> The Moscow Olympics will neither provoke war nor prevent it. They are now merely condemned to give us a laugh of historic proportions when the Russians release the usual flurry of doves at the opening ceremony and sing us songs about eternal friendship and peace.
>
> Far from staging a multi-million rouble propaganda exercise to the glory of Mother Russia, the Soviet Union has pledged to open its doors to the world at a time when its horrific ugliness has rarely been more exposed. It is too good a chance to miss.[6]

Wooldridge took his chance and went to Moscow. Nothing loath, their support of the boycott notwithstanding, the *Daily Mail* duly printed his stories. On 17 July he wrote:

> They are feeding us off the fat of someone else's land, and by way of a bargain, appealing to us daily to write the truth about the Soviet Union. Well, this is the truth. In five days here I have seen only two lurching Russian drunks and only two ladies on the game.

Things got more serious when on 19 July the Games opened, protected, in Wooldridge's words, 'by a paranoiac security cordon'. The magnitude of the problem can be gauged from a report on the Internet by the Soviet citizen actually responsible for dealing with all media issues. Lithuanian-born Henrikas Yushkiavitshus was Vice-Chairman of Soviet State Television and Radio Committee, and had to oversee negotiations with foreign media representatives for world coverage:

> During the Games, there were problems with the security people. In the television center, they set the metal detectors to such a high degree of sensitivity that an alarm would go off even if somebody had a single metal tooth. The first three days, this resulted in endless queues trying to enter the center.
>
> Just an hour before the opening ceremony, the head of the Eurovision team called me saying that security

---

6   *Ibid,* pp 10-11.

350

FROM IAN WOOLDRIDGE
IN PRICKLY MOSCOW

Really Mr B,

MOSCOW: *A senior Soviet Olympic official yesterday issued a veiled warning to the Press that journalists who insulted the Soviet Union might be expelled from the Games.*

The threat was issued by Vladimir Popov, vice-president of the Games Organising Committee, in reply to a Press conference question from a Soviet journalist.

Popov was asked for his reaction to a story in a British newspaper which analysed how the main Lenin Stadium might be vulnerable to a terrorist attack.

He said he had not read the story but if it or other Press stories were found to 'insult the national dignity of the host country' the Soviet organisers would appeal to the International Olympic Committee to take 'most decisive measures against the journalists involved'.
—REUTER

I won't

try to kill you!

AT THE risk of being rather boring about this let me make it quite clear that I have not, never have had and almost certainly never will have any ambition to assassinate President Leonid Brezhnev of the Soviet Union.

I was only pointing out, in the words I wrote about the opening ceremony of the Olympic Games, how easy it would have been to have shot him.

Yesterday around here they started mumbling things like that they should investigate the circumstances behind at least one other story which has received enormous prominence in rival British newspapers.

It concerns a number of arrests in Red Square during an incident in which the name of Sebastian Coe was mentioned. The fact is that Coe was about 11 miles away when it happened and, to this

POPOV . . . warning

moment, has not the remotest idea what it was all about.

I only write this to explain what can happen when the British Press determines to use the Olympic Games for reasons of propaganda.

Several writers have been instructed to see only evil here and write accordingly. Some have not only acceded to this request but actually embellished minor incidents into major stories, presumably in the hope of winning proprietorial approval.

There is no need to do this at all, Mrs Thatcher, while abjectly failing to stop the Games, had none the less turned this quadriennial jamboree into something of a wake.

Never has that been more vividly seen than the night before last when Duncan Goodhew won not only the first gold medal for Britain but the first for the English speaking world. His performance was stupendous, his dignity in victory supreme.

I don't know how it appeared on television but from the ninth row of the balcony it might have been Mr Smith of Luton picking up the prize for green marrows at the annual local horticultural show.

A few British supporters, led by Duncan's mum, cheered but, that apart, it was of so little interest to anyone around here that a third of the auditorium seats were empty.

Cool youngster

An hour later, by which time at previous Olympics the street would have been packed with revellers, I stood alongside a six-lane highway immediately outside the swimming venue for 20 minutes in search of a taxi and saw only six people cross the road. All six were reporters who are paid to be here anyway.

These Olympics go on in a vacuum and I must say I sympathise with the organising committee who have got so

many things right. In terms of organisation they leave Montreal and Munich for dead.

The people I am sorry for, inevitably, are the athletes themselves. If there has ever been a young Briton to entomise the characteristics that Mrs Thatcher demands for our Olympic teams it is surely Goodhew.

Calm, utterly self-controlled in a moment of enormous stress, gracious afterwards in victory, he achieved it with the disenchanted knowledge that for doing something rather good for Britain he will be reviled by half the country.

British Olympic gold medal winners in the past have usually received some recognition. Goodhew, I am sure couldn't care less but he will of course receive nothing while businessmen who have continued treating successfully with the Soviet Union will be awarded knighthoods.

It is one of the reasons why the athletes are entitled to be cynical and the atmosphere here continue to be sterile. Huge achievements pass almost unnoticed, while minor incidents are accorded major attention.

Of course we are not here to kill the President. It was purely an academic comment on how the security services actually work.

BOXER RAY STRIKES FOR A TREBLE

BANTAMWEIGHT Ray Gilbody maintained Britain's 100 per cent boxing record when he became the third man to win his opening contest in the Olympic Games yesterday.

On Sunday, Gilbody faces a dangerous Mexican southpaw Daniel Zaraguza, while Irish European bronze medallist Philip Sutcliffe

Gilbody, a painter and decorator from Warrington, gave an other classical display of British boxing when outpointing Almeida of Angola.

☐ A MAJOR upset in the soccer was provided by Nigeria when they held Czechoslovakia 1-1.

☐ SEVENTEEN - YEAR - OLD Lancashire twins, Ann and

Janet Osgerby, swim in the 100m. butterfly final tonight. It is thought they are the first twins to swim in the same Olympic final.

☐ SIXTY members of Ireland's 50-strong team have been hit by food poisoning.

☐ BRITAIN'S Mike McLeod, world's fastest man at 10,000m. last year, has shingles but intends to run in today's heats.

82. The *Daily Mail* headline (24 July 1980) which caused Ian Wooldridge so much aggravation from the KGB in Moscow during the Olympics. Copyright the *Daily Mail*.

would admit only one person per media outlet, even if the plans called for three. Things improved only after I told the Minister of the Interior that Eurovision would not cover the opening ceremony and that he would have to explain why to the world audience.[7]

By 21 July, the day of the opening ceremony attended by the Soviet President, security which had earlier seemed to Wooldridge so paranoid had suddenly become extraordinarily lax:

... the one thing you could easily have done from my seat, number 691, in the third row at the opening ceremony was to have shot Leonid Brezhnev stone dead. The fourth side of the protective marble structure in which he feebly applauded each team as it passed was open to a firing angle of 80 degrees and packed to a depth of 60 yards by photographers aiming long-lens cameras straight at his head.

Amazingly, since we are hand-searched and electronically tested every time we walk into an hotel or conference room, no one gave us a second glance as we strolled into the Lenin Stadium carrying bulging brief-cases or shoulder-bags. One would not, of course, have lived to tell the story.

Three days later, hearing suggestions that he might be kicked out of the country, Wooldridge wrote a piece in the *Daily Mail* to allay any Soviet fears about his intentions:

At the risk of being rather boring about this, let me make it quite clear that I have not, never have had and almost certainly never will have any ambition to assassinate the Soviet President ... I was simply pointing out how easy it would have been ...

Unfortunately for Wooldridge, this article was given (presumably by a sub-editor) the large inflammatory headline - REALLY MR B, I WON'T TRY TO KILL YOU! The upshot was pretty dramatic, as the journalist explained in a conversation with Tony Cash on 1 February 1999.

Ian told me the secret police came to interrogate him. They gave him a cup of coffee with a thick meniscus on it (from the movement of which they could judge how nervous he was). The grilling became more intense, and they accused him of being

7 http://www.wpfc.org/site/docs/pdf/Winning%20Press%20Freedom%20 (text).pdf What the Games taught me about press freedom.

a terrorist. Then they said: 'why are we talking in English; you speak perfectly good Russian.' They knew he had learned Russian in the Navy during his national service, though by 1980, some 25 years later, he was able to tell them truthfully that he didn't: he'd forgotten everything he ever knew. Having only two O-levels, neither in a modern language, he must have been the least qualified national serviceman to be accepted on the Russian course. Eventually, his tormentors promised to have him kicked out of the USSR. A few months later, Ian learned that the only reason they did not carry out their threat was because International Olympic Committee officials said the British athletes would withdraw if he were expelled.[8]

Tom Clarke was the sports editor of the *Daily Mail* and Ian Wooldridge's boss in 1980. In a conversation with Tony Cash in August 2011 he said that in all the twelve years he had worked with Ian, he only knew him to be frightened on one occasion – while he was in Moscow covering the Olympic Games: he complained of being followed and that they were 'listening to every word I say'.

However apprehensive he may have been, Wooldridge did not pull his punches in further articles on the Games. He was amazed by a Soviet commentator's failure to mention during live commentary that an East German football player had scored the winning goal in an important match against the USSR. Claiming that the Games were primarily intended to impress the Soviet citizens, he continued:

> ... all 259 million of them, speaking a multitude of languages and stretching through 11 different time zones between here (Moscow) and the blunt end of Alaska, USA. The Soviet Union, if there isn't to be some unrest out there, must be seen as the overlord in all that it attempts, sport not excluded. The solution if things go wrong, as they did in the soccer semi-final against East Germany, is very simple indeed. You talk through the winning goal as though it had never happened, neglect to promulgate the result and thereby produce a Utopian state of self-satisfaction in which the distasteful never occurs.[9]

---

8   The conversation was noted because Tony Cash was working up a TV proposal for a series of sports documentaries, one of which, to be called *Red Rings*, would have been an account of the Moscow Olympics; the series was never commissioned.

9   *Daily Mail*, 1 August 1980.

Bill Hetherington visits USSR in cause of peace

If asked about his attitude to the Cold War, Ian Wooldridge would undoubtedly have declared himself firmly on the side of the West. Not so former coder, Bill Hetherington, committed pacifist, honorary archivist of the Peace Pledge Union and author of *Swimming Against the Tide: The Peace Pledge Union Story 1934-2009*. He recalled a visit to the USSR in January 1982:

... in the dying days of the Brezhnev era, I was one of a 19-strong British non-aligned (i.e. not supporting either side in the Cold War) peace movement delegation (led by the redoubtable Fenner, Lord Brockway, then aged 93; I represented the PPU) invited by the Soviet Peace Committee (effectively a government agency) to visit the USSR at government expense, including Aeroflot flights there and back. Over ten days, we visited Moscow, including the Kremlin, Leningrad and, in Uzbekistan, Tashkent and Samarkand. On the first morning we were introduced to leading members of the 'Peace' Committee, including a senior official at the Soviet Foreign Office and a Red Army general in uniform; when it came to introducing ourselves, I remarked that it was unusual to find a general sitting on a peace committee - perhaps it might be more meaningful if he removed his uniform, as I, a former member of the British armed forces, had done long ago - if looks could kill! I also caused the president of one of the houses of the Supreme Soviet, at a meeting in the Kremlin, to lose his temper when I challenged him with a list of conscientious objectors then in prison for refusing to serve in the Red Army – 'Where did you get that? It must be lies; no-one ever refuses to serve in our peace-loving Red Army', which, incidentally, we were told had not invaded Afghanistan - they were invited in by the people. At a school, some teenage girls were fascinated to find someone who took Tolstoy's peace ideas seriously; they had been taught that they were only a literary fancy.[10]

10 See Bill Hetherington, 'Our Man in Russia', *The Pacifist* (PPU), February 1982. Bill also demonstrated for peace in Warsaw (1979), East Berlin and Bucharest (1980). The last occasion involved brief police detention, as did demonstrating in Yugoslavia (1963). No application to the Admiralty/MoD was made for any crossing of the Iron Curtain.

Mark Frankland on USSR's aged leaders

In his book *The Sixth Continent*, Mark Frankland wrote at length about the gerontocracy that ruled Russia for almost a decade between 1975 and 1985. He recalls the many jokes circulating among Soviet citizens about the mental and physical frailties of their leaders. Of Brezhnev in his last years, he writes:

> His speech was on occasions so slurred it could hardly be understood. People imitated it and laughed. He was given nicknames like Five Star Rotgut, a play on his fondness for medals and the Russian slang for the cheap fortified wine that heavy drinkers favoured. Someone thought up a neat variation on the old slogan 'Lenin is dead but his deeds live on,' the new one ran, 'but his body lives on.' (The pun in Russian was neat. The word for deed, *delo*, was almost the same as the word for body, *telo*.)[11]

The *bon-viveur* Brezhnev died in November 1982 at the age of 76, and was succeeded by the puritanical Yuri Vladimirovch Andropov, who was already 69 and ailing. A strictly orthodox Communist, Andropov had run the KGB for fifteen years, longer than any of his predecessors. Keeping dissident writers in check was one of his major concerns. He had literary ambitions himself but kept them well hidden: they were only revealed after his death in February 1984. In *The Sixth Continent*, Mark Frankland quotes a sympathetic birthday poem Andropov once wrote to his wife:

> Let others laugh at the poet
> But envy him twice over
> That I am writing sonnets
> To my own, not another's, wife.[12]

The year of Brezhnev's death saw Frankland back in Moscow, again as correspondent for the *Observer*. This was a period of heightened East-West tension, thanks to the continued persecution of dissidents like Sakharov and of Jews who sought permission to emigrate, but, more importantly, as a consequence of the increasingly bloody but futile Red Army efforts to subdue the Mujahideen in Afghanistan. The Soviets began to put out very tentative feelers to see what could be done to win round Western public opinion.

---

11 Mark Frankland, *The Sixth Continent*, pp 17-18.
12 *Ibid* p 38.

Mark Frankland and Tony Cash attend Soviet-British seminar

In December 1983, the Society for Cultural Relations with the USSR (generally considered pro-Soviet) and Quaker Peace and Service[13] jointly organised a 5-day seminar at a trade union sanatorium in Sochi on the Black Sea. Its purpose was to discuss the role of the media in any attempts to improve relations between the Soviet Union and the West. Among invitees were journalists, broadcasters and academics from both the USSR and Britain. There were four British participants – alongside Mark Frankland were Tony Cash (now a producer/director working for ITV's *South Bank Show*); Professor Peter Frank, of Essex University (former Army JSSL *kursant*, authority on Soviet government and, in consequence, a frequent contributor to BBC, ITV and Channel 4 news and current affairs programmes); the fourth UK delegate was a non-Russian speaker, John Eldridge, Professor of Media Studies at Glasgow University. At the seminar's conclusion, a communiqué was agreed and issued to the press. It called for more 'bridge' programmes like the one recently televised between Los Angeles and Moscow, in which kids showed their animated films and shared impressions with each other. For Tony Cash the seminar was significant, thanks to an encounter that surprised him:

> The youngest attender was Alexey Pankin. Then in his middle twenties, he was a graduate of the think-tank, the Moscow-based Institute for the Study of the USA and Canada. His English was excellent, and he clearly knew a great deal about life in the West; then, he had spent time in America. His contributions to our morning conferences were lively and quite free of the jargon that the regime's apologists usually went in for. Argument was uninhibited, often heated, but good-natured. At the end of one session, Alexey opened a newspaper package and offered a couple of us a sample of the contents to eat for lunch. It was a fish as big as a large kipper, but considerably stouter. The *vobla* is a kind of roach from the Caspian Sea, the dried version beloved of vodka drinkers as an accompanying snack. Alexey explained that his

---

13 Quaker organisation for promoting peace and humanitarian work overseas, and lead group in arranging the delegation in which Bill Hetherington was involved.

peasant grandmother, knowing that he was leaving home for a while, had packed it away for him as a treat. Older Soviet intellectuals might have felt that it was somehow *nyekul'turno* (uncultured or uncouth) to offer food in this way; that it smacked of a rustic past they were desperately trying to leave behind. Alexey's implied acceptance of at least some aspect of that past was endearing. In the afternoon, when delegates were free to stroll round Sochi and socialise, I went for a walk with him. I put it to him that those of us in the West who were interested in Russia and the Soviet Union would never have much sympathy for the country until it could frankly own up to the unpleasant facts of its history, especially the Stalin chapter. He laughed and said, 'Of course I understand that. It will change as soon as the present rulers go'.

Within three months of the Sochi seminar, Andropov, too, was dead. He was succeeded on 13 February 1984 by the 73 year-old Konstantin Ustinovich Chernenko. Frankland quotes an ordinary young Russian expressing the disappointment of many of his fellow citizens:

> ' ... now we've got this old man who can't even lift his arm to salute properly. From him we'll just get more eyewash.' ... In this atmosphere it was to be expected that the Chernenko jokes would soon follow. An epithet applied to Lenin – 'eternally living' – was rewritten for Chernenko as 'eternally living, eternally ill'.[14]

Gordon Clough gets to visit Innokenty Smoktunovsky

Chernenko was still more or less clinging on to life and power when Gordon Clough was finally allowed to return to Russia after twenty years of being refused entry. One suggested reason for the persistent refusal was that Gordon had been a spy. Normally, when a visa application is turned down, no explanation is given. Other ex-coder eavesdroppers had no difficulty in securing permission to visit the country, so it is unlikely that Gordon's having once worked in sigint operations would have affected the issue. Nor is it probable that the Soviet authorities knew of his intelligence

---

14 *The Sixth Continent,* pp 120-1.

gathering in the Baltic while he was stationed at Kiel in 1955. But they may have been infuriated by a ploy he had used to circumvent a pettifogging rule designed to stop Western visitors from consorting with Soviet citizens. In 1964 he had been in Moscow seeking permission from *Intourist* to travel to Leningrad in order to visit Innokenty Smoktunovsky: they had lunched together a few months earlier when the celebrated actor had been interviewed for the BBC's Russian Section. Gordon was denied permission to go to Leningrad, and told no hotel room was available. Smoktunovsky offered to accommodate Gordon in his own flat. This suggestion was also vetoed, on the grounds that 'It's forbidden to stay with private citizens'. Gordon's response:

> 'In that case', I said, 'I shall have to tell People's Artist Smoktunovsky that I am unable to bring him the photographs taken of him in London by the brother-in-law of our Queen'. That worked, and I handed over the [Earl of] Snowdon pictures in the ward of the Leningrad hospital where he was being treated for tuberculosis of the eye. In his modest flat the radio was touchingly tuned to the BBC Russian Service.[15]

A couple of years later the actor was back in London for a World Theatre performance of Dostoevsky's *The Idiot*, and was delighted to accept Gordon's invitation to supper at the broadcaster's home. But he never turned up. The explanation for this apparent discourtesy had to wait twenty years, until Gordon finally obtained a visa to make radio programmes in Moscow. There he met 'Kesha' who begged Gordon's forgiveness:

> 'Whatever for?' 'For not coming to your house. I was so ashamed. At the last minute they forbade me to go, even to telephone. The KGB never left my side till we were back in Moscow.'[16]

The actor's belated apology was now possible because the old geriatric regime had ended with Chernenko's death and, as Gordon concluded his obituary:

> ... the changed times, whatever their other pains, had made it possible to set things straight.

---

15 Gordon Clough, obituary of Innokenty Smoktunovsky, *The Independent*, 18 August 1994.

16 *Ibid.*

CHAPTER 15

ON THE MARGINS OF THE COLD WAR: THE GORBACHEV ERA

РЕФОРМЫ ДОЛЖЕН ЗАВЕРШАТЬ ТОТ, КТО ИХ НАЧАЛ. А НАЧАЛ-ТО ИХ Я
('The reforms must be completed by the man who started them. I started them.' – Attributed to Mikhail Gorbachev)

The energetic, humanitarian, radical reformer who rose to become head of the Soviet state on the death of Chernenko in March 1985 did so at an earlier age than any of his last four predecessors. A committed socialist, though one who put universal human values before Marxist-Leninist orthodoxy, the 54-year-old Mikhail Sergeevich Gorbachev was seen by many Soviet intellectuals as a 'child of Khrushchev' – a leader who wished to break with the past. But Gorbachev wanted to do more: the past, especially the Stalinist past, needed to be disclosed honestly and fully. Whereas Khrushchev had made his 1956 anti-Stalin speech in secret, Gorbachev committed himself to a policy of *glasnost* (openness). The other watch-word he brought into vogue during his six-year rule was *perestroika* (restructuring). The shock these policies caused to the sclerotic Soviet cardio-vascular system is conveyed in a religious metaphor by Mark Frankland:

> The mood was that of a staid church whose membership had for years attended out of conformism, social ambition, and a moderate degree of belief, but which had now fallen into the hands of evangelists.[1]

Gordon Clough reports pros and cons of *perestroika* for British radio

Soviet commentators in sympathy with Gorbachev's aims liked to talk of a 'revolution' afoot, so dramatically novel did the

---

1   Mark Frankland, *The Sixth Continent*, p 194.

proposed policy innovations seem. BBC Radio 4 soon caught on, and in 1987 commissioned a series called *Revolution Without Shots* to examine the new phenomenon. The resulting four documentaries were written and presented by Gordon Clough and Bridget Kendall (later to become the corporation's Moscow correspondent). Among those interviewed for the first episode was the sociologist Tatiana Zaslavskaya, described on air by Clough as 'dispensing grandmotherly lectures on the virtues of *perestroika*'. She explained that in the twenty years 1960-80 the USSR had effectively seen no increase in productivity - the root of the country's economic difficulties. Another academic, Professor of economics Nikolai Shmelyov, pointed to the low quality of manufactured goods as a major stumbling block – 800 million pairs of shoes that no-one wished to buy; up to a quarter of agricultural produce allowed to perish because it was not shifted quickly enough. The director of a successful publishing house indicated that he could manage just as well with only half the staff, prompting Clough to refer to the 'old Soviet bugbear of gross over-employment' – the Communists eager to make the world believe that unemployment could have no place in a socialist state.

The final programme in the series dealt with the consequences of *perestroika*. Greater freedom of expression was a boon for progressive forces but also, it was argued, for reactionary ones like the anti-Semitic organisation *Pamiat'* (Memory). During the Nazi occupation of the Crimea some 12,000 mainly Jewish Soviet citizens had been massacred at Simferopol, and secretly buried in a ditch. The programme reported allegations that supporters of *Pamiat'* had come from Moscow, and had dug up the victims of the atrocity to prise out gold teeth from the skulls. No police action followed; no reports appeared in the local or national press. However, a witness to the aftermath of the desecration was one of the Soviet Union's most eminent poets, Andrei Voznesensky, who said in an interview for the programme that it was 'like Auschwitz'. He then recited, in Russian, the opening of his poem *The Ditch*, which was translated and read by Gordon Clough:

> I speak to the skulls of my readers:
>
> Have we lost our reason?
>
> We stand here on the steppe rooted to the Crimean soil.

My skull shivers beneath my scalp,
And I felt some secret link
As if I were attached to the skulls in the ground.

Filming life of Stalin for world-wide TV audience

Radio 4's *Revolution Without Shots* succeeded in demonstrating to British listeners that serious and relatively open debate was now possible in the Soviet Union under Gorbachev. A beneficiary of this development was the Thames TV team given the opportunity to make an in-depth, three-part documentary, biography of Stalin, with full co-operation from the Soviet authorities. Before filming began seminars were organised in London, Moscow and Cambridge (Massachusetts), at which leading British, Soviet and American historians gathered to share with the production team their research findings into the despot's life and times. Tony Cash wrote, produced and directed the final programme entitled *Generalissimo* ('Supreme general', the title by which Stalin was sometimes known) dealing with the later years. He also conducted many of the Russian language interviews for the first two programmes. He has vivid memories of his travels and encounters during the filming in 1988 and 1989:

It was a credit to Thames TV that they gave a very high priority to the Stalin project, allocating a substantial budget and much more research and shooting time than would be available today. Executive producer Philip Whitehead, fellow producer/director Jonathan Lewis and I attended all three seminars, so were able to grill historians who had been leaders in this field of study – John Erickson, Robert Service, Steven Cohen, Moshe Lewin, and Yury Poliakov - to name a few more or less at random. Interviews were filmed in America, Britain and in several cities of the Soviet Union with a wide range of subjects, including Stalin's daughter Svetlana, one of his personal body guards, relatives of his purged political rivals and victims of the terror. The latters' stories of surviving years in the gulag were as harrowing as uplifting.

Moscow and Leningrad were obviously on the itinerary, but so, too, were cities rarely visited by Westerners, such as Naberezhnye Chelny (formerly Brezhnev) and Magnitogorsk, both with populations of around half a million. With its white, six-storey blocks of flats, undulating vertically over pleasant green areas dotted with trees, Naberezhnye Chelny resembled a modern Spanish seaside town rather than the base for producing the hefty *Kamaz* lorry. Street names were in Tartar as well as Russian, and many of the people I met bore Tartar names, though in appearance they were for the most part quite indistinguishable from those with purely Russian names. My reason for being there was to film interviews with a group of youngsters who had established an unusual political club: its essential aim was to bring about the rehabilitation of Nikolai Bukharin, one of the last of the old Bolshevik leaders to be bumped off by Stalin in the blood-letting of the 1930s. They seemed to believe that the adoption of Bukharin's particular brand of socialism would prove to be Russia's salvation.

Magnitogorsk could not have been more different. The city straddles the river Ural, so is half in Europe and half in Asia – like Russia itself. It seemed full of old people living in very typical, grim rectilinear blocks. From 1931 it became the powerhouse of the Soviet industrial revolution, mining the abundant iron ore in the hills around to smelt vast quantities of iron and steel. (I brought home a small but very heavy four-inch cube of rock, and asked my daughters why such an object could explain how the Soviet Union defeated the Nazis in World War II.) Here we interviewed elderly men who recalled the arduous work they had been forced to do more than half a century earlier. They were inclined to give Stalin the benefit of any doubt – principally because they attributed Russian victory over Germany to his policies.

The event that made the greatest impression on me while on location was something I saw on Russian TV. I happened to be free of programme obligations on 25 May 1989, the day the first quasi-democratically elected Soviet parliament opened – the new Congress of People's Deputies. The proceedings, chaired by President Gorbachev, were being transmitted live, and millions of Soviet citizens, were like me, simply glued to their screens. At one moment a question was raised about Boris Yeltsin, who had been prevented from standing for election despite his very considerable popularity. Was there a constitutionally acceptable way whereby he could be co-opted into the parliament? As delegates argued, it was clear that Gorbachev himself did not have the answer. But one of the delegates certainly did. With immense authority and at considerable length he spelled it out. I learned that the speaker was Anatoly Sobchak, Professor of law at Leningrad University, who had clearly taken the trouble to study the new constitutional arrangements. Everyone, including Gorbachev listened intently. And I thought how extraordinary that a Soviet leader would so readily allow his vulnerability to be on show to such a huge audience. This at a time when the British Prime Minister, Margaret Thatcher, was fiercely opposed to the televising of our own parliament.

Sobchak later went on to become Mayor of Leningrad. On his watch the city voted to change its name back to St Petersburg as it had been called in Tsarist days. One of Sobchak's protégés, and for a time deputy mayor, was Vladimir Putin.

Clifford German argues that Gorbachev needs West's support

Gorbachev's reforms were widely acclaimed in Western media, and he achieved a much better relationship with non-Communist national leaders than any previous Soviet politician. Despite their radically opposed philosophies, Margaret Thatcher famously proclaimed he was someone with whom she could 'do business together'. US President Ronald Reagan also established a friendly rapport with him - a significant factor explaining the success of summit meetings that effectively brought the Cold War to an end. Former midshipman, Clifford German, from 1987 City Editor of *The Scotsman*, felt that Gorbachev's principal negotiating partners let him down:

> I was very concerned … that Reagan and Thatcher were determined to punish Russia by stripping away its empire and leaving it to bleed to death, and I tried to advocate a 'hand of friendship' policy and a new Marshall Plan involving integrating the whole Comecon block into the Common Market.

On 18 November 1987 the *Scotsman* carried an article by Clifford arguing that Western Europe should offer some sort of economic association to Eastern Europe, not only to the small nations just beginning to throw off communist shackles, but also to the USSR itself:

> It would be remarkably short-sighted of the EC to appear to be stealing the Soviet Union's economic dependencies and its trading partners.
>
> As a matter of urgency the European Community must come up with a plan for economic co-operation between east and west as a whole, which is also flexible enough to allow the Soviet Union and its unruly nationalities to fit into.

Reports on attempted coup to topple Gorbachev

By 1991 it became clear that Gorbachev was in difficulties at home - his approval ratings there woefully lower than abroad. Opponents complained of his failure significantly to improve the country's economy, and many were unhappy that he allowed former satellite states of Eastern Europe to break free from Moscow's grip. Lithuania's unilateral declaration of independence in March 1990 prompted fears that the Soviet Union itself might disintegrate. In January 1991 Red Army troops attempted to bring Lithuania back under Soviet rule, killing fourteen people and injuring hundreds, as they stormed the new parliament in the capital, Vilnius. Gorbachev is not believed to have sanctioned the bloodshed: hardliners in the Communist Party, Army and security apparatus appear to have been responsible. It was not entirely surprising, therefore, when in August of that year a group of conspirators from these power blocs organised a coup against their President. Gorbachev himself was held prisoner while on holiday with his family in a villa on the Black Sea, as the plotters tried to persuade him to declare a state of emergency or transfer power. Failing to obtain Gorbachev's agreement, they returned empty-handed to Moscow, where tanks had entered the streets to enforce the conspirators' will. Mass resistance to the putsch was led by Boris Yeltsin, the very popular President of the Russian Federation, directly elected the previous year. He was able to count on the support of significant elements of the Army which had refused to obey orders.

In Moscow during the coup attempt was former coder, Peter Hoare, attending a large conference of the International Federation of Library Associations. He was billed to deliver a talk about a

Russian librarian who had visited Western Europe in 1859, and written a fascinating account of his travels:

> My slot was the first one on the Monday morning of the putsch, and one of my Russian friends stood up when I'd finished and thanked me for reminding everyone that links between Russia and the West were not something new and fearful, but had gone on for many years. He also commented that he wanted to say this now, since tomorrow he might not be able to. I think this was the same chap who took me through the barricades on Tuesday to join the crowds at the White House, listening to speakers including Elena Bonner, wife of Andrei Sakharov, and welcoming delegations from the Ukraine and other republics which were heading for 'independence' (of course the appearance of the 'new' Russian flag over the Kremlin, replacing the Red Flag, was a significant moment).

The August 1991 Moscow 'events' were observed more closely by Chairman of the Frinton Society, Robert Avery, who between 1978 and 1985 had run the Russian refresher courses for former midshipmen *kursanty* at the Britannia Royal Naval College, Dartmouth. His account of the conspiracy was published in the Society's news letter the following month. In it, he charged the initiators of the coup of being:

> ... trapped in the mind-set of late Brezhnevism: leaders are changed by inner coups and intrigues; those deposed are said to be ill and have asked to be relieved of their now burdensome duties; tanks are sent out onto the streets not to shoot at people but by their massed and menacing presence to convey the forcible impression that these things are best left to those who know about these things – i.e. the Politiburo and perhaps the Central Committee. It was clear that putting tanks on the streets was not the first stage of the plan to seize power – it was the whole plan.

Mark Frankland was now back in Moscow for the *Observer* and was equally dismissive of the plotters. In an article published on 25 August he depicted the figurehead leader of the coup, Gennadi Yanayev:

> ... with trembling hands and the collapsing face of a humourless Frankie Howard.[2]

---

2   Mark Frankland, 'The Russian Revolution', p 101.

83. Mikhail Gorbachev and Boris Yeltsin in the Soviet Parliament in 1991 shortly before the USSR fell apart. Courtesy RIA Novosti.

Mark named the other seven leading conspirators and their positions in the hierarchy, and commented:

> In these eight persons were united all the Soviet institutions that must be swept away or castrated by reform.

Both Frankland and Avery made much of the Russian citizens' will to resist the usurpers, even though the demonstrators crowding into the square in front of the White House – home of the Russian (as opposed to all-Soviet) parliament – numbered in the tens rather than hundreds of thousands. Both commentators remarked, too, on the oratory and persuasive powers of Boris Yeltsin, whom the plotters had grossly underestimated. Everything about him, Frankland stated, fitted the role he had to play:

> ... his bulk, his healthy looks, his voice – especially his voice, which is not beautiful but which at crucial moments, such as declaring the plotters must be brought to trial, took on the mercilessness of a power-saw ripping through balsa wood.[3]

Alongside Avery's report in the Frinton Society newsletter of September 1991 is a facsimile Russian text of the appeal written by Yeltsin on 19 August, calling on members of the armed forces not to allow themselves to become:

> ... the blind weapon of the wilfully criminal group of adventurers who have trampled on the Constitution and laws of the USSR ... They can erect a throne of bayonets, but they cannot sit on it for long.

The appeal concludes with the words:

> The honour and glory of Russian arms will not be stained with the people's blood.

Yeltsin was writing in his capacity as President of the Russian Federation, the major, but only one, of the Soviet Union's fifteen republics. Gorbachev was still President of the USSR as a whole. In the light of future events there is a highly significant passage in the proclamation to the military from which we have been quoting. It refers to the issuing of an order (*Ukaz*) in accordance with which:

> ... all the territorial and other organs of the MVD [Ministry of Internal Affairs], KGB [Committee for State Security] and of the Ministry of Defence on the territory of the RSFSR [Russian Socialist Federal

---

3   *Ibid*, p 102.

Soviet Republic] are obliged immediately to carry out all commands of the President of the RSFSR, of the KGB of the RSFSR, the MVD of the RSFSR and of the RSFSR State Committee for Defence.

It reads like a unilateral declaration of independence, and did not augur well for the continued existence of the Soviet Union.

The cement which had held together the fifteen republics for so many decades was the Communist Party. When, on 29 August 1991, the Soviet Parliament voted to suspend the activities of the Party, the break-up of the USSR was probably inevitable. On Christmas Day that year, Gorbachev resigned from office and the hammer and sickle ceased to fly on the Kremlin

In an article for the *Observer* of 25 August, Mark Frankland had used, appropriately for a former midshipman, a maritime metaphor to convey the futility of the whole Soviet Communist project, likening the Soviet Union to a:

> ... great liner trapped in savage seas and just about to founder ... a ship, built with unimaginable cruelty and waste, had set out with high hopes but equipped with crazy charts for a port that never existed.[4]

---

4   *Ibid,* p 101.

COLD WAR TIMELINE

The back-drop to the story we have been telling is the Cold War - the necessary, sufficient, perhaps even the only reason for the then British government to launch the JSSL operation in 1951. Since the conflict features very prominently in this publication, we thought it might be useful to provide readers with a brief timeline of the most relevant historical events.

Hostility between Russia and western nations goes back centuries. Its severest manifestations were the Napoleonic and Crimean Wars in the 19th century, and the First World War of 1914-18. In all three conflagrations, Russia endured foreign occupation and humiliating military failures. Following the Bolshevik revolution of 1917, some fifteen western countries, including Britain, intervened in the ensuing civil war, eager to forestall a Red victory. Even when the Soviet Union joined forces with western states against Germany after the unprovoked Nazi invasion in June 1941, mutual suspicion between the allies remained endemic. In a sense, Cold War was the status quo – the default scenario – so nominating a starting point for our timeline is tricky.

The imposition of communist rule in East European states at World War II's end; Churchill's 1946 Fulton speech complaining of an 'iron curtain' imposed by Stalin to preserve the USSR and its satellite countries from western influence; the 1948-49 blockade of Berlin, when the Soviets hoped to assimilate the western, Allied, sectors of the city; the setting up by western states in 1949 of the North Atlantic Treaty Organisation – all these events exacerbated the conflict, if they did not initiate it. However, deep-rooted antagonism only escalated to wholesale bloodletting as a result of the incursion into South Korea of communist North Korean forces in June 1950. Britain followed the USA in backing the United Nations' call for a military response, and sent regulars and national servicemen to Korea to repel the invaders. The very first coders were fully aware that choosing the Russian course via the Navy was a sure-fire way to avoid possible posting to that benighted peninsula.

For the purposes of this book, we deemed the outbreak of hostilities in Korea a suitable starting date for a Cold War timeline:

1950

June	North Korean forces invade South Korea. UN Security Council authorises US intervention in support of South Korea.
July	US forces under the UN banner land in South Korea.
September	UK extends length of compulsory military service to facilitate UK support of UN forces in Korea.
October	UN forces enter North Korea.
November	Communist Chinese forces enter North Korea in its support, advance to South Korea; local conflict becomes major international war.

1952

October	UK explodes its first atomic bomb.
November	USA explodes the first hydrogen bomb.

1953

March	Stalin, USSR dictator dies.
June	Uprising in East Berlin against authoritarian regime is suppressed.
July	Armistice ends Korean War, with peninsula reverting to 1945 division on 38th parallel.
August	USSR explodes its first hydrogen bomb.
September	Nikita Khrushchev becomes de facto new Soviet leader, by election as First Secretary of the Communist Party.

1954

July	After defeat of French colonial power at Dien Bien Phu, Geneva Conference settles division of Vietnam between communist North and supposedly democratic South.

1955

May — West Germany is recognised as sovereign Federal Republic, joins NATO; Berlin remains under four-power occupation. USSR and its Eastern European communist allies create military alliance, the Warsaw Pact, to counter the US-led North Atlantic Treaty Organisation (NATO), founded in April 1949.

1956

February — Khrushchev makes secret speech to the Soviet Communist Party hierarchy denouncing Stalin.

October — Combined Anglo-French-Israeli forces invade Egypt in attempt to take back the Suez Canal, nationalised three months earlier by President Gamel Nasser; UN pressure supported by the US leads to withdrawal.

November — USSR troops and tanks crush liberalising revolution in Hungary.

1957

July — The Moscow International Youth Festival provides one of the first openings to the world of the Khrushchev era.

August — UK explodes its first hydrogen bomb.

October — USSR launches the sputnik, first man-made satellite to orbit earth.

1958

April — First major Aldermaston March, supported by newly-founded Campaign for Nuclear Disarmament (CND).

1959

January — Fidel Castro seizes power in Cuba.

July — US Vice-President Richard Nixon visits Moscow

for opening of the American National Exhibition, at which he tangles with Khrushchev over the relative merits of communism and capitalism - the so-called 'kitchen debate'.

September   Khrushchev visits the USA and meets President Eisenhower.

1960

May   US U2 high altitude reconnaissance aircraft is shot down on a spying mission over USSR and its pilot, Gary Powers, taken prisoner; summit meeting with US President Eisenhower is cancelled by Khrushchev.

1961

April   Anti-Castro forces supported by USA invade Cuba at the Bay of Pigs, but are defeated.

August   East Germany, with active USSR support, builds the Berlin Wall to prevent its citizens defecting to the West.

1962

October   The Cuban Missile Crisis arises from USSR decision secretly to install nuclear weapons on Cuba, which USA counters by imposing a naval blockade and threatening to treat any nuclear attack by Cuba as an attack by the USSR. The missiles are removed in return for USA agreeing to withdraw nuclear warheads from Turkey and promising not to topple the Castro regime.

1963

June   USA and USSR agree to set up a telephone 'hot line' to manage international crises more effectively.

August   UK, USA and USSR sign treaty undertaking to cease all atmospheric nuclear weapon tests. In contrast to previous purported voluntary cessation of tests, the treaty is observed by all three parties.

1964

October   Khrushchev is deposed as USSR leader, to be replaced by Leonid Brezhnev.

1965

March   Following a sustained bombing campaign of communist North Vietnam, in reprisal for communist insurgency in the South, first US combat troops arrive in South Vietnam.

1968

August   USSR and allied Warsaw Pact troops invade Czechoslovakia to suppress the liberal 'Prague Spring' version of communism being experimented with by the Czech government.

1973

February   USA signs agreement withdrawing from Vietnam.

1975

April   North Vietnam overruns South, and Vietnam becomes a single state.

1979

December   USSR forces invade Afghanistan.

1980

July   Moscow Olympics open, despite boycott by USA and some allies. Prime Minister Margaret Thatcher supports US action, but several British athletes participate.

1982

November   Brezhnev dies, succeeded by Yury Andropov, former Chairman of KGB, USSR secret police.

1985

March   Mikhail Gorbachev becomes leader of USSR following the death of Konstantin Chernenko, Andropov's successor.

November   Summit meeting between US President Ronald Reagan and Gorbachev establishes rapport.

1986

April   Nuclear power plant, Chernobyl, Ukraine, USSR, explodes, contaminating wide area.

1987

June   Gorbachev calls for reforms, which he labels glasnost and perestroika – transparency and reconstruction.

1989

February   Final exit of USSR troops from Afghanistan.

March   First multi-party general elections in USSR since 1918; Boris Yeltsin defeats official Communist Party candidate; many others are also rejected.

June   Communist China crushes embryonic democracy movement in Beijing's Tiananmen Square.

September   Communist Hungary dismantles border fence with Austria to allow citizens from communist East Germany to travel to West without hindrance.

November   The Berlin Wall is broken through by popular nonviolent uprising; later dismantled. Similar uprisings lead to fall of other 'satellite' regimes.

1990

October   The formerly Communist, German Democratic Republic reunites with its Western neighbour, the Federal German Republic.

1991

August   Hard-line Communists attempt to oust Gorbachev from power, but are foiled by Boris Yeltsin and his supporters.

December   Following resignation of Gorbachev as President, USSR is dissolved.

GLOSSARY AND LIST OF ABBREVIATIONS

A-level

advanced, upper, level of the GCE examination instituted in 1951, taken by sixth formers and usually leading to higher education.

AB

able seaman, a sailor whose rating is above ordinary seaman and below leading seaman, equivalent to a trained Army private.

Admiralty

government department responsible for the Navy; merged into MoD, 1964.

Adrift

as an adaptation of the strict nautical sense, the word is used of a rating not reporting punctually when and where required.

AFP

the French news agency Agence France-Presse.

AGI

American sailors' jargon for a Soviet auxiliary intelligence-gathering vessel.

AIB

Admiralty Interview Board, the committee which selected candidates to be officers in the Navy.

Air Ministry

government department responsible for the RAF; merged into MoD, 1964.

AK

a rifle of Soviet/Russian manufacture named after its inventor, Mikhail Kalashnikov.

ALS

Applied Language School, where technical and military Russian terminology was learned.

AM

when used in relation to radio transmission and reception means 'amplitude modulated'.

Andrew (the)

naval slang meaning the Navy itself. The term derives from the name of a notorious eighteenth-century lieutenant of that name who led a particularly successful press gang dragging young men off the streets and forcing them into the service.

AWOL

UK armed forces acronym for absent without leave; also used as a noun, referring to an absentee without leave.

BA

Bachelor of Arts

a first degree usually conferred by an institute of higher education on successful completion of a three- or four-year course.

Badge

When used in the RN without further description means a chevron worn on the left sleeve denoting four years good conduct; up to three, totalling twelve years, could be awarded.

BAOR

the British Army of the Rhine, signifying all British armed forces stationed in West Germany; 1945-55, an occupation force in the British Zone; from 1955 a NATO force hosted by West Germany.

Berlin

historic capital of Prussia, and then of Germany on first unification in 1871. In 1945 the city, wholly within the Soviet occupation zone, was divided by the occupying powers into four sectors. The three western sectors became jointly self-governing as West Berlin, while the Soviet sector was treated effectively as if it were part of East Germany. Formal status as an occupied city ceased only on the final reunification of Germany in 1990.

Blue-liners

special issue, duty-free cigarettes with a blue line along their length. Sailors were entitled to purchase 200 a month for personal consumption only.

Brummie

colloquial noun or adjective deriving from the name of the city Birmingham.

Buffer

nickname for the boatswain's (pronounced bosun's) mate responsible for conduct of a ship's routine and piping of all orders.

Bundeswehr

literally, 'federal defence'; collective term for West German armed forces, established 12 November 1955.

Captain

Navy rank equivalent to Army colonel; also post of officer commanding ship or shore establishment, irrespective of rank held.

Captain's Defaulters

naval disciplinary session in which a rating charged with an offence is ordered to appear before the Captain for a hearing of the matter, and punishment ordered if the Captain finds the offence proved. Serious offences are remitted to a court-martial.

CB

Commander of the Most Honourable Order of the Bath, an award given for conspicuous services to the Crown.

CCF

Combined Cadet Force; established in 1948 (superseding earlier cadet corps) and comprising school-based uniformed cadet units that include sections representing all three armed forces; funded by, but not formally part of, the armed forces.

Chippie

naval slang for ship's carpenter.

CIA

Central Intelligence Agency, the USA's principal secret service.

CinC

Commander in Chief.

CL

Chinese linguist, airman studying that language.

CND

Campaign for Nuclear Disarmament, founded 1958.

CNN

US-based Cable News Network providing 24-hour news coverage to cable TV subscribers.

C of E

Church of England.

CO

Commanding Officer.

Committee of 100

anti-war organisation set up in 1960 advocating non-violent resistance and civil disobedience to further its anti-nuclear aims. Among its 100 public signatories was the philosopher Bertrand Russell.

CPO

chief petty officer, naval equivalent of army staff sergeant and air force flight sergeant.

Comecon

Council for Mutual Economic Assistance, created in 1949 by the USSR and its East European allies to strengthen economic ties.

cri de coeur

French expression meaning 'cry from the heart' or 'anguished appeal'.

CW

Commission and Warrant, branch of Admiralty responsible for recruiting officers.

Deus ex machina

Latin expression translated from Greek, literally, 'god from the machinery', denoting a god descending from the sky in a play to resolve an issue.

D/F

direction finding, the art of detecting where a radio signal is coming from.

Divisional officer

naval officer having responsibility for oversight and welfare of a number of ratings.

Divisions

a formal naval parade within a ship or shore establishment.

DNI

Director of Naval Intelligence.

Doeskin

see No. 1s.

DSC

Distinguished Service Cross, a medal awarded to naval officers below the rank of captain, for gallantry in action.

DSO

Distinguished Service Order, a medal awarded to officers in all the armed forces for especial service in action.

East Germany

common, but unofficial, name for the German Democratic Republic, formed from the post-WWII Soviet occupation zone of Germany; ceased as an entity on German reunification in 1990.

EM2

electrician's mate second class, equivalent rating to ordinary seaman

Enigma machine

sophisticated German mechanical device used by the Nazis during WWII for coding and decoding messages.

E-boat

'Enemy boat', name given by the British to German motor torpedo-boat, *Torpedoboot*, used in World War II; not to be confused with the really fast post-war Mercedes-Benz 'spy boats'.

FOCRIN

Flag Officer Commanding Royal Indian Navy.

Fore-and-aft rig

term referring to a specific arrangement of sails on a ship. When used of dress it denotes uniforms comprising shirts and ties and conventional jackets and trousers.

Four-ringer

slang for Naval captain, who has four gold rings on the lower part of the jacket sleeves. Similarly, a two-ringer is a lieutenant; a two-and-a-half-ringer, a lieutenant commander; and a three-ringer, a commander.

FRINTON Society
a club for Former Russian Interpreters of the Navy.

FT
the *Financial Times*

GCE
General Certificate of Education instituted 1951, at two levels: O-level replacing the School Certificate, and A-level replacing the Higher School Certificate.

GCHQ
Government Communications Headquarters (Cheltenham); responsible for providing the political and military authorities with signals and other intelligence.

GI
naval Gunnery Instructor; also, in American slang, a private in the US army (derived from 'government issue').

Goskontsert
the Soviet state agency responsible for putting on concerts.

GRU
Russian initials for the Chief Intelligence Directorate of the General Staff, a branch of the Soviet armed forces comparable in power and authority to the KGB.

Gulag
the acronym for the state administration responsible for Soviet prison camps.

Haus der Jugend
German for House of Youth, or youth centre.

Heads
naval term for lavatory. 'Captain of the Heads' was an ironic term for a menial task.

HMS

his (her) majesty's ship, including shore establishments so designated.

in flagrante delicto

Latin term meaning caught in the very act, caught 'red-handed'.

HSC

Higher School Certificate, replaced in 1951 by A-levels.

Inter alia

Latin expression meaning 'among other things'.

IPCS

Institute of Professional Civil Servants.

IQ

intelligence quotient

term usually preceding the word 'test'. Such tests were in common use in the 1940s and 1950s to select candidates for different forms of education or work.

ITV

Independent Television, the first (1955) commercial TV channel in Britain and the BBC's long-standing rival.

Jankers

Army slang word for an official punishment such as being confined to barracks or camp.

JIC

Joint Intelligence Committee; on behalf of the Cabinet, controls activities of the United Kingdom's intelligence agencies and GCHQ; in our period a sub-committee reporting to the three armed forces Chiefs of Staff (there was no Chief of Defence staff before 1964).

Jimmy

naval slang for the officer, second in command of a ship or establishment. Also known as 'No. 1', but more formally as the 'first lieutenant', a post held irrespective of the actual rank of the holder.

JSSL

Joint Services School for Linguists; also in the planning period and after the JSSLs closed the initials JSSL stood for Joint School for Service Linguists.

KBE

Knight Commander of the Most Excellent Order of the British Empire, knight commander is the second highest rank in an order of chivalry.

KCB

Knight Commander of the Most Honourable Order of the Bath, an award for conspicuous service to the Crown.

KGB

Russian initials of the Committee for State Security, Soviet secret police; replaced MGB, Ministry of State Security, 1953.

Killick

slang for anchor, but more commonly for a leading rating, derived from the anchor badge worn on the left sleeve denoting the rank.

Kolkhoz

portmanteau abbreviation of the two Russian words *kollyektivnoye khozyastvo*

collective farm.

Kriegsmarine

literally, 'war navy', the German equivalent of the Royal Navy, military as opposed to merchant.

Kursant
from the Russian word (*kurs*) meaning 'course', hence 'student on a course'.

Kursanty
plural of *kursant*.

Land
German word indicating one of the 16 states constituting Federal Germany.

Leading hand
generic term for holder of a 'leading' rate, equivalent of an Army full corporal.

Ldg Cdr
abbreviation for leading coder.

Liberty boat
small vessel ferrying sailors from a ship in harbour ashore for leave, but also used in relation to shore establishments for motorised transport or even just the time of day when a sailor has permission to leave the base.

Light Programme
precursor of BBC Radios 1 and 2; it broadcast music and light entertainment 1945-67.

MA
Master of Arts, denoting the holder has gained a second degree usually conferred by an institution of higher education on successful completion of a one- or two-year course. In Scottish universities the MA is awarded as a first degree.

Master at arms
most senior Naval rating on a ship or establishment, the rank roughly equivalent to that of an Army regimental sergeant major.

Matelot

French word for sailor, often used jocularly of themselves by British sailors.

Matrosen

German for sailors.

MBE

Member of the Order of the British Empire, an award conferred by the monarch on selected worthy individual.

MGB

see KGB.

Mick

sailors' slang abbreviation of 'hammock'.

MI5

Military Intelligence, section 5 - the Service responsible for protecting the UK's national security.

MO

Medical officer; in RN, an officer of the Medical Branch; in Army, an officer of the Royal Army Medical Corps.

MoD

Ministry of Defence; set up 1946 to co-ordinate the three armed forces ministries; subsumed them completely in 1964.

Mot(s) juste(s)

French expression meaning 'the exactly appropriate word(s)'.

MT

military term for motor transport.

NAAFI

Navy, Army and Air Force Institutes, providing retail, leisure and catering services. The term is frequently used to denote specifically the building on base where food and drink, including alcoholic drink, can be purchased, and servicemen can relax. It was very common for the NAAFI to have a piano.

NATO

North Atlantic Treaty Organisation - a military alliance of western states, created in 1949 in response to the perceived threat from the eastern/Soviet bloc.

NCO

non-commissioned officer.

No. 1s

a sailor's best outfit, usually made of doeskin with gold insignia, not issued to national servicemen, but could be purchased.

No. 8s

a sailor's working clothes.

Novosti

the Soviet state news agency; the word means 'news' in Russian.

NYJO

the National Youth Jazz Orchestra.

O-level

ordinary, lower, level of the GCE, determining whether pupils are qualified to proceed to A-levels, preparatory to entering university, but also qualifying for acceptance on some vocational courses. When it was instituted in 1951 there was a rule that one had to be at least 16 at the time of sitting the examination, but from 1952 head teachers could apply for permission for exceptional individual pupils to sit at a lower age.

Omerta
Italian word for the the mafioso's vow of silence under pain of death.

OSA
Official Secrets Act. There were actually two Acts in the 1950s, the 1911 Act and its 1920 complement, expanding the provisions. Communicating secret information to a person not authorised to receive it carried a possible penalty of two years imprisonment.

OSNAZ
acronym for certain Soviet military forces existing 'for special purposes'.

Pigs
term commonly used by ratings to denote naval officers.

PO
petty officer, Navy equivalent of an Army sergeant.

Pompey
familiar name for Portsmouth.

Pour encourager les autres
French expression meaning 'to encourage the others', famously cited by Voltaire as the reason for the naval execution (by firing squad) in 1757 of Admiral John Byng, after his failing, with a poorly equipped squadron, to relieve blockaded Minorca; he had been acquitted of treachery and cowardice and recommended to mercy; see also chapter 11.

PPU
the Peace Pledge Union, founded 1934 the oldest, non-sectarian pacifist organisation in Britain.

Probationary rating
equivalent of seaman's 'ordinary' rating; used for coders and some other functions. Coders were uprated from probationary six months after first joining, with a small enhancement of pay.

PSI

President of the Services Institute, usually referred to in connection with the fund established to pay for serving men's leisure time activities.

PTI

physical training instructor.

Pusser

term indicating that someone adheres strictly to the Navy's rules and regulations; also an adjective denoting naval supply of e.g., food, furniture, working equipment. The word is a colloquial corruption of 'Purser', the officer responsible for accounts and supplies.

QRAIs

Queen's Regulations and Admiralty Instructions, frequently abbreviated further to QRs.

Quantum sufficit

Latin expression used in medicine, and meaning 'as much as is necessary'.

RAF

Royal Air Force.

raison d'être

French expression: reason for existence.

RL

Russian linguist.

RN

Royal Navy.

RNB

Royal Naval Barracks.

RNR

Royal Naval Reserve, formerly comprising members of the Merchant Navy volunteering as a reserve force, but from 1958 also including the former RNVR.

RNSR

Royal Naval Special Reserve, comprising former full-time national servicemen of the Royal Navy fulfilling their reserve liability.

RNVR

Royal Naval Volunteer Reserve. Analogous to the Territorial Army; volunteers were committed to regular training/ exercise sessions, and liability to call-up for continuous service in an emergency; merged into RNR, 1958.

RSM

regimental sergeant major

the most senior Army non-commissioned officer in any regiment and roughly the equivalent of a ship or naval establishment's master at arms.

Samizdat

'self-published' - unofficial hand produced document or literature intended to escape the Soviet censor.

Samovar

Russian word sometimes translated as 'tea pot', but it is actually more like an urn for boiling water, with a lid and a tap. A samovar may be quite ornate, and is often a source of pride for its owner.

Satellite countries

East European countries either occupied by Soviet troops and/or under communist rule subservient to the USSR.

Sick berth attendant

rating in the Medical Branch acting as nursing orderly/ paramedic.

Sigint

portmanteau word from 'signals intelligence'

information acquired from operators' eavesdropping. Also 'siginter'

someone engaged in gathering intelligence. Similarly, 'elint' is 'electronic intelligence' derived from non-voice communications such as radar and satellite transmissions; and 'humint' is 'human intelligence' obtained by agents.

SIS

the British Secret Intelligence Service (often referred to as MI6). Its essential role is to collect foreign intelligence.

Soviet

literally, 'council', used adjectively of matters relating to the USSR, as Soviet Union, a short form for the state; Soviet Army etc; or 'the Soviets', people or government of the USSR.

Sprog

naval slang for novice, or a sailor's wife's baby.

Square-rig

term referring to the arrangement of sails on a ship, but when applied to uniform means traditional sailor's dress, namely bell-bottomed trousers, tight-fitting shirt (or jumper if winter), a jersey over the shirt/jumper, a 'sailor' collar, a short black silk scarf, a lanyard, and a nearly round, peakless hat with a ribbon (slang, 'tally') showing the name of the wearer's ship. Quite a palaver to dress correctly.

SRC

the Soviet Relations Committee of the British Council.

SU

signals unit.

Taiga

coniferous forest lying between tundra and steppe, Siberia

TASS
initials of the Telegraph Agency of the Soviet Union, the Soviet press agency.

TTY
refers to a teleprinter or teletypewriter, an electromechanical device facilitating direct electronic communication. If monitored, its output yields one form of elint.

Third Reich
term devised by Adolf Hitler to denote Germany 1933-1945 under his regime. *Reich* means 'empire' - the first was the Holy Roman Empire, and the second, the *Kaiser* period, 1871-1918.

Tickler
duty-free loose tobacco made available to naval ratings as an alternative privilege to duty-free cigarettes.

Tiffy
abbreviation of artificer, a trained mechanic.

TNA/ADM
The National Archive/Admiralty papers.

TNA/CAB
The National Archive/Cabinet papers.

UB
the initials of the Polish Secret Service.

Ukaz
Soviet government edict or decree

UPI
United Press International

an international news agency.

USS
United States ship.

USSR

Union of Soviet Socialist Republics, which came into being in 1922 by the combining of the Russian Soviet Federal Socialist Republic with other 'soviet socialist republics' which had emerged from the Russian Empire after the 1917 Bolshevik revolution. With the collapse of communism, the USSR disintegrated at the end of 1991.

V1, V2

respectively, unmanned flying bomb and powerful explosive rocket, launched by the Germans towards the end of WWII and causing damage mainly in London.

VHF

very high frequency (used of radio waves).

Vicky B

Victoria Barracks in Portsmouth where coders until approximately 1955 joined the Navy and did their basic training.

WAAF

Women's Auxiliary Air Force established 1939; renamed Women's Royal Air Force, 1948.

War Office

government department responsible for the Army; merged into MoD, 1964.

Wehrmacht

literally, 'defence force', collective name for Nazi armed forces; sometimes used informally just for the army.

West Germany

common, but unofficial, name for the Federal Republic of Germany, formed from the post-WWII American, British and French occupation zones; ceased as an entity on German reunification in 1990.

Whaler

a seaworthy rowing boat, capable of being used as a lifeboat or for other emergency purpose.

Wren

rating of the Women's Royal Naval Service (WRNS, collectively known as 'the Wrens').

WWII

common abbreviation for the Second World War.

Y station

an establishment set up by GCHQ or on its behalf for the purpose of monitoring and recording signals intelligence.

ZOMP

a Soviet acronym from the initial letters for the Russian words meaning 'Protection against Weapons of Mass Destruction'.

READING LIST

Admiralty: *Naval Rating's Handbook*, B.R. 1938, Naval Training Department, N.T. 97/48, promulgated on behalf of the Lords Commissioners of the Admiralty, 19 October 1951, 'for the information and guidance of all concerned'.

Aldrich, Richard J: *The Hidden Hand - Britain, America, and Cold War Secret Intelligence*, London, John Murray, 2001, and New York and Woodstock, The Overlook Press, 2002. Also, *GCHQ - the Uncensored Story Of Britain's Most Secret Intelligence Agency*, London, Harper Press, 2010.

Aru, Mart: Estonian who, as Soviet soldier, did intercept work during the Cold War. *Mart's Life as a Spy* at http://www.langeleben. co.uk/draftproject/draft_010.htm.

Boiling, Graham: *Secret Students on Parade - Cold War Memories of JSSL*, Crail, Plane Tree, 2005. ISBN 1-84294-169-0.

Botting, Douglas: *One Chilly Siberian Morning*, Macmillan, 1965.

Boyd, Douglas: *The Kremlin Conspiracy - A Long, Hot and Cold War*, Hersham, Surrey, Ian Allan Publishing, 2010. Boyd was an RAF RL at RAF Gatow in 1959, but arrested in the Soviet sector of Berlin and held by the *Stasi* in six weeks solitary confinement; he was released apparently to prevent a second Soviet interrogation. He argues uncompromisingly that Russian/Soviet foreign policy has not changed in essentials in a thousand years and has been continuously supported by a programme of dirty tricks.

Cash, Tony: 'Observing Omerta', *East-West Review* (Journal of the GB-Russia Society), 2011, vol. 10, no. 1 (Issue 26). The article examines implications of the Official Secrets Acts for former RLs.

Cavendish, Anthony: *Inside Intelligence*, London, Collins, 1990. Cavendish was a MI6 officer in West Germany in early Cold War years, running agents in East Germany informing on Soviet troop movements, new weapons etc.

Clayton, Aileen: *The Enemy is Listening*, London, Hutchinson, 1980; Crecy Books, 1993. The author had fluent colloquial German acquired in Germany, 1938-39; joined WAAF at outbreak of war; describes in detail the tactical use of intercepts by RAF Y teams, starting in early 1940, continuing during the Battle of Britain and early days of the blitz.

Cobbold, Peter M: *The National Service Sailor*, Wivenhoe, Essex, Quentin Books, 1993. Interesting as sharp contrast to coders, as Cobbold was a seaman; demonstrates difficulty of getting into the Navy as national serviceman.

Drummond, John: *Tainted by Experience - a Life in the Arts,* London, Faber and Faber, 2000. Autobiography of the late Sir John Drummond, Navy JSSL alumnus; has chapter on JSSL. He was later Director of the Edinburgh Festival and BBC Promenade Concerts.

Elliott, Geoffrey and Harold Shukman: *Secret Classrooms - a Memoir of the Cold War,* London, St Ermin's Press, 2002. A very lively, often amusing account of the JSSL experience with the emphasis largely on the recollections of those on interpreter courses, especially Army and RAF *kursanty*. It does include some discussion of the intercept work of all three services, though this is not the book's primary purpose.

Faulks, Sebastian: *The Fatal Englishman - Three short lives,* Hutchinson, 1996, Vintage, 1997. Three biographical essays, the last dealing with life and tragic death of Jeremy Wolfenden, former midshipman interpreter, including his JSSL experiences 1952 -54 and work for the *Daily Telegraph* in Moscow (pp.209-307).

Frankland, Mark: *Child of my Time - an Englishmen's journey in a divided world,* London, Chatto and Windus, 1999. Frankland was trained to interpreter standard, and was *Observer* correspondent in Moscow for two lengthy spells. Also, *Khrushchev,* Stein and Day, New York, 1967, paperback 1969; *The Sixth Continent - Mikhail Gorbachov & the Soviet Union,* Harper & Row, 1987, Perennial Library, 1988; and 'The Russian Revolution', in *The Observer at 200* Donald Trelford (ed), Quartet Books, 1992.

Hetherington, William: 'Open Secrets - Confessions of a Siginter', *Peace News,* 25 August 1978, pp 6-9. It describes his experience as a coder 1952-54, includes image of Cuxhaven log sheet and text of the *Isis* article (26 February 1958), and compares that case with the 1978 'ABC' case involving sigint. He is also the subject of the article in *Peace News,* 10 May 1963, p 12, 'Official Secrets Man Renounces Undertakings', recounting his renunciation of the Official Secrets Acts. Author of *Swimming Against the Tide: The Peace Pledge Union Story 1934-2009,* Peace Pledge Union, 2010.

Hinsley, F H and Stripp, Alan (eds), *Code Breakers: the inside story of Bletchley Park,* Oxford University Press, 1993.

Hunt, Reginald; Geoffrey Russell and Keith Scott: *Mandarin Blue - RAF Chinese Linguists, 1951 to 1962, in the Cold War,* Hurusco Books (84 Butler Close, Oxford, OX2 6JQ; email: RAFChinese@gmail.com), 2008, ISBN 978-0-9560235-0-6. 190 pages detailing the training and work of some 300 Chinese linguists in the RAF.

Kidd, Angus B S: 'I Spy' (Reminiscences of an out-of-the-ordinary National Service sailor during the Cold War), on the website www.royalnavyresearcharchive.org.uk/Memories 26 February 2010.

Lee, Michael: 'The Joint Services School of Linguists', *The Linguist,* 38 (4), pp. 118-19. The title has a minor error - JSSL stood for Joint Services School *for* Linguists.

MacDonell, Donald: *From Dogfight to Diplomacy - a Spitfire Pilot's Log, 1932-58,* ed Lois MacDonell and Anne Mackay, Barnsley, Pen and Sword Aviation, 2005. MacDonell rose to air-commodore rank and was Air Attaché in Moscow 1956-58. In preparation he took the Cambridge Russian course under Lisa Hill, 1951-52, and was principal, JSSL Coulsdon, for nine months from May 1952. The memoirs were edited as cited after his death in 1996; a chapter on his Coulsdon experience will interest more than students there at the time, as it demonstrates the uneasy relationship between a camp commandant and a JSSL principal of equal rank; the only memoirs of a JSSL principal known to us, apart from Lisa Hill's.

Miller, John: *All Them Cornfields and Ballet in the Evening,* Kingston-upon-Thames, Hodgson Press, 2010. Miller was an Army RL in one of the two very early intakes to Bodmin in autumn 1951; the book mainly deals with his work in the Soviet Union for Reuters and the *Daily Telegraph.*

Mills, Dennis R: *My Life as a Coder Special,* 2005, unpublished; copies deposited at King's College, London, War Studies Department (c/o Prof Andrew Lambert); University of Leeds Library, Russian archive; Royal Naval Museum, Portsmouth; and Imperial War Museum; also available at http://www.royalnavyresearcharchive. org.uk/People_Mills.htm.

Mills, Dennis R: 'Signals Intelligence and the Coder Special Branch of the Royal Navy in the 1950s', *Intelligence and National Security,* vol. 26 (5), October 2011, pp.639-55. Based partly on once-secret Admiralty documents and coder recollections.

Muckle, James: *The Russian Language in Britain - a historical survey of learners and teachers,* Bramcote Press, 2008. By a RAF *kursant,* it is a thorough and readable survey of the subject from 16th century to present day, including a section on JSSLs.

Potter, Dennis: *Lipstick on Your Collar* (script of six-part Channel 4 TV series of that name), Faber and Faber, 1993. Like the drama's hero, Potter was an Army RL, but the hero is engaged in analysing the spoils of *Operation Tamarisk*, involving retrieval and sanitisation of soiled Red Army bumf, which, for want of proper toilet paper, could be pages of military manuals, phone directories, letters from home etc.

Proctor, Patrick: *Self Portrait*, Weidenfeld and Nicolson, 1991. The artist's autobiographical memoir, written at the height of his fame as painter, recounts experiences in the Navy learning Russian as trainee interpreter and participating in Russian-language plays at JSSL, London; includes accounts of several trips to the Soviet Union.

Riordan, Jim: *Comrade Jim - the Spy who Played for Spartak*, London, Fourth Estate, 2008. Jim learned Russian as a RAF national serviceman. A member of the Communist Party of Great Britain, he studied at the Moscow Higher Party School. He was later emeritus professor of Russian Studies, University of Surrey.

Roberts, John C Q: *Speak Clearly into the Chandelier - Cultural Politics between Britain and Russia 1972-2000*, London, Curzon Press, 2000. John was a RAF member of the JSSL, London, October 1951 intake. For many years he ran the Great Britain-USSR Association (now the GB-Russia Society), through which he made many contacts with leading Soviet intellectuals, artists, writers and performers.

Rosenthal, Jack: *Jack Rosenthal - An Autobiography in Six Acts*, Robson Books, 2005. The late Jack Rosenthal was a coder special, October 1953 intake to Coulsdon. Written as a screenplay, the book contains extracts from his TV drama *Bye-Bye, Baby* (Paravision production for Channel 4, 1992), a remarkably authentic, quasi-fictional account of the coder special experience, much of it supposedly at Cuxhaven.

Ross, Alan: *Blindfold Games*, London, Harper Collins, 1986, 1988; also, Faber and Faber, 2010. Autobiography recounting joining the Navy as seaman after five Oxford terms reading German and French; 30-page chapter on East Coast convoys, and his intercepting messages exchanged within E-boat flotillas coming from Netherlands and Germany to attack them; later he was commissioned as an intelligence officer and returned to the Fleet to do similar work to that done as a rating.

Roxburgh, Jack: An Army *kursant* in the very first intake at Bodmin, October 1951. See http://homepage.ntlworld.com/john.roxburgh/nationalservice/jssl.html.

Thomas, Ned: 'Cold War Classrooms - on learning Russian during National Service', *Planet*.160 (August 2003), pp 75-79. Also, for Welsh readers, Ned Thomas: *Bydoed*, Lolfa 2010, 190 pp; personal memoir, with chapter on National Service on the Army Russian course (Bodmin-London-Crail).

Thompson, Paul co-author with William Miller (neither formally attributed): 'Frontier Incidents - Exposure', *Isis* (Oxford University student magazine), 26 February 1958. The article led to their trial and imprisonment for breaching the Official Secrets Acts.

Vice, Sue: *Jack Rosenthal*, Manchester University Press, 2009.

Wheeler, Jeremy: *History Project* (chapter 10) on www.langeleben.co.uk is concerned with work of Army siginters in West Germany; also contains *Mart's Life as a Spy,* memoir by an Estonian, Mart Aru, who, as a Soviet soldier, did intercept work during the Cold War.

Woodhead, Leslie: *My Life as a Spy,* London, Macmillan, 2005. Personal account by RAF equivalent of a coder special, with particular reference to Crail radio school and intercept work at RAF Gatow in the late 1950s. Leslie also wrote, and presented for the BBC's documentary strand *Storyville*, a TV programme under the same title.

Zinoviev, Alexander: *Yawning Heights,* trans. Gordon Clough, The
Bodley Head, 1979.

ACKNOWLEDGEMENTS

TO Dr DENNIS R MILLS

One could perhaps describe Dennis Mills, a former coder, as the midwife of *The Coder Special Archive*, though the Latin formulation *fons et origo* would be a more accurate description of his role, for he has been the 'source' of some of the content of this book, besides originating what is now a larger enterprise. It all began in the oddest of circumstances, hinging on the slenderest of threads.

In April 2009 Dennis got a letter from the Lincolnshire Archives Office (where he is a frequent visitor). Enclosed was yet another, mysterious letter, this with a Monaco post stamp. 'What plutocrat could be mailing me from there' thought Dennis. The answer proved to be Graham Young, ex-leading coder (special), who had resided in Hut 44 at Coulsdon in 1953, along with Dennis and about fifteen others, with whom he was now trying to re-establish contact. Coincidentally, former midshipman Clifford German had been trying to locate *another* Graham Young, but instead had stumbled on GY2 of Hut 44. Clifford and GY2 then exchanged the names of men they were searching for, and one on GY's list struck Clifford as vaguely familiar – Dennis Mills – though the association was much more recent. In a *eureka* moment he remembered that a bloke named Mills had written a good deal on the Victorian census, a subject Clifford had been reading up in connection with his own research. It was suggested to Clifford that he try the Lincolnshire Archives Office, as many of Dennis's examples were from that county - hence Graham finding a route to communicate with his former hut mate. Dennis had remembered Clifford, who was midshipman of his watch at Cuxhaven, so at a stroke he was connected in two different directions. After he had got over the surprise, he decided to contact as many ex-coders as possible with a view to publishing an article on the Coder Special Branch. One was duly published in May 2011 in the *Naval Review*, and a longer version, incorporating suggestions from Professor Richard Aldrich, appeared in the October 2011 number of *Intelligence and National Security*.

The response from ex-coders was so great that Dennis also conceived the notion of creating for future historians a comprehensive, digital archive of the Coder Special division of the Royal Navy. In existence for little more than ten years, this part of the Navy was shrouded in mystery because of its unique role defending Britain in the Cold War. The 1,500 or so national service conscripts accepted were among the brightest of their generation, judging by success in examinations and especially linguistic talent. The project Dennis had in mind would combine in-depth research with former coders' verbatim recollections of their experiences. To deliver the latter he had to contact survivors, who by 2009 were all well into their seventies. He managed to get in touch, principally by email, with around 70 who were willing, usually eager, to share reminiscences and even ransack attics and cellars for old papers, photographs, ephemera and other mementos of their days in the Navy. It soon became clear there was enough sufficiently diverse matter for a book, and in 2010 Dennis co-opted Tony Cash, another former coder, to write it with him. The book draws on three types of source material: documentation, especially from the National Archives; recollections; and secondary sources.

Unfortunately, over the next year increasingly uncertain health and eyesight problems prevented Dennis from continuing as co-author. In November 2011, he decided that he ought to concentrate his energies on collating and cataloguing all research material and written submissions for eventual storage on a disc that will be distributed to historians of the period. Ex-coder Mike Gerrard stepped in as co-author of the book. Mike and Tony acknowledge a huge debt to Dennis not only for having initiated the whole undertaking, but for commenting on what we have written, and for making invaluable suggestions about content, structure and style of presentation. Needless to say, any errors or faults the reader may find are entirely the responsibility of the credited authors of the book.

Sincerest thanks are also due to every former *kursant* named in this volume, not all of whom, sadly, have lived long enough to see it published. Invidious though it may be to single out individuals, we are especially grateful to Mark Frankland (who, sadly, died before the book was completed), Clifford German, Peter Hill, James Muckle, Gareth Mulloy, Bill Musker, Alan Smith and Graham Young, all of whom have contributed extremely helpful advice and suggestions over a good many topics. Bill Hetherington, who bravely agreed to proof read the publication, has worked prodigiously hard to check that our account of naval rites and practices as well as our Cold War narrative are factually based. Nevertheless, any historical bloopers must be attributed exclusively to the authors.

INDEX

420

Germany x, xvii, xix, 1, 16-17, 59, 86, 93, 104, 109, 144-145, 182, 189, 209, 221, 223, 229-230, 232, 235, 239-240, 243, 250, 254, 300-301, 305, 336-337, 349, 352, 362, 369, 371-372, 374, 378-379, 382, 386, 393-394, 398, 402
  Nazi 1, 71, 86, 104-105, 108, 182, 229, 243, 253, 321, 327, 360, 369, 394
  see also Cuxhaven
  see also Kiel
Gerrard, Mike i, ii, iii, ix, xix, 18, 42, 63, 73, 103, 115-116, 123-124, 138, 144, 147, 155, 161, 175, 177-178, 205, 274-275, 277, 406
Gestapo 93
Gieves 124, 267
Glasgow 167, 355
  University Media Studies 355
Glasnost 359, 374
Glenn Miller Story, The 116
Gloucestershire 69, 161
Goddard, Lord Chief Justice 215
Godfrey, Vice-Admiral John 27
Godlewski, Jozef vii, 79, 88, 106-111
Goethe 233
Gogol, Nikolai 65
Goons, the 181
Gorbachev, Mikhail Sergeevich v, x, 61, 291, 330, 359, 361-364, 366-368, 374-375
Gorbatov, Alexander 327
Gorky (city) 343
Goskontsert 341, 383
Gosling, Alan 12
Grammar school xi, 5, 28, 31, 32, 111, 264, 266, 314,

Greenland 55-56, 300-301
Grenoble 25
Griffin, Cardinal 109
Griffiths, John 38, 75, 99, 105-106, 201, 225, 240-241, 315
Grimsby vii, 28-29
Grog 51-52, 179
GRU 293, 383
Guardian, The 211
Guernsey 209
Gulag 327, 335, 343, 383
Gulag Archipelago 343

H

Hague, The 61
Hamburg 185, 221, 223, 230, 233, 240-241, 254-255, 282, 305
Hamlet x, 48, 61, 283-284, 324-325
Hammerlund 191
Hammersmith 105, 108, 110
Hammock vii, 38
Hampshire 42, 135
Hancock, Terry 3
Harvey-Jones, Lt-Commander John 17, 189
Harwell 29
Harwich 221, 261, 272
Hastings 29
Haus der Jugend 230, 383
Hawkins, Nigel 30, 269, 271, 279
Heazell, Paddy 195, 197, 202, 206, 254
Heligoland ix, 236-237, 239
Henry II 118
Henry, Mr 97
Herman, Woody 235
Hero of Our Time 66
Hetherington, Norman 178

434

Lightning Source UK Ltd.
Milton Keynes UK
UKOW031338160912

199099UK00001B/11/P